A FAITHFUL ACCOUNT OF THE RACE

The John Hope Franklin Series in African American History and Culture

WALDO E. MARTIN JR. and PATRICIA SULLIVAN, editors

A FAITHFUL ACCOUNT OF THE RACE

African American Historical Writing in Nineteenth-Century America

STEPHEN G. HALL

The University of North Carolina Press *Chapel Hill*

Designed and set by Rebecca Evans in Bembo
Manufactured in the United States of America

The paper in this book meets the guidelines for permanence
and durability of the Committee on Production Guidelines
for Book Longevity of the Council on Library Resources.

The University of North Carolina Press has been a member
of the Green Press Initiative since 2003.

A portion of this book was drawn from Stephen G. Hall, "A Search
for Truth: Jacob Oson and the Beginnings of African American
Historiography," *William and Mary Quarterly* 64, no. 1 (January 2007):
139–48. Used by permission.

Library of Congress Cataloging-in-Publication Data
Hall, Stephen G. (Stephen Gilroy), 1968–
A faithful account of the race: African American historical writing
in nineteenth-century America / Stephen G. Hall.
p. cm. — (The John Hope Franklin series in African American
history and culture)
Includes bibliographical references and index.
ISBN 978-0-8078-3305-6 (cloth : alk. paper)
ISBN 978-0-8078-5967-4 (pbk. : alk. paper)
1. African Americans—Historiography. 2. Historiography—United
States—History—19th century. 3. African Americans—Intellectual
life—19th century. 4. African American historians—History—19th
century. 5. African American intellectuals—History—19th century.
6. African diaspora—History—19th century. 7. United States—
Intellectual life—19th century. I. Title.

E184.65.H35 2009
305.896'073—dc22   2009026113

CLOTH 13 12 11 10 09 5 4 3 2 1
PAPER   13 12 11 10 09 5 4 3 2 1

For my parents,

CLYDE ALLEN HALL (1930–1996) & GERTRUDE HALL (1926–2002),

with love and respect for your many sacrifices

Contents

Acknowledgments

IN THE LONG COURSE OF WRITING A BOOK, one incurs many debts, which are, in many cases, life altering. My undergraduate years at Morgan State University in Baltimore proved foundational for the types of interests and scholarly work I have pursued since graduating from the institution. Rosalyn Terborg-Penn provided a solid skill set in historical methodology and deepened my developing interest in historiography, African American women's history, and the African Diaspora. Elaine Breslaw, Susan Chapelle, and JoAnn Robinson exposed me to early American urban history and modern American history. Henry Robinson taught a demanding course in Russian history peppered with interesting anecdotes about his years at M Street High School (Dunbar High) in Washington, D.C., and the experiences of African Americans at elite northeastern universities and European schools in the first half of the twentieth century. Charles Chikeka offered several upper-level courses on Africa that provided a good foundation for subsequent work. One of my most significant influences was Benjamin Quarles. An emeritus professor during my undergraduate years, Quarles maintained an office in the main library on campus. I recall fondly his willingness to engage in conversations with historical neophytes such as myself. He was a regular presence in the department, often attending events. His prodigious scholarly production, rigorous intellect, discipline, and devotion to African American history as a humanistic discourse, as well as his soft-spoken demeanor, made a lasting impression on me. Like Quarles, Walter Fisher, another emeritus member of the history faculty, took me under his wing and exposed me to good art, literature, and high culture, in general. The late Augustus Adair, a political science professor and first executive director of the Congressional Black Caucus, eased the transition from high school to college for me through his genuine belief in nurturing students. His political acumen, encouragement, support, and erudition still inform my life today. Other faculty members served as mentors and offered sage advice at crucial stages of my undergraduate career: James Haynes, Gossie Hudson, Timothy Kim, Glenn O. Philips, and Clayton Stansberry. I am also indebted to students who assisted me in innumerable ways: Manu Ampim, Damon Freeman, Vanessa

Phears, and Derek Willis. I am also deeply grateful to my "second family," Randy and Brenda Jews.

Immediately after completing my undergraduate education, I spent a summer in Oxford, England, at St. Hugh's College (Oxford) sponsored by the University of Warwick, that provided a wealth of new experiences and exposure to scholars whose work continues to shape my understanding of African American history. I am indebted to Leonard Harris, who skillfully organized the trip and continues to support my career in indirect ways. I took classes with Cedric Robinson, Charlotte Pierce Baker, and Manthia Diawara and spent time with Houston Baker, Dennis Brutus, and David Dabydeen. A subsequent meeting with Robinson, after he delivered a paper at Ohio State, renewed our acquaintanceship and helped to crystallize my thoughts on David Walker's *Appeal*.

My time as a graduate student at the University of Wisconsin was a scholar's dream. The university's resources in African American history are among the best in the country. James Danky helped me to navigate the State Historical Society's holdings. William Van DeBurg helped to develop my work on Alrutheus Ambush Taylor. Brenda Gayle Plummer's teaching and scholarship in modern African American history fundamentally reshaped my understanding of the discipline and pointed me more clearly toward a deeply interpretive and nuanced understanding of African American history. The late Herbert Hill's irascible nature and quick wit allowed a firsthand glimpse of an active participant in many of the titanic struggles waged by the NAACP to secure labor rights for African Americans. Hill was living and breathing history. I am also grateful for the support of Sandra Adell, Stanlie James, Freida High Tesfagiorgis, Richard Ralston, Michael Thornton, and Craig Werner. I am also grateful to Matt Bachman, Stephanie Felix, Jacqueline Francis, Melvina Johnson, Anthony Lewis, and Darryl Graham, who provided a real and sustaining community.

Ohio State University proved a natural fit for doctoral work because of its long history of graduating substantial numbers of African American Ph.D.s. My graduate experience was greatly enhanced by a strong, close-knit group of African American students whose involvement with the Diop Historical Association, a thesis and dissertation support group, enhanced all of us. I am grateful to all of the members of this association but especially to Steeve Buckridge, Robert Decatur, Carol Gibson, Cherisse Jones, Lawrence Little, Michael Lomax, Tiwanna Simpson, Siri Rudholm, and Oscar Williams. Marshall Stevenson recruited me into the doctoral program and served as my first graduate adviser. I am grateful for his early interest in my work. John Rothney provided much-needed guidance on a paper written in a historiography seminar on Earl Thorpe. He introduced me to Merton Dillon and remained interested in my work and welfare long after the seminar ended. I was fortunate to interact with a number of scholars who broadened my perspectives and deepened my interest in the African Diaspora, including Ahmad Sikianga, Claire Robertson, and Donald Cooper. Cooper encouraged me to think critically about Latin America and the Caribbean, and his graduate readings course on Mexico and subsequent courses on the Caribbean, Brazil, and Central America were very useful for my work.

As a faculty member, I found Ohio State an ideal location for writing a book. At every stage of this manuscript's development, Steven Conn championed the project and provided useful advice and suggestions to improve it. My departmental mentor and colleague Mansel Blackford offered sage words of advice and strong support throughout this process. Words cannot express the debt of gratitude that I owe to Stephanie Shaw, my colleague and friend. She shepherded this manuscript from its early incarnations as an amorphous set of ideas into a book manuscript. Along this path, I have benefited greatly from her deep erudition, careful readings and rereadings of drafts, and continued encouragement, support, and true friendship. At my lowest moments in this process, when I was uncertain if it were possible, she remained steadfast in her belief in the importance of the work and provided deep and sustaining assistance at every juncture. If I can become half the colleague and friend that Stephanie has been to me, then my life will be rich indeed. Numerous colleagues at Ohio State have offered support in word and deed over the years. I am eternally grateful to Ken Andrien, Les Benedict, John Burnham, Alan Beyerchen, Cynthia Brokaw, Philip Brown, Joan Cashin, Jon Erickson, Carol Fink, the late John Conteh-Morgan, Kenneth Goings, Harvey Graff, Alan Gallay, Matt Godish, Donna Guy, Barbara Hanawalt, Marilyn Hegarty, Daniel Hobbins, Michael Hogan, Thomas Ingersoll, Ousman Kobo, Chris Reed, Nate Rosenstein, Claire Robertson, Lelia Rupp, David Stebenne, and Judy Wu. Staff in the History Department at Ohio State were immensely helpful to me at every stage of my career. I am indebted to Joby Abernathy, James Bach, Chris Burton, Steve Fink, the late Marge Haffner, Maria Mazon, Gail Summerhill, Jan Thompson, and especially Rich Ugland. My graduate students, old and new—Anja Heidenreich, Nicole Jackson, Gissell Jeter, and now Brandy Thomas—provide me with youthful energy as I try to impart some of the wisdom that has been distilled in me. My scholarly life is deeply enriched by all the members of the Journal Club for African and African American History and Related Areas.

Colleagues at Central State University offered assistance at an early stage in the project. Anne Steiner, Terrance Glass, Lovette Chinwah-Adegbola, Deborah Stokes, and Kwawisi Tekpetey offered encouragement and support at every juncture. Jeff Crawford befriended me immediately after my arrival on campus in the summer of 1999 and offered useful advice on early drafts of proposals and on several book review essays. My students Diane Ward and Diretha Jennings continue to maintain contact. The opportunity to contribute to their growth and maturation has been life altering.

I have received considerable financial support to complete this study. I am indebted to the John Hope Franklin Center for African American Documentation at Duke University, the National Endowment for the Humanities, the Gilder Lehrman Center, the Ford Foundation, the W. E. B. Du Bois Institute at Harvard University, the Schomburg Center in Black Culture, the American Historical Association, and the Ohio State University College of Humanities for a book subvention.

My experience at Harvard University as a Du Bois fellow was extremely productive. Having the opportunity to conduct research in the Rare Books Room proved indispensable for many aspects of this study. I had the privilege to share an office with the late John Conteh-Morgan. His scholarly presence continues to loom large in my life. He is sorely missed. Joan Bryant's interest in black theology and intellectuals and willingness to question standard interpretations of black history offered a good sounding board for my ideas. Her willingness to painstakingly read several early drafts has improved this book immeasurably. I am grateful for her friendship. At the Schomburg Center, I encountered a very helpful staff and equally engaging fellows. Sharon Howard gracefully accommodated me during my stay in New York. Diana Lachatanere answered all of my questions. Colin Palmer took an early interest in my work and helped me in many ways. The monthly presentations by fellows allowed me to sharpen my work considerably. I benefited from the suggestions of all of the fellows regarding various aspects of my project, especially the first half. Since my departure, I have continued my association with the Schomburg. I am also grateful to Sylviane Diouf, whose directorship of the Mellon Humanities Institute at the Schomburg Center each summer for the past three years has allowed me to present my ideas regarding the evolution of African American history to advanced undergraduates and graduate students. These intellectually rich conversations have allowed me to rework many of the arguments in the manuscript. My work has been deeply enriched by these interactions.

Roy Finkenbine, Dickson Bruce, and Mitch Kachun expressed interest in this project from its earliest conceptualizations and read countless drafts. Presentations at conferences and the opportunity to interact consistently with these individuals have strengthened this study immensely. I have been fortunate to meet or interact with other scholars who have encouraged and supported this work: Rafael Allen, Randall Burkett, Mia Bay, John Ernest, Pero Dagbovie, Eric Duke, Kevin Gaines, Nghana Lewis, and Marshanda Smith.

I am especially grateful for the help and assistance of my longtime friend Tim Greene, a high school history teacher in Jersey Shore, Pennsylvania. We met as graduate students at Ohio State. He has been a constant sounding board for my ideas via phone, during his many trips to Columbus, and on my visits to his home in Jersey Shore. As a consummate student of American history, his rich insights have provided useful information for many aspects of this study.

Librarians and archivists at the Amistad Center, Atlanta University Center, Hampton University, Howard University, the Historical Society of Pennsylvania, the Library of Congress, the Tuskegee Institute, and Wilberforce University provided important assistance through this long process. Eleanor Daniels, Leta Hendricks, and David Lincove offered assistance at Ohio State University in locating obscure materials through interlibrary loan.

I am grateful for all of the assistance I have received from the UNC Press. Waldo Martin's interest in the manuscript aided and abetted this project. Chuck Grench and Katy O'Brien moved this project along very efficiently and expeditiously. Paul Betz has answered all of my technical questions in an incredibly efficient manner. I am grateful to John K. Wilson, the copyeditor, for his careful editing of the manuscript. I am also grateful to the anonymous reviewers for their careful and helpful reading of my manuscript.

My in-laws have also been supportive of this long process. I am grateful to my mother-in-law, June Barton, for her continued support and tangible actions for the family, and my sister-in-law, Sheron Barton, a Washington, D.C., attorney, whose constant debates about one issue or another have helped me to appreciate how to articulate my particular viewpoint to a wider audience. I appreciate the generosity of Sheron and my brother-in-law, Orrin (Tony) Barton, especially their willingness to open their homes to accommodate me during research trips or conferences in the Washington, D.C., area. I am especially grateful to my late father-in-law, Dr. Winston E. Barton. Although trained as an economist, he was an avid student of history. His insights about his native Guyana and interest in Caribbean history always provided lively conversations and interesting material for my work.

My immediate family has been a constant source of support. My children, Marcus, Marton, Morgan, and Makaela, enrich my life in countless ways. All of them were born during my graduate school years and the first years of my career, and I learned early to balance my academic and familial responsibilities in useful and productive ways. Many days and nights have been spent balancing paper production with diaper changes and bottle feedings; and later it was homework help I was balancing with teaching, writing, and thinking. I owe all that I am and hope to be to my wife, Roshawne. For more than twenty years she has been my constant companion, intellectual partner and co-parent. When we met at nineteen, as undergraduates at Morgan State University, I was intensely attracted to her radiant smile and inner and outer beauty. Our affection and love was natural from the start, and it has grown immeasurably over the years. We have literally grown up together, tackling the tough business of balancing a two-career household and four children. Always good-humored, meticulous, savvy, and courageous, her love and acumen inspire me to be a better husband, father, and person. For this I am deeply grateful.

Lastly, my parents, Clyde and Gertrude, are an incredible source of inspiration. It is from them that I learned all that is essential in life. For me they were and still are the greatest intellectuals, despite the fact neither graduated from high school. They tutored me in the essential business of life and taught me the importance of hard work, discipline, and personal sacrifice. My mother helped to develop in me a deep appreciation for the written word. Armed with a library card, I remember visiting the local library at every available opportunity with my mother. She was an avid reader. I would sit in our small library, located between the living room and the master bedroom, and observe my mother reading books of all types. She and my father insisted that I watch the news daily and read the newspaper often. They nurtured a strong appreciation for education, discipline, and refinement for which I am extremely grateful. My father, a soft-spoken man and Korean War veteran, worked hard, often two jobs, to support the family. His constant admonition to pursue education and make something of myself still has resonance today. Always active in my education, my parents visited my schools every year from kindergarten through 10th grade. Their presence enriched my academic experiences and sketched out vistas of possibility. They saw worlds and experiences that I could not and urged me ever patiently towards them. As with many things in the long course of producing a book, both my parents passed away. At many difficult and demanding moments in this long process, I often hear their voices or sense their warmth pushing me or encouraging me to press on. In my mind's eye, I see my mother, lying on the bed in the master bedroom, reading, or my father, perched in his usual space at the kitchen table watching the news or reading the newspaper. I know they would be proud, and this book is dedicated to their memory.

A FAITHFUL ACCOUNT OF THE RACE

Introduction

NOT TEN YEARS AFTER the end of the Civil War and two years before the formal collapse of Reconstruction, William Wells Brown, fugitive slave and abolitionist, authored one of the earliest race histories of the postbellum period, *The Rising Son; or, Antecedents of the Colored Race* (1874). No stranger to racial agitation or prognosis, Brown had been an active participant in the antislavery movement. During the controversy over the Fugitive Slave Law of 1850, he fled to England to avoid recapture and reenslavement and played an important role in the transatlantic abolitionist community, a closely knit group of black abolitionists who lectured throughout Europe from the 1830s to the beginning of the Civil War. It was no surprise, then, that Brown, as he had done throughout the antebellum period, utilized the power of the pen to right the injustices of the past and present. The rapid-fire publication of *The Black Man* (1863), a compilation of biographical sketches of prominent men and women of African descent, and *The Negro in the American Rebellion* (1867), one of the earliest African American histories of black participation in the Civil War, set the stage for Brown's larger race history, *The Rising Son*, which provided one of the earliest models for postbellum racial history.[1]

Brown's use of the word "son" is obviously a play on the word "sun." Like so many race advocates of his day, Brown wanted to herald the coming of a new day for African Americans. Associating the rising of a son, the offspring of a slave race, with the rising of the sun, the dawn of a new day for the race, suggested untold possibilities that loomed on the horizon for what noted postbellum author and race man William J. Simmons described as a "progressive and rising race." Less concerned with "the dark night of slavery," Brown sought to write the history of the race in new terms and from the vantage point of a new race stirred in the cauldron of the Civil War and created in the legislative enactments of the Reconstruction period. This subjective posturing explains Brown's positioning of his race narrative. His title not only creates a certain perception about the present but also tells us how Brown wanted his readers to think about the African American past. But his prefatory remarks reminded readers that, "After availing myself of all the reliable information obtainable,

David Walker

the author is compelled to acknowledge the scantiness of materials for a history of the colored race. He has throughout endeavored to give a faithful account of the people and their customs, without concealing their faults." Thus, he relied on his authority as a historical eyewitness to suggest at least two things. First, he wanted the reader to appreciate the difficult task he was undertaking. Second, and directly related to the first point, that the task of reconstructing African American history is difficult because of the limited sources available. One could also add the traditions of an inadequate methodology and an uncritical and celebratory discourse to the list of challenges he faced. Given these impediments, Brown hoped the reader could understand why a critical and serious textual African American discourse did not arise during the late eighteenth century or the first half of the nineteenth.

One might argue, as I do throughout this study, that the scope and methodological sophistication of textual African American historical writing were much more developed, and its origins much deeper, than Brown suggested in the book's preface. His table of contents alone shows that the book's scope is truly diasporic. It encompasses the black experience in Africa, Latin America, and Europe as well as the United States. *The Rising Son* also relies on a wide variety of sources, ranging from travelers' accounts to diaries and slave narratives. Although the book is primarily descriptive, Brown interjects a substantial amount of historical analysis. Some of this commentary relies on the work of earlier black writers, ranging from the fiery abolitionist David Walker to the staunch integrationist William C. Nell. Lastly, the book's length, more than five hundred pages, suggests a different conclusion about the availability of resources than Brown himself had drawn.[2]

Like many of his contemporaries, Brown understood that the challenges African Americans faced in the postbellum period dwarfed those experienced in their previous history. Race histories, including Brown's, not only mapped the racial past but instilled pride and provided a roadmap for how the race might adapt to freedom. Re-creating the past to inform the present proved important, but in order to facilitate adaptation to freedom, it was necessary to look into the future. In charting the future by reconfiguring the past, Brown's work placed less emphasis on the harshness of the slave regime and focused instead on the varied ways African Americans resisted its most damaging effects. Rather than harsh masters and compliant slaves, Brown presented interracial dramas of aggressive agitation against the slave regime. He presented freedom as a teleological process and as a moment of unfettered possibility.

Postbellum history, however, did not constitute the totality of black history, and Brown pointed out that his work relied on a number of "antecedents." These antecedents ranged from writings of classical antiquity, the Bible, and volumes of world history by European and American writers to the vindicationist literature of abolitionists and half a century of writing by African American intellectuals. These antecedents provided powerful proof of an abundance rather than a "scantiness of materials for a history of the colored race."

Scholars today often privilege nontextual manifestations of black culture as the dominant modes of early African American historical expression.[3] Studying oral, vernacular, and commemorative culture and historical memory has become a prominent means of examining the ways African Americans re-create their past. The nontextual approach for researching black experience seems reasonable, given the relatively high illiteracy rates among African Americans throughout much of the nineteenth century. Still, such examinations have the effect of casting the African American subject as essentially one who functioned within a very narrow portion of the cultural realm, primarily related to performance, while implying a somewhat deficient (and even absent) intellectual tradition.[4] Ultimately, privileging nontextual manifestations of black culture adds tremendously to our understanding of the historical period, but also presents an incomplete picture of the African American experience.

Highly nuanced understandings of the black experience produced during the nineteenth century actually do exist. Sometimes just beneath the surface, but often in plain view, there is a rich *textual* historical and cultural tradition among African Americans that was crafted, as Elizabeth McHenry has convincingly shown, in both individual and communal settings. John Ernest has also made this point persuasively in his recent study of African American history in the early republic (1789 to 1830) and the antebellum period (1830 to 1861). Indeed, historians can gain a great deal by looking more carefully at the complex terrain of nineteenth-century historical practice and attending to the ways African Americans engaged the larger culture as readers and writers. Reading the terrain of nineteenth-century historical practice as a complex site where African American writers carved out an identity allows us to reenvision the intellectual landscape and enlarge the frame of African Americans' culture, life, and production beyond what might be expected, given the conditions in which they lived; that is, beyond the narrow confines of the slave trade, the Middle Passage, North American slavery, and general oppression.

The central purpose of this study, then, is to chart the origins, meanings, methods, evolution, and maturation of African American historical writing from the period of the early republic to its professionalization in the twentieth century. Central to the articulation of a black historical voice was textual production, especially extended, book-length works, and its influence on and connection to the subsequent scholarly development of the field. Three underlying themes are central to the process of charting the genealogy of African American historical writing prior to 1915: the selective appropriation and complex interchange with the ideological and intellectual constructs from larger, mainstream movements including the Enlightenment, Romanticism, realism, and modernism; the creation of discursive spaces that simultaneously reinforced and offered counternarratives to more mainstream historical discourse; and the influence of the African diaspora, especially as it relates to Haiti and Africa on the development of historical study.

In addition to establishing a clear genealogy of African American historical production, this study shows that the rich vein of such production embodied nuanced understandings of black identity. This idea is best reflected in the way the nineteenth-century black classicist William Saunders Scarborough summed up his life story as a journey from "slavery to scholarship." Historical work by African Americans early on served to construct a complex black subject who transcended the narrow confines of nineteenth- and early twentieth-century life. Likewise, in this study, my goal is to shift the perspective from the external conditions that African Americans experienced for more than half of the nineteenth century, manacled as they were by chains and fetters, and to look at their historical production through their own eyes, dreams, and visions. Here, African Americans represent more than stolen property, chattel in the bottom of slaves ships, and beasts of burden in the Americas. They are also thinking, rational, and critically engaged human beings. Focusing on their textual production brings this point into broad relief.[5] The texts under study here tell a uniquely nineteenth-century story of the emergence of the book as an increasingly important indicator or measure of intellectual worth and ability in a larger society determined to negate black humanity. Books served as barometers of what types of contributions blacks could make to racial as well as national literature.[6]

Denied access to education, many blacks used formal and informal networks to acquire basic literacy and to educate themselves. Literacy, however, did not always set its bearer above or beyond the reach of racism or discriminatory treatment. Moreover, literate persons in the black community, many of whom had escaped from the jaws of slavery, were autodidacts (self-taught), or trained by sympathetic whites in America or abroad. These individuals understood the plight of the nonliterate and constructed discursive spaces to address these realties. Commemorative celebrations (including festivals and parades), slave narratives, black newspapers, conventions and orations, and literary and historical societies, which other researchers have discussed in detail, were just a few of the ways blacks re-created and reconstructed aspects of their past. But in addition to creating and taking advantage of institutions within the black community, black thinkers and writers engaged in what literary historian Rafia Zafar described as "instances of appropriation from and accommodation to the European mainstream as trials and experiments in the development of an African American [historical] consciousness."[7]

Beyond appropriation and accommodation, however, African American intellectuals were conversant with the larger intellectual culture in which they lived. While a great deal of work has been done on the sophistication of black popular or mass culture, we have not fully applied these lessons to how African Americans engaged the intellectual culture of their day, especially as it pertained to historical writing. They skillfully utilized tools and concepts drawn from the American and European Enlightenment, the Bible, classicism, and Romanticism, during the first half of the nineteenth century, and from realism and scientism and objectivity by century's end.[8] Examining the engagement of black writers with the complete intellectual toolkit of America in the nineteenth and early twentieth centuries yields fascinating insights into the development of African American historical traditions.

From the outset, history was at the center of public discourse in the black community. Texts, in part, shaped in the cauldron of historical and literary societies, newspapers, and the convention movement, allowed black intellectuals unique spaces wherein they crafted the rhetoric and substance of their arguments to reflect the validity and importance of the complex black subject. Within such spaces, writer Jacob Oson, orator and abolitionist David Walker, and orator and self-trained preacher Maria Stewart, to name a few, offered some of the earliest examples of historical production during the years of the early republic. In doing so, their writing served as the catalyst for the production of numerous treatises on the black experience up to the Civil War.[9]

During the early republic and antebellum periods, African American writers engaged the intellectual trends then current in the American and Euro-American mainstream. These trends offered black intellectuals the means for creating discursive spaces for a critical examination of the past. Their techniques and ideas included essence history, an attempt to identify forces that defined human society; history as progress; and the use of literary devices in historical writing.

David Walka

European Romanticism offered the concept of *historicism*, which meant that change could be explained by examining history as a process, rather than a science. The *jeremiad*, as a rhetorical technique, allowed for the interjection of religion and the acknowledgement of God as an operative force in human affairs. But by the 1840s and 1850s, American Romanticism challenged both the rationalistic approach of the Enlightenment and the appeal to Providence, and the jeremiad began to lose some of its explanatory power. Romanticism accentuated the qualities and actions of humankind rather than God in propelling events in an often chaotic universe. The human being as the arbiter and best example of his/her own destiny is a concept ultimately embodied in the idea of *representative* men and women serving as models for human behavior. Classicism, along with biblical knowledge, offered an important space for making scholarly claims about blacks in the biblical and ancient worlds. Although scholars regularly overlook or misinterpret this fact, as classicist Michele Ronnick has shown, blacks were deeply engaged in classicism throughout the nineteenth century.[10]

African American historical writing in the nineteenth century cannot be reduced to terms such as "anticanonical" or only understood in terms of more recent phenomena such as the Great Books controversy of the late 1980s and 1990s.[11] Black intellectual life indeed reflected larger societal trends. As historian Thomas Bender has noted, American intellectual life in the first half of the nineteenth century was organized around civic professionalism in the institutional structures of the major urban centers. This was no less true for African Americans: black literary, historical, and cultural societies flourished there as well. In addition to being important locations for abolitionist activity, these cities and sites served as cultural and intellectual centers where African Americans could gain access to what book historians have termed, "technologies of power"—newspapers, books, pamphlets, and other reading materials. From the first black newspaper, *Freedom's Journal*, started in 1827, to one of the last significant antebellum African American publications, *Anglo-African Magazine* (1858), antebellum newspapers and magazines played an important role in disseminating historical information within the black community.[12]

As influential as Euro-American ideologies and intellectual constructs were, African American intellectuals did not adopt them in a wholesale fashion. By the 1830s, when white historians began to construct American history in increasingly nationalistic ways, drawing on Romanticism to construct ideal historical personalities and deriving crucial lessons from the immediate rather than the distant past, black writers, led by black abolitionists trained in various clerical traditions, challenged this approach by trumpeting the authority of sacred, ancient, and modern history. In this way they preserved a more complex black subject who emerged from a review of *world* history rather than *national* history. Although these intellectuals usually derived their authority from clerical and abolitionist sites, by the 1850s the momentum generated by the demise of Northern slavery and the growth of secular organizations in the black community led to the inclusion of other voices in the debate over black personhood and humanity. The passage of the Compromise of 1850, with its infamous fugitive slave provision, deflated integrationist possibilities and pitted integrationist ideology against diasporic notions of black identity. The rise of a secular group of free blacks who had limited experience with slavery but were closely associated with the abolitionist community emerged in the forefront of historical production. Using the American and Haitian Revolutions as signifiers of democratic possibility, these writers reconceptualized the relationship of African Americans to America and the history of the African diaspora.[13]

Black abolitionists, former leaders in the rhetorical and literal war to end slavery, played an important role in producing historical writing in the years following the Civil War. William Wells Brown and William Still used historical writing both as a means of recalling the horrors of slavery and as a vehicle for looking forward to the possibilities of freedom. Their work prepared the intellectual terrain for a more reflective mediation on the Emancipation in the form of race history, which emerged with the publication of George Washington Williams's *History of the Negro Race* in 1883.[14] But the mid- to late nineteenth century witnessed, as historian Thomas Bender also noted, a shift from civic to disciplinary professionalism, a professionalism framed around the university. Among black intellectuals, owing to social, political, economic, and societal constraints, the process was somewhat different, not as linear, and some of the influences of the preprofessional milieu of historical writing still obtained.[15]

Throughout the postbellum period of the late nineteenth and early twentieth centuries, a larger and more diverse group of works on the African American experience appeared. In particular, African American history in the form of emancipation narratives, race textbooks, and collective biographies (biographical catalogs) proliferated. And especially significant, African American women, encouraged by the organization of prominent groups such as the National Association of Colored Women (NACW), challenged the masculinist focus of what Kevin Kelley Gaines calls "uplift philosophy." By including the historical writing of Anna Julia Cooper, Pauline Hopkins, Leila Amos Pendleton, and

Gertrude Mossell, this study adds another dimension to, and compliments the work of, scholars such as Rosalyn Terborg-Penn, Cynthia Neverdon-Morton, and Stephanie J. Shaw who have examined the contributions of African American women to various forms of institutional and intellectual endeavor.[16]

Perhaps the most important aspect of the development of African American history in the late nineteenth century was the growth of avocational sites for historical understanding, such as literary and historical societies and educational institutions, where black intellectuals also involved themselves in the collection and preservation of important artifacts relating to African American history. The Bethel Literary and Historical Society (1881) and the American Negro Academy (1897), both in Washington, D.C., and the Afro-American Historical Society (1897), in Philadelphia, among others, played important roles in extending the antebellum interest in African American history while also serving as catalysts for the professionalization of the field. Some of the earliest proto-professional models of historical engagement, individuals on the cusp of professionalization, were men like Robert Adger, a member of the Afro-American Historical Society; Arturo Alonso Schomburg, a prominent Puerto Rican bibliophile who also contributed to Alain Locke's seminal Harlem Renaissance work, the *New Negro*, and lectured widely on the importance of including the study of black history in colleges and universities; and John Cromwell, an active member of the American Negro Academy, close friend of Carter G. Woodson, who founded the Association for the Study of Negro Life and History.[17]

Despite the limited historical training of many black bibliophiles, lay and amateur historians, and members of literary and historical societies, it is from among their ranks that the first disciplinary interest in history emerged. Joseph Wilson published his book *Emancipation: Its Course and Progress* (1882) with the Normal Steam Printing Press, the school press for Hampton University. William Still sent Daniel Payne, president of Wilberforce University in Xenia, Ohio, a copy of the 1883 edition of his book *The Underground Railroad*, for inclusion in the school's library. William Henry Crogman, coauthor with Henry F. Kletzing of *The Progress of a Race* (1898), enlisted Booker T. Washington, principal of Tuskegee Institute, to write the book's introduction. Edward Johnson, author of *School History of the Negro Race* (1899), taught at Shaw University and maintained close ties with Washington through the National Negro Business League, and he urged Washington to use this study for courses at Tuskegee Institute. *The Negro in America History* (1912) by John Cromwell, amateur historian and author, became required reading at Tuskegee Institute.[18]

These few examples suggest some new avenues for investigation into the development and dissemination of African American history. First, while a number of scholars have discussed aspects of the rise of race history or documented the existence, career, and importance of literary and historical societies, few have discussed their connection to the process of professionalization within the nascent black academy. This study also departs from earlier studies that isolate the growth of race history from the rise of departments of history. While most studies treat history departments in the context of specific institutions, here the professionalization of history is viewed as an important outgrowth of the rise of race history, and colleges, universities, and seminaries played an important role in the process. They not only offered courses but many sponsored conferences and symposia on various aspects of the "Negro Question."[19]

The historiography on the development of black history is only about two generations old. And in this short time, two discernible approaches, one modernist and one postmodernist, have come to dominate the literature. In the first instance, because early work on the development of black history often viewed its origins as a byproduct of American racism or as a characteristic American quest for a historical tradition, a common tendency in this scholarship is to dismiss work produced prior to the late nineteenth century as largely heroic or preprofessional. I see the insistence on using current historical standards (of professionalization, for example) to judge work produced in the nineteenth century as modernist or as imposing a modernist approach. The modernist approach places more emphasis on postbellum historical production, especially historical work that is closer in form to twentieth-century historical production, rather than earlier manifestations of black history and historical consciousness. Some of the best examples of this approach include the work of John Hope Franklin, August Meier, and Elliott Rudwick. Franklin, using a generational approach that began with George Washington Williams's publication of *History of the Negro Race* in 1883, reflected the modernist approach by positioning Williams as the father of modern black history. Williams's work represents the institutional model because its form, Franklin contends, is similar to other works published in the professional era. Meier and Rudwick's *Black History and the Historical Profession* (1986) also gives credence to the institutional model by focusing almost exclusively on the post-1915 evolution of the field under the auspices of Carter G. Woodson, the founder of the Association for the Study of Negro Life and History, the first professional historical organization for African Americans.[20] The postmodernist approach is best illustrated in John Ernest's

Liberation Historiography (2004). Ernest's work builds on recent work in African American historiography that has emphasized the influence of Emancipation Day celebrations, commemorative occasions, monument culture, and historical memory and their impact on nineteenth-century historical production. Ernest persuasively argues that black writers faced numerous intellectual challenges as they sought to situate African Americans in a historical narrative from which they had been largely excluded. In this construction, history is conceptualized as a destabilized and decentered narrative rather than a holistic one. As white historians were attempting to "cobble together" a history, which, Ernest argues, would ultimately be predicated on a white nationalist narrative, black writers grappled with the monumental task of reconstituting a historical past that had largely been disrupted by the trauma of the Middle Passage and enslavement in the United States. Given this contested contextual space, black writers constructed black history largely as a metahistorical narrative that simultaneously transcended and reinterpreted mainstream historical narratives. Ernest's insistence on the complexity of black writing in the nineteenth century and his belief in the serious nature of black historical production in this period creates an important foundation for my work to build upon.[21]

My study, however, builds on *both* the modernist and the postmodernist approaches. Like the modernists, it privileges form, method, and style as operative indicators of the character of black historical production, but my work sees evidence of this much earlier than most studies. And similar to the postmodernists, this study is sympathetic to the complexities of black historical production and the myriad ways in which black writers crafted a historical discourse, notwithstanding the limitations in their training and constraints of their experiences. It also recognizes, as modernists and postmodernists do, that African American intellectuals sought to present a more balanced portrait of African American history to mainstream American audiences.

Despite these similarities to modernist and postmodernist approaches, my approach seeks a third way to interrogate the genealogy and underlying theoretical and methodological thrust of nineteenth-century African American historical production. To understand the development of African American history, I place more emphasis on situating discussions squarely on the terrain of eighteenth- and nineteenth-century historical practice, which relied, at different times, on the authority of biblical, classical, universal, and modern history.

Beyond modernism and postmodernism, black history has popular meanings that sometimes compete with academic understandings of the discipline's origins and development. Popular understandings locate the evolution of African American historical writing and even the discipline itself as arising from a cauldron of black protest and agitation in the 1960s. Even some academics believe that W. E. B Du Bois and Carter Woodson inaugurated black history in the 1920s. As this study shows, these understandings are mired in contemporary notions of what constitutes history as much as they are informed by our perceptions of what a nineteenth-century black public sphere might have looked like. In our popular visions, perhaps, the black public sphere consisted of a circumscribed and reactive space informed by slavery, racism, and marginalization. In this study, however, I am less interested in binaries and more engaged with how to think differently about the origins and varied meanings of black historiography. The nineteenth-century black public sphere was not simply a reactive space created in response to the vicissitudes of a hostile white world, nor was it a place that operated totally apart from the larger mainstream. What I suggest throughout this study is that the black public sphere, a term that I do not use explicitly in the text, is deeply informed by the broader realities of American and European intellectual life, and people of color throughout the nineteenth and early twentieth centuries viewed themselves in terms articulated by David Walker, as "citizens of the world." As Walker recognized, it is clear that throughout the nineteenth century and up to the early twentieth century, black intellectuals drew upon the twin reservoirs of African American communal and intellectual culture and American and European intellectual traditions ranging from classicism to scientism and objectivity to fashion a historical tradition. If the work of the last few years on free black communities and black life has taught us anything, it suggests that the black community was not monolithic or one-dimensional but vibrant, engaged, and culturally, especially intellectually, diverse. The black public sphere that these writers created reflected all of these complexities, and it is evident in the depth and sophistication of the work they produced throughout the period covered in this study.[22]

This study explores the complex ways in which African Americans maintained and utilized historical knowledge during the nineteenth and early twentieth centuries by discussing the intellectual process through which they created and maintained historical traditions. The study is also concerned with attending to the complex ways in which African Americans obtained and utilized historical knowledge during the nineteenth and early twentieth centuries by discussing and analyzing the development of intellectual sensibilities among African Americans related to history. African Americans understood history not simply from the limitations of their deeply contentious present in the nineteenth century, shaped as it was by the realities of slavery and marginalization, but from the wider scope and range of their presence as complex historical subjects from the "first ages of the world." The histories they created also symbolized their desire for a more enlightened and complete citizenship in the future. They saw themselves as subjects, citizens, and actors in the human drama, and they used history and their historical work to amplify this point.

My approach to the evolution of the African American historical project is significantly influenced by the work of Benjamin Quarles and Earl Thorpe. Quarles established the importance of the antebellum period as a formative moment of historical discourse. He also noted that antebellum historians established the parameters for the African American historical enterprise used earlier—namely, the Haitian Revolution (1791–1804)—to broaden the scope of African American history while utilizing a contributionist discourse centered on black participation in America's wars and activism to eradicate slavery. Thorpe devised one of the first and most useful periodization schemes for black history. He divided black historiography into four schools: The Beginning School, Justifiers of Emancipation, 1800–1896; the Middle Group, 1896–1930; Negro Historical Societies and Late Nineteenth- and Twentieth-Century Historians; and the New School, 1930–55. Although in this early study he downplayed the impact of the Beginning School, the model still provides a useful periodization scheme for historical production in the nineteenth century and an analytical framework for the examination of black writing throughout this period.[23]

In a reassessment of this work, shortly before his death in 1989, Earl Thorpe called for a rethinking of the contours of African American historiography. As Quarles had done before him, Thorpe called for examination of the *motivations* of black historians in writing history, a more nuanced discussion of numerous neglected black historians, and a critical understanding of the genealogy of black history. This study heeds Thorpe's call by locating black historical production within the context of the development of black social ideology and historical consciousness, examining these phenomena throughout the entire nineteenth century and up to 1915. One simply cannot fully assess the black tradition of historical production without examining it over a long sweep of time.[24]

In selecting the works and writers to consider in this study, I have largely followed the lead of literary historians, including Dorothy Porter Wesley, Vernon Loggins, and Blyden Jackson, and historians Earl Thorpe, John Hope Franklin,

August Meier, Elliott Rudwick, and more recently Wilson Jeremiah Moses, Mia Bay, Mitch Kachun, Dickson Bruce, John Ernest, and Joan Bryant. While there is a strong consensus on the intellectuals and works that comprise the nineteenth-century historical canon, few historians have discussed the ways in which these works informed subsequent historical production and the professionalization of the field—an omission that this study seeks to correct.[25]

I have designed a periodization scheme that allows us to account for the intensification of social and historical consciousness in the African American community during the nineteenth century while maintaining an appreciation of the shifting intellectual terrain of the period. Therefore, for the first period, I begin with the 1817 publication of Jacob Oson's pathbreaking treatise *A Search for Truth* and end in 1836, the year before the publication of Hosea Easton's *Treatise on the Intellectual Character, and the Civil and Political Condition, of the Colored People*. American and African American scholars recognize this as a period during which the new nation began to take shape socially, politically, and most important, intellectually. For African Americans, this period witnessed the establishment of churches, schools, literary and historical societies, the black press, and other important community institutions. These developments set the stage for a more developed tradition of historical writing between 1837, the year Easton's work appeared, and 1850, the year of the Compromise, which date my second period. This period also witnessed the publication of important treatises on the black experience by James W. C. Pennington, Robert Benjamin Lewis, Ann Plato, and Henry Highland Garnet and featured the domination of historical writing by clergy associated with the abolitionist movement.[26]

The periodization for the remainder of the study follows the chronology agreed upon for African American and American history generally: 1850, the year of the historic Compromise, to 1863, the year William Wells Brown's *The Black Man* was published, form the boundaries of the third period. The Emancipation Proclamation took effect on January 1, 1863, and the Battle of Gettysburg later that year turned the Civil War's tide in favor of the Union. All these events had an important impact on the nature of black life and historical production. The fourth period, 1863 to 1882, was largely transitional. It facilitated the transformation in African American historical writing from antebellum to postbellum modes of writing and analysis and laid the groundwork for the rise of race history. The final period, 1883 to 1915, is one in which history, in general, and black history, in particular, became more professionalized. I see the process of professionalization as informed by changes in historical writing as well as the growth of historical interest in the black academy. The founding of the Association for the Study of Negro Life and History signals the achievement of that professionalization.[27]

The study is divided into six chapters. Chapter 1, "Troubling the Pages of Historians: African American Intellectuals and Historical Writing in the Early Republic, 1817–1837," examines the intellectual and rhetorical uses of history among African Americans from the publication of Jacob Oson's *A Search for Truth* (1817) through the founding of *Freedom's Journal* (1827) to the publication of Hosea Easton's *Treatise* (1837). This chapter examines the emergence of book-length textual discussions. Instead of looking solely at what I term the usual "driving engines" of black historicism—vindicationism, contributionism, or Afrocentricism—to understand the influences on nineteenth-century African American historical production, I argue for the consideration of traditional, mainstream humanist paradigms as an explanation for how and why black intellectuals engaged in historical writing in the ways that they did. Chapter 2, "To Present a Just View of Our Origin: Creating an African American Historical Discourse, 1837–1850," discusses the creation of a historical discourse in the antebellum period focusing on black intellectuals associated with the church and why that association did not relegate them to a predictable or essentialist approach to the past. Members of enlightened and sophisticated clerical traditions, these authors skillfully integrated a wide range of scholarly traditions. Using the work of Martin Delany, Hosea Easton, James W. C. Pennington, Ann Plato, Robert Benjamin Lewis, and Henry Highland Garnet, this chapter builds on the previous one through an analysis of how African American intellectuals used the intellectual culture of the nineteenth century, namely biblical, classical, and modern history (American antiquities and Holy Land mania) to frame a complex humanistic portrait of African American history that transcended the rise of the West with its attendant horrors of the Middle Passage and slavery and extended back to the "first ages of man."

Chapter 3, "The Destiny of the Colored People: African American History between Compromise and Jubilee, 1850–1863," juxtaposes black historical discourse on the American Revolution with that of the Haitian Revolution through an examination of the writings of William C. Nell, George Boyer Vashon, William Wells Brown, and James Theodore Holly, major history writers of these years. Chapter 4, "The Historical Mind of Emancipation: Writing African American History at the Dawn of Freedom, 1863–1882," begins with the publication of William Wells Brown's *The Black Man* (1863) and ends with the publication of Joseph Wilson's *Emancipation: Its Course and Progress* (1882). This period served as a bridge between antebellum discourse featuring the centrality of the classics and the Bible and the rise of postbellum discourse, which slowly began to professionalize by the end of the nineteenth century. The work of William Wells Brown and William Still's *Underground Railroad* serve as representative examples of the shifting priorities of black writers.

Chapter 5, "Advancement in Numbers, Knowledge, and Power: African American History in Post-Reconstruction America, 1883–1915," examines the development of race history from the publication of George Washington Williams's *History of the Negro Race* (1883) to the founding of the Association for the Study of Negro Life and History (ASNLH) in 1915. While considering the work of various authors, male and female, and the forms their history assumed, especially emancipation narratives, race textbooks, and biographical catalogs, this chapter pays particular attention to the historical writing of Anna Julia Cooper, Fannie Barrier Williams, Frances Watkins Harper, Lelia Amos Pendleton, and N. F. Mossell and helps to broaden the usual interpretations of their historical writing as woman-centered. In this chapter the work of these women is joined to the larger historical discourse of the period.

Chapter 6, "To Smite the Rock of Knowledge: The Black Academy and the Professionalization of History," looks at the intersections between the rise of race history and the development of history curricula in the leading liberal arts colleges and normal schools of the late nineteenth and early twentieth centuries. An examination of the course offerings and publications supported by these institutions reveals other aspects of intense interest in history, namely the development of historical studies over time and the emergence of a fully trained professional class of historians by 1915.

As with any study of this scope, there are important caveats to note. My focus here is on historical writing, especially the ascendancy of texts. While I engage the black press, literary and historical societies, and the convention movement and present them in my study where relevant, Frankie Hutton, Mia Bay, Laurie Maffly-Kipp and Elizabeth McHenry, Philip Foner, and John Ernest have examined these institutions in more detail, especially in the antebellum period. Second, in the postbellum period, I am more concerned with larger trends that led to the institutionalization of African American history in colleges and universities and the ultimate professionalization of African American history. Next, the structure of this study does not allow systematic study of historical literature produced by black clerics in the late nineteenth century, the sheer volume of which warrants a study in itself. My goal is simply to trace the ways that black intellectuals negotiated and contributed to the construction of a nuanced, expansive, complex, and humanistically grounded historical discourse throughout the nineteenth century and to show the relationship of this textual production to the wider intellectual culture of the time.

Although no study of this size can consider all, or even most, of the historical work produced during the time period under study here, *A Faithful Account of the Race* nevertheless presents the development of historical production as much more than the intellectual undertakings of the few, but as an important part of African American life. It shows that African American intellectual history can shed significant light on all facets of African American history. It relates this history and historical production to larger national and intellectual movements. While departing from African American historiographical orthodoxy by focusing less on racial vindication or black liberation as the primary determinant of African American historical discourse, this study takes seriously the intellectual and scholarly contributions such works made, based on their own internal logic (methodology, argumentation, and sources). Finally, while considering the construction and dissemination of history in the African American community, this study also helps to establish the intellectual and ideological underpinnings of black historical scholarship.

Perhaps, most significant, however, it is critical to emphasize the importance of situating all of these works within the historical milieu in which they were produced. In doing so, one can clearly see not only the obstacles inherent in re-creating the past at these points in time, but, perhaps more important, the tremendous determination of these writers to present an engaging and enduring record of the past. Their work represented both the best efforts and the unique limitations of black historical writing during the nineteenth and early twentieth centuries. Fettered by slavery, circumscribed in freedom, and marginalized in the larger society across time, black intellectuals harnessed the power of the pen to create a holistic tradition of historical writing that served as the basis for the subsequent professionalization of the discipline. This writing laid the groundwork for the evolution of college and university programs in African American history and studies. This tradition of historical writing was not static but proved amazingly adaptable both to the changing condition of African Americans and developments in the larger intellectual community. Constructing "a faithful account of the race" meant more than simple hagiography, but a careful reconstruction of a history that re-created the past, complicated the present, and charted the future condition and possibilities for the race.

CHAPTER 1

Troubling the Pages of Historians

African American Intellectuals and Historical Writing
in the Early Republic, 1817–1837

> I have been for years troubling the pages of historians, to find out what our
> fathers have done to the white Christians of America, to merit such condign
> punishment as they have inflicted on them, and do continue to inflict on us
> their children. But I must aver, that my researches have hitherto been to no
> effect. —DAVID WALKER, *Appeal to the Coloured Citizens of the World, 1829*

THE ERA OF THE EARLY REPUBLIC WAS, without a doubt, a hopeful and
promising moment in American history. Not only had the country expanded
demographically and spatially after the Louisiana Purchase in 1803, it abolished the Atlantic slave trade in 1808 and successfully weathered a significant
challenge to its sovereignty by defeating the British in the War of 1812. Yet,
African Americans searched, often in vain, for recognition of, and appreciation
for, their contributions to this national development and their achievements
in this process. David Walker recognized the incongruity; he also understood
the stakes involved in an accurate representation of the past. As Walker's *Appeal to the Coloured Citizens of the World* suggests, and literary historian Elizabeth
McHenry's recent work on black reading habits demonstrates, "troubling the
pages of historians" became an important cause among black intellectuals and
could very well serve as a central metaphor for their efforts during the era of
the early republic. They "trouble[d]" the pages of historians as they searched
existing documentary/historical records for evidence of other African Americans' contributions to historical developments. And the evidence they found
went to produce new texts, which, no doubt, also served to "trouble" the pages
of historians who, to that point, had written history almost as if African Americans had no past.[1]

The emergence of African American historical texts coincided with the explosion of print culture in the United States. Determined to present a nuanced

and complex portrait of themselves as citizens and actors in the human drama, black intellectuals began to use and produce texts that accentuated their humanity in a world where slavery and black degradation were commonplace. While it is clear, as others have argued, that oratorical and commemorative historical expressions played a significant role in conveying historical messages in the African American public sphere, texts, especially pamphlets and later books, played an increasingly important role in shaping historical understandings in the black community.[2] Rooted in the desire of an expanding, educated, and literate population to define itself as more than slaves or circumscribed citizens, black intellectuals' engagement with history centered on the interrogation of texts in the effort to understand and name the complex realities of African American existence in the modern world.

Naming the realities of black existence in the modern world required more than oratorical eloquence or rhetorical flourish, as important as both were. To be especially effective, it depended on the ability of intellectuals to penetrate the central texts of the Western canon, namely universal, classical, and biblical history. In doing so, these writers demonstrated their deep engagement with Enlightenment-driven modes of rationality, which in this case privileged reason over speculation and the written over the oral. Texts, in these intellectuals' minds, not only provided access to the past but also helped to preserve that past and create new possibilities for the interpretation of black life and history.[3]

In 1817, African American intellectuals comprised a small, but vocal minority, concentrated in well-established, primarily free communities, such as New Haven, New York, Boston, Philadelphia, and Baltimore. Most were self-trained, some had matriculated at American liberal arts colleges, and a few had enjoyed access to educational institutions abroad. The creation and expansion of domestic institutions such as schools, churches, and literary and historical associations contributed to the growth of this small intellectual class. Black intellectuals, like African Americans in general, however, faced severe proscription in the public sphere. As members of a group conceptualized as a perpetual problem and nuisance in the North, and increasingly as "hewers of wood and drawers of water" in the South, black intellectuals faced an uphill battle in their effort to construct more promising and complex portraits of racial possibility. Although they usually rejected the tendency common among Enlightenment theorists to divide the world into a classic binary—the civilized and the savage—these intellectuals were strong proponents of the Enlightenment vision of the world suffused with reason.[4]

The strategies these early black intellectuals adopted came directly from historical methods common in the eighteenth and early nineteenth centuries. For example, the idea of *Providence* posited God as an operative force in human affairs and the Bible as a major historical source. This concept, drawn from Puritanism, held that God played an active, even interventionist, role in human affairs. The jeremiad, a series of biblical injunctions that reminded believers of God's original promises and commandments, complete with stern injunctions to encourage the faithful to follow them, were mainstays of historical writing not only during the colonial and revolutionary periods, but George Bancroft, the nation's premier historian, continued to employ these traditions through the end of the nineteenth century.[5] Another important concept was *universal history*, the eighteenth- and nineteenth-century term for *world* history, but more than that, the history of humankind from its advent to the present. Universal history in historical conceptualizations put the ancient world on center stage. Caroline Winterer described the tradition as the "culture of classicism," a systematic engagement among educated Americans from the eighteenth to the late nineteenth century with the intellectual products of ancient Greece and Rome—from the poetry of Horace and Ovid, to the philosophical writings of Plato and Aristotle, to the historical commentary of Herodotus and Thucydides.[6] A third strategy involves the idea of *progress*, perhaps the most important mode of eighteenth-century historicism. Drawn from the work of European thinkers such as Montesquieu, Rousseau, and Condorcet, progress meant that the historical past offered a roadmap to chart the possibilities of humankind. More often than not, progress was conceptualized in cyclical and millennial ways as eighteenth-century thinkers argued that human history advanced from simple societies to complex civilizations. Despite a growing belief during the eighteenth century that casual rather than providential forces determined historical outcomes, American intellectuals clung to a belief in the exceptional qualities of the new republic, and God's hand loomed large in the events and occurrences of the period. Because of this thinking, more often than not, historical conceptualizations embodied a curious mixture of the sacred and the secular.[7]

This chapter explores some of the earliest manifestations of textual historical production among African American intellectuals through these lenses. Building on, as well as critically engaging, the work of Wilson Jeremiah Moses and John Ernest, I explore early nineteenth-century black historicism in the broadest possible terms in order to showcase the complexity of historical styles and approaches of that period. This chapter views these early historical works as far more than vindicationist—a defense of black humanity against racist disparagement. And they are more than contributionist in their focus on how African Americans have contributed to American society. Freemasonry played a role in these texts, as Joanna Brooks and Maurice Wallace have persuasively shown, but its influence is not adequate to explain the constant references in these texts to the ancient world, especially Africa. Moreover this study presumes that recent interpretations by Moses that frame early black historicism as Afrocentric and that Ernest calls "liberationist historiography" perhaps reflect as much about the post–civil rights movement moment out of which these interpretations came as they do the nineteenth century that produced the texts. The challenge here, therefore, is to revisit all of the common assumptions underlying scholarly beliefs about the driving engines of black historicism and, as much as possible, to keep the texts in the context in which they were created. Doing so will not necessarily negate any of the conclusions others have drawn about these texts. Nevertheless, it will reveal how much richer and more revealing they are. African American history was closely connected to European historical methods, but the point is not to "legitimize" the historical production of black intellectuals by connecting it to Europe. Rather the point is to emphasize that it was more than "race" work and racial writing. Without apologies or explanations (suggesting none were necessary), these writers and thinkers engaged the world of ideas and provided, *themselves*, a legitimate expression of and contribution to nineteenth-century historiography.[8]

Literary and historical scholars generally see the development of print culture in the black community during this early period in two distinct phases: writings that appeared in the early republic from 1789 to the late 1820s, and those written from the late 1820s through the 1830s. The first period of African American print culture was influenced by the American Revolution, the rise of post-revolutionary ideologies that called into question the nation's commitment to freedom and equality for all its citizens, critiques of the continued existence of slavery, and the growth and expansion of free communities of color. The latter period witnessed the development of a defined African American identity, the formation of important institutional sites such as the press, literary and historical societies, and the convention movement, and a decided shift from the antislavery tactics of the eighteenth century to the immediate abolitionist goals of the antebellum period.[9]

The explosion of African American print culture in the 1790s coincided with the post-revolutionary quest to reconcile the principles of liberty and equality contained in the Declaration of Independence with the discriminatory and exclusionary realities faced by a burgeoning African American population.

Alongside other forms of historical expression, ranging from public festivals and displays to commemorative celebrations of seminal events such as the 1807 abolition of the slave trade, black intellectuals produced pamphlets, sermons, tracts, and other textual pieces to plead the case of African Americans and used the written word to construct what Richard Newman, Patrick Rael, and Phil Lapansky have termed "pamphlets of protest."[10] Pamphlet culture, as historian Lewis Perry noted, represented and contributed to a "reorganization of knowledge" that fueled print and intellectual production and allowed for the growth of the printing press and the production of chapbooks—small, inexpensive pamphlets that were literally read to pieces. These pamphlets, written primarily by ministers, lay community leaders, and antislavery activists, used a wide variety of approaches ranging from vindicationism and contributionism to moral suasion and sentimental advocacy to present their claims for black equality to the American public. In the process, they covered a wide range of subjects, including the plight of free blacks in the aftermath of the American Revolution, the ending of the Atlantic slave trade, and growing debates over the colonization movement. Nevertheless, one of the most frequently discussed topics in these early pamphlets was the history of Africa.[11] Partly because of this focus on Africa, modernist scholars tend to argue for the centrality of vindicationism, contributionism, and Freemasonry as driving forces in this early history.[12] But these works reveal much more.

Early historical narratives written by Puritan writers such as William Bradford and the subsequent histories of the American Revolution written by David Ramsay and Mercy Otis Warren had little to offer that provided a complex and nuanced discussion of the Americas. George Bancroft's providential narrative gained wide acceptance as American history began to take shape between the 1840s and 1890s, but when black intellectuals looked to American history in this earlier period, they were more interested in discussing the gulf between American promises of liberty and equality embodied in the Declaration of Independence and the Constitution, on the one hand, and the continued existence of the slave trade up to 1808, and after that, of slavery itself. Consequently, black writers selectively turned to eighteenth-century European historicism because, significantly, American historiography was in its infancy. European writers such as Montesquieu, Voltaire, David Hume, Edward Gibbon, and William Robertson produced magisterial treatises that discussed progress, historical causation, universal history, classical antiquity, and the history of the Americas. Although these histories were steeped in European national and ethnic prejudices, superiority and inferiority complexes, progressive and degenerate views of history, as well as a host of other limitations, this eighteenth-century historiography was, nevertheless, useful because it preserved some aspects of Renaissance humanism and, in some instances, expressed serious concerns about the colonization in the New World. It also continued to rely largely on classical and biblical models. These models allowed useful discussions of human progress that could transcend the limitations of the American present. Thus, they were especially useful to black writers.[13]

But in addition to the influence of eighteenth-century European antecedents, early black historicism included elements of the culture of classicism that permeated the *American* public sphere and higher education in the eighteenth century and for much of the nineteenth. Because of the focus in recent analyses on black Masonry as a driving engine for black interest in Africa (Egypt and Ethiopia), scholars have overlooked African American intellectual engagement with the classics. In other instances, references to the premodern world in early black histories appear to be a nascent form of Afrocentricism.[14] But black intellectuals, as others have also noted, were much more sophisticated in their scholarly production, appealing to classical texts of Herodotus, Strabo, and Diodorus Siculus as well as early Church writers such as Josephus, Jerome, and Eusebius precisely because this history predated the rise of the Western hemisphere, which significantly inaugurated the slave trade. This approach allowed these writers to use the Western canon to offer a more complex portrait of themselves in the human drama in part by presenting a much longer genealogy of black involvement in world affairs than their introduction to the Americas primarily as slaves.[15] Thus, as useful as modernist and postmodernist approaches are for aiding our understanding of these nineteenth-century texts, we can look squarely at the eighteenth and nineteenth centuries for even greater insights into black historicism.

Orations, subsequently published as pamphlets, not only provide some of the best illustrations of the complex approaches to the past utilized by black intellectuals, but also demonstrate how they deployed print culture to situate African American history in the larger and longer stream of universal and classical history. The first pamphlets, which primarily focus on the slave trade, include John Marrant's *You Stand on the Level with the Greatest Kings on Earth* (1789); Peter Williams's *Abolition of the Slave Trade* (1808); and William Hamilton's *O' Africa* (1815). Although all of these pamphlets predate the stated starting point of this study, their inclusion allows us to see some of the eighteenth-century roots of early nineteenth-century historical writing.[16]

John Marrant's *You Stand on the Level* is an excellent example of early black historicism. Marrant, one of the earliest black preachers in the English colonies and chaplain of Prince Hall's African Lodge, offered a cursory overview of ancient Africa. One of the central purposes of Marrant's pamphlet, as demonstrated by the pamphlet's title, is the vindication of the race. Drawing heavily on the institutional knowledge provided by black Masons about ancient Africa, Marrant reconstructed its history prior to the rise of the slave trade, ranging from the origins and development of ancient kingdoms to early advances in the arts and sciences. Marrant did not disguise his interest in and indebtedness to the ancient arts of Masonry throughout the text. Indeed, black Masonry figured prominently in African American social, institutional, and intellectual culture in the early republic.[17] But a closer look at his methodology and sources shows they are firmly grounded in even broader eighteenth-century historical approaches.

Marrant demonstrated his knowledge of the classics and their connection to biblical exegesis when he referenced the writings of the Roman philosopher Seneca in his discussion of the duties of human beings to one another. Seneca was one of the first Roman thinkers to depart from the Aristotelian notion articulated in *Politics* and the *Nicomachean Ethics* that certain groups were not usually destined for slavery. Seneca not only promoted the idea of humanity's consanguinity but insisted that slaves be treated with kindness. Marrant's knowledge and use of the classics is also apparent in his discussion of early human history, especially the story of the Garden of Eden, which the ancients believed was located on one of the four rivers at the corners of the earth (Tigris, Nile, Ganges, Euphrates). Marrant's reference was not based exclusively on the Bible but on the opinions of "the learned" whom he cited as early Christian writers, including Josephus, Eusebius, and Jerome. In fact, he cited Josephus to support the assertion that "Paradise did, as it were, border upon Egypt, which is the principal part of the African Ethiopia, which the ancient writers hold is meant there." In another instance, when citing the great ancient builders of civilizations honored by Masonry such as Nebuchadnezzar (Babylon), Cyrus (Persia), Julius Caesar (Rome), and Herod the Great (Judea), he referenced Josephus's description of the erection of the Second Temple by Herod.[18]

Marrant did not limit his concerns to the past but also reflected on the present, noting that slavery was not the natural state of African Americans. Although his claim was common among black intellectuals in this period, its validity hinged on an examination of universal history. In short, to make this claim, Marrant had to "trouble the pages of historians." He was clear about his purpose: "For if we search history, we shall not find a nation on earth but has at some period or other of their existence been in slavery, from the Jews down to the English nation, under many Emperors, Kings, and Princes." Marrant further elaborated, pointing out that slavery's existence corrupted ancient empires (as it did civilizations in the modern period) by using a story drawn from universal history of an incident that occurred before Gregory I became pope and recorded in the *Life of Gregory the Great*. In this story, Gregory described a Roman slave market populated by enslaved subjects from Britain in the sixth century, which served to demonstrate the universal nature of slavery and its devastating effect on humanity.[19]

While John Marrant's pamphlet heralded the beginning of the early republic, Peter Williams's oration and subsequent pamphlet signaled a similarly auspicious occasion in the African American "commemorative calendar," the abolition of the slave trade in 1808. Williams filtered history through the lens of commemorative culture, which, as historian Mitch Kachun has shown, played an important role in shaping African American historical consciousness. An Episcopal priest, cofounder of the St. Phillips African Church in New York, and subsequent cofounder of *Freedom's Journal* in 1827, Williams spoke forcefully about the slave trade, which he described as an "inhuman branch of commerce." In a clear use of what Wilson Moses has termed "sentimental Afrocentricism," a mode of historicism tending to portray African character as being in harmony with "nature, communalism, art and music," Williams argued that Africans lived in a veritable Eden, a state of "simplicity, innocence, and contentment." The rise of the Western powers brought devastation and destruction, especially as Europeans explored the western coast of Africa. Williams's discussion of the African past and the changes occasioned by European penetration of the western coast of Africa represented a highly politicized exercise that persuaded African Americans and whites of the horrors of the slave trade and slavery while celebrating the trade's demise.[20]

Using the lens of classical and universal history, Williams's presentation becomes part of a conversation with broader sentiments in American society about black worth that are deeply engaged with even larger eighteenth-century ideas about indigenous cultures. Even though the work clearly adhered to a cyclical understanding of history, a historiography of decline, it also showed that Africa's demise was hastened by inhumane traits and events that corrupted humanity. Williams's harsh critique of the slave trade and at least one of its instigators, Christopher Columbus, not only represented black indignation and a desire for vindication, but a skillful use of eighteenth-century ideas about the degeneracy and backwardness of the Spanish. He ascribed their motivations to greed: "Gain induced the first colonists of America to cross the waters of the Atlantic, surpassing the bounds of reasonable acquisition, violated the sacred injunctions of the gospel, frustrated the designs of the pious and humane, and enslaving the harmless aborigines, compelling them to drudge in the mines."

Williams's reference to Spanish rather than British colonial depredations against the indigenous population has important antecedents. He cited William Robertson's *History of America* (1777) as a source. Robertson, a prominent eighteenth-century Scottish historian, was viewed as one of the greatest historians of his generation, ranking with David Hume and Edward Gibbon in popularity and book sales. His *History of America* was steeped in providential history and the acceptance of Spanish backwardness, codified in what historian Charles Gibson popularized as the Black Legend, which has come to characterize negative treatments of the Spanish imperial project in the New World. The Black Legend originated in the pronouncements and writings of Bartolomé de Las Casas, a Dominican priest whose *Devastation of the Indies* offered the most thoroughgoing critique of the impact of Spanish colonization on the indigenous people. Although a proponent of the eighteenth-century notion of impartiality, an early form of objectivity in which historical writers attempted to distance themselves from the historical past in order to relate it more accurately to contemporary audiences, Robertson's discussion of "primitive civilizations" such as the Amerindians tended to frame them as simplistic, naïve, and in harmony with nature. This approach represented a shift from seventeenth-century historiographical traditions in which Europeans attempted to juxtapose Amerindian civilizations they encountered in the New World with the civilizations of classical antiquity. Despite his criticism of some indigenous groups, Robertson praised the highly advanced civilizations of the Aztec and the Inca. In this account, Edenic as well as comparatively sophisticated civilizations coexisted in the Americas prior to Europeans' arrival. Williams's presentation of African societies, in ways similar to the eighteenth-century critique of indigenous American life, combined these assessments with characterizations based on nationality rather than race. Many black writers used similar approaches in their discussions of the black past, suggesting, among other interpretations, a keen awareness and active use of popular eighteenth-century notions of historical causation.[21]

William Hamilton's *O' Africa* (1815) contains features similar to those found in John Marrant's pamphlets. One of the most prolific orators and writers of the early republic, Hamilton founded the New York Mutual Relief Society and was active in many different capacities in New York's free black community.

O' Africa, according to historian Dickson Bruce, utilized techniques found in vindicationist literature such as Henri Grégoire's *An Enquiry concerning the Intellectual and Moral Faculties and Literature of Negroes*, an admirable defense of African American intellectual capacity, and works of the English writer Thomas Map. When analyzing Hamilton's textual production, historians have focused on the caustic nature of his indictment of European involvement in the slave trade. And, indeed, Hamilton not only criticized the slave trade in harsh terms but was particularly critical of European involvement: "The trade was begun by white men, and by Europeans . . . they set to work that low, sly, wicked cunning, peculiar to the Europeans, to the creating of jealousies and animosity, one horde or nation with another. To these princes who were proof against their vile craftiness, they administered draughts of their intoxicating spirituous liquor and then distilled in them their base purposes." At another juncture in the pamphlet, Hamilton conjectured that some nations portrayed the devil as white.[22]

Hamilton's assessment of whites was really an assessment of their behavior and relied on two important components of eighteenth-century historiography: the use of cyclical and millennial conceptions of the past, and the relationship between civilization and barbarism. Giambattista Vico, like other eighteenth-century historians, maintained a belief in the idea that all civilizations cycled from barbarism to advanced achievements and back again, guided by Providence. Hamilton may have used this approach when discussing the involvement of various European powers in the slave trade, and, by extension, the nature of whiteness. Hamilton's application of Vico's cycles of civilizations played an important role in making this argument. He pointed out that Portugal, "the first trader in African blood and sinews," and Spain, "the base followers of so base an example," not only were in a state of decay but this state of decay led them to barbaric actions like the institution of the slave trade. This approach also followed other interrogations of eighteenth-century histories that were highly critical of the Spanish imperial project and promoted the idea of Portuguese and Spanish barbarism. By these accounts, the decline of both nations led not only to a state of "effeminacy, weaknesses and degradation," but caused them to engage in "barbaric acts" against African people. In eighteenth-century historicism, barbarism naturally accompanied decline, which may explain the numerous instances in Hamilton's speech where he juxtaposed ideas of European superiority with actual behavior towards enslaved Africans. Hamilton singled out Columbus and Cortes for their roles in the conquest of the New World and insisted that if they had not been successful then Africa might have been spared from the worst manifestations of the slave trade.[23]

Eighteenth-century writers were also interested in the correlation between Providence and progress, which, in an age of mercantilism, referred to the establishment of sophisticated civilizations, complete with commercial enterprises. Convinced that commercial and economic motives played an important role in the inauguration of the slave trade, Hamilton asked the reader, "What was all this butchery set on foot for? I will tell you my brethren; for sordid gain, the white man's God." Hamilton suggested further that Africans replaced Native Americans "to do the drudgery of the new found world." The intersections of commercialism, a preference for modern civilizations, and concern for humanity may explain all of the human interest stories as well as vivid descriptions of humanity's plight in the pamphlet. Hamilton vividly described the enslavement of African people: "They purchased the captives taken in war for gewgaws and for draughts of that intoxicating liquor that is sometimes the bane of the peace of families among themselves, and sold them again at an advanced price." He also detailed the abuses of the Middle Passage by providing an account of the murder of an infant who would not eat. "The savage captain with his knotted cat whipped it until its body and legs were much swollen, he then ordered it placed in water so hot, that its skin and nails came off." In these cases, rather than commerce illustrating progress and Providence, it revealed the corruption of European humanity.[24]

Proponents of the modernist school frequently note the absence of sources in nineteenth-century black writing to place them outside the modernist tradition. While this is true in some cases, Hamilton's and Williams's audiences were clearly aware of common sources of information about the black past. As Dickson Bruce has shown, black literary writers drew from Christian and British abolitionist writing to create a literary tradition, and the same is true of black intellectuals who wrote history—often the same people. The commonly accepted sites of eighteenth-century knowledge drew heavily on the Bible and classical authorities, writers whom these authors referred to as "ancients" or the "the learned." Given the existence of common sites of knowledge, one can reasonably infer that their detailed descriptions of Africa were based on some combination of knowledge embedded in the work of eighteenth-century thinkers from Comte de Buffon to Herder and possibly the accounts of Herodotus, Strabo, and Pliny. Hamilton's specific discussion of Egypt clearly echoed that of Herodotus as well as eighteenth-century "learned" individuals. Moreover, since classical knowledge held sway in the early republic, it is easy to see the classics as a source of this information.[25]

Although it is clear that vindicationism, contributionism, and Masonry played important roles in the development of African American historicism in the early republic, the narrow focus on these aspects of black historicism has often prevented detailed attention to other approaches, especially universal, biblical, and classical histories used by African American intellectuals to make more sense of the past. This narrower focus has also shifted attention away from the broader humanistic discourse that was an integral part of black historicism in this period. The humanistic discourse considered the role of greed and degeneracy in the development of the African slave trade and saw the treatment of Africans and indigenous people not just as empire building (or progress) but as a sign of decline. One of the best examples of how black intellectuals grounded their concerns firmly in the complex use of eighteenth-century historiography is Jacob Oson's *A Search for Truth*. This pamphlet skillfully combined more traditional approaches to black historicism while taking advantage of changing sensibilities in black writing in what historian Dickson Bruce has called "the Age of Colonization," which featured the formation of the American Colonization Society. Because the ACS favored the removal of free and enslaved blacks beyond the borders of the United States, its existence and ideology forced a more transparent discussion by black intellectuals of the African role in the development of Western as well as American civilization.[26]

Jacob Oson's writing, even more profoundly than the earlier works, points to the start of a broadly conceptualized humanistic African American historical tradition. In 1817, three months after the eventful meeting of black Philadelphians at Mother Bethel African Methodist Episcopal Church to denounce the objects and aims of the recently formed American Colonization Society, Oson, a Connecticut minister and schoolteacher and self-described "descendant of Africa," addressed the free black population of New Haven, Connecticut, and later that year, New York City. His address, *A Search for Truth; or, An Inquiry for the Origin of the African Nation*, assessed the place of Africa and African Americans in the rise of Western civilization. "My thoughts run on my people and nation," wrote Oson. "I wish to inquire, who was our common father, and from whom we sprang? And whether our ancestors were such a vile set of beings as we, their descendants, are considered to be." Cognizant of the difficulties he faced in reconstructing the African past because of slavery and its impact on free and enslaved alike, Oson did not entertain wishful or fanciful notions regarding the difficulties of his inquiry but grounded it in a biblical search for truth: "I well know the task is arduous to inquire into this subject, on account of our opposers, for they are many; but ought I give up the inquiry after Truth on this account? Certainly not."[27]

In the world of the early nineteenth century, Jacob Oson is a historical enigma. Most of the material regarding his early life, as religion historian Randall Burkett has shown, appears in the diaries of Frank Croswell, a well-known Episcopal cleric in New Haven during the early republic. The diaries present Oson, who was probably born in the West Indies, as an individual who possessed excellent reasoning, writing, and oratorical skills.[28] Benefiting from the critical groupings of persons of African descent in various Connecticut cities such as Fairfield, New London, and to a lesser extent New Haven, which historian William Piersen has described as encompassing a black subculture, Oson drew upon the resources of these communities, lay and professional, and eventually became a schoolteacher in New Haven.[29]

Absent from the historical record for more than ten years after the publication of *A Search for Truth*, but present in the diaries of Frank Croswell, Oson resurfaced in the pages of *Freedom's Journal* in 1828. Apparently, with Croswell's encouragement, Oson unsuccessfully sought to obtain ordination in the Episcopal Church throughout the first half of the 1820s. Discouraged, Oson eventually formed an Episcopal congregation, but it is unclear whether this enterprise succeeded or failed. Admitted to the holy order of deacons in a special ceremony at Christ Church in Hartford, Connecticut, on February 16 and 17, 1828, by the Right Reverend Bishop Brownell, Oson eagerly anticipated missionary service in Liberia. But less than seven months after his ordination, and before embarking into the missionary field, Oson died. Despite an untimely demise, his historical production raises suggestive questions about the ways black intellectuals looked to biblical, classical, and universal history to understand their world.[30]

In twelve pages, Oson's *A Search for Truth* addressed many of the central components of African American historical understanding in the early nineteenth century. His address centered on answering basic questions regarding black origins, descent, and identity. Answering these questions, as the proliferation of print literature suggested, was central to establishing the humanity of African Americans. To obtain the evidentiary material necessary to assert black humanity required culling information from the twin sites of nineteenth-century authority: sacred history (the Bible) and profane history (works of classical antiquity).[31]

Black origins, a site of unbridled contestation during this period, figured prominently in Oson's account. Racial theorists of the eighteenth and nineteenth centuries looked to the Bible to explain race and justify the maltreatment accorded to black people. Oson confronted his people's detractors directly by naming the aspersions: "Some people say we sprang from the accursed race of Ham; others say from the devil and that we have no soul and must consequently perish like the beasts." Two of the most popular biblically based explanations about black origins suggested the condition of blackness emanated from Noah's curse on Ham for mocking him during Noah's drunken stupor after disembarking from the Ark and from God's placement of a mark on Cain for murdering his brother, Abel. But biblical evidence coexisted with eighteenth-century scientism to explain various aspects of the black condition. Writers like Samuel Stanhope Smith argued that the physical environment affected skin color and other bodily characteristics as well as moral traits.[32]

Aware of the wide range of concerns evident in black pamphlets in this period and their ability to merge social and historical messages, Oson remained convinced of the inadequacy of these explanations of blackness and cast his lot with what he referred to as a third class, probably a reference to antislavery proponents, who believed "we [blacks] are human and have souls to be saved or lost." Not content simply to take sides, Oson also provided evidence. He recited the biblical story of creation to establish firmly the paternity of Noah and his three sons, Shem, Ham, and Japheth, as "the common fathers of all human beings without any distinction of colours, nations, languages or tongues." Clearly using the Bible as his source of authority, Oson offered a similar approach in assessing the relationship between the races: "It is obvious to every impartial person that we sprang from one common father and are united by consanguinity."[33]

Rather than sentimental Afrocentricism, a clear conception of Africa's meanings in world history drawn from biblical, classical, and universal history emerges: "Holy writ speaks more of our nation and land," wrote Oson, "than of any land or people, except the Israelites, who wrote it." Much the same is true of his use of the writings of classical antiquity. He cites Josephus, a Jewish historian of classical antiquity, as the source for the contention that "Greece is indebted to Egypt for science." He gave some credit to another unnamed author enlisted to show that "Nubia was the seat of learning; and from which, probably science sprang, and that they were a powerful and polished nation." Oson also pointed to the contributions of Africa to the early Christian church by listing the early African clerical leaders such as "Divinus, Turtulian [sic], Julius Africanus, Armobius, Sactantins, and St. Austine [sic]," showcasing their contributions as "bishops" and "cornerstones" of the early church.[34] More than a nod to what we now refer to as Afrocentricism, establishing Africa's place as a contributor to the rise of the West in biblical and secular history, prominently

→ cased
tiger

figured in nineteenth-century historical methodology. Prior to the turning of attention to Egyptian antiquities in the 1820s, although few claims were made about race, most historical writers acknowledged the centrality of Egypt to the rise of Western civilization. Like many of his contemporaries, Oson also invoked cyclical history, especially the belief in the restoration of formerly great empires and the rise and fall of nations: "I am well aware that nations have their rise and fall, both in trade and science, which goes from one nation to another, and this is a well known fact."[35]

Oson's discussion of the African American plight is not solely focused on the distant past but also on the contemporary condition of the descendants of Africa. In juxtaposing these realities, he argued that conditions of subjugation and marginalization in the public sphere prevented African Americans from achieving their greatest potential. In discussing the shortcomings of Christian nations, Oson argued that "had the Christian nations been as ambitious to train up our minds to religion and piety as they were to enslave and live upon their ill gotten wealth, by injustice and cruelty, our minds would have never been as degraded as they are represented to be." Comparing African Americans to a caged tiger, Oson stated further that, "the strength of a tyger [sic], or his agility, is not known in his cage, but uncage him and then see whether he would be made the sport and derision of men, women and children around him—so uncage us." In another instance, Oson linked the image of the majestic lion with the suggestion of restoration: "Let the majesty of the Lion be unbound, and he will resume his former prerogative: so let us be emancipated from our encumbrances, and then, where ignorance and darkness reigns, religion and true science would abound."[36]

Oson's assertions regarding the use of the term "Negro" illustrate his use of history as a humanizing force and anticipate what historian Sterling Stuckey has described as the "names controversy." At a moment when the term "African" predominated as the designation for persons of African descent, in Oson's mind, "Negro" proved problematic. Possibly because the term's use disconnected such people from their ancestral homeland, it ran contrary to the naming of African American organizations, especially churches, schools, meetinghouses, and fraternal groups, and as Oson suggested, it set persons of color on a lower intellectual and human plane. Oson used a combination of intellectual and empirical observations to explicate the varied meanings of black existence. Turning to the biblical assessment of all humanity as sinners and wretches, Oson persuasively argued that "Negro," loosely defined as mean wretch, has, at some moment been applicable to "every son and daughter of Adam." As such, it seemed particularly inappropriate to "select us out and brand us with a character that belongs to all mankind." Clearly, no one race had a monopoly on virtue or evil, and this assertion of a common moral character humanized African Americans by connecting them to the larger stream of human history.[37]

Oson's *A Search for Truth* demonstrates how African American intellectuals merged both sacred and secular sensibilities to bolster claims for the importance of Africa as a geographical space and its inhabitants as important contributors to world civilization. Biblical authority deepened secular appreciation of the "benighted sons and daughters of Africa" and made a powerful statement about Africa's importance in terms of place rather than race and the debt Western civilization owed to it.

Here was an asylum to flee from hunger and persecution—here it was that

> Abraham and Sarah found relief in time of famine, that the name of Israel should be held in everlasting remembrance—that is the land where Moses was born and educated—the same Moses that spoke to God face to face, and gave us the moral law—and here it was also that the angel of the Lord commanded Joseph to flee with the child Jesus from the persecuting rage of Herod—here innocence was protected, that it might be fulfilled as it was spoke by the prophets saying, "Out of Egypt have I called my Son." And now, why should the Christian nations boast of the Law and Gospel, and of their supremacy over us? For if they would consider its rise, and obey its precepts, they would be as humble as we poor Africans.[38]

Oson's sophisticated discussion of black origins, identity, and racial designation served simultaneously to present African Americans as complex human actors and subjects in universal and contemporary history. In Oson's account, Africa appeared not as a "heroic or monumental civilization," but as the progenitor of the humanistic values of Western society. Moreover, Oson did not lament the demise or decline of Africa. He was more concerned with discussing the continent's contributions to Western civilization. His analytical style, methodological rigor, and engagement with the Western canon foreshadowed the subsequent work of David Walker and Maria Stewart, who not only built on the work of Oson but integrated themselves fully into the dynamic print culture of the late 1820s and 1830s.[39]

In those decades, as the social and political conditions of black life shifted, newspaper publications contributed to the efforts of black intellectuals to present more sophisticated examples of textual historicism and characterizations of Africa. These efforts were fueled, ironically, as Jacob Oson's work suggests, by the formation of the American Colonization Society (ACS) in 1816 and its organ, the *African Repository*, which, throughout the 1820s, provided intelligent discussions of the African interior, emphasizing the diversity of the African continent. Antislavery proponent Benjamin Lundy's *Genius of Universal Emancipation*, founded in 1825 and headquartered in Baltimore, Maryland, echoed the projects of the *African Repository* by excerpting material from it related to the African past.[40] Discussions of Africa were, however, changing. Although Africa had been an important site for European exploration since the late eighteenth century, funded by commercial outfits, motivated by the Industrial Revolution, and further encouraged by the British establishment of Sierra Leone in 1787 and the British abolition of the slave trade in 1807, the era of free trade (1830–80) made Africa a bountiful field for commercial acquisition, and extensive exploration of the African interior occurred. Popular nineteenth-century visions of Africa as the stereotypical "dark continent," on the one hand, and as a potential commercial haven ripe for exploitation, on the other, clearly conflicted with descriptions of the continent in classical antiquity or in universal history, which had promoted Africa in its greatness.[41]

In challenging popular nineteenth-century beliefs, however, black intellectuals demonstrated their commitment to the importance of primary accounts or textual evidence, which though written generations after events had taken place, offered more authenticity than contemporary sources, which were tinged with notions of black inferiority. The most authoritative sources, therefore, remained the Bible and classical antiquity, but they were joined by eighteenth-century writers who often read the classics in the original Greek or Latin. The more sophisticated use of these sources made its appearance in the pages of the black press.[42]

The 1827 founding of *Freedom's Journal*, by Samuel Cornish, a Presbyterian minister, and John Russwurm, one of the earliest African American college graduates, fundamentally altered the historical terrain. Not only did *Freedom's Journal* serve as a showcase of the social, political, and intellectual life of blacks in the early republic, it also provided one of the first institutional glimpses of African American textual historical production. Early issues of *Freedom's Journal* and its successor, *Rights of All*, featured historical articles with wide-ranging coverage of various issues and events. Appeals to ancient history, especially classical antiquity, to rectify stereotypes and misperceptions about the African past were important features of these articles. One, written by the ex-slave, Haitian scholar, and diplomat Baron Pompée de Vastey demonstrates this point. An official in the government of Christophe, the fiercely monarchical leader of

Haiti's southern regions in the 1820s, Baron de Vastey merged his knowledge of the classical past with his participation in the present triumphs of Haitian nationalism. His editorial "Africa" used eighteenth-century ideas about the origins of civilization, but placed Africa in a more favorable light than contemporary discourse did. He wrote, "The enemies of Africa wish to persuade the world that for five out of the six thousand years the world has existed, Africa has been long sunk in barbarism. Have they forgotten that Africa was the cradle of the arts and sciences? If they pretend to forget this, it becomes our duty to remind them of it." Rather than brutish Africans, in this account, Europeans, or more precisely Greeks, appear as the low nation in the order of humanity. "Everybody knows that the Greeks, so celebrated for their polish of manners and refinement of their taste, were in a state of the grossest barbarity, living like beasts upon herbs and acorns until civilized by Egypt." Biblical genealogy also figured prominently in De Vastey's castigation of white intellectuals who, he argued, suffered from historical amnesia as they subjected African Americans to the same conditions that they previously endured. "These unworthy descendants of Japeth [sic], forgetful of their own history, calumniate their brethren and reproach them with that very state of ignorance and barbarity in which they were plunged upwards of five thousand years."[43]

Another eighteenth-century source figured prominently in the effort to clarify the condition and state of ancient society and the role Africans played in its creation. Count Constanin Volney, who wrote *Travels in Syria and Egypt* (1783) and *Ruins; or, Mediations on the Revolutions of Empires and the Law of the Nature of Empires* (1791), buttressed some of the claims of these intellectuals. In *Ruins*, Volney, a European who traveled extensively in Egypt and Syria during the late eighteenth century, relied heavily on eighteenth-century notions of history that privileged empires as the apex of human civilization. As artistic and aesthetic sites, "ruins" proved both the glory of bygone days and the fleeting nature of power, and they offered important lessons to understanding human development as well. In *Ruins*, Volney explains that Africans were the people to "whom the Greek were indebted for their arts, their learning and even their religion," although by the early nineteenth century, Africans seemed to be in a "dark and prostrate condition in the bosom of a country calling itself Christian." Volney spoke with authority because he, like most intellectuals of his day, read the work of classical writers, including Herodotus and Strabo, in the original Latin and Greek. *Ruins*, like the excerpts published in *Freedom's Journal*, illustrated the primacy of Africa and Africans as central to the development of Western civilization.[44]

John Russwurm in "Mutability of Human Affairs," serialized in successive issues of *Freedom's Journal* in 1827, used Volney's work to substantiate Africa's contribution to the rise of Western civilization. Routinely presented by historians
as a classic example of the historiography of decline, Russwurm's essay, when
read through the lens of universal and classical history, provides unexpected
insights. Decline, as Russwurm and other black intellectuals indicated in their
work, was a function not only of African reality, but a universal condition. To
prove this point, Russwurm, trained in a classical curriculum at Bowdoin College, looked to universal history for examples. There he found ancient societies
like the Greeks and Romans and modern nations like Spain, France, and a host
of others, who had declined from their previous glory. Russwurm's designation
of the plight of these nations reflected eighteenth- and nineteenth-century
prejudices. He echoed, for example, ongoing Christian opposition to Muslim
incursions in Greece, the site of one of the greatest civilizations of classical
antiquity, and Turkey, the former site of the Eastern Roman Empire with the
rich culture and art of Byzantium. He also lamented the current state of Rome.
He called on the Greeks to summon the spirit of a second Leonidas, the Spartan
general who protected the pass at Thermopylae from the invading Persians, to
"arise in this time of need and drive the Crescent [Muslims] from the second
land of freedom, arts and refinement." Rome, the ancient civilization most directly responsible for the rise of the West, suffered a similar fate. In a scene that
could easily have been drawn directly from Volney's *Ruins*, Russwurm detailed
the state of Rome's decline and its implications for the present:

> O' how unlike is Rome in the nineteenth century, to the Rome of the
> Scipios and the Cesars [*sic*]! But while she remains, like her coliseum, after
> having passed successively into the hands of the Herculi, the Ostrogoths
> and the Lombards, until the final dissolution of the Western Empire, by
> Charlemagne; Constantinople, her sister, for whose prosperity the most
> Christian Emperor Constantine was so solicitous, has had her share of
> adversity; her holy temples erected to the worship of God profaned with
> Mahomedan rites, and the haughty Turk reigns over her provinces.[45]

These assessments not only reveal a concern about Africa, they also use a
historiography of decline to level the playing field among nations by bringing
contemporary African history into line with other national and racial experiences. If all civilizations experienced cyclical patterns, then the African state of
decline was not lamentable; rather it was unavoidable. Worse circumstances existed for the founts of Western civilization, Greece and Rome, which not only

were in decline but also under Muslim rule, a fate that, for nineteenth-century Christians, was intolerable. Given this situation, Russwurm conceptualized the present state of Africans as an opportunity to reshape and reassert themselves as actors in the making of the modern world. A different configuration of world affairs did not negate African achievements in the past and the possibilities of African greatness in the future. In fact, after talking about decline as a historical occurrence for all nations, and perhaps anticipating his own return to Africa as a missionary, Russwurm pointed to Africa's role in human civilization through the lens of universal history. He wrote, "We are informed that the gospel was first received in the burning sands of Africa with great eagerness." Although he did not name his source, he also noted that "African Christians soon formed one of the principal members of the primitive church. During the course of the 3rd century, they were animated by the zeal of Tertullian, directed by the abilities of Cyprian and Origen and adorned by the eloquence of Lactantius." Not content simply to sit on the sidelines, Russwurm evidently abandoned the United States and participated in efforts to colonize Liberia.[46]

Although critically important in reconfiguring understandings of the past, Africa was not the only site writers examined. Haiti, a constant symbol in the diasporic imagination, played an important role. African American imaginings of Haiti, however, were less monolithic than one might assume. The island's factitious history did not lend itself to an uncritical embrace of its possibilities. Consequently, in an effort to elevate the Haitian people, intellectuals carefully embraced various schemes, ranging from sympathetic writing about the republic to supporting emigration schemes to bolster its flagging prospects in the years following the tumultuous Haitian Revolution. One of the most interesting examples in *Freedom's Journal* is the anonymously written "Scrapbooks of Africanus," which merged classical understandings with the glorious history of Haiti. In these half-dozen short presentations, "Africanus" appropriated vindicationist language to justify the Haitian Revolution and to chart the progress of the republic in the revolution's aftermath.[47]

Freedom's Journal also featured articles on François Dominique Toussaint L'Ouverture, the mulatto leader of the Haitian Revolution, that were excerpted primarily from the *British Quarterly Review*. These writers understood the need to present him not only as a capable general and diplomat but as a role model. Constructing the Haitian Revolution as exceptionialist, one unnamed editorialist believed that Toussaint's life and the history of Haiti since the revolt conclusively showed that the race possessed "hearts pregnant with heroic energies and hands capable of wielding the sword of war, or swaying the rod of empire."[48]

As important as Africa and Haiti were to black intellectuals during the early years of the American republic, a reverence for classical antiquity, especially awareness and mastery of classical knowledge and the Bible, continued to carry much weight. This is especially apparent in the coverage of *Freedom's Journal*'s successor, *Rights of All*, edited by Samuel Cornish. Topics in the *Rights of All* ranged from advice columns on the value of knowledge to discussions of ancient biblical kingdoms. The inclusion of a regular column, the "Literary Department," provided a showcase for the maturing of intellectual life in the black community. These endeavors revolved around the acquisition of knowledge about history, often in the form of national history. Information about the "moral and physical resources of a country," many observers believed, excited "enterprise and virtuous ambition" among the members of the race. Confirming the power of classical learning, another installment boasted, "a few years ago our most privileged men were but babes in learning, now we boast our classical scholars." Samuel Cornish's column "Babylon" married two functions of classical learning, Babylon's role as an ancient empire and its prominent role in biblical history. Some of these column topics, if not based on, certainly paralleled those in mainstream magazines such as the *North American Review*, which promoted the classical model of education by urging instruction in Greek and classical studies. Black newspapers provided venues for discussions of works like these by John Marrant, William Hamilton, Jacob Oson, and others, and in reprinting for dissemination parts or all of these works, they established a public intellectual sphere for the perpetuation of these and other historical and literary productions.[49]

The early historical work of black writers not only displays their intellectual sophistication but also the deeply humanistic messages they worked to convey to the wider society about the origins of black people and the need to correct the injustices of the past and present. The maturation of African American print culture in the late 1820s and early 1830s meshed with the increased sophistication and communal shifts among African Americans. Determined to tell their own unique story, black intellectuals not only looked to earlier conceptions of historicism informed by moral suasion, vindicationism, and contributionism, but increasingly turned to a critical examination of classicism and universal history to make a more compelling case for black parity with whites in the public sphere. They drew on the efforts of the American Colonization Society's organ, the *African Repository*, to frame more complete visions of Africa. Moreover, not content to rely on white antislavery or abolitionist proponents to argue their case, and aware of the importance of intellectual organizations to promote their cause, black intellectuals actively constructed and promoted the black press, literary and historical societies, and the convention movement, all of which played important roles as incubators for historical thought. David Walker and Maria Stewart clearly benefited from these institutional sites and were actively engaged in helping to craft the knowledge contained in and dispersed by them. Walker's case for urgent and decisive action and Stewart's simultaneous appeal to and subversion of "true womanhood" and moral piety, combined with critical and analytical assessments of classicism and universal history, helped lay the groundwork for a black historical tradition that used history to question the tenets of the American Enlightenment. That questioning involved an active effort on the part of black intellectuals to reread the claims of reason, rationality, and empiricism as markers of the civilized and enlightened mainstream culture and to juxtapose them to the unenlightened and barbaric treatment of enslaved and free blacks in the United States and elsewhere in the world. By questioning the failure to apply enlightened thought to the treatment of African Americans, Walker advocated a more "enlightened" discussion on how African Americans should be treated, especially given their history in classical antiquity and the biblical era.

David Walker's *Appeal to the Coloured Citizens of the World* is one of the best examples of black historical writing at the end of the early republic era. Not only is it an eloquent treatise on the evils of slavery, but like Oson's work, it makes a case for the respect owed to black humanity. Drawing upon a well-established tradition of pamphlet writing in the early republic, but radically different in style, focus, and emphasis, , it serves as a harbinger of a burgeoning and expansive historical discourse in the antebellum period. Typically cast in the tradition of protest literature, the *Appeal* has all the components of history written during this period: utilizing universal history, biblical, classical, and eighteenth-century sources. In constructing what Herbert Aptheker described as "one continual cry" against the cruelties and injustices of slavery, Walker made a most important contribution to the evolution of historical thought among black intellectuals.[50]

Born free in North Carolina in 1795, Walker met prominent African Americans such as Samuel Cornish, abolitionist Henry Highland Garnet, and Bishop Richard Allen, founder of the African Methodist Episcopal (A.M.E.) Church, when he journeyed north in the 1820s. In Boston, he befriended Maria Stewart and Hosea Easton. He later served as an agent for *Freedom's Journal*, and he eventually joined the city's General Colored Association.[51]

At least since the 1970s, black scholars have regularly read Walker's *Appeal* exclusively as an antislavery or nationalist exhortation. Such a perspective seriously limits what Walker accomplished not only as an appeal to African Americans but also as a critical reading of Euro-American society during the early republic. In challenging Thomas Jefferson's *Notes on the State of Virginia*, Walker's *Appeal* signifies on the American Enlightenment, with its insistence on reason, rationality, and written expression of ideas and thoughts.[52]

Jefferson's *Notes*, written in the best of empiricist traditions of the time, offered an extensive set of observations on various aspects of eighteenth-century life and thought. Its detailed observations on topics ranging from the flora and fauna of Virginia to slave capacities afford critical glimpses into intellectual production during the American Enlightenment. Walker clearly set out to refute Jefferson's *Notes*, and he did so by offering an Enlightenment-inspired, reasoned, alternative black response.[53]

Walker understood Jefferson's centrality to American political traditions and letters as well as the influence his writing continued to exert in mainstream intellectual circles. It is equally likely that during some of his travels Walker read or witnessed some of the public debates that were taking place between Republicans and Federalists. Most of these debates revolved around the role the federal government should play in the lives of citizens. Federalists believed in a more expansive role, while Republicans supported a less intrusive governmental structure. These debates dominated the public sphere until the "Era of Good Feelings" in the early 1820s, at which point Republicans became the majority in the Congress and the Federalist Party withered away. Jefferson's death, on July 4, 1826, probably brought even more attention to his contributions to the fledgling nation's revolutionary heritage. When, only three years after Jefferson's death, Walker published his *Appeal*, he asked, "Do you know that Mr. Jefferson was one of the greatest characters as ever lived among the whites? See his writings for the world, and his public labors for the United States of America. Do you believe that the assertions of such a man will pass into oblivion unobserved by this people and the world?"[54]

Jefferson's understanding of slavery reflected his religious and moral beliefs as well as essentialist and fixed notions of race prevalent in the eighteenth century. Thus, his belief that the circumstances of blacks depended on biology as opposed to condition (environment) held sway in his writings. While antislavery proponents argued that racial slavery in the United States was one of the most unique and harshest forms of human servitude that existed in the modern world, Jefferson sought to demonstrate the opposite. Jefferson's refutation might have been based partly on the fact that the institution was crumbling in New England, and the antislavery movement, domestically and internationally, had gained momentum in the late eighteenth century. But still, Jefferson's positions seem rather defensive, especially in light of those changes underway. Utilizing the Enlightenment concepts of rationality and empiricism and the rhetorical style of Cato, the Roman orator, Jefferson argued that various aspects of the slave economy in classical antiquity were more severe than those structures in nineteenth-century America. He pointed to the tradition of selling all assets when they were no longer useful, including old tools, wagons, and slaves. He also pointed out the torture of slaves to elicit evidence and the use of severe punishments as commonplace.[55]

Walker's *Appeal* challenged many of Jefferson's contentions by using history to validate alternative claims. Walker, however, went much further than Oson and others by using his text to enact a careful reading of the classical tradition that offered demonstrable proof of black intellectual achievements. Rather than rationality being reserved exclusively for whites, Walker's *Appeal* applied Enlightenment principles to African Americans. Enacting African American agency required positing African American exceptionalism. Exceptionalism, in this case, situated African Americans, rather than white Americans, as unique historical agents because of the unprecedented level of brutality perpetrated against them by the practice of racial slavery in the United States. Centralizing this concept required a number of literary strategies, including rhetorical questions that dramatized the African American condition, examinations of ancient and biblical history, and the use of dramatic, almost hyperbolic, language to make various points regarding opposition to colonization and slavery. But most especially, Walker looked directly to Enlightenment rationality to buttress his claims.[56]

Empirical observation, travel, and "accurate observations of things as they exist" characterized the work. Walker tied his observations to the historical record to make factual claims about the nature of the "peculiar institution" of slavery. Referencing ancient societies, Walker concluded that "heathen nations of antiquity had but little more among them than the name and form of slavery, while wretchedness and endless miseries were reserved apparently in a phial, to be poured out upon our fathers, ourselves and our children, by Christian Americans!" As further proof of the deliberate degradation of African Americans, Walker invoked the names of two important ancient historians prominent in the Western tradition. "The causes, my brethren, which produce our wretchedness and miseries, are so numerous and aggravating that I believe that only the pen of a Josephus or Plutarch can well enumerate and explain them." The twin poles, then, of rationality and reason were the historical traditions that allowed Walker to "penetrate, search out, and lay open for inspection" the wretchedness of the African American condition.[57]

Using Enlightenment ideas and history, he questioned the tradition that upheld black inferiority. Though he undoubtedly agreed that "coloured people of the United States are the most wretched, degraded and abject set of beings that ever lived since the world began," he proved that it was white society that had degraded them. If any doubts remained in readers' minds, he admonished them that "These affirmations are so well confirmed in the minds of unprejudiced men who take the time to read histories that they need no elucidation from me."[58]

Walker inverted Jefferson's *Notes* and cited the biblical cases of Joseph and Moses as two examples of slaves ascending to positions of honor and respect. For Walker, this suggested that the ancients treated their slaves more humanely than nineteenth-century whites did. For him, the treatment of the ancient Israelites by the Egyptians also served as an interesting case study. He asserted that the Egyptians were "Africans or a coloured people, such as we are—some of them yellow and others dark—a mixture of Ethiopians and the natives of Egypt." As such, rather than being a "gang of devils," which Walker alleged Jefferson called them, the historical record showed that the Egyptians treated the Israelites humanely. Ultimately, Walker inveighed, "I call upon the professing Christian, I call upon the philanthropist, I call upon the tyrant himself to show me a page of history, either sacred or profane, on which a verse can be found, which maintains that the Egyptians heaped the insupportable insult upon the children of Israel by telling them they were not part of the human family."[59]

To prove his point, and as Jefferson had done before him, only differently, Walker presented a genealogy of slavery's development (in ancient history) to dismiss Jefferson's claims about the mildness of American slavery. Although slavery existed among the Romans, for Walker it appeared as "no more than a mere cypher when compared to ours under the Americans." Strengthening his case, Walker argued, "Everybody who has read history, knows that as soon as the slave among the Romans obtained his freedom, he could rise to the greatest eminence in the State and there was no law instituted to hinder a slave from buying his freedom." Contrasting the history of the ancient world (or universal history) to that of America, Walker asked, "Have not the Americans instituted laws to hinder us from obtaining our freedom. Do you deny the charge? Read the laws of Virginia, North Carolina &c." Not only did these laws prevent African Americans from obtaining respectable positions in the state, but they also denied black humanity.[60]

For Walker, the history of European civilization offered lessons that were as instructive as those from ancient history. In assessing the conduct of Europeans in both classical antiquity and the modern age, Walker concluded that European behavior, whether referring to "heathen or Christian," differed little. In Greece, Walker opined, "we see them there, cutting each other's throats—trying to subject each other to wretchedness and misery." Across time, from Britain to Greece, violence characterized civilization. Christianity, as practiced by white Americans, not only did not correct or ameliorate the treatment of African Americans, it increased the level of cruelty, Walker opined. "Take them as a body," he wrote. "They are ten times more cruel, avaricious and unmerciful than ever they were before." Walker's characterizations of European civilizations dismantled the myth of superiority and exposed the contradictions inherent in Enlightenment thought, especially in its application to African Americans.[61]

Rethinking the African American role in Western civilization required a systematic engagement with black achievements, ancient and modern. Walker turned to classical sources to make an important point about the place of Africa in the history of the world: "When we take a retrospective view of the arts and sciences—the Pyramids and other magnificent buildings—the turning of the channel of the river Nile, by the sons of Africa or of Ham, among them learning originated and was carried thence into Greece, where it was improved upon and refined." Haiti, an emerging nation, easily served as proof of recent black progress and worth. In a sarcastic challenge to prevailing historical traditions that he himself employed, Walker asked, "what need have I to refer to antiquity, when Hayti, the glory of the blacks and the terror of the tyrants, is enough to convince the most avaricious and stupid of wretches." Conversely, he used Haiti in the same passage to issue a jeremiad warning to the slavocracy: "Read the history of Hayti particularly, and see how they were butchered by the whites, and do you take warning."[62]

Walker's threat of impending retribution came most directly from the Bible. He traced God's instructions or "dispensations" from Moses through successive generations, and Europeans received the last dispensation. Instead of heeding the laws of Christ, the Europeans, like the Israelites, disobeyed God and used the "dispensation to aid them in their infernal depredations upon us." These infernal depredations violated the original promise. Because Europeans deployed God's dispensation in unjust ways, they would have to correct their attitudes toward and treatment of African Americans in order to achieve redemption. Christians' misuse of God's law to justify the oppression of African Americans began in the sixteenth century when Bartolomé de Las Casas, a Franciscan priest who opposed Indian slavery, proposed to the Spanish monarch Charles V that African labor replace Indian labor. Spain began shipping Africans to the Americas after 1503, and Charles V's 1511 *Asiento* led to a precipitous increase in the number of African slaves in the Americas. Although Walker viewed Christianity as a rational religion, he viewed "professed Christians" as little better than "heathens."[63]

The last article of the *Appeal* focused on one of the most explosive issues confronting the African American community of the day—colonization. Like Oson and a host of other black orators, Walker believed that the remedy to slavery's cruelty did not lie in colonization, which he argued would benefit the slaveholding class by removing free blacks from their useful station in relationship to enslaved blacks. And so he appealed to the authority of educated men in the African American community to work in opposition to the movement. Borrowing some of A.M.E. bishop Richard Allen's authority to gain additional support, Walker reprinted an Allen letter in which he insisted that it made much more sense to educate African Americans in the United States than to send them abroad to Africa, where, given the current state of affairs there, they would only sink deeper into wretchedness.[64]

The *Appeal* closed where it began, by appealing to the power of history, historical witnesses, empirical observation, and modernity. If it was not Thomas Jefferson's *Notes* that compelled Walker to trouble the pages of historians, he at least was not intimidated by Jefferson's fame. Instead, Walker directly asked "the candid and unprejudiced of the whole world to *search the pages of historians diligently*." They could determine for themselves whether or not *any* of the ancient civilizations such as the "Antediluvians, Sodomites, Egyptians, Babylonians, Persians, Macedonians, Greeks, Romans, Mahometans and Jews ever treated a set of beings as the white Christians of America do us, the blacks, or Africans." And, ultimately, Walker invoked the sum of historical witnesses, the totality of humankind, civilizations prior to and subsequent to classical antiquity, to trumpet the cause of an African American search for truth.[65]

Walker's *Appeal* indeed offered African Americans a unique way to read history. On the one hand, it affirmed the millennial and teleological speculations of Protestantism present in the culture since the colonial period. In another and possibly more important sense, Walker's treatise marshaled historical facts to deliver an indictment of American slavery and the practice of Christianity. In offering this indictment, Walker called into question Western society's claims of rationality by juxtaposing them to the torturous realities of African

American life in the early republic. The historical record revealed a long and distinguished genealogy for African Americans as the initiators of civilization. And in the *Appeal*, African Americans represented America's only hope for redemption. Walker longed for the day when God "shall raise up colored historians in succeeding generations, to present the crimes of the nation, to the then gazing world." Ultimately, he was certain that African American historians would eventually produce a venerable tradition of scholarship to challenge the domination of white intellectuals. They would shed light on a race and a history previously buried in "obscurity and degradation," and that history would elevate black people to a position of "preeminence."[66]

Black women never had the platform that some men had, but they too, played an important role in the development and dissemination of history among African Americans in the early republic. Preaching women such as Jarena Lee, Amanda Smith, and Sojourner Truth regularly and publicly challenged prevailing conventions about women's roles in the public sphere as they offered their own wisdom about the African American condition. Self-taught preacher, exhorter, and activist Maria Stewart was, in some ways, very much like them. Following in the tradition of black women preachers and building upon the work of her friend and confidant, David Walker, Stewart offered critical assessments of the African American condition through examinations of biblical, classical, and universal history.[67]

As is true of other black writers of this time period, what is known of Stewart's early life is sketchy. Details of it must be gleaned from speeches in which she framed her personal biography in terms that would have been familiar to most of her contemporaries. In the introduction to "Religion and the Pure Principles of Morality, the Sure Foundation on Which We Must Build," published in the *Liberator* in 1831, Stewart recounted the specific dimensions of her life's calling in a manner reminiscent of Old Testament stories. Tracing her journey from physical bondage to spiritual liberation, she tells how she became an orphan at age five and was bound out to a clergyman. "Deprived of the advantages of education," her "soul thirsted for knowledge." Leaving "bondage" to marry James W. Stewart in 1829, but widowed after only three months, Stewart's subsequent life followed a course familiar to many women, black and white, who claimed space for themselves in the public sphere. She experienced a religious conversion, and it justified her brand of activism. She avowed that, if necessary, she "would willingly sacrifice life for the cause of God and brethren." And the two, God and her brethren, became the defining poles of much of the rest of her life.[68]

Conscious of contemporary expectations related to proper feminine behavior, Stewart delivered most of her exhortations as messages of morality and piety, but she often infused her discussions with classical and universal history. She knew that she was challenging many current conventions, but she took refuge in a spiritual authority that justified her actions and would protect her in case of difficulty. "Many will suffer for pleading the cause of the oppressed," she wrote, "but I am firmly persuaded, that the God in whom I trust is able to protect me from the rage and malice of mine enemies, and from them that will rise up against me; and if there is no other way for me to escape, he is able to take me to himself, as he did the most noble, fearless, and undaunted David Walker." One must take note that the manner in which she offered herself as a potential martyr in the cause of racial and gender equity relied, as much as it did for the intellectuals, on biblical and classical authority. Throughout her brief speaking and publishing career, she searched for and relied on history to support whatever specific cause she was trumpeting.[69]

The exclusive nature of the public sphere made it difficult for anyone who was not white and male to make inroads into it. And ultimately, these male-privileged biases combined with notions of true womanhood and domesticity to derail Stewart's aspirations as a public speaker. When opposition to her public role proved too great for her to bear, she retired. But she did not go quietly. Insisting that God had ordained her to carry a message to the benighted African people, in her "Farewell Address" she defended all her earlier efforts by examining the role of women in classical and universal history. She asked, "What if I am a woman; is not the God of ancient times the God of these modern days?" She pointed to the importance of women as actors in the public sphere and their centrality to the survival and extension of religious principles, citing Deborah's role as a judge in Israel, Queen Esther's role in saving the Jews from imminent destruction, and Mary Magdalene's declaration of Christ's resurrection. She argued that because "holy women ministered unto Christ and the apostles and women of refinement in all ages," they "more or less have had a voice in moral, religious and political subjects." In her "Farewell Address," Stewart cited her "Sketches of the Fair Sex," in which she had argued that the ancients held women in high regard because of their ability to see the future. She highlighted the role of women among the Greeks as interpreters of the Oracles, as Sibyls among the Romans, and as psychics among the Egyptians. Stewart focused on the multifaceted role of women in intellectual life: as preachers and interpreters of Greek and Hebrew, as scholars and divines, as "apostles, martyrs and warriors." She wondered what if "such women as are here described should rise among our sable race? Moreover, it is not impossible. For it is not the color of the skin that makes the man or woman, but the principle formed by the soul."

Throughout her short career, Stewart was forced to confront and defend her right as a woman to pursue so public a role. But even more, this defense often involved defending the race. The most explicitly historical of Stewart's oratorical productions, "A Speech Delivered at the African Masonic Hall," used the jeremiad, biblical prophecy, and history to assess the position of African Americans in the Western world and to establish their right to equal access. Like Oson and Walker, she began her speech by asking questions about the nature of black existence. Although she presented whites as emblematic of achievement and progress, she was determined to find "the names of our illustrious ones" as well.[70]

Stewart enlisted the authority of history and religion to chart the rise and fall of African civilizations, the ruin of empires, as Volney would have termed it, that were once comparable to the contemporary West. In a veiled reference to Herodotus, Stewart wrote that "History informs us that we sprung from one of the most learned nations of the whole earth—from the seat, if not the parent of science; yes, poor despised Africa was once the resort of sages and legislators, was esteemed the seat of learning, and the most illustrious men in Greece and Rome flocked thither for instruction." For Stewart, like Oson and Walker before her, Africa's fall had nothing to do with the inferiority of its inhabitants but the natural cycles of history. In this counternarrative, Africa's decline also has the spiritual dimension and quality of a jeremiad. Utilizing an exceptionalist construct, Stewart, like Walker, envisioned the African race as a chosen people. Like the Israelites, Africans turned their backs on God and committed "gross sins and abominations that provoked the Almighty to frown heavily upon us and give glory to others."[71]

As a corollary to her counternarrative and in an attempt to sketch out the present condition of African Americans, Stewart recognized the importance of universal and biblical history in juxtaposing American civilization with that of ancient Babylon. Indeed, Babylonian captivity served as an essential part of Judeo-Christian heritage, marking the first stage of the Jewish diaspora—the dispersion of the chosen people. According to Stewart, America, like Babylon, was "a seller of slaves and the souls of men; she has put them completely beneath her feet and she means to keep them there." Stewart integrated her rhetoric into biblical conceptions of redemption for His chosen people and cyclical notions of history prevalent in the nineteenth century. If Babylon was once great but was punished because it transgressed the will of God by worshipping graven images and selling the chosen people into slavery, America could not possibly escape a similar fate for its transgressions against a modern chosen people. In order to achieve redemption, one could not look solely to earthly forces, but the power of God. For Stewart, God's power undergirded claims for citizenship rights: "Powerful sons and daughters of Africa will shortly arise, who will put down vice and immorality amongst us and declare by him that sitteth on the throne, that they will have their rights." While Walker envisioned the rise of historians in the redemption of the race, Stewart cast racial redemption in religious and millennial terms.[72]

Using biblical, classical, and universal history to claim her humanity as a black woman, Stewart's work carved out an important space for discussions of the place of black women in the public arena. Treated differently, ostracized, and ultimately denied public space, she cloaked her rhetoric in the garb of religious piety and true womanhood, but managed to articulate her concerns publicly for only a short time. A stalwart of freedom, a gifted orator, and persuasive writer, her life and work would, nevertheless, subsequently occasion comment from other black intellectuals throughout the antebellum and postbellum periods.[73]

While it is clear that during the first period of African American historical production, vindicationism, contributionism, and sentimental Afrocentricism played important roles in the arguments of early black thinkers, they also drew heavily on the European and American Enlightenment, cultures of classicism (sources from classical antiquity), and the Bible to ground their calls for African American rights, dignity, and improvement and to reframe current constructions of the contemporary world. Appealing to these varied traditions allowed African Americans to establish a historical genealogy whose beginnings transcended the narrow confines of the hold of slave ships in the Middle Passage or the long rows of cotton and tobacco in the agricultural South. It also transcended the marginality and tenuous nature of life for free blacks in the newly industrializing Northern states. Black intellectuals viewed their history as wholly intact and accessible by grounding it in a wider span of human existence than just the nineteenth century. The genealogy they created featured African Americans as significant contributors to, if not architects of, some of the most important aspects of the Western tradition. Not lowly or subjugated, these sons and daughters of Ham bequeathed knowledge and wisdom to the civilizations of antiquity, and in turn, aided in the development of modern nations. Appeals to classical sources and references to Egypt and Africa were more than precursors of Afrocentricism; they were complex markers of a culture deeply interested in the authority of the classical world as a site for knowledge and wisdom.

This early period also witnessed a moment of change in historiography. On the one hand, black intellectuals looked to eighteenth-century historiography, which trumpeted progress, Providence, and cyclical, millennial visions of the past, present, and future. Eighteenth-century historians maintained active attention to the humanist interests of humanity. And despite the rising specter of science, they continued to utilize classical antiquity, universal history, and the Bible as viable sources to re-create the richness and dynamism of human existence. This longer time span, from the creation of humankind to the present, offered African Americans a much longer genealogy, one in which they appeared in a wide variety of capacities in the human experience, and it could be utilized to debunk the idea that the nineteenth-century condition of African Americans was a providentially ordained mandate rather than an aberration rooted in greed and the corruption of the best ideals of humanity.

It is clear that Oson's appeals to the sacred record, David Walker's call for an end to slavery, and Maria Stewart's agitation for increased recognition of women's roles in the public sphere attempted to force white Americans to acknowledge African contributions to universal/world history, the role of Europeans in the destruction of African civilizations, white American's involvement in debauching the race, and the evils of slavery which, despite the American Revolution, America continued to preserve and defend. The gulf between the teleological promise of American possibilities and the degrading institution of slavery was apparent to anyone who dared to notice.[74]

But even more than these obvious conclusions, these writers were consciously and effectively "troubling the pages of historians," perhaps all the history that was available to them, to construct new narratives of the past that presented a more holistic portrait of human history. They presented these new narratives in speeches, pamphlets, newspaper articles, and other sites. They were by no means professional historians, and we might even debate whether to call them "intellectuals." But it remains the case, nevertheless, that in their efforts to vindicate the race they called the broader European and American intellectual traditions into service and situated their contributionist, vindicationist, liberationist, and even Afrocentric narratives squarely into mainstream historiography.

CHAPTER 2

To Present a Just View of Our Origin

Creating An African American Historical Discourse, 1837–1850

> Every close observer must have seen that we suffer much from the want
> of a collection of facts so arranged as to present a just view of our historical
> origin. —JAMES W. C. PENNINGTON, *Textbook of the Origin and History of the
> Colored People* (1841)

> I would remark that of the woolly haired Africans, who constitute the princi-
> pal part of the inhabitants of Africa, there is no history and there can be none.
> That race has remained in barbarism from the first ages of the world.
> —NOAH WEBSTER TO AMOS BEMAN, 1843

JAMES W. C. PENNINGTON AND NOAH WEBSTER represent two distinct
understandings of black history during the antebellum period. Pennington, in
ways similar to earlier black intellectuals, called for a serious interrogation of
black origins that transcended the narrow confines of the American present.
Noah Webster, convinced of the idea of permanent black inferiority, erased
black achievement not only from the present but since "the first ages of the
world." Both of these approaches speak to the ways intellectuals grappled over
the place of blacks not only in the American present but in the human experience. They also clearly demonstrate the social and intellectual challenges African American intellectuals confronted in the period between 1837 and 1850.

The antebellum period saw decisive changes in the direction of American development. Slavery became entrenched in the South and rapidly spread
westward. Proof of the power of the emboldened slavocracy was demonstrated
by the success of its members in extending their sway over the U.S. Congress,
engineering the infamous "Gag Rule" that not only led to the cessation of
congressional debate on slavery but to the censorship of antislavery literature
throughout the South. The 1837 murder of prominent abolitionist and newspaper editor Elijah Lovejoy outside of his printing press in Alton, Illinois, came
to symbolize the slippery slope the nation was descending.

There were changes in intellectual thought also. Although American historical writing remained in its infancy, a new wave of interest in building an American historical tradition linked to historical preservation and documentation swept the nation. Increased public support at the local and national levels encouraged the publication of historical texts in the form of documentary and biographical collections. One of the best known of these collections, the *Library of American Biography* by Unitarian minister and future president of Harvard University Jared Sparks, helped to fuel the production of romantic histories.[1]

Romanticism as an intellectual movement challenged Enlightenment ideas of reason and rationality, favoring, in the words of Susan Conrad, an "organic interpretation of nature, the cosmos and humanity," drawing its potency from defining knowledge symbolically and metaphysically rather than in concrete ways. Despite these apparently mundane and harmless attributes, Romanticism, in the hands of American intellectuals, created some difficulties for African American writers. Older sensibilities, such as the notion of *representative* men and women, and the passion for American antiquities, figured prominently in this new historical construct, which relied extensively on classical notions of exemplary individuals, perhaps best dramatized in Plutarch's *Lives*. The romantic interest in antiquities operated in the same ways as veneration of the classical past but also included American antiquities. Thus, American Indians figured prominently in this formulation, functioning as a threat to the nation's dreams of unfettered expansion on the one hand and as a somewhat heroic but vanishing race on the other. The problem for black intellectuals arose because of the ways romantic histories of the nineteenth century emphasized local distinctiveness and other human qualities thought to be uniquely American, such as ruggedness, thriftiness, and patriotism. These qualities found their greatest expression in the multivolume *History of the United States*, published by George Bancroft, and in the work of Richard Hildreth, a staunch Federalist who, unlike many of his contemporaries, criticized the institution of slavery. Black historians had no difficulty incorporating the Bible, classical antiquity, and universal history into their texts, but the emphasis on exceptionalism, essentialism, and Manifest Destiny, which celebrated the triumph and distinctiveness of Western civilization, was linked to the West, "discovery," and empire, and thus to slavery. This emphasis on the present, or modern history, rendered the long-range view of the rise and fall of empires unimportant. African American histories would have to find a way to subvert this.[2]

This chapter explores more fully, and within the context of a period of rapidly changing ideas about black humanity, how African American intellectuals utilized history to challenge the consolidation of what John Ernest has characterized as "a white nationalist historiography," a racially exclusive historical discourse predicated on white supremacy and dominance in an emerging American providential narrative. The consolidation of this historical narrative attempted to relegate African Americans to the margins of human history and raised serious concerns for black writers who interrogated the Western canon to reframe developing ideas about the rise of the West, black identity, and their role in the burgeoning republic in the period 1837 to 1850. Although slavery was ever-present, the active antislavery movement that facilitated the end of the slave trade in 1808 had crystallized, and the British abolition of slavery in their possessions in 1833 also encouraged historical reflection. In this atmosphere, black intellectuals understood the necessity of focusing their challenge on contemporary nineteenth-century constructions of history that privileged the rise of the Western hemisphere as the starting point for American history. For the black writers, the rise of the West coincided with the development of the slave trade and the demise of Africa. To respond to these changes, black writers, in more expansive ways than they had done between 1817 and 1836, honed a well-crafted historical discourse that accentuated their complex role in human history and that, more often than not, appeared in longer, book-length treatments rather than pamphlets or speeches. These book-length treatments presented more extensive and expansive forums for a critical reading of evidence about the black past contained in biblical, ancient, and modern history. A longer historical genealogy, which transcended the rise of the West, was indispensable to black intellectuals as they sought to vindicate themselves and their race. But they also understood that if they could use the Western canon to show how contemporary understandings of history distorted the past, then their story would have a greater degree of legitimacy. Much of this approach was also related to a desire by these writers to situate black history beyond the stream of the slave trade, the Middle Passage, and slavery, which effectively yoked the black experience to a problematic present, and to transcend this limited historical view by accentuating the black presence in the broader humanistic and collective experience. History was, in the words of cleric James W. C. Pennington, an attempt to "unembarrass the origin and show the relative position of the colored people in the different periods among the different nations." Their ability to craft a more sustained response to contemporary nineteenth-century historicism was fueled by the continued expansion of the black public through increased institutional organization, the utilization of a broad range of moral and political tactics to end slavery, and an expansion of the number of extended treatises and historical books of an explicitly historical nature produced by black intellectuals.[3]

The writers in this chapter are those generally recognized in the literature as substantial contributors to African American social, political, and intellectual life, a fact that allows us to understand the connection of history to larger social, political, and economic realities in antebellum America. Imposing modernist assumptions on works like these easily relegates them to the fringes of historical legitimacy because of the writing style, form of argumentation and methodological approaches. Likewise, they may be dismissed in light of postmodernist assumptions rooted in a much later historical moment that privilege the political and liberationist underpinnings of black historicism. Rather than relegating these writers to the margins or privileging more recent ideas about black liberation or the political agenda of their writings, the point here is to historicize the complex processes by which these works drew on classical history, eighteenth-century universal histories, and literal readings of the Bible to craft a history of black people that transcended the limitations of an enslaved reality.

While the desire to "trouble the pages of historians" was central to the intellectuals in chapter 1, the black writers in this chapter took this charge a step further and worked consciously and aggressively to "present a just view" of black origins. In doing so, they moved from simply interrogating the sources and production of speeches and small pamphlets to more lengthy and extended treatment of historical issues. The presentation of this material in longer form reflects the explosion in book publication in this period as much as it reflects changes in the internal logic (organization, argumentation, and sources) of the works that allowed and sometimes demanded more space. Differences between these intellectuals and those featured in chapter 1 are also evident in other ways. First, unlike the black intellectuals of the early republic who were primarily self-taught, black intellectuals in the antebellum period were more formally (and sometimes very well) educated. Many of them were abolitionists and clergymen, and their better education, their positions of responsibility at the head of important community institutions such as churches, and their literary efforts in support of the antislavery movement provided them greater access to the large religious, reform, and political networks of the period. The earlier writers undertook their work at a hopeful time for the race, due to the trend during the revolutionary era of abolishing slavery or gradually emancipating enslaved populations, especially in the North. In that context, it was important to create a humanistic narrative that accentuated the role of black people in aiding the process of "civilization," as understood in the late eighteenth and early nineteenth centuries. They also put their history in a humanistic narrative that made their story a part of the universal tradition of the rise and fall of civilizations. And finally, antebellum writers witnessed and confronted not only the entrenchment of slavery and an increasingly militant proslavery movement but also more problematic constructions of race, which increasingly turned on physical evidence linked to the nascent physical sciences rather than biblical authority.[4]

Biblical History

Recent scholarly literature describes African American engagement with the Bible during the nineteenth century as part of an institutional approach to social, political, and economic empowerment, helping to incubate black leadership and reflecting providential discourse embedded in ideas of African American and American exceptionalism.[5] Black use of the Bible, however, went beyond these approaches to include a belief in *biblical inerrancy*, the use of the Bible as a literal source, and provided the genealogy of biblical time that incorporated Africa into the history of the early Christian church. Examining these traditions in this manner casts new light on our traditional understanding of black engagement with the Bible and the use of the jeremiad and the Hamitic myth in black historicism during the early portion of the antebellum period. Black intellectuals used the Bible as a historical source to subvert the contemporary understandings of blackness that were embedded in scientific presentations of race that became increasingly popular by the 1840s.

In the nineteenth century, black and white intellectuals, especially those in reform movements and connected to various Christian denominations, viewed the Bible as an indispensable tool in re-creating the past. For many, it not only served as a reliable historical source but affirmed the theological underpinnings of classical education prevalent throughout the period. Lyman Beecher, the famed New England minister and father of Henry Ward Beecher and Harriet Beecher Stowe, put it best when he wrote, "we can only say the history contained in it, is the only well authenticated history, which reaches beyond the fabulous ages and carries a beam of light to the creation." Eighteenth-century historians, whose work figured prominently in the work of black intellectuals, displayed similar sentiments about the importance of the Bible as a legitimate historical source. Alexander Fraser Tytler, Lord Woodhouselee, a Scottish universal historian, in his immensely popular *Elements of General History* (1801), stated similarly, "From the earliest periods of the history of the world, we have no records of equal authority with the Sacred Scriptures. They ascend to a period antecedent to the formation of regular states or communities, they are long prior to the authentic annals of the profane nation, and they are, therefore, our only lights on those distant and dark ages of the infancy of the human race." James W. C. Pennington certainly concurred: human history could only be valued "in proportion as it has the coincidence of sacred history."[6]

As unimportant as biblical chronology seems today, during the eighteenth and nineteenth centuries, it provided not only a way of making sense of the Bible, but more important, a foundation for understanding the history of humankind. James Ussher's chronology was one of the first to gain wide acceptance. Ussher, a Scottish clergyman, adopted 4004 B.C. as the date for the creation of the world, based on calculations drawn from close readings of three important religious texts. First, the Hebrew Bible, or Pentateuch (the five books of Moses), or the Torah, gave a period of 1,656 years for the earth's existence. Second, the Septuagint, the collection of Jewish writing that comprises the Old Testament for Greek-speaking Christians, provided a figure of 2,242 years. Third, the Samaritan translation of the Bible dated the creation of the world at 1,307 years.[7] Alexander Tytler, relying exclusively on Ussher, presented the three traditional sources for marking the creation of the world in his major work.[8]

Although scholars have regularly pointed to the abolitionist influences on the work of these early black historians, the universal histories they utilized (which also used the Bible as a historical document) were equally, if not more, important. Black intellectuals used biblical notions of time especially to establish a chronological order of human history. Hosea Easton's *Treatise on the Intellectual Character, and the Civil and Political Condition, of the Colored People of the United States*, like Tytler's *Elements*, used the Hebrew text of the Scriptures to document the earth's creation and biblical chronology to provide a history of humankind—or "each race," as he put it, blacks and Europeans. Thus, in Easton's account, "Misraim, son of Ham, found[ed] the kingdom of Egypt" in 2188 B.C. Pennington's 1841 *Textbook of the Origin and History of the Colored People* relied on Ussher's biblical chronology, which suggested that two thousand years of the creation period was essentially void, thus resulting in a four-thousand year figure. Pennington wrote in his *Textbook*, "We live in a period rising unto six thousand years from that in which Jehovah spake and caused the earth with its appurtenances to come into being." Robert Benjamin Lewis's *Light and Truth* featured a forty-page chronological table that began with 4004 B.C., the date of the world's creation drawn from the Hebrew Bible and Ussher's chronology, which Lewis used to order human history.[9]

Biblical genealogy, or the Table of Nations, was also important to black writers for establishing a clear historical framework for the relationships between and among nations and historical epochs. As historian Mia Bay has argued, black intellectuals centralized the notion of consanguinity, the idea that all humankind originated from one creation, and Robert Benjamin Lewis's *Light and Truth* provides a good example. But historians and literary scholars have criticized Lewis's work for framing the genealogy of human events in ways favorable to Africa.[10] In one instance, Lewis asserts that the "first people were Ethiopians or blacks." Usually read as a racially chauvinist assertion, Lewis actually based his conclusion on "biblical inerrancy" and a literal reading of biblical dictionaries of the period. He asserted that the words *Adam*, *Adaman*, *Adami*, and *Admah* refer to "earth" in ancient Hebrew, and "the earth is a rich, dark, substance and from it our first parents were taken, and if Dr. Brown and other Bible dictionaries are correct in their explanation of the meaning of the terms, then the deduction must be that Ethiopia (Gen. 2.13) was black and the first people were Ethiopians or blacks."[11] For Lewis, Ethiopia rather than Egypt became the logical starting place for a history of black people. In another instance, Lewis cited Josephus's assertion that *Adam* means "red," and so Lewis was clearly flexible in his definitions of "earth" and his descriptions of Adam. The point, however, is his location of the origin of people of color.[12]

James Pennington's *Textbook* also devoted a considerable amount of space to biblical genealogy. And his and Lewis's approaches were standard during the nineteenth century. Genealogy provided ways to subvert the nationalist and racist discourse of the American present. Sketching out a history of blacks or human endeavor anterior to the rise of the West reflects more than a reactionary racial chauvinism; rather, it involved fairly sophisticated thinking that relied on the Western canon, of which the Bible is a part, to construct a longer genealogy of human existence that extended and expanded the narrow timeline of popular nineteenth-century romantic histories.[13]

Lastly, black intellectuals also celebrated Africa's role in the early church. But they saw Africa as a geographical location closely connected to the politics of nation (place) rather than simply as a metaphor for race. The history of the Christian church in Africa, according to many African Christians, stretched back to a.d. 44, when St. Mark reputedly brought the Gospel to Africa, especially North Africa, the home of many early Christian writers such as Origen, Tertullian, and, most notably, St. Augustine of Hippo. Jacob Oson's *Search for*

Truth, one of the first historical discussions produced during the early republic, situates Africa as *the place* where important events occurred in the Bible: Abraham and Sarah found refuge there during a time of famine; it is where Moses grew up; and Joseph and Mary were there when they received instructions from God to flee with Jesus in order to escape the rage of Herod. Oson and other black writers during the antebellum period looked to the role of Africa in the early church to make claims for the broader humanity of black people.[14]

Consistent with this tradition, Henry Highland Garnet's oration and pamphlet, *The Past and the Present Condition, and the Destiny, of the Colored Race*, focused on the presence of Africa in the Old Testament. He referenced the fact that Solomon married non-Jewish women from various parts of the world, and "the most favored queen was a beautiful sable daughter of one of the Pharaohs of Egypt." Garnet's reading of this extended to an analysis of the one of the Songs of Solomon known as the "Canticles," or "Solomon's Song." The more familiar connection between Solomon and the broader world, however, is the story of the queen of Sheba. As biblical scholars have noted, Josephus presented the story in the *Antiquities of the Jews* and referred to the queen of Sheba as the queen of Egypt and Ethiopia. This was, undoubtedly, an exaggeration; she was probably of Arabic origin; but these early histories characterized her as African, and black intellectuals, using the most widely accepted biblical sources of their day, could do no less. For Garnet, however, the queen of Sheba is only one of the great luminaries in Africa's connection to the Bible. Garnet praised early Christian writers associated with the early African church including Cyprian, Origen, and Augustine.[15]

These basic understandings about how black intellectuals used the Bible as a historical source, understood biblical genealogy, and recognized Africans in the history of the early Christian church can help us to understand more fully how they used other traditional strategies such as the jeremiad and the Hamitic myth, which are central to current conceptualizations of African Americans' use of the Bible. The use of the Bible in black intellectual rhetoric clearly reflected the ongoing role of biblical authority during this period, and it also served as the basis for an explicit attack on the entrenchment of slavery and the reduction of the black experience to its lowest set of variables. Often, the "righteous discontent" of these authors found its greatest voice in the jeremiad, which served as an extension of messianic black nationalism and ideas related to African American destiny. Much of the jeremiad's appeal is attributable to the ministerial affiliations of black intellectuals as well as the widespread belief among reformers in the millennial aspects of God's judgment upon the wicked and unrighteous. The jeremiad, through the pens of these writers, both reminded America of its democratic promises and guaranteed punishment for those who failed to bring their actions in line with its warnings. It also admonished black people to accept their responsibilities and actively work to "uplift" the race.[16]

For all of these writers, the promise of heavenly retribution for the treatment of African Americans was very important. Henry Highland Garnet's *Past and Present Condition* urged America to hear the voices of African slaves crying from the "dark holds of slave ships, rice swamps, plantations of cotton and tobacco." It necessarily followed that the mistreatment of God's children would invoke his wrath, culminating in severe consequences for American slaveholders: "You have slain us all the day long—you have no mercy. Legions of haggard ghosts stalk through the land. Behold! See, how they come: Oh what myriads. Hark hear their broken bones clatter together! With deep unearthly voices, they cry: We come, we come! For vengeance we come! Tremble, guilty nation, for the God of Justice lives and reigns."[17] Hosea Easton, a minister in the A.M.E. Church, also combined the jeremiad with an actual prediction of a millennial age for Africa and its descendants in his *Treatise*. Easton asserted that "when that time shall arrive, the lapse of a few generations will show the world that her sons will again take the lead in the field of virtuous enterprise, filling the front ranks of the church, when she marches into the millennial era."[18] Alluding to Africa's early role in the history of Christianity, Easton's comments predicted a millennial intervention but also turned the jeremiad upon Northern and Southern leaders who sanctioned slavery. James W. C. Pennington appealed to the anti-Catholic biases inherent in Protestantism, which also emanated from a continued adherence to eighteenth-century histories that were critical of the Spanish role in the colonization of the New World. He boldly asserted that slavery's growth emanated from the "Romanish church," which promoted a return to the "dark age," a moment of relative intellectual backwardness inconsistent with the notion of progress trumpeted during this period of history. Pennington wrote:

Slavery is an institution of the dark age! Did the monarchs, patriarchs, and prophets of the south ever think of this? Yes slavery was bred, born and nurtured in the will of Charles the Fifth of Spain, second only to Nero of Rome; this rebel ghost who was capable of fulminating, and figuring in the darkest of the darkness of the dark age; this great patron of the mother of abomination; this stoutest of the co-workers with the Pope of Rome, in his persecution of Luther and the reformers; *he was also the first patron and patriarch of the institution which is so peculiar at the South.*[19] (emphasis in original)

One editorial writer summed up this view by uniting the condemnation of the slave trade and the promise of providential retribution: "We are deeply humbled before God and tremble in view of his avenging rod, when we consider the connection of the church with the great national sin, slavery, for God will someday make inquisition for blood."[20]

Black intellectuals did not blame whites for all of their problems. They also used the Bible to point out internal shortfalls. Polytheism, the worship of more than one god, was the culprit—a practice, according to Pennington, invented by Nimrod and adopted by Ethiopians of the second generation. In practice it blossomed from the simple veneration of ancestors to the worship of "imaginary personages, thence to images, and thence to beasts and to birds, &c." This literal reading of the Bible as source and Pennington's recognition that Nimrod is actually "Belus or Baal in sacred history," preserved a providential reading of black history while simultaneously locating that history in a universal historical stream. For Pennington, "our venerable ancestors provoked God to give them up to the influence of their folly, open[ing] the door to the slave trade" and causing Africans to be "riven up . . . into petty tribes and ready to be made dupes of." Pennington believed that in order to "recover from this degradation from which we have sunk we shall need to rely eminently upon God."[21] Thus, Pennington did not see slavery as a "fortunate fall," a benefit to Africans by allowing them to access the Christianized world and ultimately escape from barbarism. Rather, it represented an unfortunate consequence of his ancestors' disobedience regarding religious belief and practice.

Antebellum black writers also challenged the Bible's use by proslavery forces to rationalize black inferiority. The Hamitic myth, as well as the supposition that blacks were descendants of Cain, played a dominant role in this construction. The Hamitic myth, according to which Ham's mocking insult of his father Noah's drunkenness caused Noah to put a curse on Ham's son Canaan and all Canaan's progeny down through the ages, was widely believed to be about Africans. Focusing less on biblical justification and more on popular lore about the diabolical nature of blacks, proponents of the Hamitic myth also tried to link the race with Cain who, according to the biblical record, committed the world's first murder upon his brother Abel.[22]

James W. C. Pennington took the lead in the debate on the Hamitic myth during the antebellum period. A cleric and leading abolitionist of his day, he understood the importance of destroying the potency of these myths and made it a central goal of his *Textbook*. In answering the question, "who and whence are the colored people," the foundational question of his treatise, which he saw as essential in presenting a "just view" of black origins, he first dismissed the popular supposition that blacks were the seed of Cain. "Had the framers of this argument done their homework," he maintained, "a quick glance at a school boy's textbook would have revealed that Cain lived before the Great Deluge and that all his prosperity were swallowed up in the deluge." But Pennington's critique also included a lengthy analysis of Adamic genealogy. As Robert Benjamin Lewis's *Light and Truth* suggested, this engagement with biblical genealogy was an essential part of historical practice and demonstrated the authority of the biblical record, especially from "the earliest history of man." Carefully constructed genealogies were needed in a historical moment when erroneous ones buttressed ideas regarding black inferiority, ideas so pervasive in the public sphere, wrote Pennington, that they were "trumpeted about by barroom and porter-house orators, with as much gravity as a judge charges a jury who are to decide in a case of life and death." Listing Adam's sons beginning with Seth and ending with Noah to find evidence that Africans most likely did not descend from Canaan, Pennington suggested that Africans probably descended from Cush and Misraim, who were also sons of Ham. Dismissing the Curse of Ham as a justification for degrading black people generally, Pennington pointed out that the universally accepted definition of the term *Cush* was "black," *aithiops* in Greek, or *aethiops* in Latin. Pennington took umbrage with those who "theorize themselves into the right to oppress, and to hate and abuse their fellow men!" These "ministers and professors," he contended, not only have "desecrated their holy profession, but they have taken God's word and construed it into a commission to shed the innocent blood of his creatures," for Noah's curse of his grandson should not "doom the black man and constitute the white man [as] the slaveholder."[23]

Carefully examining some of the myth's illogical suppositions, Pennington's efforts diminished the mischaracterization of black people as simply "hewers of wood and drawers of water." The fact that Ham received Noah's blessing immediately after disembarking from the ark seemed inconsistent with a generational curse. Also, he pointed out, no mention was made of Ham's name in Noah's curse. Noah's curse did not affect his first three sons, from whom Africans more likely descended. Only Canaan's name appeared. Finally, Pennington also called the idea of Noah's curse into question by pointing out the patriarchal blessings and curses following Noah as well as the stipulation in Ezekiel 18:20 that the sins of the fathers do not pass to subsequent generations.[24]

Rather than focusing on the Hamitic myth, Henry Highland Garnet's address, *The Past and the Present Condition, and the Destiny, of the Colored Race* (1848), was more reminiscent of the work of Oson and Walker. It highlighted events in the Bible to show the role of place rather than race, to posit the essential unity of humankind, and thus to disrupt then-current perceptions of African and African American inferiority. This schema of place located Africa in the center of world or universal history as an active site of important, if not seminal, events in the rise of Western civilization. Garnet wanted his readers to be very clear about his sources of information. "Moses is the patriarch of sacred history. The same eminent station is occupied by Herodotus in profane history. To the chronicles of these two great men we are indebted for all the information we have in relation to the early history of man."[25] Garnet's claim regarding Moses, the great lawgiver and first recorder of human history, was quite common in the nineteenth century. One need only turn to the universal histories used by these black authors to make this case. Tytler's *Elements of General History* makes this point succinctly: "The books of Moses afford the earliest authentic history of the ages immediately following the deluge."[26] For Garnet, Africa's place in Western civilization was undisputed.

Writing at a moment when Egypt's role in the construction of Western civilization was under assault, and at a time of hardening and territorial expansion of slavery in the Western hemisphere, Garnet understood the importance of Africa as a place. Where biblical genealogy informed Garnet's decision to name Ham as the first African and founder of Egypt, one could argue that "African" referred to the inhabitants of Africa regardless of race. According to Garnet, Moses's fame emanated from the fact that he acquired "all the learning of the Egyptians." Ethiopia enjoyed a similar status, a point that James W. C. Pennington and Hosea Easton highlighted in their historical work. However, Garnet reminded readers that "Ethiopia is one of the few nations whose destiny is spoken of in prophecy." He cited the Psalms prophecy that "Princes shall come out of Egypt and Ethiopia shall stretch forth her hands unto God." Although it might be appropriate to see Garnet's comments as an expression of Ethiopianism, the idea of a providential connection between Africa and its diasporic descendants allowed Garnet to celebrate Africa's central role in the early church. It is not surprising, then, that the first illustration Garnet used to frame this issue was the willingness of the Ethiopians to accept Christianity, as evidenced in the baptism of the Ethiopian eunuch, a member of the Ethiopian queen Candace's household, by the apostle Phillip. This event demonstrated the willingness of some Africans and, by extension, all of Africa, to accept Christian doctrines.[27]

Without a doubt these early writers used the Bible to dislodge its misuse in both the proslavery tradition of using biblical authority to justify slavery and nationalist readings that related to Manifest Destiny. But it is equally important to understand and assess the centrality of biblical literalism and its impact on black intellectuals' use of the Bible. Biblical chronology played an important role in locating black people in a longer stream of universal and human history that transcended the limitations and constraints of American slavery. The Bible served as a trusted source of history as well as a social, cultural, and ideological guide to the past. African Americans connected to the clerical constructs of their day understood how the Bible's symbolism could work not only to vindicate but also to reconfigure negative nineteenth-century constructions of blackness.[28]

Ancient History

Ancient or profane history held a similar place of reverence to biblical history among antebellum writers and offered just as many useful lessons. Rather than obstructing vision with "mists or shroud of history," a phrase commonly used in the literature, ancient history offered a more concrete terrain on which to fashion the highly didactic lessons of nineteenth-century history. Its handmaiden in this enterprise was classicism. As historian Caroline Winterer observed, "Next to Christianity, the central intellectual project in America before the late nineteenth century was classicism." Linking classicism's pervasive presence as a signal of intellectual activity with popular views of black inferiority, John Calhoun infamously noted that, "If he could find a Negro who knew the Greek syntax, he then would believe that the Negro was a human being and should be treated as a man." African American engagement with classical literature, however, related to even more than these sentiments. It emanated as much from individual and collective desires to promote intellectualism through literacy and literary taste.[29]

Black scholars used classical sources in diverse ways for diverse reasons. Some were used to juxtapose the current condition of the race with its past glory. Others were instructive, offering information about various facets of the ancient world, ranging from specific historical information to lessons about the rise and fall of empires. Lastly, they often offered lessons concerning morality and proper deportment in the public sphere. In short, if the Bible was the foundation, classical sources provided the structure for fully comprehending the past for African Americans. Here in the realm of the classics, black writers transcended the narrow confines of the American experience and crafted universal portraits of black possibility.[30]

One of the best examples of how African American intellectuals utilized classical sources is the work of Robert Benjamin Lewis. In the 1836 preface of his book, *Light and Truth*, Lewis skillfully located his project in the nexus of biblical and classical authority. He wrote, "It has been a general and true observation that darkness has gradually vanished at the increase of light and knowledge. . . . I have therefore searched for light and truth, in sacred and ancient history, in those works translated by English historians—truths which have long been concealed from the sons of Ethiopia—and will now present the result of my investigations to the public." Lewis described the works of Herodotus and Josephus as among his most important sources, "next to the historical books of the Old Testament, the most ancient history worthy of perusal." Pliny's *Letters*, Eusebius's *Ecclesiastical History*, Sallust's *History of Rome*, Xenophon's *History of Greece*, Livy's *History of Rome*, Plutarch's *Notable Lives*, Dionysius Halicarnassus's *Roman Antiquities*, Tacitus's *Histories* and *Germania*, Polybius's *General History of the Greeks and Romans*, and Isocrates's *The Orations and Epistles* figured prominently in his account.[31]

Knowledge of the works of classical authors did more than demonstrate black erudition; it also served as the basis for presentations of African civilization and persons of African descent that affirmed the authority of *eighteenth-century* (rather than nineteenth-century) historical conceptions of blackness and the place of Africans in the ancient world. Lewis used these sources to show the greatness of African civilizations such as Ethiopia and Egypt. He also took care to note the presence of learning and intellectual life on the African continent: "The Library of Alexandria—richest in the world," wrote Lewis, "contained four hundred thousand valuable manuscripts."[32] If one views these statements as important comments on Africa as place rather than a metaphor for race, these claims deflated assertions, common in the public sphere during the nineteenth century, that Africa was simply a vast, uncharted wilderness, devoid of light and reason.[33]

Discussion of African American engagement with the ancient world, especially Egypt, raises the specter of Afrocentricism. Such a reading is difficult to avoid when nineteenth- and twentieth-century writers are brought

Afrocentrism

together to make a larger point about the continuity of an Afrocentric strain of thought.[34] Such an approach not only erases serious aspects of the work of black intellectuals in the nineteenth century but fails to appreciate the more complex ways black intellectuals engaged the past using the scholarly models of their day.[35] The recent tendency to link nineteenth- and twentieth-century black writers who engaged the ancient world perhaps resulted from late twentieth-century concerns and debates about the utility of classical knowledge or the modification of the Western canon, especially Great Books courses in which competing claims arose regarding how to represent and credit various groups for their contributions to the rise of the West. Many of these concerns were also outgrowths of the clash between modernist and postmodernist thought and the result, at least in the minds of many defenders of traditional ideas regarding the Western canon: disciplinary fragmentation.[36] Such concerns would have been foreign to our nineteenth-century predecessors who produced knowledge in a moment when disciplinary boundaries were not only permeable but in some instances nonexistent. Black nineteenth-century writers, drawing on the Bible and classicism, simply sought to make Africa a complex subject rather than a dejected object. Thus, rather than positing Afrocentricism or racial romanticization as the explanations for the engagement of black intellectuals with the classical world, we would do well to locate the historical production of antebellum black writers squarely in the contested terrain of nineteenth-century racial politics. In short, these writers sought to reconstruct the image of Africa in the public sphere and in the midst of a shifting public debate over race during the antebellum period.[37]

By the 1840s, rather than explaining race in religious terms or through Linnean systems of rationalization such as the "Great Chain of Being," white intellectuals increasingly turned to physical explanations of racial difference, which were tangled up with scientific theories and proslavery social ideology.[38] Samuel Morton, a Philadelphia doctor whose *Crania Americana* (1839) garnered critical acclaim, emerged as one of the pioneers in this project. Morton argued for a correlation between skull size and the capacity for civilization. In what we now understand as stunningly pseudoscientific terms, he reasoned that blacks, who possessed the smallest brains in his study (whites possessed the largest, and browns were somewhere in between), possessed the least capacity for civilization. In a remarkable manifestation of interest in Egyptian antiquities, his *Crania Aegyptiaca* (1844), which featured an examination of skulls from ancient Egypt, concluded that blacks predominated in ancient Egyptian society, but possessed lowly stations as servants and slaves.[39]

Not surprisingly, given the focus on what seemed to be inherent physical differences between races, it was not long before racial typology began to undermine religious and monogenetic theories of race. Scientists and anthropologists posited polygenesis, multiple and separate creation of races, as a more plausible explanation of racial difference. Promoted by prominent scientists and anthropologists associated with the American School of Ethnology such as Josiah Nott, Samuel Gliddon, and Louis Agassiz, essentialist constructions of race became more prevalent than ever.[40]

These scientific explanations of race, which began to trump biblically based understandings, further encouraged black writers to rely on history to disentangle them. One especially obvious way to do that was to turn to the idea of consanguinity, the belief that all humankind shared one common origin. According to James Pennington, God made "them male and female and he destined them to propagate their own kind," and Pennington affirmed this fact was "the root of all true history of the human family." Hosea Easton, in his *Treatise*, put the issue more succinctly by quoting the Bible: "I conclude that, by this time, the one great truth is acknowledged by Christendom, viz—God hath made of one blood all nations of men for to dwell on all the face of the earth."[41]

The work of dislodging nineteenth-century racial science required, however, a more direct attack than presentations on consanguinity allowed. James Pennington's 1841 *Textbook*, largely overlooked for its racial commentary, offered a succinct dismissal of nineteenth-century ideas regarding race. Pennington was particularly concerned about discussions regarding black complexion. Not only did he call the subject "nonsense" but described the reasoning as "a tissue of foolery." He presented the arguments of Hanneman, who supposed that black complexion derived from Noah's curse on Ham, and the work of the anatomist Meekel, who posited that complexion emanated from the color of the brain. After posing affirmative and opposing views, Pennington concluded, relying on the work of the ethnologist Samuel Stanhope Smith, that climate was more responsible for complexion than other factors. He also based his conclusions on the work of Buffon, Camper, and Blumenbach as well as "common sense."[42]

Easton's 1837 *Treatise*, drawing on eighteenth-century assessments of European character, also challenged the physiological arguments about race. As was the case for Lewis before him, he saw race not as the sum of physical characteristics, but rather of a number of constituent parts, including culture, temperament, and intellect. Intellect, while bound by laws, he believed, followed a different path not proscribed by physical characteristics. If intellect did not follow physical law, then what governed it? He responded by arguing for the centrality of public sentiment.[43]

Easton believed public sentiment served as a driving force in society, not only influencing the development of the mind, but also the progress of nations. Intellect, an essential subject of Enlightenment thought and, as David Walker and Maria Stewart suggested, one of several determinants of the rise and fall of nations, established the fitness of African Americans as participants in American life. Sketching public sentiment and its impact on intellect through classical antiquity offered Easton another vantage point from which to view its importance. Uncontaminated by racial slavery or hegemonic theories of racial inferiority and second-class citizenship, the past, especially classical antiquity, offered a fertile field for examination of this question.[44]

Rather than a lowly and accursed place, the Africa Easton presented included a wide range of racial and ethnic groups and served as a fount of wisdom for the Western world. He asserted, "it is evident from the best sources extant that the arts and sciences flourished among this great branch of the human family, long before its benefits were known to any other." A similar statement appeared in the 1836 edition of Lewis's *Light and Truth*: "This kingdom [Egypt] bestowed its noblest labors and finest arts upon the improvement of mankind. And Greece was so sensible of this, that its most illustrious men, Homer, Pythagoras, Plato and even its greatest legislators traveled into Egypt to complete their studies and draw from that fountain whatever was rare and valuable in every kind of learning."[45] These writers tapped into eighteenth-century historical conceptualizations of universal history that put the Mediterranean world, which included Egypt (Africa very broadly defined), Greece, and Rome, at the center of the construction of the West's intellectual foundations. The immensely popular eighteenth-century historian Charles Rollin, whose work Pennington, Easton, and Lewis all utilized, helps to illustrate this point.[46]

Best known for his multivolume work, *Roman History from the Foundation of Rome to the Battle of Actium* in seven volumes (1730–41), and *The Ancient History of the Egyptians, Carthaginians, Assyrians, Babylonians, Medes and Persians, Grecians and Macedonians* in ten volumes (1738–41), Rollin's work is impossible to ignore as the source of at least some of the nineteenth-century black writers' conclusions. One need only compare Lewis's remarks, quoted above, to Rollin's remarks quoted below.

Egypt was ever considered, by all the ancients, as the most renowned school for wisdom and from whence most arts and sciences were derived. The kingdom bestowed its noblest labors and finest arts on the improvement of mankind; and Greece was so sensible of this that its most illustrious men, such as Homer, Pythagoras, Plato, even its great legislators, Lycurgus and Solon, with many more whom it is needless to mention, traveled into Egypt, to complete their studies, and draw from that fountain whatever was rare and valuable in every kind of learning. God himself has given this kingdom as glorious testimony; when praising Moses, he says of him, that he was learned in all the wisdom of the Egyptians.[47]

Rollin's conception of history (and Easton's, subsequently,) employed both didactic and cyclical understandings of history. It also drew from both biblical and classical sources. In *Ancient History* Rollin affirmed his belief regarding the pinnacle of learning and civilization: "The nearer we approach those countries inhabited by the sons of Noah [the Middle East and Africa], in the great[er] perfection we find the arts and sciences." Notwithstanding his 1843 slur of Africans generally, Noah Webster offered a similar conclusion: "Letters were invented in the East, and appear to have been first cultivated in Assyria. From Assyria to Egypt to Greece, and to Rome, letters were propagated, and the rude inhabitants were instructed in the arts and sciences."[48]

Despite the important eighteenth-century historical understandings, which offered an alternative portrait of Africa, centralizing Asia and Africa as important contributors to human civilization, nineteenth-century notions of Africa remained deeply contested. Because of the interest in and demand for Egyptian antiquities, borne of the brief Napoleonic occupation of Egypt, in 1799–1806, the interpretation of the Egyptian phenotype became less Ethiopian and more Arabic or Semitic. Consequently, for nineteenth-century intellectuals, the issue of how to describe Africa became even more challenging. At the end of the eighteenth century, European explorers including William Barrows, Mungo Park, and a host of other adventurers were just penetrating the interior of Africa, almost wholly unknown to Europeans in previous centuries, but their travel accounts slowly filtered into the public perception throughout the nineteenth century. Because many were still wedded to classical understandings of Africa, the continent presented an intellectual challenge of how to map its inhabitants, geographically and racially. Charles Anthon's *Classical Dictionary*, published in numerous editions during the antebellum period, provided a guide for both white and black writers of his day. Anthon, one of the preeminent classicists of the period and a faculty member at Columbia College (part of Columbia University), cannot logically be ignored.[49]

Anthon's entry on Africa reflected the continued reliance on classical knowledge—namely Greek and Roman—to make sense of the complexities of the continent. Some of the complexity arose from the eighteenth-century scholarly concurrence that Egypt was geographically a separate country prior to the invention of three continents—Africa, Asia, and Europe—in the ninth or tenth century. In classical antiquity, Africa, or Libya, constituted the smallest of the three continents. Using Herodotus, Anthon suggested that the appropriate classifications of its peoples were "Africans" (or "Libyans") and "Ethiopians." The former occupied the northern part of the country, while the latter occupied the southern part. He placed the "Moors and the Negroes" under the designation "Ethiopian." Despite making what seem to be definitive statements, Anthon opined, "Nothing, however, can be more indeterminate than the terms Ethiopia and African; and it is certain that many distinct races were included under the later denomination." After a lengthy discussion of the varied accounts of the ancients, especially Strabo, regarding geographical details of the country, Anthon, seemingly throwing his hands up in exasperation, wrote, "In the midst of so many contradictions, and in a region still almost unknown, the boldness of ignorance may hazard any assertion, and pretend to decide any point, while the modesty of science resigns itself to doubt."[50]

Distinguishing between the two areas of inhabitants became more and more common. As early as 1815, just eight years after the end of Napoleon's occupation of Egypt, Noah Webster's *Elements of Useful Knowledge*, a commonly used source in this period, asserted that the inhabitants of Africa belonged to two distinct classes: "the blacks of the interior and Southern parts and the swarthy descendants of the Arabs and Carthaginians." *Anthon's Classical Dictionary* raised the possibility that the Egyptians migrated from Arabia. "Aegyptus [Egypt], as the son of Belus and a brother of Danaus, inherited Arabia from his father, but subsequently conquered Egypt." By the mid-1830s, European and American writers were less likely to concede that ancient Egyptians were of African origin.[51]

Interest in Egypt's place in the ancient world persisted, and black intellectuals used this to their advantage. Hosea Easton, however, subverted the uncertainty of the earlier conclusions. For him, Africa's importance was not simply racial but also deeply rooted in the civilization the continent produced. Easton claimed Egypt's culture and civilization, based on its location on the African continent, without getting into the intellectually contentious issue of the "race" of its inhabitants. While he suggested that Africa and Africans made important contributions to the West, he never made any explicit racial claims about the Egyptians and instead referred in quite general terms to Africans—that "great branch of the human family." Following the lead of Herodotus and Diodorus Siculus, he applauded the sophisticated nature of governmental and commercial structures in Africa. He did not limit his praise to Egypt: "Africa could once boast of several states of eminence, among them are Egypt, Ethiopia and Carthage; the latter supported an extensive commerce, which was extended to every part of the then known world." Clearly, Easton viewed Africa as a place consisting of several different empires and, presumably, different peoples. For Easton, place trumped race in the quest for a meaningful historical discourse about Africa.[52]

Easton used his work to make certain claims about the general character of Africans, a discussion fueled by the endemic belief during the period that national character resulted from the history of a particular group or race. The idea that Africans were generous, good-spirited, and willing to share their good fortune with the nations of the world undergirded this presentation: "This noble people were not content with the enjoyment of luxury and ease, to the exclusion of their neighbors," wrote Easton. Instead, at "an early period they are found carrying the blessings of civilization into Greece; and although repulsed in their first attempt by the rude barbarity of the Greeks, yet their philanthropy soon inspired them to resume the enterprise, which resulted in the settlement of two colonies, one in Argos and the other in Attica."[53]

Easton's historical chronology of European and African civilizations, predicated on a belief in difference, involved a strategic use of history to rewrite and reinterpret the relationships between these civilizations. Only by juxtaposing African and European civilization, Easton believed, could readers clearly understand the historical evolution of these civilizations for themselves. The intellectual terrain upon which Easton operated was not of his making or choosing. As historian George Price, arguing for a humanist understanding of Easton's work, suggests, Easton was "attempting to reveal an environmental cause and effect relationship between worldwide historical events and the degradation of all humanity, which eventually and inevitably shaped the abysmal state of interracial relations in antebellum America."[54] Arguments like Easton's were necessary to create an intellectual foundation for toppling the slave power that was slowly, but unmistakably, developing in America. These arguments also made a persuasive case for complex notions of black humanity.

While biblical examinations of early human existence provided black scholars indisputable historical evidence of black origins and genealogy, or what scholars referred to as "biblical inerrancy," many also conceded that human history did not really begin until civilizations, defined in the nineteenth century as societies organized around clearly defined governmental structures, came into existence. Civilizations, more often than not, took the form of empires, which represented the apex as well as the limitations of human achievement. Nineteenth-century historical writers recognized several empires—Babylonian, Medo-Persian, Macedonian, and Roman—as central to the formation of the ancient and modern worlds. As Charles Rollin noted, historians and intellectuals wanted to not only "know by what methods those empires were founded, but by what steps they rose to the exalted pitch of grandeur which we so much admire; what was it that constituted their true glory and felicity; and what were the causes of their declension and fall." It was particularly important for African-American historians to juxtapose the grandeur of the African condition in the ancient world with the realities of the nineteenth century. Ann Plato's *Essays* summed up the sentiments of many black writers of her day regarding the issue of empire and its connection to civilization: "Egypt that once shot over the world brilliant rays of genius is sunk in darkness."[55]

Aware of the shifting nineteenth-century perceptions of the racial composition of Egyptians and Ethiopians, Pennington, while illustrating all of the aforementioned historical traditions, seemed determined to show connections between the two empires. His work was partly in response to assertions like that in Webster's *Elements of Useful Knowledge*: "The interior of Africa is little known, being inhabited by savages and ferocious wild animals. It is to be remarked that in Africa, no inland seas exist to invite commerce and civilization, nor will the rivers bear large ships to the interior country. This country, therefore, seems abandoned to the savage and wild beast." Rather than accept that areas south of Egypt lacked civilization, Pennington argued for the parity of Ethiopian and Egyptian civilizations to shore up his claims regarding the capability of black civilizations. As one might by now expect, he relied on biblical, ancient (Herodotus's *Histories*), and eighteenth-century historical accounts (Rollin's *Ancient History*) to present his case. In discussions of "race" and even culture, Pennington's account viewed the Egyptians and Ethiopians as two distinct groups. Using biblical genealogy, he opined, "It is beyond all dispute that Misraim settled Egypt, as it is also that Cush settled Ethiopia, and that these settlements were made contemporaneously." Despite the fact that the two nations, "confederated in the same government, and soon became the same people in politics, literature and peculiarities," two distinct racial groupings existed.[56]

In Pennington's mind, Ethiopian genius was no less awe-inspiring than that of the Egyptians. "Down to the time of Herodotus," he wrote, "eighteen of three hundred Egyptian sovereigns were Ethiopians." This fact offered Pennington ample evidence that the two nations were "equals in the arts and sciences for which Egypt is admitted on all hands to have been so renowned." To buttress his argument for difference but intellectual parity, Pennington used an excerpt from Herodotus that told how the Persians under Cambyses easily subdued the Egyptians, but enjoyed less success with the Ethiopians. This story demonstrated the prowess of the Ethiopians as well as the arrogance of ancient rulers. The retelling of it functioned as a history lesson. As detailed in *Histories*, book 3, Herodotus's allegory described the ill-fated mission of Cambyses, king of Persia, to conquer Ethiopia. Apparently, the Persian king sent messengers to the Ethiopian king with the ulterior motive of their doing some much-needed reconnaissance for a planned attack. Aware of the ruse, the Ethiopian king rejected the dubious offer of alliance as well as gifts of a purple robe, a gold chain, armlets, an alabaster box of myrrh, and a cask of palm wine. The king then handed the messengers a large bow, a symbol of Ethiopia's strength and malleability, and instructed them that when they could bend the bow with ease they would be adequately prepared to attack. Insulted by the Ethiopian king's gesture, Cambyses embarked on a disastrous mission that reduced the Persians to cannibalism, and he was ultimately forced to abandon his plan.[57]

Pennington's discussion of Carthaginian origins displayed the same nuance as his assessment of Egyptians and Ethiopians. His approach relied on an understanding of what nineteenth-century intellectuals viewed as natural historical cycles. The Egyptian and Ethiopian Empires gave way to the Carthaginian Empire, and it, in turn, gave way to the Roman Empire. In a chapter titled "Were the Carthaginians Ethiopians?" Pennington stated, "I do not mean to ask whether the Carthaginians were Africans. They were Africans. However, African does not mean the same as Ethiopian. Ethiopian is a name derived from the complexion of the inhabitants, while Africa is a name given to a tract of country inhabited by nations of various complexions." He went on to make the point explicit: "To me, it appears that Carthaginians cannot in any proper sense be considered Ethiopian." Moreover, Pennington knew and accepted, as did most writers of this period, the story drawn from the *Aeneid* about Carthage's establishment by a colony of Tyrians lead by Queen Dido.[58]

Aware that no record of extensive contact between the Ethiopians and the Carthaginians existed, Pennington could not argue that the Carthaginians were black. Moreover, citing Herodotus, he pointed out that the Persians were actively conquering parts of Africa and that the Carthaginians escaped this fate because the Phoenicians refused to take up arms against their descendants. The Persians, however, did participate in the unsuccessful assault against the Ethiopians previously described. Moreover, during the infamous Punic Wars launched by Rome against Carthage during the republic, Pennington suggested, Rome had "no spite against the Ethiopians, while their aim seems to have been to exterminate the Carthaginians."[59]

Following closely on the heels of Easton's and Pennington's studies, the 1844 edition of Robert Benjamin Lewis's *Light and Truth* offered the most expansive historical text published by an African American during the antebellum period. A committee of "distinguished colored men" including Thomas Dalton, head of the Massachusetts General Colored Association, and James Scott, abolitionist and clothier, endorsed the work. The book's title, *Light and Truth: Collected from the Bible and Ancient and Modern History, Containing the Universal History of the Colored and Indian Race from the Creation of the World to the Present Time*, represented Lewis's attempt to construct a history that conformed in style, scope, and substance to the universal histories of the eighteenth century extensively cited throughout the work. Like Rollin before him, Lewis provided information on various civilizations, including the Ethiopian, Egyptian, Assyrian, Persian, Macedonian, and Roman Empires. The second edition, which at four hundred pages was more than double the size of the 1836 edition, traced the contributions of people of color to biblical, ancient, and modern history, and it represented Lewis's "determination that a correct knowledge of the Colored and Indian people, ancient and modern, may be extended freely, unbiased by any prejudicial effects from descent or station."[60]

Lewis's history, eclectic by modern standards, conformed closely to the eighteenth- and nineteenth-century universal histories upon which it was modeled. Still, it differed considerably in content. One of the central differences is that Ethiopia, as opposed to Egypt, figured prominently in Lewis's account. Following a widely accepted practice in the nineteenth century, Easton accepted in his *Treatise* that "Ham was the son of Noah, and founder of the African race, and progenitor to Assur, who probably founded the first civilization after the flood," a reference to the Egyptians. Lewis disagreed with the accepted genealogy of the earth's settlement after the Great Deluge and concluded that Ethiopia was "the first country founded after the flood." He described the Ethiopian empire as large, consisting of more than forty-five kingdoms and cities. He also proudly proclaimed, using Diodorus Siculus as his source, "that Ethiopians consider the Egyptians as one of their colonies."[61]

Perhaps the most significant difference in Lewis's work compared to others is the complex racial and ethnic terms it incorporates. As mentioned earlier, these writers knew, and Lewis especially knew, that not all Africans were Ethiopians even though they used the term very broadly. For instance, Lewis wrote, "Africa, in general, and Egypt, in particular, are called the land of Ham." In another instance he wrote, "Ham's descendants are Egyptians—blacks with frizzled or curly hair." This statement, read literally (and in isolation), could lead one to conclude that Lewis meant that Egyptians are black. But at another point, when describing the genealogy of the Egyptians, and using biblical sources, he wrote, "a portion of the Egyptians seem to have been the descendants of Abraham, by Hagar; and of Esau, by Bashemath, the daughter of Ishmael." Hagar, widely reputed to be the progenitor of Arabs, could not be Ethiopian by any standard. Nor was Ishmael, whom Lewis considered "founder of the red race," which probably refers to Semitic people, black. Rather than an uncritical reading, Lewis blended ancient and modern knowledge regarding the physical characteristics of the Egyptians and acknowledged the Semitic and Asiatic origins of the Egyptians while not ruling out African influences. Lewis's discussion of the inhabitants of Lower Egypt, which is the northernmost portion of the country, suggested that they were not of African origin, but "colonies from Syria and Arabia." For Lewis, the importance of Cyrene, a Phoenician colony on the Mediterranean, lay not in the race of its inhabitants but in its contributions to ancient history. The site of the Christian day of Pentecost, when Jesus is reputed to have given the church the gift of the Holy Ghost, Cyrene was also the birthplace of the poet Callimachus, the historian Eratosthenes, and Simon the Cyrene, "who bore the Savior's cross." Regardless of its racial makeup, Cyrene offered valuable evidence of Africa's importance to Western ideas and civilization.[62]

It is easy to mistake Lewis's descriptions of Strabo, Euclid, Homer, and Plato as Ethiopians for the conclusion that he thought all these individuals were black. While none of them was of African or Ethiopian descent, they were all reputedly associated with Africa during some point in their lives. The geographer Strabo traveled extensively and spent considerable time in Egypt. Euclid, the famed mathematician, is reputed to have had some association with Alexandria, although the claim is of doubtful origin. According to Herodotus, Homer and Plato spent time in Egypt studying in the mysteries school. Association, rather than racial origin, seems to be the engine that drove Lewis's understanding of Africa's contributions to the wider world.[63]

Drawing on reputable sources of Western knowledge, all of the writers discussed here situated Africa and Africans as important contributors to Western civilization. Their work, however, more clearly distinguishes between the two than it might appear. Given the shifting discourse on the racial makeup of Egyptian society and the imprecise nature of nascent scientific formulations, it proved intellectually strategic to focus on the more concrete realities of place rather than race. However, even within that construct, the black intellectuals did not limit themselves to the modern, romantic type of history that was becoming popular. Rather than limiting themselves to the present, antebellum black writers, as did those before them, skillfully juxtaposed the biblical and ancient condition of Africans with the current state of African Americans. Because of their more advanced education and their closer (than earlier writers') readings of ancient history, they could and did do more than prove black contributions to Western development: they positioned themselves to attack directly the relative failings of a society that preached equality and liberty but tolerated inequality and practiced slavery.[64]

Modern History: Using the Past to Understand Black Origins in the Present

One of the most pernicious contentions of the antebellum period was that Africans' lack of civilization gave rise to the slave trade. Not only did such a claim provide a foundation for commenting negatively on the black past but also for justifying the antebellum condition (especially enslavement) of African Americans and theories of black inferiority. Through an analysis of modern history, early antebellum black intellectuals turned assertions of black inferiority on their head by contradicting (perhaps even helping to deflate) the celebratory American nationalism and the belief in teleological progress prevalent in mainstream historical works of the day. It was particularly important for black scholars to continue to look at the past through the lens of universal history and to pay particular attention to the rise and fall of empires. But because the European age of exploration and the slave trade that created new, modern empires also occasioned the rise of racialized slavery and attendant theories of racial inferiority, it was especially important to connect universal history to contemporary (or modern) notions of Western culture and civilization.

Although the only source Easton cited in this regard was Diodorus Siculus, his *Treatise* probably also drew heavily from the work of the eighteenth-century

English historian Edward Gibbon. Gibbon's influence on Easton's writing is evident in two ways. First, Easton's work is explicitly indebted to that of Robert Benjamin Lewis's *Light and Truth*, which clearly relied on Gibbon's *History of the Decline and Fall of the Roman Empire*. Second, Easton's caustic treatment, in tone and language, of Europe during the Dark Ages is reminiscent of Gibbon's treatment of the Germanic tribes in *Decline and Fall*. Gibbon's work, first published in 1738, is a classic lament for the destruction of one of the greatest representatives of classical antiquity, the Roman Empire. It also offers a scathing critique of the Germanic tribes. Enamored of the "glory that was Rome," Gibbon attributed its decline and fall to the equally insidious forces of barbarism and Christianity. His conception of history relied on cyclical theories and remained stuck in a peculiar antiquarianism. Colored by his undying admiration for the Romans, in his description of the Germanic tribes, Gibbon blended Herodotus's discussion of the Scythians, inhabitants of the region around the Black Sea and the Caspian, with accounts from the more moderate portrayal by the Roman historian Tacitus, which appeared in *Agricola*, *Germania*, and *The Histories*.[65]

Gibbon, possibly relying on some combination of biblical genealogy and European myth and fable, stated that the Germans descended from Japheth. European descent from Japheth was not only a central contention in Easton's work but figured prominently in the work of all of the black intellectuals who wrote history in the early republic and antebellum periods. It served as a marker of the distinct differences between "branches of the human family." Given his particular dislike of Christianity and the Germanic tribes, Gibbon painted a particularly odious portrait of Germanic origins, indicating that they "received their existence from the gradual union of some wandering savages of the Hercynian woods." Given the problematic origins, it naturally followed that the Germans were "warlike and fierce—without cities, letters, arts or money." Easton offered a similar account in his discussion of these groups: "Wherever the barbarians marched, their route was marked with blood. They ravaged or destroyed all around them." Tribes that descended from the Germanic people, Lombards, Scandinavians, and Bulgarians, fared no better. They had hands like dogs, or they drank the blood of their enemies, and some inhabited places no better than the homes of beavers.[66]

Easton's comparative model did, however, transcend Gibbon's work. Rather than the expression of a simplistic polarity between the Romans and Germans, Easton was interested in questioning the social, political, and intellectual foundations of European civilization, a necessary exercise in a historical moment in which racial achievement seemed directly related to the attainment of civilization. He accomplished this by relating the history of feudalism in Europe to the development of slavery in the modern world. Thus his claims about the connection between ancient and modern history did not end in Europe but extended to America. In ways similar to American slavery, feudalism subjected a large proportion of the population to servitude, and under it, the serfs were "fixed to the soil" and transferable "from one proprietor to another, by sale or conveyance."[67]

In other assessments of national character, Easton suggested that some European kings, rather than displaying the high arts of statehood, led their subjects on missions of conquest in neighboring lands. Once the land was conquered, the chiefs or generals parceled out the captured land to their lesser officers. These men, in turn, became part of an armed force sworn to protect the king's standard. The lesser officers would also impose this standard on their dependents. Whereas the Egyptians waged war only when provoked, Europeans, Easton maintained, "for the smallest pretext would make war with one another and lead their slaves on to conquest."[68]

While it would be easy to argue that Easton linked the relatively uncivilized Germanic tribes to Americans in an uninterrupted chain, it would be historically misleading. Easton's hyperbolic language about Europe drew attention, by contrast, to characterizations of Africa, and by extension, to Africans, as devoid of civilization.

Europe and America present a different spectacle. There is not one foot of God's earth which is now occupied by them but was obtained, in effect, by the dint of war, and the destruction of the vanquished, since the founding of London, a.d. 49. Their whole career presents a motley mixture of barbarism and civilization, of fraud and philanthropy, of patriotism and avarice, of religion and bloodshed. Yet, it must be admitted that almost every nation in Europe, and especially Americans, retain in principle, if not in manners, all the characteristics of their barbarous and avaricious ancestors.[69]

Henry Highland Garnet, probably also drawing from Gibbon, offered a similar assessment of the condition of Europe and Europeans before the rise of modern Western civilization. Garnet remarked that the "ancestors of the now proud and boasting Anglo-Saxon were among the most degraded in the human family. They abode in caves underground either naked or covered with the skins of wild beasts. Night was made hideous by their Wild shouts and day was

darkened by the smoke which arose from bloody altars, upon which they offered human sacrifice."[70] Europe's barbarism, according to the black-authored
histories, served as a significant casual factor in the development of modern
slavery.

Black writers not only looked to the European past to discuss modern history but, more important, examined the meanings of this type of history in
the settlement of the Americas. Proslavery arguments contended that blacks
were naturally inferior to whites and justified the ever-expanding slave power.
James Pennington's narrative of modern history in the *Textbook* challenged
these contentions. He pointed to the fact that the Spanish used indigenous
Indian populations in Central and South America as slaves before the importation of Africans. The main culprit in this enterprise, the Spanish monarch
Charles V, Pennington argued, "reduced the aborigines to a state of vassalage,
and compelled them to work the soil." Once it became clear that Native Americans could not withstand the workload, Africans became a "natural" substitute.
Slavery, then, in Pennington's mind, had little to do with African inferiority, but related directly to the conquest of the Americas. Slavery's invention
resided with the conquerors, not the conquered or imported persons, or the
Africans.[71]

Pennington extended this argument to its logical conclusion by looking to
the emerging literature from assorted European and American explorers on
the continent during the era of free trade (1830–80). Although some of these
works, like those in the *African Repository*, were obviously designed to provide
favorable accounts of the African continent to facilitate exploitation of natural
resources, black writers found these works useful to counteract the contention,
prevalent in Noah Webster's work, that Africa, especially the interior, lacked
any traces of civilization. Listing a series of explorers like Anna Falconbridge,
T. J. Steadman, and others, Pennington boldly proclaimed in his *Textbook* that
they "have visited that country since it has begun to be drenched with blood
by the manstealer, and have seen the arts in a highly cultivated state. These have
also given accounts of their rulers, their states, or kingdoms."[72]

The use of universal history allowed African American intellectuals to combat the idea of alleged black inferiority caused by the supposed backwardness
of Africa. They argued that many early civilizations followed well-established
patterns as they developed from less-refined states and moved in cyclical patterns towards progress. Moreover, nineteenth-century accounts of Africa, although they helped pave the way for colonialism, provided a critical forum
for more nuanced and verifiable descriptions of the interior, especially in civic

and political institutions. Although very broad and somewhat biased, these characterizations offered important insights into the breadth of black thinking in the period. Modern history, like the sacred and ancient, offered a means of presenting a more complete portrait of the African American past. How, these writers wondered, could white Americans justify the institution of slavery, given the contributions of Africa and its inhabitants to Western civilization? And how could white America ignore the example African Americans provided of progress? How could white America argue that black Americans were slaves because of innate inferiority, when different kinds of people (including whites) had at one time or another been slaves? And how could they forget that that they themselves had racialized slavery? Rather than an uncritical racial chauvinism, these writers attempted to provide a more faithful account of the history and evolution of human societies, using the historical tools of the eighteenth century.

They did not, however, ignore the intellectual toolkit of the nineteenth century. Black scholars also used Romanticism to discuss the complexity of the black past and present. While Romanticism, the dominant American intellectual movement from the 1830s to the 1860s, offered a somewhat limited historical trajectory with which to work, it nevertheless offered important ways of framing historical discourse consistent with the goals of black writers. One of its most important components was the literary device of portraying representative men and women, which situated the lives of notable individuals as symbolizing the potential of all human beings.[73] Black representative men and women revealed the intellectual parity of African Americans who, according to James W. C. Pennington, "distinguished themselves in the midst of slavery" with whites. And particularly important, the device of representative men and women was highly compatible with contributionist discussions inherent in the use of sacred and ancient history and in the production of modern and universal history. Notably, it also accommodated the use of the jeremiad and providential approaches to history.[74]

Abbé Grégoire's *On the Cultural Achievements of Negroes* (1808), Lydia Maria Child's *An Appeal in Favor of That Class of Americans Called Africans* (1833), and to a lesser extent, Wilson Armstead's *Tribute for the Negro* (1848) provided useful mainstream models for the type of presentations black writers constructed. Magnifying African abilities merged seamlessly with the highlighting of exceptional talents in James W. C. Pennington's *Textbook*, which included, for example, a sketch of Anthony Amo, a Guinean who received a doctorate from the University of Wittenberg in Germany in 1734. Pennington also included information about Thomas Fuller, known as the "African calculator" because of his ability to perform sophisticated mathematical feats despite the inability to read and write, and Jacobus Eliza Capitein, an African-born recipient of a doctorate from the University of Leyden in 1729 who was proficient in several ancient languages. Each of these men's lives demonstrated the capacity of Africans to achieve outstanding intellectual feats, and, thus, suggested the possibilities for the larger group.[75] Henry Highland Garnet reached back in the ancient world to African achievements. Recalling ancient glories in a traditional approach, he praised "beautiful Cleopatra, who swayed and captivated the heart of Anthony," and Hannibal, the Carthaginian general who, during the Punic Wars, crossed the Alps and threatened Rome. Intent upon referencing the glories of the African past and discussing the representative nature of Africa's contributions to the early church, Garnet referenced Terrence, Euclid, Cyprian, Origen, and St. Augustine.[76]

The Romantic device of using representative men and women served larger purposes than vindication. Pennington used it to comment on Thomas Jefferson's assessments of blacks in *Notes on the State of Virginia*: "O that he reflected for a moment that his opinions were destined to undergo a rigid scrutiny by an improved state of intellect assisted by the rising power of an unbiased spirit of benevolence," wrote Pennington. "Had he done this, he would, as a wise man [have] modified that ill judged part of his work which relates to the colored people."[77] As if to provide the final word on Jefferson's pronouncements, Pennington added, "He makes a labored effort to conclude his proof [of intellectual inferiority] against us, and reasons throughout as if he intended to claim the case, but his conclusion is a budget of confusion."[78] This critique offered the first realization of David Walker's desire to see a generation of black scholars who would challenge the pronouncements of white scholars on issues of race.

When Ann Plato presented Western notables such as Isaac Newton, John Milton, and Walter Scott as examples of her representative men, it was part of an attempt to deflate the concept of race as fixed in biology and nature by arguing that genius emanated from mental discipline rather than natural endowment. The involvement of women in historical writing had increased dramatically by the antebellum period, as Nina Baym has shown, and their general visibility in the public sphere dramatically increased during Plato's lifetime. The women Plato selected, however, did not fit the traditional definition of representative women. They did not produce visible literary works, nor did they enjoy fame and fortune outside of the communities in which they lived, worked, and died. The fact of their nonrepresentative nature breaks with the contributionist and vindicationist approach of Lydia Maria Child and Henri Grégoire, mentioned earlier. Nevertheless, Plato presented the lives of ordinary black women as extraordinary and thus representative. As Kathryn Bassard notes, Plato's focus on these black women may have been an attempt to dramatize the limited options available to middle-class, free black women. Whatever the case, their representative qualities included their piety and devotion to service. Louisa Seabury, for example, was "guided in and preserved in the paths of rectitude and goodness; so that she was not only free from the stain of vice and vanity in her later rising years, but looked to things superior to the world and its vain and trifling amusements." Julia Ann Pell, Elizabeth Loomis Sherman, and others shared the pious lifestyle. These women, whom Plato knew and respected, were not extraordinary in the traditional way, but they, like her race, deserved a history—for someone to know their names. And Plato's focus on piety, at least in this context, showed her distinctly nineteenth-century reliance on clerical and religious forms of expression to convey points about history and the place of historical subjects. It even raised questions about what constituted the historical subject.[79]

Robert Benjamin Lewis also broadened the scope of the individuals represented as representative men. Those who helped to uplift the race, in word and deed, received honor. In addition to Jacobus Eliza Capitein, Anthony Amo, and Paul Cuffee, Lewis included intellectuals who wrote history; the most important of whom was David Walker. Lewis considered him "an African and distinguished friend, a good writer and a warm advocate for the miserable condition of his brethren in slavery." He also noted that Walker's "celebrated *Appeal* in behalf of his afflicted brethren is highly esteemed by wise men." Hosea Easton's *Treatise* "is a profound production," wrote Lewis, "and gives a true sketch of the condition of this class of people." And, of particular note, Lewis included women in his discussion. Recalling the achievement of women in the ancient world, he praised the work of two well-known Alexandrian poets, Cornelia and Hypatia. Cornelia devoted herself to culture and learning while Hypatia excelled in mathematics, astronomy, and philosophy. Lewis linked the ancient and the modern, praising Phillis Wheatley's literary production and reprinting several of her poems, while assuring the reader that they would be "favorable to African genius." He closed the chapter of *Light and Truth* with a tribute to Maria Stewart for her appeal on behalf of oppressed blacks and her steadfast manner in promoting African rights.[80]

The merger of vindicationist literary devices and the romantic technique of representative men and women provided a useful means for black intellectuals to offer a more nuanced presentation of black possibility. Highlighting individuals allowed their achievements, respectability, and noble bearing to be used to represent the larger possibilities of the race. And there was one more characteristic of the romantic movement that informed black historical writing—attention to American antiquities.

Europeans tried to reconcile the theoretical musings of the ancients with practical, current realities related to discovery and its outcomes. Native Americans easily figured as part of the formulation. On the one hand, American ethnographers tried to account more precisely for the origins of Native Americans, and in doing so, to create a genealogy for America to rival that of Europe. But on the other hand, the place for Native Americans in America was shifting and would complicate these romantic constructions. Sometimes conceived as "noble savages" in the eighteenth century, a concept no doubt drawn from the classical perception of German tribes prior to the destruction of Roman civilization, Native Americans often fit into similar protective rubrics designed to preserve their culture and heritage within the context of a free and undistributed wilderness. However, as the expansionist discourse of the Jacksonian era, fueled by the excesses of the market revolution, gained prominence, Native Americans became a threat to unfettered expansion and came to be viewed as simply savage. Despite the existence of the so-called five civilized tribes along the Eastern Seaboard, Jacksonians seemed less concerned with acculturation within Indian territories and more determined to seize Indian land to benefit white settlers. The result was the Trail of Tears, a forced march in 1830 from Indian lands in the East to government allocated land west of the Mississippi.[81]

Within this atmosphere of relocation, displacement, and dispossession, black intellectuals easily appropriated "popular imaginings" of the Western hemisphere prior to the European age of exploration. Samuel Drake's *Biography and History of North America* (1837) relied on Diodorus Siculus, Hanno, Plato, and particularly Aristotle, which was an important source for him. These earlier scholars had conjectured that another continent existed on the other side of the world. Perhaps taking advantage of that idea, and explicitly relying on the subsequent work of Elias Boudinot and Ethan Smith, two prominent Indian ethnographers, Lewis cited similarities in birth and death rituals, language, and myths of the Native Americans and ancient Hebrews. He included a recitation of more than thirty ethnographic works written by various authors on the question, and an etymological chart listing English, Native American, and Hebrew words. After this detailed presentation, Lewis exclaimed, "Can a rational doubt be entertained whether the above Indian words and parts of sentences were derived from the corresponding words and parts of sentences in Hebrew?"[82]

Lewis's discussion of Native Americans in the romantic tradition of American antiquities is closely related to the black intellectual project of "present[ing] a just view of [their] origins," or creating a reliable historical discourse. Not only was the connection real for him—Lewis had a biracial background (Native American and African American)—but Native Americans, like blacks, were seen as marginal characters in the American public sphere. However, while blacks were important to the nation's economic possibilities, Native Americans had become dispensable objects, revered as part of a mystical past, but disregarded in the progressive present. Lewis appealed to the same reformist impulses that drove the antislavery movement by decrying the "foul deeds that Europeans perpetrated against Native Americans" and pointed out that they were "the only true Christians in the land," which he supported by reprinting several Native American speeches to white settlers. Lewis challenged the notion of the "vanishing Indian" and argued in favor of Native American sovereignty.[83] Black writers expressed concerns about Native Americans, with whom they shared blood and experience. These discussions, based neither on simple veneration nor on nostalgia for the past, focused on the amelioration of injustices in the past and present.

Within the broad framework of Romanticism, interest in American antiquities was second only to what was popularly called during the antebellum period "Holy Land mania," the veneration of ancient sites and ruins from the Bible. Although the Holy Land as a source of inspiration continued and matured well into the late nineteenth century, its manifestations in black writing are rarely explored. Among black intellectuals, Holy Land mania's most potent manifestations appeared in newspapers, especially the *Colored American* (originally the *Weekly Advocate*), widely viewed as a showcase of black thought in the antebellum period.[84] In 1840, the *Colored American* featured a series titled "Sacred Geography and Antiquities," which highlighted the paper's interest in both biblical antiquity and history. It featured descriptions of ancient empires and their demise during the four historical epochs: the Babylonian, Medo-Persian, Greek, and Roman periods, a common division of historical chronology in the works of mainstream and African American intellectuals alike. Additionally, in 1841, the paper published a series of articles and etchings of various biblical cities in each issue. The paper's interest in history and antiquities was not only an indicator of their importance in the black community, but also possibly a

reflection the influence and interests of James W. C. Pennington and James Mc-
Cune Smith, ministers as well as writers, who were associated with the paper
as contributor and coeditor, respectively.[85]

The first installment in the antiquities series appeared in May 1840, one year
before the publication of Pennington's *Textbook of the Origin and History of the
Colored People*. It featured a discussion of the Chaldean city of Babylon. According to the writer, although highly revered as a magnificent city whose inhabitants wielded great political and economic influence, "its pride, idolatry and
abominable wickedness provoked the almighty." Not surprisingly the theme
of idolatry figured prominently in Pennington's *Textbook* as an explanation of
African American decline. The assessment of Assyria by the series' writers is
similar to that of Babylon. Much, if not all, the historical information on the
kingdom was found in the writings of various ancient historians, including
Diodorus Siculus, Tragus, Justin, Castor, and Eusebius, even though the authors
were critical of these sources. Despite a history of more than five hundred
years, many believed Assyria's government and social organization were insuf-
ficient to escape the wrath of God, because the rapid expansion of the kingdom
had been occasioned by corruption and murder. According to biblical history,
the city of Nineveh escaped destruction only because of the preaching of the
prophet Jonah.[86]

Black engagement with antiquities presented a decidedly modern spin on
the biblical and ancient worlds. Babylon and Assyria figured prominently in the
biblical sources as well as classical antiquity and universal history. Both empires
experienced unchecked expansion that led to social, political, and economic
decline, and both, according to the series' authors, declined because of religious
systems based on polytheism, a common conclusion regarding the decline of
empires. This particular aspect of black historical writing did more than display
an engagement with historical and biblical antiquities, given the nineteenth-
century focus on nations; it also functioned as a veiled jeremiad comparing the
history of ancient empires with the contemporary United States in an attempt
to caution American policy makers. Rapid expansion and the worship of slavery as the nation's idol would occasion God's wrath in the form of assault on
the slave regime.[87]

The continuation of the newspaper's sacred antiquities series in 1841 worked
in much the same way as material on Babylon and Assyria. Here the authors'
interest was in not only recording the rise and decline of these empires but
juxtaposing their past glory with their present state. The writers in the *Colored American* excerpted material from Charles MacFarlane's *Seven Apocalyptic*

Churches, published in 1832. Each account served to comment on the enduring power of Christianity, the decline of pagan idolatrous worship, and the fact that the Ottoman Empire, which had existed since 1453 (and would last until 1919), controlled much of the area that constituted the Holy Land. Largely because of centuries-old animosities dating back to the Crusades, Christians contested and lamented Muslim control of the Holy Land but were comforted by the fact that the Ottoman Empire was largely in decline throughout the nineteenth century, and they commonly referred to it as the "Sick Man of Europe." Its death proved the ultimate triumph of Christian and Western religious doctrine (also reflected in the paper's presentation of etchings from MacFarlane's work).[88] MacFarlane's *Seven Apocalyptic Churches* showcased the seven churches in the apostle John's visions in Revelations. Whether he was interested in eschatological issues or not is unclear. It is clear, however, that MacFarlane worked to weave into his accounts the glory of each of these churches in the biblical account and their present decline in the contemporary world.[89]

The antiquities series fits nicely with the ministerial editorship of the paper, but this material amplified themes common during the period. Charting the historical genealogy of the early Christian church spoke to larger issues of progress and decline. The articles also indirectly used religion to address the failings of proslavery arguments that were also grounded in religion. Articles mirrored nineteenth-century prejudices regarding the role of Muslims, especially the Ottoman Empire's role in world affairs and its relationship to the wider world. But finally the appearance of this material in the *Colored American* must also be viewed as consistent with the interests of the paper's readers and demonstrative of the complex images and influences on black writers (and readers) of the period.[90]

AFRICAN AMERICAN HISTORICAL WRITING in the early antebellum period drew from a set of three distinct historical traditions: the biblical or Mosaic tradition, classicism and universal history, and modern history—nineteenth-century historical conceptualizations that included Romanticism, American antiquities, and Holy Land mania. Not only did these traditions allow black writers a substantially longer historical time frame through which they could analyze the African American past and juxtapose the condition of blacks with whites in various historical periods, they also allowed them to produce a compelling counternarrative to the dominant discourse on African Americans in antebellum America, especially regarding their origin and their present and future possibilities in the world.

African Americans' use of the Bible here is less connected to an essential religious sensibility that supposedly permeates communities of color than an important means of conceptualizing and cataloging black participation in world history and an essential element in framing intellectual understandings of the past. Black intellectuals used the Bible to craft a more complete story about the African past than existed in mainstream publications to that point. It is not surprising that the majority of writers in this period were associated with the ministry. For much of the nineteenth century, divinity schools and seminaries constituted one of the few, and most important, sites of advanced training beyond the undergraduate degree available to African Americans. Ministerial training not only involved exposure to the texts of the biblical period but also required facility with ancient languages. While it is certainly the case that the importance of formal training in seminaries limited women's ability to participate in these efforts to the same extent as men, the exposure to and reverence for the biblical world permeated the wider world of letters and impacted all black intellectuals in the period, women included.

Biblical authority also served, for much of the nineteenth century, as a bulwark against the early advances of science. Forced increasingly to deal with the nascent authority of science in this period, which relied less on spiritual measures of human compatibility and more on physical designations that could presumably be measured in precise ways, black writers' continued reliance on the authority of the Bible helped to soften the worst manifestations of racism and bigotry and blunt the perception of these issues in the public sphere. Surely, black intellectuals understood, as Mia Bay has suggested, that the Bible's powerful narrative of humanity's interconnectedness offered incontrovertible proof of African American equality in a society that trumpeted this principle but did not practice it. Examining language closely, interrogating semantics, and privileging the Old Testament story of creation over theories of polygenesis provided a way to suggest the limitations, rather than the advantages, of science in a world where black existence grew more tenuous and contested by the day. The Bible as a site of authority worked to hold the power of science at bay and in check within the American intellectual sphere. But still, in the traditional way for Christians, the Bible was simply an incontrovertible disseminator of truth.

The classical tradition worked in much the same way, and black engagement with this literature provided additional evidence of erudition. Black thinkers and writers engaged these works not only to make vindicationist or contributionist arguments about their place in the ancient world, but also to show their understanding of the foundations of the Western intellectual tradition. By situating this concern within the nineteenth-century world of intellectual production, we are better positioned to understand the complex ways in which African Americans engaged these works. Consider, again, for example, the work of Robert Benjamin Lewis, which appears to many to be little more than a random catalog of facts. In fact, Lewis viewed Africa as a dynamic geographical space with unique connections to the advent of the modern world. In Lewis's argument, one has to consider race *and* place in order to understand the many ways African history is connected to the cultures of classical antiquity, namely Greece and Rome, as well as events discussed in the Bible. And although some of Lewis's evidence, viewed very critically (negatively) today, was based on the observations of the ancients, the authority of the ancients held sway in most credible historical work at that particular moment.

As history turned from the universal to the national, black intellectuals embraced facets of Romanticism, which looked to the organic world and human nature as arbiters of human reality. In doing so they utilized methodologies of representative men and women and American antiquities, which nicely dovetailed with contemporary understandings of biblical and classical history. The use of nineteenth-century intellectual tools by black intellectuals demonstrates how conversant they were with scholarly trends in the period. It also shows their determination to use these tools to construct a counternarrative to challenge mainstream thinking about Africa and the place of African Americans in the past and present.

While subsequent black intellectuals drew on the clerical and reform tradition, within the context of their particular historical moment, in some ways their approach was an extension of the work discussed here and above. The ultimate aim of their writing was to use the divisive politics surrounding race to make a statement about the limitations of American exceptionalism, especially as it related to African Americans. They used the concepts of emigration, revolutionary memory, patriotism, and republicanism to make larger points about the limits of black participation in a republic that prided itself on its democratic ethos and equalitarian sensibilities. As they had done with universal histories, they did so by skillfully excavating their role as actors and agents at two critical moments in the rise of modern history: the American Revolution and the Haitian Revolution. For writers between 1850 and 1863, these two events came to define the realities of the American past, present, and future as they tried to contest the idea that American slavery could logically exist alongside American freedom.

CHAPTER 3

The Destiny of the Colored People

African American History between Compromise and Jubilee, 1850–1863

> So the bill for the recapture of fugitive slaves has passed the Senate! That it
> will pass the House, I have no kind of doubt. Let the slavecatchers try to put
> it into force. Let the marshals of different districts come to our houses on
> the devil-sent errand of capturing our wives and our children. Not a black
> man must go unprepared for such a contest as the exigency of our cause
> demands. . . . There is but little to be expected from our friends. We must
> depend on ourselves. —SAMUEL RINGGOLD WARD, "Fugitive Slave Bill," 1850

INCREASING CONTROVERSY over the place of black people in American life
marked discussions of the 1840s. During that decade, the debate between proslavery and free-soil advocates heated up, with Free-Soilers not necessarily opposing slavery but simply its expansion. Suggesting just how divided the nation
was even among traditional allies, leading black antislavery activists repudiated
Garrisonian abolitionism and adopted a posture that called for an immediate
end to the "peculiar institution." This decade also featured the renewed popularity of emigrationist thought. Some free blacks concluded that they would
never be fully incorporated into American life and, therefore, they should simply leave. The turmoil resulting from all these ideologies made it particularly
urgent for black writers to create a historical narrative that forcefully addressed
the present state of African American life. A particularly efficient way of constructing this narrative was to connect their histories of participation in the
Revolutionary War with the contemporary rhetorical war in opposition to
slavery. Almost three-quarters of a century had passed since the patriots won
the Revolutionary War, and still, not only had citizenship rights not accrued to
all free Americans but even the memory and record of black contributions to
the American struggle for freedom were being neglected and lost. Black writers used historical writing to recover and preserve them and to reconfigure the
basis of American freedom, citizenship, and democracy.[1]

By the 1850s their work seemed even more urgent. In succession, the infamous Compromise of 1850 and its treacherous fugitive-slave provision, the Kansas-Nebraska Act and the skirmishes that preceded it, the *Dred Scott* case and decision, and John Brown's raid on Harpers Ferry made clear that the "paradox," as Edmund Morgan called it, created by the presence of slavery and freedom, was not even close to resolution. While the nation deliberated over the place of African Americans in the republic, black writers' move away from ancient and classical texts and toward the more recent Revolutionary War record reminded the nation of black people's contributions to the successful outcome of the effort—to America's history—and confronted the nation's failure to fulfill the republican promises made, ostensibly, to all its citizens. In the process, these writers and activists produced historical writing that became an important part of the final chapter of the antislavery war.[2]

Despite this look back to the Revolutionary War era and the continuing use of biblical, ancient, and universal history by some authors, the substance of black thought increasingly focused on contemporary issues. The 1850s represented an intense moment during which a coterie of black writers focused on an intractable American dilemma—whether or not the nation could live half slave and half free and continue to exist. While this was not a new preoccupation—a well-developed body of literature existed on the topic—black historical writers brought fresh perspectives to the debate as well as a highly developed literary and historical sensibility honed in the struggles against the slave power during the early republic and antebellum eras.[3]

This literal and rhetorical war made it emphatically clear that the abolitionists were determined to stop slavery's spread to newly acquired territory and defeat the proslavery forces popularly known as the "slave power." Still, simply arguing that the Revolutionary-era rhetoric had established the principle of citizenship as a *right* would not be enough. Antislavery activists had to combine their tactics of moral suasion with the threat of outright revolt, an example of which the Haitian Revolution provided. But the example provided more than a threat. It also enabled black writers to combine the history of black involvement in the American Revolution and the example of Haitian independence to enact a powerful new conceptualization of the possibilities of democratic promise, based partly on the leadership of free black men and women and the assistance of the enslaved.[4]

When juxtaposed with the American Revolution, the Haitian Revolution offered a different kind of legacy for public consideration. Long considered outside the pale of revolutionary legitimacy by American republicans, the Haitian example had coursed through the intellectual currents of black writing from 1804, the year of independence, to the 1850s. But black intellectuals understood that the island's prospects were limited and, in some instances, severely constrained by internal divisions, periodic instability, and financial difficulties. Consequently, while the significance of the Haitian *Revolution* was indisputable among, and agreed upon by, the African American writers, their characterization of Haitian *independence* was never monolithic or uniformly celebratory of the defeat of the continental European powers. Rather, the rhetoric was always cautious and restrained and often even critical. Historical discourse before 1850 sought to justify the island's existence and laud its success in the face of seemingly insurmountable obstacles. But the politically charged atmosphere of the 1850s changed the discourse on Haiti. The rewriting of this narrative required the authors to rethink and reconceptualize traditional understandings of patriotism, republicanism, and democracy in order to make it relevant to the political struggle going on in the United States right then.

The writers of this period differed substantially from those who came before. First, rather than exclusively abolitionists associated with the church, writers in the 1850s were primarily secular in their orientation. They lacked direct experience with slavery and were more likely born free in the North. They were also more consistently formally educated. These differences had some impact on what and how they wrote. Less likely than their predecessors to appeal solely to the authority of classical antiquity, although the classics still mattered in some of this work, these writers framed history within the context of the nation-state, the United States and Haiti. They used the past differently as well: the past, more often than not, provided the basis for an analysis of the present rather than providing part of a longer sweep of universal history. And finally, there was also a change in the role of the writers, intellectuals, and historians. Although the earlier writers were undoubtedly important leaders in the effort to construct a usable past, in the 1850s writers, true elites in many ways, expanded both the breadth and depth of the historical discussion of revolution in their effort to understand and to shape the contemporary "destiny of the colored people." An important part of that "destiny" mandated a new, explicit focus on free blacks and the leadership roles they would play in this struggle.

The new attention to free blacks and their leadership roles had at least two important origins. First, new legal developments, in the *Dred Scott* decision for example, had far-reaching implications that imperiled the few liberties that even free blacks enjoyed. But second, Haiti also presented the opportunity to hail the role of blacks in attaining their freedom through revolutionary struggle. The example proved blacks' ability to be leaders and highlighted the

centrality of slaves in the liberation process. But it also re
ers themselves, even if only indirectly, for leadership in tl
war ongoing in America.

This chapter discusses the advent of a uniquely America.
cal discourse framed around self-elevation and destiny and reflec.
the lens of the American and Haitian Revolutions. Not only had issues o. .
ery and freedom reached the boiling point by the 1850s but this moment represented great possibility for abolitionist forces even as restrictive legislation such
as the Compromise of 1850, the Kansas-Nebraska Act, and the *Dred Scott* decision became law. Black writers integrated themselves more fully into the language of nationhood, a project that began in the early republic, in which they
affirmed their belief in the core civil and human rights to which all members
of a nation were entitled. As the nation invoked the memory of the American
Revolution, black people argued for *their* centrality in the founding drama. And
finally they also looked to the Haitian Revolution, which threatened American
pretensions to life, liberty, and the pursuit of happiness just at the moment the
United States was emerging as a new nation.

Martin Robinson Delany, Emigrationist as Historian

The work of Martin Delany begins our look at the shift in African American historical production. First, rather than turning to biblical and classical
texts to construct a universal history, his work used modern history to connect
the past and the present of black people for the specific purpose of creating
a roadmap for navigating the difficulties faced by African Americans in the
1850s. Delany used his work to make concrete linkages between destiny, self-
elevation, emigration, and institutional constructs and the contemporary realities of African Americans. Second, Delany dramatically refined the traditional
argument about the rise and fall of civilizations, claiming simply that in every
historical age various groups have found themselves oppressed and degraded,
denied equal privileges, and deprived of political, religious, and social rights.
Injustice was more than a byproduct of European racism; it was an ideological
framework with roots in the human condition and in history. Delany's focus
on political economy, the intersection between political policies and economic
processes, as an important determinant of the status of African Americans deflated the falsehood that slavery existed as a result of God's disfavor, an essential
claim of proslavery clerics who continued to trumpet the Curse of Ham as the
rationale for black degradation. And finally, locating claims for citizenship in

Martin Delan

ular realm allowed Delany to posit the question: "What claims then have olored men, based upon the principles set forth, as fundamentally entitled to citizenship? Let the living records of history answer the enquiry."[5]

Delany's The Condition, Elevation, Emigration and Destiny of the Colored People of the United States (1852) shows that he clearly understood that one had to look beyond contemporary American realities to understand these complex questions. But when he looked to classical antiquity, he focused on political economy, and he coupled this with some utilization of modern history as well. The practical pursuits of Africans and their contributions to commerce, trade, and industry in Africa and later as laborers in the United States figured prominently in his discussion. According to Delany, "from the earliest period of history, Africans had been known as an industrious people, cultivators of the soil. The grains fields of Ethiopia and Egypt were the themes of the poet and . . . the subject of the historian." Delany drew an analogy between Africa in antiquity and nineteenth-century America in this discussion of commercial and economic strength. "Like the present America, all the world went [to Africa] to get a supply of commodities. The massive stone pile of masonry, their skillful architecture, their subterranean vaults, their deep and mysterious wells, their extensive artificial channels, their mighty sculptured solid rocks, and provinces of stone quarries, gave indisputable evidence of the hardihood of that race of people." The travel reports of John and Richard Lander, two Britons who explored the west coast of Africa in the late 1820s, established the existence of an equally developed agriculture in a "high state of cultivation, clothed in the verdure of husbandry, waving before the gentle breezes with the rich products of industry—maize, oats, rye, millet and wheat." These descriptions by the Lander brothers of Africa's agricultural pursuits gave evidence of its importance as a contributor to contemporary civilization.[6]

African industry extended to the United States, where enslaved Africans continued to make significant contributions to the American political economy. Delany noted that there were no "laborers known to the colonists from Cape Cod to Cape Lookout, than those of the African race." Having worked as farmers, herdsman, and laborers in Africa, "they required not to be taught to work and how to do it, but it was only necessary to tell them to work and they at once knew what to do and how it should be done." In fact, Africans were the "only skillful cultivators—the proprietor knowing little or nothing about the art save that which he learned from the African husbandmen."[7]

Delany extended his analysis by commenting on the attainments of African Americans in the civil, social, and business arenas. "There has never been in the history of nations any people thus situated who have made equal progress in attainments with the colored people of the United States." In another attempt to link African industry and African American ingenuity and to challenge the idea of superior white blood, Delany added that among those who have "stood and shone the brightest in the earliest period of our history, there are those of pure and unmixed African blood." Delany praised the work of intellectuals such as James McCune Smith, Henry Highland Garnet, and James W. C. Pennington—two of whom traced their origins directly to Africa.[8]

Not content simply to look at questions of social and civil development in isolation, Delany turned to a discussion of emigration, which he viewed as one of the cornerstones of political economy. Individuals, groups, and nations constantly searched for better opportunities and greater possibilities. Delany's examples from the Bible and classical antiquity included the Jewish exodus from Egypt, Dido's migration from Tyre to Mauritania, and the "hundreds of modern European examples." The most memorable of these was, of course, the "emigration of the Puritans in 1620 from Great Britain, the land of their birth, to the wilderness of the New World, at which may be fixed the beginning of immigration to the continent as a permanent residence." Delany's invocation of Puritan emigration not only validated his support for movement by African Americans to Africa, the Caribbean, and Canada in the 1850s, but presented the phenomenon as an important manifestation of human determination to effect a change in social, political, and economic circumstances. If Puritans could seek a New Jerusalem abroad, why should African Americans not do the same?[9]

Delany's preoccupation with political economy, his interest in and support of emigration, and more important, his ongoing linkages between an African past and a contested American reality continued in *The Origins and Objects of Freemasonry: Its Introduction into the United States and Legitimacy among Colored Men*. Like the earlier treatise, *Origins and Objects* relied on a combination of more traditional approaches to historical presentation grounded in the Bible and classical antiquity and applied to modern history. The fact that Masonry transcended the American reality proved the antiquity of the black race and established the legitimacy of the organization among African Americans. As already noted, Masonry was more than an uncritical celebration of a lost Africa or a romantic attempt to re-create an Afrocentric past, which is the way it figures prominently in Robert Levine's analysis of the phenomenon. Delany used the past instead to discuss concrete rather than abstract aspects of black reality in the contemporary world. He, like subsequent writers of this period, talked about the African past only in relationship to how it could explicate the

realities African Americans faced in the 1850s. This issue was of critical importance in that period because of the debate over whether or not blacks could
legitimately practice the Masonic arts.[10]

Delany delivered *Origins and Objects* by invitation before St. Cyprian Lodge
No. 13 in Pittsburgh, Pennsylvania. Echoing the sentiments of Prince Hall, the
founder of the Prince Hall Masons, Delany traced the evolution of Masonry
from its inception among the Egyptians and Ethiopians to its formal establishment in the seventeenth century. Themes of exclusion, black worth, and
the legitimacy of black organizations figured prominently in this work. And
being more than an antebellum invocation of vindicationist discourse, and thus
transcending the narrow constraints that had been placed upon it, *Origins and
Objects* represents an extension of Delany's practical concerns and interest in
history. As popular publications lampooned African Americans for their participation in various Masonic rites, Delany defended their intellectual capacity
and organizational legitimacy.[11]

The first charge that Delany challenged was the belief of some white Masons
that blacks had no legitimate claim to Masonry membership. Delany argued that
African engagement and involvement with the ancient practice preceded the
biblical record. By this account, Africans contributed to the underlying ideas
of both modern Christianity and Masonry. Unlike James W. C. Pennington,
who criticized the polytheistic practices in ancient African societies, Delany
skillfully skirted discussion of these practices by pointing out that although
they were "heathens, their mythology was of a high and pure order, agreeing
in regard to the attributes of the Deity with the doctrine of Christians in after
ages." In fact, the monotheistic god, Jupiter Ammon (Aton, Aknathon) was
one of the first monotheistic conceptions of God in the ancient world. Delany
went further, stating that "the wise men of Egypt and Ethiopia understood the
great attributes of the Deity: omniscience, omnipotence and omnipresence."
This bears some similarity to the idea of the Christian Godhead—the Father,
Son, and Holy Ghost—as three separate entities operating as one.[12]

Delany's treatise also addressed the issue of Masonry's introduction to the
United States. In 1776, Prince Hall received sanction from an Irish regiment of
the British army stationed in Boston to organize a Masonic lodge, the African
Lodge No. 1. Hall applied for and received a charter from the Mother Grand
Lodge of England in 1784. The Duke of Cumberland upheld the earlier Irish
regiment's actions by issuing a separate charter for the operation of African
Lodge No. 459. The charter, dated September 29, 1784, was personally delivered
to Prince Hall by James Scott, a sea captain. As the early republic progressed,

disagreement arose between the First African Grand Lodge of North American and African American Masons in Philadelphia. The Philadelphia group formed another Masonic organization known as the Hiram Grand Lodge of the State of Pennsylvania. In 1847, these factions met, settled their differences, and formed a complete union under the auspices of a National Grand Lodge, directed by John T. Hilton and with William E. Ambush as secretary. The settlement of differences among black Masons, however, did not quell the anti-Masonic sentiment among the American populace or the prejudice and exclusionary tendencies of white Masons.[13]

The opposition to black Masonry attempted to discredit its legitimacy and to deny its origins in the African world (place, not race). One of the ways frequently used by white lodges to discredit the legitimacy of black lodges was to conduct an examination of the black Masons. One such incident occurred in Philadelphia when a committee from the Grand Lodge of Pennsylvania examined a black lodge "to prove or disprove their capacity as recipients of the ancient and honorable rituals of the mystic order." In this case, they found the black group fully qualified to be Masons. Despite the black Masons' success in that test, Delany criticized its administration because it compromised the autonomy of the group, rendering their legitimacy dependent on the decision of a white review board rather than on the established historical record of black participation in Masonry in Africa and the United States. He pointed to the fact that ethnic groups such as the Scotch, Irish, and Welsh had certain social, political, and economic issues that prevented them from direct association with the Grand Lodge of England. They consequently established separate lodges and received the sanction of the Grand Lodge of the British Empire. By presenting these facts, Delany wondered, "Can there be a greater demand for an independent jurisdiction of masonry among the Scotch and the Irish than among the colored men of the United States?" His answer to the question was "Certainly not!"[14] And in response to Jacob Brinkenhof's 1851 speech before the Masonic Fraternity of Ohio, in which he claimed that no descendant of a slave could be a Mason, Delany went to the historical record to remind readers that Moses, a slave and a descendant of slaves, studied in Egypt, performed miracles before Pharaoh, was prime minister, and among the wise men of Africa demonstrated the fitness of blacks to be Masons. In fact, Delany asked, "Are we as Masons, and the world of mankind, indebted to him the Egyptian slave—may I add the fugitive slave—indebted for a transmission to us of the Masonic Records—the Holy Bible, the Word of God?" Delany even compared Louis Kossuth to a slave (since Austria controlled Hungary from the sixteenth century until the

Revolution of 1848); and yet, upon visiting the United States in 1851 (when he disappointed abolitionists by refusing to denounce slavery) Cincinnatians made him a Mason. For Delany, the condition of slavery was less important than race prejudice in this example. Normally, the requisite requirement of free birth would not apply to those who had lost their liberty in an involuntary manner. In the biblical period, only those who had lost their liberty as a result of a criminal act or who, like Esau, bartered their birthright away were denied Masonic privileges.[15]

Delany's skillful ability to connect history and destiny marked an important component of historical writing in the 1850s. As is clear from earlier discussions, he was not the first writer to make tangible connections between the distant past and the present. He did, however, begin to recognize the urgency of the matter. With the struggle over slavery reaching fever pitch, black writers used history, sacred and profane, ancient and modern, to explicate events in the contemporary world. This skillful merger of the ancient and modern figured even more prominently in the work of William Nell, William Wells Brown, George Vashon, and James Theodore Holly. Although the work of each of these writers utilized biblical and ancient history, their common goal was to bring the present into conversation with the past in an effort to defeat proslavery proponents.

To Confer with the Living and the Dead: Constructing an Antislavery History from the American Revolution

In the opening to his groundbreaking studies, *Services of Colored Americans in the Wars of 1776 and 1812* (1851 and 1852) and *Colored Patriots of the American Revolution* (1855), William Nell announced his intention to reconstruct an accurate record of black participation in the Revolutionary War. He was mindful that he was undertaking a difficult task, given that the denial and erasure of that record seemed commonplace at the time. Still Nell, undaunted, persevered while reminding readers of *Services of Colored Americans* of the difficulties of his undertaking. "Imperfect as my first edition may prove," he wrote, "journeys have been made to confer with the living, and even pilgrimages to graveyards to glean the shreds and patches for a presentation." In the second edition of that book and in *Colored Patriots of the Revolution*, Nell substituted "fast disappearing records" for the "shreds and patches" to emphasize the urgency of his mission.[16]

William Nell

One of the most poignant aspects of the late antebellum constructions of the history of black participation during the Revolutionary War relates to how conscious these writers were of the fact that the nation had not moved aggressively to preserve that history in its founding dramas. William Yates, a noted black abolitionist speaker who published *The Rights of Colored Men* in 1838, commented on the urgency created by the loss of sources. He sought "to mine, from the records of the past, some of the many testimonies to be found of the rights and services of the colored men." Yates knew that the records he needed to produce history, which he defined as an accurate representation of the services of colored Americans to the nation, were quickly disappearing. "It is to be regretted that effectual efforts were not made at an earlier date to furnish a history of the services of the men of color," he wrote. "The materials were more abundant—a greater number than at present were living, who were witnesses of their services; then the task would have been comparatively easy." Still, he believed, the subject contained great possibility: information gleaned from the War Department, especially pension records, and the private correspondence of individuals actively involved in the abolitionist movement could yield good results.[17]

Although Yates's remarks indicated that written primary sources were still available, the natural loss of witnesses, through death, was a lamentable fact. No doubt partly because of that, Nell went so far as to point out that even the documentation he had once been able to glean from cemeteries (probably tombstones or other grave markers) was disappearing. Retelling a story originally told by Theodore Parker, recalled in a speech by William Day, Nell reported that the remains of black soldiers who fought on Long Island in 1776 had been unearthed during the construction of a dry goods store. In an obvious reference to constructions of race prevalent in the 1850s, Parker had noted that the skulls were unmistakably those of Africans. Parker continued: "[T]he bones of these forgotten victims of the Revolution are shoveled up . . . , carted off and shot into the sea, as the rubbish of the town." He added, "had they been white men's relics, how would they have been honored with sumptuous burial anew, and the purchased prayers and preaching of Christian divines? Now they are the rubbish of the street!" Nell enlisted Parker's words from Day's speech before a black convention in Cleveland, Ohio, in 1852, to sum up the task at hand: if whites failed to preserve the record of black participation in the conflict, the responsibility fell to blacks. Day believed that these records constituted a living and breathing history in need of recovery and restoration to their rightful place. He encouraged readers to become actively involved in its recovery, for it "lies upon the soil watered with their blood; who shall gather it? It rests with their bones in the charnel house: who shall exhume it?"[18]

Despite the neglect of black participation in the war, there did exist several significant histories of the war itself. In the Revolution's aftermath, white writers offered biographical, diplomatic, and general historical narratives of the important event. Popular works ranged from Parson Weems's valorizing *Biography of George Washington*, to the encyclopedic compilations of Jared Sparks, *The Diplomatic Correspondence of the American Revolution* (1829–30) and *Works of Benjamin Franklin* (1836–40). Patriot histories also appeared. David Ramsay's *A History of the American Revolution* (1793) and Carlo Botta's three-volume *History of the War of Independence of the United States* (1821) figured prominently in this group.[19] And writers during the late antebellum period, like their early republic counterparts, offered celebratory assessments of the Revolution to consolidate its legacy as a major turning point in American history. Benson Lossing's *Pictorial Fieldbook of the Revolution* (1850, 1852), William Gilmore Simms's *Life of Francis Marion* (1844), and Lorenzo Sabine's *American Loyalists* (1847) contributed greatly to these visions of the American Revolution.[20]

Black intellectuals shared some of the interests of their white counterparts regarding the Revolution. Black writers compiled volumes that documented African American contributions, valorized their heroes, celebrated their accomplishments, and heralded the patriotism of the participants. Still, these writers offered a significant counternarrative. Rather than uncritically celebrating the Revolution's legacy, they highlighted the race's service in order to remind the nation of its unpaid debt, the guarantee of freedom and citizenship. As the life-and-death struggle against proslavery advocates reached fever pitch, even free blacks living in America faced severe proscription. The Compromise of 1850 and its Fugitive Slave Law resulted in the indiscriminate enslavement of free African Americans and fugitive slaves alike. And the *Dred Scott* decision, which affirmed that blacks were not citizens of the United States, further weakened their already tenuous position in the national life. These historical realities strengthened Nell's resolve to record faithfully the services of those who fought "in those times that tried men's souls" and to position black people's historical commitment, contribution, and sacrifice in the middle of the nation's current upheaval over race and slavery. Thus, the effort to reconstruct the history of black participation in the Revolutionary War, as difficult as it was, was also an integral part of the antislavery war.

The opening salvo of this war probably came in 1837, the year of the congressional "Gag Rule" and the publication of Hosea Easton's *Treatise on the Intellectual Character, and the Civil and Political Condition, of the Colored People of the United States*. Most obviously, Easton reminded his readers of black involvement in the war. He noted that when the Continental Congress established an army of twelve thousand men and later raised the number to twenty thousand, "it is well known [that] hundreds of men of which this army was comprised were colored men and recognized by Congress as Americans." But, equally important, as if in anticipation of the *Dred Scott* decision, Easton also used his pamphlet in another way to prove that black Americans were legitimate citizens. He argued that African Americans were citizens because they had been slaves when the American colonies were governed by England, but once the colonies declared independence "they were no longer held by any legal power." The only law in the land was martial law, Easton contended, which recognized no one as a slave. According to Easton, neither in the various meetings convened in the colonies to discuss the Revolutionary cause, nor at the Continental Congress convened in Philadelphia in 1776, did the delegates mention color.[21]

Easton's attention to the citizenship of black Americans was an important step in using history to prove (if not create) a legitimate place for black Americans in the American republic. William C. Nell's account of the American Revolution, however, focused on the patriotism and tangible contributions of blacks to the revolutionary cause and was much easier to prove. As historian Elizabeth O'Leary has noted, the nation's sense of patriotism in the years before the Civil War was ill-defined and mired in local and regional politics. Consequently, Nell's commentary was not only central to efforts to enact an explicitly African American history but also to use that history to intervene in and contribute to contemporary debates about the failures and the future of democracy. He accomplished this goal by juxtaposing the "services of the Colored Americans in the Wars of 1776 and 1812" with the nation's course of disenfranchising and erasing African Americans from the public story of national life.[22]

William C. Nell, born in Boston on Beacon Hill in 1817, was an outstanding student as a youngster, quickly attracting the attention of William Lloyd Garrison, who hired him as an errand boy for the *Liberator*. A firm believer in equal rights, Nell later led successful campaigns to integrate Boston schools; he participated in several antislavery societies, including the Boston Committee of Vigilance and the Western Antislavery Society; he served as secretary for the Adelphic Union, Boston's premier literary and historical association; and he worked briefly as an editorial writer and publisher for Frederick Douglass's

North Star. Much of this work regularly put Nell in contact with white abolitionists, with whom he discussed his interest in reconstructing black participation in the Revolutionary War.[23] In letters to his friend Wendell Phillips,
founder of the *Liberator* and Nell's benefactor for a time, Nell raised the possibility of writing a biography of Crispus Attucks, one of the first victims in
the Boston Massacre. Upon reviewing the authoritative sources of his day, Nell
lamented: "I have been unable to find much of the history of Attucks, the first
martyr in the revolutionary conflict." But enough information existed in the
sources he consulted, particularly Botta's *History of the American Revolution* and
George Twelve Hewes's *Memoirs of the Boston Tea Party*, to convince Nell that
Attucks was a central figure in the Boston uprising, his fame and eminence
established by the fact that "he was buried from Faneuil Hall as one of the
strangers who fell in the struggle."[24]

Nell's first edition of *Services of Colored Americans*, written just one year after
the passage of the Fugitive Slave Law, spoke as much to the contested realities
of the 1850s as it did to the missing and incomplete documentation of the past.
Nell's account foregrounded the 1851 refusal of the City of Boston to erect a
statue in memory of Crispus Attucks. His reprinting of the *Boston Transcript*'s
incendiary opposition to the monument served to buttress his point. The *Transcript* disparaged Attucks as the "very firebrand of disorder and sedition, the
most conspicuous, inflammatory and uproarious of the misguided populace,
and who, if he had not fallen a martyr, would have richly deserved hanging as
an incendiary." Nell's indignation was clear in his response, which concluded
that the "rejection of the petition was to be expected if we accepted the maxim
that a colored man never gets justice done him in the United States, except by
mistake."[25]

Although Nell's original study was only twenty-eight pages in length, he
managed to make a substantial case for the active involvement and patriotism
of the black participants in the war. He peppered the work with quotes from
the speeches and pronouncements of white public officials, including Governor
Eustis of Massachusetts, John Hancock, a signer of the Declaration of Independence, and Calvin Goddard, a judge in Connecticut, to establish a record
of valiant service by African Americans in the war despite discrimination and
prejudice. Using biographical details of the lives of black patriots, he wove the
past and the present together to make the case that blacks' past public or military service and patriotism warranted citizenship rights. To make this point,
Nell recounted the experiences of Charles Black, an impressed seaman during
the War of 1812, whom British officials offered nine hundred dollars to fight

against his country. Black refused the bribe and served America valiantly. Still, he received no pension and later became the victim of a vicious beating during the Philadelphia race riots in 1842.[26]

While there are no extant records documenting the sales or popularity of Nell's work, a limited second edition appeared in 1852. Produced under the same constraints as the first one, it nevertheless included several new components. It was forty pages (as opposed to the twenty-eight pages of the first edition), and the coverage of black activities was expanded to include the South and the West. More important, Nell was able to reprint tangible evidence from blacks concerning their participation in the war. Of particular interest is a speech delivered in Cleveland in 1852 by author and abolitionist James W. C. Pennington in which, continuing arguments advanced in his 1841 *Textbook of the Origin and History of the Colored People*, Pennington renewed his claims of black patriotism and for black citizenship. Nell reported Pennington's display of archival materials from the State of New York showing the significant role black people had played in Revolutionary War service as well as an autographed petition presented to the governor of Connecticut after the war asking him to comply with the promise to manumit all slaves who bore arms in the struggle for independence.[27]

Reviewers of the second edition fully understood the relationship between this historical study and the contemporary crisis over black slavery and citizenship, and they commented extensively on it. "No reviewer presenting true sensibility, can read these proofs of the loyal devotion of the free people of color to their country in the hour of danger and disaster and remember the ingratitude and cruel injustice that it has returned to them without a sense of sadness and shame," insisted one writer. William Howard Day, editor of the *Aliened American*, focused on the importance of preserving the history of the race in his review: "We feel that the idea of preserving these records is just as important as any other. The facts in Mr. Nell's book are not generally known. Let us spread them by adding in the circulation of this work and confirm them by collecting all others we can." An advertisement for Nell's *Colored Patriots of the American Revolution* in the *Anti-Slavery Bugle*, May 26, 1855, stated that, "as a means of enlightening public sentiment on an interesting and much neglected department of American history, the subscriber has been induced to make a compilation of facts portraying the patriotism and bravery exhibited by Colored Americans, on land and sea, in the times that tried men's souls—embracing the old French War of 1855, the Revolution of '76 and the struggle of 1812, and subsequent periods." Indicating that access to sources had increased since *Services of* the Colored Americans was first published, these "facts," the circular stated, were gleaned from a plethora of primary sources ranging from military records to private correspondence and fireside conversations.[28]

Nell's evidence of black patriotism, subsequent abuse, and even enslavement indeed came from diverse sources. Theodore Parker's *American Anecdotes* provided the tale of an elderly slave "distinguished for bravery and other soldierly qualities" during the Revolutionary War whose owner subsequently sold him for one hundred dollars. The new owner, in Mobile, Alabama, put the elderly man to work raising poultry and tending a chicken coop. From the *Charleston Standard and Mercury* came the details about a veteran of the Revolutionary War who participated in the defense of Fort Moultrie and served as a ship's cook after the war ended. The veteran was falsely accused of poisoning a crewmember who subsequently died. At the trial, no one mentioned his military service, and the court ignored evidence regarding the desertion of several crew members (possibly the murderers). Nell added that the "real proof, no doubt, was written in the color of his skin, and in the harsh and rugged lines of his face." He was found guilty and subsequently executed. The trial, according to the Charleston paper, "must excite the feelings of every benevolent heart against the ruthless prejudices engendered by the foul and leprous stain of slavery." Clearly justice had not been served. Despite the man's past patriotism, his contribution to the freedom of the country had counted for nothing in his effort (his right) to a fair trial.[29]

Despite the fact that Nell's book seems to document a litany of abuses against black veterans, this information provided a much-needed spotlight on their service in the war effort. Nell reported details provided by a letter from Parker Pilsbury that the names of two soldiers, Lambo Latham and Jordan Freemen, were separated from those of their white counterparts on a Connecticut monument commemorating the storming of Fort Griswold. Although both men played critical roles in the battle — Latham, by killing the British officer who had killed Lieutenant General William Ledyard, and Freeman, by killing Major Montgomery, the British commander of the assault on the fort — they did not receive the treatment normally reserved for heroes. Not only did their names appear below those of their fellow soldiers, but Lambo's name appeared as "Sambo." The affront was particularly galling because both men were killed at Fort Griswold in Connecticut in September 1781.[30]

Perhaps it was because of this neglect that when Nell discussed black participation in the Battle of Bunker Hill, he highlighted the services of particular individuals: Titus Colburn, Alexander Ames, and Barzillai Lew of Andover,

Massachusetts, and Cato Howe of Plymouth, Massachusetts. It was just as important to put their names in the record as it was to prove their patriotism. But the most poignant example of both goals involved James Forten, the famous Philadelphia sail maker and abolitionist. Nell reprinted an excerpt from Robert Purvis's 1842 eulogy of Forten. In a brilliant use of classical imagery, not unlike historian Mary Beth Norton's "Republican Mothers," Purvis characterized Forten's mother as a "Roman matron" who, yielding to the solicitations of her son, "gave the boy of her promise, the child of her heart and hopes, to this country; upon the altar of its liberties she laid the apple of her eye, the jewel of her soul." Forten volunteered as a powder boy on the *Royal Louis* commanded by Stephen Decatur. Captured by the British, Forten received several inducements—offers of freedom, a good education, and money—to abandon the colonists' cause and escape to England. Nell's recitation of Forten's refusal to abandon his country in a time of need proved the depth of his patriotism and provided a stellar example of one who should have, at the time of his death, been enjoying all the rights and privileges of citizens.[31]

It was undoubtedly important that Nell prove that black people deserved citizenship rights if for no other reason than that their history of active participation in the American Revolution warranted it. But his chapter "Conditions and Prospects of Colored Americans" best captures his effort to intervene, as a writer, in the antislavery war. In addition to lengthy excerpts from the writings and speeches of Hosea Easton, Frederick Douglass, Charles Lenox Remond, and John Rock on citizenship and elevation, Nell compared contemporary struggles in the antislavery war to the Revolutionary War. For him, the revolutionary spirit of 1776 necessitated a "second revolution no less sublime than that of the regenerating sentiment in favor of Universal Brotherhood." Here, he referred to it explicitly as an "Antislavery War," "waged for the last twenty-five years, prolific in noble words and deeds and remarkable for the succession of victories, always the reward of the faithful and preserving." In Nell's mind, this war justified the "historical propriety in setting forth the services of those colored Americans who, in the day of small things, labored earnestly in the welfare of humanity. If others fail to appreciate the merit of the colored man, let us cherish the deserted shrine. The names which others neglect should be the more sacredly our care."[32]

The black and abolitionist press celebrated Nell's accomplishments as they highlighted his evidence of black patriotism and the proof of black rights to citizenship. A reviewer in the *Liberator* praised Nell for bringing together a "large mass of interesting and valuable facts, relating to the colored people and the services they rendered to the country." The *Liberator* also printed the endorsement of Nell's old friend, John Greenleaf Whittier, whose words made the case that African Americans should and must take the lead in recording their own history in any effort to lay claim to their natural citizenship rights:

> It is due to the colored men that they should wrest from their ungrateful and mean oppressors the acknowledgement of the services of their fathers in the Revolution. If anybody deserves honor for fighting heroically the battles of their country, the black men who sat at Valley Forge—who tracked with naked and bloody feet the snows of Jersey,—the stream of whose life blood mingled warm and red with that of their white comrades at Red Bank and Monmouth—are entitled to it, in spite of all the false-hood of historians writing with the fear of "Massa" before their eyes.[33]

A writer in the *Radical Abolitionist* opined that Nell's book was "well-calculated to put our spurious Christianity and our sham Democracy alike to the blush of shame for the cruel prejudice against the colored people."[34]

Other authors noted Nell's general contribution to restoring the historical record. Radical black abolitionist Martin Delany, in his emigrationist mani-festo, *The Condition, Elevation, Emigration and Destiny of the Colored People* (1852), acknowledged his debt to Nell's published history and recommended *Services of the Colored Americans* to "every American the country through." Prominent abolitionist William J. Watkins, in *Our Rights as Men*, quoted extensively from Nell's work to support the contention that African Americans' service to their nation entitled them to exercise their rights as citizens of the United States. Charles Langston borrowed heavily from Nell's work in an address before white citizens in Columbus, Ohio, in December of 1855, on behalf of the right of blacks to serve in the local militia: "Have we proved ourselves enemies to our country? Have not our fathers stood side by side with your fathers in the battles that gave glory to American arms!" In that speech, Langston appropri-ated Nell's discussion of a petition presented by black Philadelphians, *Memorial of Thirty Thousand Disenfranchised Citizens of Philadelphia* (1855), in which the petitioners used black participation in the Revolutionary War as proof of citizenship.[35]

The failure of others to acknowledge black services to the republic also figured prominently in Nell's account. Less racially inspired than tactical in deployment, these were issues that Nell knew resonated with white and black abolitionists in a historical atmosphere characterized by contestation over black citizenship. White and black abolitionists, orators, and petitioners used the work with great profit to themselves and the antislavery cause. Its greatest usefulness, however, occurred when Nell rendered his text a symbol by hosting a series of commemorative celebrations to remind the nation of black participation in the nation's revolutionary conflicts. Nell's commemorations, to borrow Geneviève Fabre's language on memory and commemorations, were "subjunctive, focusing not simply on the past, but 'the ought and should.'" This subjunctive mode is consistent with Nell's active juxtaposition of the services of black patriots in the Revolutionary War with the tenuous position of blacks in the United States in the 1850s. Nell was not only concerned with the past simply on its own terms, but how it could contribute to a more just life for black people at that time.[36]

Celebrations and commemorative culture generally were not a new development in the black community. In the eighteenth century, Election Day and Pinkster celebrations were common across the North. From the abolition of the slave trade in 1808 through West Indian Emancipation in 1833, black people used the public sphere to dramatize the injustice of slavery and celebrate its demise. Thus, Nell drew on a wellspring of black culture to construct his commemorations of what he dramatically described as "the Boston Massacre of March 5, 1770, the day, which, by the valor, patriotism and martyrdom of the Colored American Crispus Attucks and his associates, has been selected by history as the dawn of the American Revolution." The March 5, 1858, Faneuil Hall celebration linked the revolutionary accomplishment with a lively protest against the *Dred Scott* decision. Important abolitionists, including William Lloyd Garrison, Charles Remond, Theodore Parker, and John Rock addressed the eager crowd. As historian Mitch Kachun has shown, these commemorations were important spaces in which blacks could convey information in a straightforward manner to large numbers of people about their condition and the steps necessary to ameliorate it.[37]

Nell's program presented diverse types of historical evidence to commemorate the black contribution to the war. One of the most interesting components of the program was the use of Revolutionary War artifacts including "emblems, relics, engravings, [and] documents." Nell displayed a goblet and powder horn that belonged to Attucks; a certificate with George Washington's signature discharging Bryster Baker, a black soldier from Connecticut; a letter from Captain Perkins to Brigadier General Green to arrest Lieutenant Whitmarsh for abusing a black soldier on Long Island in 1776; and the flag presented by John Hancock to black soldiers in front of his mansion on Beacon Street in grateful appreciation of their services to the country. The celebration included a reenactment of the March 1770 scene on State Street which precipitated the Boston Massacre. And the presence of the widows of Barzillai Lew and Alexander Ames, participants in the Battle of Bunker Hill, solidified linkages between the past and the present.[38]

All of these forms of historical documentation served to challenge the pronouncements of contemporary figures such as Stephen A. Douglas, the Democratic candidate for president in 1860, a fierce opponent of racial equality and sponsor of the Kansas-Nebraska Act in 1854, which allowed these states to chose whether or not they wished to enter the Union as slave or free states; and Roger Taney, chief justice of the Supreme Court, who wrote in the *Dred Scott* decision that African Americans had no rights that whites were bound to respect. Nell concluded that their spurious claims that blacks were not entitled to the benefits of citizenship caused "white Americans to ignore many of the prominent and significant facts in the early history of the country." Nell demonstrated through his historical labors and commemorative celebrations that "facts could be piled Olympus high in proof that the Colored American has ever proved loyal and ready to die, if need be, at freedom's shrine." That loyalty ought to have guaranteed their citizenship rights. But it did not. And Nell continued to merge textual representations of black history with commemorative culture, staging other celebrations in 1859 and 1860.[39]

Nell's work, more than that of any other late antebellum intellectual, offered engaging reconstructions of black participation in the Revolutionary War. Undoubtedly he was inspired by John Greenleaf Whittier's 1847 article in the *National Era*, in which he wrote, "Of the services of the Colored Soldiers of the Revolution, no attempt has been made to preserve a record, they have no historian." Nell challenged the nation's limited understanding and incomplete reconstruction of black participation in that war. When government officials subsequently dedicated battlefields as important historic sites, they had to acknowledge that black and white soldiers served, bled, and died together. When new monuments replaced earlier ones celebrating the success of the war, Peter Salem, Lambo Latham, and John Freeman could not legitimately be placed in the background, separated from their white counterparts. And when the nation reflected on the invaluable services of the martyrs who sacrificed their lives on State Street, in Boston, in 1770, the incident that sparked the Revolutionary War, it had to acknowledge the centrality of blacks in the conflict. Indeed thirty-some years after the *Boston Transcript* cast Crispus Attucks as little more than a thug, the city in 1888, erected and dedicated a monument in his honor.[40]

Rereading the Haitian Revolution and the Possibilities of Independence

While the legacy of the American Revolution served as an important ideological battleground in the antislavery war and a legitimate site of revolutionary discourse, Haiti, given the success of the slave revolt there in 1804 and the fear and tremors it sent through the Western world, offered other possibilities. The site of the only black republic in the Western hemisphere, Haiti reemerged in the nation's public discourse, offering a place for potential emigration and a symbol of ultimate triumph in the antislavery war.[41] But that war, in an American context, was more than a simplistic contest between anti-and proslavery forces. It also operated as a war of ideas and rhetorical strategies that revolved around defining, appropriating, and applying terms usually reserved for white populations and extending them to African American populations and other diasporic communities of color. Concepts of democracy, patriotism, republicanism, self-government, moral propriety, and civic and social responsibility figured prominently in the social reform lexicon of the day. It was equally important in the historical work of black writers.[42]

The most prominent writers on the intersections between the Haitian and American Revolutions were George Boyer Vashon, William Wells Brown, and James Theodore Holly. Highly visible in the abolitionist community, Vashon and Holly traveled to Haiti in the late 1840s and 1850s. Although Brown never visited the country, he actively participated in the transatlantic abolitionist community, traveling extensively in Europe and lecturing on the abolitionist circuit. All of these writers built on Martin Delany's *Condition, Elevation, Emigration and Destiny of the Colored People of the United States* (1852) and William Nell's *Colored Patriots of the American Revolution* (1855). Delany's work offered emigration as a viable alternative to African Americans' remaining in the United States, and he historicized the concept of emigration by addressing its role in the formation of the United States. Delany also included a lengthy discussion on other potential sites for emigration, from Africa to the Caribbean, assessing their social, political, and economic benefits for potential settlers. His manifesto resonated with the feelings of hurt and betrayal experienced by free black populations in the North. Nell's *Colored Patriots* affirmed the sense of exclusion and uncertainty experienced by African Americans, rendering Delany's proposed solution even more important for some.[43] The works of these five men had common goals. One was to raise the specter of revolt in the minds of white Americans, some of whom not only had little interest in ending slavery in the United States but successfully rebuffed many efforts even to talk about it through, for example, the 1837 Gag Rule. Another was to prove the capacity of black people (i.e., former slaves) to govern themselves and, thus, to justify their emancipation. While earlier writers were more cautious in how they invoked the symbolism of the Haitian Revolution, later writers used this imagery more aggressively to intervene in the national impasse regarding whether to expand or end the peculiar institution in the United States.

Initially a site of fear and uncertainty for the slavocracy of the Western hemisphere and a source of pride for African-descended populations, Haiti's independence in 1804 did not assure its unfettered entry into the community of republican nations. Rather, its incendiary meanings threatened to destabilize the institution of slavery in the whole of the Western hemisphere. Throughout the revolutionary period, many white planters fled the island with their families and slaves, carrying with them lurid tales of a violent slave uprising complete with stories of planters murdered in their beds by bloodthirsty slaves. These individual stories as well as immigrant tales of the destruction and plunder of Cap Haitien in 1792 quickly melded into an image of the revolution characterized as "the Horrors of Saint Domingue." The "horrors," rather than the possibilities, figured prominently in the pre-1850 relationship between Haiti and the United States.[44]

Although scholars regularly suggest that African Americans uncritically embraced Haiti and its incendiary meanings from the republic's inception up to the 1850s, the relationship between African American intellectuals and Haiti was much more complex.[45] While black intellectuals certainly embraced the republic as an example of black governance, the ebb and flow of Haiti's fortunes during the tumultuous period following its establishment lessened the possibility they would hold a uniformly positive view of the nation. In fact, one can distinguish two topics of discussion in the record, one on the revolution and another on independence. For all of these writers there was no way to read slavery, colonialism, and all the attendant exploitation as anything but bad, and so the revolution was a noble cause to them all. But the reading of the aftermath of the revolution (and even some of the particular tactics of the actors during the revolution) was never so consistent. Chronic instability, frequent changes in government, colonial intrigue, *and* the refusal of the United States to recognize the fledgling nation contributed to a cautious strain in the discussions of Haiti. Equally important, the intellectuals understood the revolution's history well enough to know that it was more than the culmination of a successful slave revolt. The Haitian government's pledge of citizenship to persons of African descent, however, proved attractive enough that beginning in the 1820s numerous African Americans immigrated to the island. While some remained, many did not, and the mixed reputation generated by their reports also tended to moderate the scholarly conclusions.[46]

Despite the problems, black intellectuals were, indeed, optimistic about Haiti's prospects. Because of the importance that the example of Haiti provided of the capacity of black people to govern themselves, the writers often went to great lengths to refute the erroneous characterization of the revolution as simply the "Horrors of Saint Domingue." James McCune Smith's "Lectures on the Haytien Revolution" (1841) dramatizes this point. Smith, a distinguished member of New York's free black community who trained as a physician at the University of Glasgow, affiliated with several abolitionist organizations, including the American Anti-Slavery Society, the Society for the Promotion of Education among Colored Children, the Statistics Institute, and the Philomathean Literary Society, almost as soon as he returned to the United States. From the outset, drawing on articles from the *British Quarterly*, D. M. Brown's *History of St. Domingo*, and Vide's *History of St. Domingo*, Smith's "Lecture on the Haytien Revolutions" aimed to vindicate the struggles of the Haitian people to establish a republican form of government and situate Haiti as an indisputable example of the benefits of immediate emancipation. In the process, he did more than simply valorize the slaves' efforts in their emancipation; he examined the plight of slaves, caste distinctions, the treatment of the free colored population, and the topographical features of the island, all of which facilitated the revolution.[47]

But of special importance is Smith's rewriting of the revolution. Rather than focusing on a single explosive event, a central component of the "Horrors of Saint Domingue" legend, Smith's lecture offered a more complex discussion of the evolution of the Haitian Revolution. He convincingly presented it as the result of a series of events involving a multiplicity of actors, including St. Domingue's *grand blancs*, the planters and slave owners; *petit blancs*, the small farmers, artisans, and overseers; and *affranchis*, or *gens de couleur*, the free black population, as much as it was influenced by the slave population. For example, Smith noted that, concerned more with the profitability of sugar cultivation than the condition and plight of the slaves, the *grand blancs* seemed unaware of the ramifications of importing large numbers of African slaves into the colony. The growing animosity between the *petit blancs* and free people of color added additional fuel to the fire.[48]

In Smith's genealogy, the outbreak of the French Revolution in 1789 sparked the forces of dissension and class warfare between *petit* and *grand blancs* in Haiti.

By Smith's account, it was they, not the slave population, who exacerbated an already tense situation. The refusal of the *grand blancs* to allow *petit blancs* representation in the new government sparked an armed conflict between the two groups. Smarting from their rebuttal by the *grand blancs*, the *petit blancs* organized themselves into an army with the intention of expelling the attorney general and the *intendant* at Port-au-Prince. Rather than face expulsion, both men voluntarily left the island. This already tense situation became even more complicated with the arrival of Vincent Oge, a member of the *affranchis*, who had traveled abroad seeking support for the demands of the free people of color on the island. Oge returned to the island to secure compliance with the 1790 decree of the French legislative assembly allowing all (free) persons age twenty-five and above to vote in the formation of a national assembly. Instead of complying with the request, the colonial assembly sent a force of six hundred men to capture Oge. After his capture and execution, the French National Assembly decreed equal rights for all French citizens regardless of race, but rather than implementing the new law, the governor and Colonial Assembly in Saint Domingue convened to circumvent the law's passage and tighten restrictions on the slaves.[49]

Smith's presentation of Saint Domingue's internal racial and class politics was, indeed, a rather complex construction of the history of the Haitian Revolution. Still, his account masks as much as it presents. For example, he was conspicuously silent about Vincent Oge. Smith's silence speaks to the relative uncertainty of how to present the leaders of the revolt because of their often tenuous and sometimes oppositional relationship to the masses. Smith was also silent about the initial revolt of free blacks after it became clear that the Colonial Assembly would not recognize or even receive Oge's petition. Oge was not simply a humble petitioner who threw himself on the mercy of the Colonial Assembly. And although Smith did not stereotype him as a heroic military leader, neither did he show that Oge was a hesitant insurgent whose inferior force was defeated by a vastly superior one. In short, Smith masked much about Oge by presenting him as a supplicant who was rebuffed, taken prisoner, and executed. Oge was, in fact, a free black man whose hands were dripping with blood. He led a revolt for the benefit of free blacks. But such an image was anathema to those who opposed the use of politics or violence to effect the abolition of slavery. Perhaps more important in this instance, while the apparently selective lapse in the rendition seems to be an effort to represent the Haitian Revolution unilaterally as a glorious and noble event, by not commenting on Oge, Smith's early account kept the focus on the success of the revolution, which he rightly portrayed as more complex than any others had done to that point.[50]

Altogether, Smith's presentation begged the question (one as apt for people in the United States as in Haiti): How long can people justifiably wait for freedom without taking action to make it a reality? This question seems to lie at the heart of Smith's inquiry. Given the general fear of slave rebellions in the United States and the myth that emancipation of slaves led to outright murder and other outrages committed against whites, Smith reminded his readers that the "insurrection was the legitimate fruit of slavery, against which it was a spontaneous rebellion. It was not therefore the fruit of emancipation, but the consequence of withholding from men their liberty." Following from this supposition, Smith turned to settling questions surrounding the 1792 destruction of Cap Haitien, another important component of the "Horrors of Saint Domingue," which Smith sought to dispense with once and for all. The survivors' tales maintained "that the first use of their liberty made by the slaves, was ruthlessly to imbrue their hands in their former master's blood." Smith reminded readers that although the army of slaves consisted of more than one hundred thousand, only three thousand actually attacked the town. He compared the level of violence visited upon slaveholders to the uprising of Spartacus, one of the largest slave revolts in the Roman Empire. In fact, Smith believed the damage inflicted on the planters by the slaves paled in comparison to the number of slaves killed by white insurgents.[51]

Having asserted the right of human beings to rise up and throw off the yoke of oppression, Smith situated Haiti as a legitimate revolutionary example in hemispheric history, deflated the potency of the "Horrors of Saint Domingue" legend, and then turned to shoring up the vindicationist edifice he had erected to glorify the Haitian Revolution by celebrating the ability and capacity of blacks for self-government. For Smith, Toussaint L'Ouverture embodied this capacity, and his fame proved the one constant in African American and Haitian relations. Unlike his successors, Dessalines, Rigaud, and Christophe, whose motives and tactics were questionable, he remained above reproach.[52] He not only defeated French, British, and Spanish forces on the island but also proved a capable administrator. His imposition of strict labor laws allowed the colony to regain much of its former strength as a site for sugar, coffee, and indigo production. He also promulgated a new constitution guaranteeing equality before the law. In time, however, Toussaint's fortunes changed, which did not bode well for Haiti. Smith attributed his demise to Napoleon's "dark spirit[,] glutted but not satiated with the gory banquet afforded at the expense of Europe and

Africa." Although Napoleon's plan to reinstate slavery never came to fruition, his capture of Toussaint set the stage for the bloodiest portion of the revolt, led by Generals Dessalines and Christophe, and about which, as already suggested, Smith withheld comment.[53]

Smith's clever manipulation of the meanings of the Haitian Revolution necessitated a discussion of the revolutionary "moment," which included: an initial revolt by the mulattoes led by Oge and Chavannes; a slave rebellion; an invasion by Spanish and British forces and their subsequent defeat by Toussaint L'Ouverture; an internal civil war between Toussaint and Rigaud, who was defeated and exiled to France and who returned with Leclerc's invasion force in 1800; the subsequent capture, imprisonment, and death of Toussaint L'Ouverture; and the last and bloodiest phase of the revolution, led by Dessalines, Christophe, and Pétion. Altogether, the revolution offered an unsettling and unflattering picture of wanton destruction, intraracial and interracial warfare, and a country in ruins. This is not the image Smith wished to project at a time when free black leaders, no doubt influenced by the British example of emancipation of black slaves in the Caribbean, wished to present the example of a smooth and orderly transition to freedom.[54]

The 1850s offered different conditions than existed when Smith wrote in the early 1840s. Texas had come into the Union as a slave state, and the slavery controversy flared up again when it was California's turn and the state's admission was coupled with the Compromise of 1850, which included the odious Fugitive Slave Law allowing for the recapture and return of actual and suspected fugitive slaves to their owners with only the flimsiest proof of identity or residence. American "Manifest Destiny," a term widely used by politicians during the 1840s, would, it seemed, forever include slavery. And so the antislavery war needed new ammunition. That ammunition would come from the pens of Brown, Holly, and Vashon, who turned more directly to the leadership of Haiti than did Smith. They would also use the *revolution* to focus on the *independence*. By their accounts, the Haitian Revolution became a template for the American antislavery war, and they used it to warn the United States of its possible future if slavery were not abolished. The focus on Haitian independence also provided proof of blacks' ability for self-governance, giving the lie to the stereotype of their inferiority.

George Vashon, an 1840 graduate of Oberlin College, worked briefly in 1844 with Martin Delany's short-lived newspaper, the *Mystery*. Although he trained for a career in law, the Alleghany County bar refused him admission due to an 1838 statute in the Pennsylvania constitution, which limited the franchise and citizenship to white men and thus prevented access to the bar for African Americans. Upon relocating to New York, Vashon became the first African American admitted to the bar in that state.[55] William Wells Brown, a runaway slave who first attracted broad-based public attention with the publication of his autobiography, *The Narrative of William Wells Brown* (1847), worked as an agent for the Massachusetts Anti-Slavery Society and published a songbook, *The Anti-Slavery Harp* (1847). Best known for his controversial novel, *Clotel; or, The President's Daughter* (1852), he spent considerable time on the European antislavery circuit, during which time he published *Three Years in Europe; or, Places I Have Seen and People I Have Met* (1852) and *The American Fugitive in Europe* (1852).[56] Like Vashon, James Theodore Holly was also freeborn. Born in Washington, D.C., in 1820, he enjoyed the benefits of a classical education in his youth. After completing his formal education in Burlington, Vermont, he took increased interest in the work of the American Colonization Society. Less interested in immigrating to Liberia than to Canada, Holly soon became a volunteer correspondent for Henry Bibb's *Voice of the Fugitive*.[57]

All three men saw great potential in Haiti as an important symbol in their struggle for democracy in America. Haitian politics, and its political leaders in particular, figured prominently in their work. Each man, for example, found a useful example in Faustin Solouque, or Emperor Faustin I. Elected in 1848, and self-proclaimed emperor in 1849, Faustin, a black leader, associated himself with the island's black traditions. He employed Freemasons, and because he did not discourage the practice of vodun, or voodoo, as earlier leaders had done, it became more pronounced during his reign. More important as proof of the political capability of black leaders, Faustin notably imposed a state monopoly on the importation of sugar and coffee, curtailing the influence of local and foreign merchants in the economy, and organized state-controlled houses to regulate imported goods.[58] Vashon, who traveled to Haiti but never met the leader, commented favorably on the early years of the regime (which lasted for ten years) in a series of epistolary exchanges that appeared in Frederick Douglass's *North Star*. Holly arrived in Haiti six years after Vashon. On a mission sponsored by the Episcopal Church, he met with the emperor and presented a plan to settle immigrants on the island, complete with stipulations to exempt settlers from the military and to facilitate the importation of tools and other personal possessions. Although Faustin never officially endorsed Holly's plans, Holly remained optimistic about Haiti's prospects for African American settlement.[59] For George Boyer Vashon, it was the leadership of Vincent Oge that proved most useful. Less intimidated by Oge than was Smith, or perhaps simply more knowledgeable of him, Vashon published a highly romanticized portrait of the mulatto leader. Vashon's formal, classical education allowed him to adopt one of classical literature's most enduring forms—the epic poem—to memorialize Oge, make the case for his important role in Haiti's revolutionary history, and position Haiti and its independence in the stream of legitimate revolutionary activity in the Western hemisphere.

First published in Julia Griffiths's *Autographs for Freedom* in 1854, Vashon's poem "Vincent Oge" appropriated the most powerful intellectual imagery of his time, namely the progressivism and poetics of Romanticism and the imagery of classical antiquity in the form of heroism.[60] The highly romanticized portrait of the Haitian mulatto leader began, however, by drawing tangible connections between the French and Haitian Revolutions. In this account, freedom is a teleological force often preceded by tyranny and undemocratic systems of government that are ultimately transformed into a positive force. The French example was embodied in the splendor and power of the monarchy beginning with Louis XIV, also known as the Sun King, and ending with the beheading of Louis XVI. Vashon wrote:

> The visions of grandeur which dazzlingly shone,
> Had gleamed for a time and all had suddenly gone.
> And the fabric of the ages—the glory of the kings,
> Accounted most sacred mid sanctified things,
> Reared up by the hero, preserved by the sage,
> And drawn out in rich hues on the chronicler's page,
> Had sunk in a blast, and in ruins lay spread,
> When the altar of freedom was reared in its stead.

The marriage between freedom and destiny also joined France to Haiti in that "a spark from that shrine in the free-roving breeze, / Had crossed from far France to that isle of the seas." Once there, the liberatory light of the spark gave rise to feelings of "vengeance, hatred and despair." Most strongly felt among free blacks and slaves, owing to their exclusion from the island's political life, freedom's spark ignited the need for the redress of previous grievances; so much so, wrote Vashon, that

> When they burst, they wildly pour
> Their lava flood of woe and fear,
> And in one short—one little hour,
> Avenge the wrongs of many a year.[61]

In Vashon's romantic portrait, Oge represents the highest echelon of free black populations. Educated, sophisticated Oge embodied all the qualities of a leader, and he was a member of the highly influential Friends of the Negro, a prominent group of French abolitionists that included Abbé Grégoire; Antoine Pierre Barnave, a lawyer and a liberal; and Jacques-Pierre Brissot de Warville, founder of the Friends and a Girondonist leader in the General Assembly. When Oge, the voice of the mulatto elite, traveled to Europe, he intended to return to Haiti and force the Colonial Assembly to accept the proclamation of March 8, 1790. Instead, he was rebuffed by the assembly, and according to Vashon, free blacks then had no other choice but to let "other torrents louder roar"—thus, armed revolution.[62]

Not surprisingly, given Vashon's intimate knowledge of the classic and romantic devices, one hears the voice of the Spartan mother in "Vincent Oge." In this case, however, she is the Afro-Caribbean woman. From the start, she played a traditional (feminized) role in the nation as citizen: she reared strong children who would become important to the cause. And when it became necessary, her involvement was direct: she bid the troops, the freemen, her figurative sons, farewell, sending them into battle. Her voice authorized and sanctioned the struggle for freedom, and sacrifice for freedom was made a noble cause:

> And there's the mother of Oge,
> Who with firm voice, and steady heart,
> and look unaltered, well can play
> The Spartan's mother's hardy part;
> And send her sons to battle-fields,
> And bid them come in triumph home,
> Or stretched across their bloody shields,
> Rather than hear the bondman's doom.[63]

Vashon's construction of Oge's actions as heroic celebrates, by extension, the leadership qualities of the free black population. But Vashon was very selective in his use of evidence in his portrait of Oge. As historian C. L. R. James noted, despite having procured weapons and support from abolitionist Thomas Clarkson, Oge seemed unsuited to the contingencies of revolution. Instead of initiating a revolt, which he was equipped to do, Oge supported the slave system, issuing two high-sounding proclamations calling for mutual cooperation between (free) blacks and whites to alleviate some of the odious restrictions on the free black population. Despite the willingness of free blacks to compromise on the issue of full black equality, the island's white citizenry remained determined to block free blacks' participation in the political forum.[64]

Vashon again deployed romantic and classical imagery to capture the desperation of the freedmen after their rebuff by the white factions on the island. Despite the nobility of their cause, "it availeth them nought / With the power and skill the tyrant brought." The freeman, "like Sparta's brave sons in Thermopylae's straits," failed to overcome the power of a superior foe. The simile was especially fitting. Oge's force consisted of far fewer men than their white opposition numbered, and the Spartan force comprised only Leonidas and 350 men. And like the Spartans, who were unable to secure the pass at Thermopylae because of the treachery of a fellow Greek in showing the Persians a route around the Spartan soldiers guarding it, Oge's forces were unsuccessful. Also like the Spartans, the Haitian freemen represented a privileged class. Although they did not possess the military genius of the Spartans, they occupied the best position from which to launch an insurrection against the white planters. As the Spartans sacrificed themselves for Greece, so the free blacks sacrificed themselves for Haiti.[65]

Vashon captured the martyrdom of Oge in compelling tones. These brave "Spartans," as Vashon conceived them, gave their all to the cause of freedom in Haiti. After their capture, Oge and Jean Chavannes experienced a grueling trial, after which, under torture, both confessed their crimes. Chavannes never lost his resolve, but Oge broke down under pressure and begged for mercy. The next day, Oge's brother was condemned along with the other conspirators. Whereas in the case of the Spartans, Leonidas's body, after a great struggle for possession of it by the warring parties, was preserved by the remaining Greeks, the state literally destroyed the bodies of Oge and his brother: both men were placed on the rack and their limbs broken and their bodies dismembered. Yet, as the preservation of the body of Leonidas ensured his fame for the Spartans, the brutal execution of Oge and his brother preserved their names for posterity and served as the catalyst for subsequent developments in the quest for Haitian independence.[66]

William Wells Brown continued the heroic presentation of free black Haitians in his account, making tangible connections with the American Revolution. Brown's speech, "St. Domingo: Its Revolution and Its Patriots," reminded readers of the earlier participation of Haitian patriots, as he called them, in the Siege of Savannah during the American Revolution in 1779. Brown's calling them patriots was undoubtedly a deliberate attempt to expand the meaning of the term beyond the American Revolutionary context. Brown hoped, by linking the two patriotic traditions, to clarify and exonerate the contributions of both to the revolutionary history of the Western hemisphere.[67]

In his analysis of the debates preceding the issuance of the March 8 decree and the actions of various components of the Haitian populace, Brown quoted Antoine Pierre Barnave, who in seconding the claims of mulatto rights put forth by Vincent Oge, exclaimed, "Perish the colonies rather than the principle!" Brown called it "Noble language this!" and wondered, "Would that the fathers of the American Revolution had been as consistent." When describing the massacre of five hundred faithful servants who refused to bear arms to put down the rebellion, Brown echoed the words of the American revolutionary Patrick Henry by pointing out that the struggle was for "liberty or death." If the slogan could justify the actions of the American patriots in their effort to rid themselves of British control, then it could do no less in the Haitian struggle against the French.[68]

James Holly's "Vindication of the Capacity of the Negro Race for Self-Government," published two years after Brown's lecture, presented a contributionist and vindicationist portrait of black involvement in the revolutionary uprising. Reflecting his role as a minister, Holly's account invoked the jeremiad, characterizing the slave population as inspired by the "Lord of Hosts, who directed their arms to be the instruments of His judgment on their oppressors, as the recompense of His violated law of love between man and his fellow." But Holly's lecture also included several common features in historical presentations of the period: he viewed the revolution as progressive in size, scope, and import. And altogether, the Haitian revolution and its aftermath, independence, not only vindicated the mental and moral capacity of blacks for self-government, but "was one of the noblest, grandest, and most justifiable outbursts against tyrannical oppression that is recorded in the pages of world history."[69]

Like Vashon, Holly viewed the free black population as the class of destiny. After describing the restrained behavior of the slave population in the face of the rapidly growing tide of revolution on the island, he turned to the free black population. This population exercised even more restraint than the slaves, Holly thought, considering that their wealth and education should have entitled them to political power in the colony. Aware that their patience might be misunderstood and labeled as ignorance, Holly pointed to the fact that these classes of men were "educated in the seminaries of France" and were "patrons of that prodigy of literature, the Encyclopedia of France." Nor were they cowards, as some might surmise, because they were the ones who served, as Brown had pointed out in "St. Domingo: Its Revolution and Its Patriots," as the "voluntary compeers of the Revolutionary heroes of the United States; and who, under the banners of France, mingled their sable blood with the Saxon and the French in the heroic battle of Savannah."[70]

Holly seemed more trenchant than Brown in his claims that the Haitian Revolution "surpassed the American Revolution, in an incomparable degree." Deflating the importance of the American Revolution while trumpeting the benefits of the Haitian one, he strengthened the case for its legitimacy. Ultimately, Holly cast the Haitian Revolution as something the American Revolution could never be. The Americans were free, highly enlightened, and their greatest grievance seemed "the imposition of the three pence pound tax on tea." Holly argued that leaders of the Haitian Revolution were largely menial and uneducated slaves and were not just taxed on their consumption but paid with their lives. Their opponents consisted of both a mother country and its colonial government, the latter of which played an active role in attempting to suppress the revolt. Given the sum total of these conditions, Holly concluded that compared to the Haitian Revolution, the America Revolution was but a "tempest in a teapot."[71]

There were, however, complications in this romanticization of the Haitian Revolution and the effort to position it properly in the history of recent world revolutions. The complication pertained to the position of most free blacks in the early revolutionary struggle. Although it was clear in these narratives that they, as a potential leadership class, were key figures in outlining "the destiny of the colored race," they were not always (some were never) on the side of the slaves. Clearly aware of the few prerogatives they possessed, determined not to lose them and, in fact, to add to them, free blacks, including Oge, at first made the proverbial deal with the devil—one they would eventually have to abandon. Without denying this, the black American writers managed to present their story in a manner that fit the larger goal of using the Haitian Revolution, which resulted in independence *and* freedom, to criticize the American Revolution, which left some people enslaved and others free but as something less than citizens. Such a representation situated Haiti in the mainstream of world revolutions, and it drew necessary attention to Haitian independence.

Arguing for the inherent ability of African Americans to govern themselves, and deeply committed to a civilizationist project, Holly focused on presenting Vincent Oge as representative of the ability of free blacks to negotiate contested political terrain. Aware of the opposition in the colony to black rights, Oge appears here as a calculating politician, one who attempts to judge the mood of the people and take the most appropriate action. Rather than return-ing immediately to Haiti from Paris, where he argued for the rights of free blacks, Oge sought support from other European nations, and Holland gave him the rank of lieutenant colonel and membership in the Order of the Lion. When Oge returned to Haiti with an armed escort, he immediately became aware of opposition to his position. His selfish attempt to privilege the posi-tion of free blacks by devising a Faustian bargain—the tacit acceptance of black slavery—with the landed whites proved unfruitful. Despite the implications of this scenario, rather than ignore it as Smith had, Holly tactfully offered an interpretation of it. "This specific assurance on the part of Oge, although its does not speak much for his high sense of justice . . . shows as much wisdom and tact in the science of government, as evinced by the sap-headed legislators of this country, who make similar compromises to the oligarchic despots of this nation." Glossing over the obvious betrayal of the slave population by the free black population, Holly interpreted this move as a political strategy no different from those employed in the Northern antislavery war of the 1850s or by politicians, in general, in this period. In an attempt to encourage selective historical remembrance, Holly essentially urged the reader to forgive Oge for his early actions toward the slave population and to focus instead on "the ig-noble and unworthy fate" he suffered "at the hands of those monsters of cruelty in St. Domingo."[72]

Brown's "St. Domingo" also portrayed the mulattoes as an oppressed and grieving class. Brown concurred with Holly that they received few benefits as a result of their class position, but Brown located the spark of freedom in Eng-land rather than in France, probably because of Britain's then-current role in humanitarian, and especially abolitionist, movements and Brown's admiration of the reformers he had no doubt met during his travels in Europe in the early 1850s. Brown also differed from Holly in his view of the slave population's role in the war. Brown, who had lived as a slave and a fugitive, depicted slaves as a primary factor in the revolt. The slaves awoke, Brown wrote, "as from a dream, and demanded their rights with sword in hand." Fire consumed the island, de-stroying villas, factories, and farms. The slaves' fury seemed justified for Brown because their "ancestors had been ruthlessly torn from their native land and sold in the shambles of St. Domingo." Holly's view of slave involvement in the insurrection was more cautious. Suspicious of the capacity of slaves to conduct themselves rationally, he presented them as awakening "from [their] slumber of degradation to the terrific power of brute force." Bouckman, "the Spartacus of His Race," directed the work of devastation on the island. In a manner almost indicative of brute, unthinking force, he "continued to ride on the storm of the revolution in its hurricane march, with a fury that became intensified as it progressed." But like Oge, he too fell under the vindictive weight of the colonists. His death cleared the way not only for a "triumvirate of Negro and mulatto chieftains," but for what Holly termed the "Auspicious Dawn of Negro Rule," the ascendancy of Toussaint L'Ouverture.[73]

For Brown, the revolutionary legacy began not in 1804, with the declaration of Haitian independence, but 1799, the year Toussaint L'Ouverture emerged as the leader of the colony. His comrades Rigaud, the mulatto general, and former slaves Christophe and Dessalines also figured prominently in the discussion. When the main contingent of the French army landed at Cape City and a smaller force at Port-au-Prince, the main commanders of the slave force, Toussaint and Christophe, like "Nat Turner, the Spartacus of the Southampton Revolt," fled into the mountains, ostensibly to begin a campaign of guerilla warfare against the insurgents. In describing the numerous atrocities committed by the black general Dessalines against white planters, Brown pointed out that this should serve as an omen for American slaveholders: "Let the slave-holders in our Southern states tremble when they call to mind these events." Given the belief in the tangible and ongoing nature of the American Revolutionary heritage, Brown applied this same concept to the Haitian revolutionaries. He believed that the father of the Haitian Revolution, Toussaint L'Ouverture, and its patriots would reappear in the Southern United States. Their spirits were already there, as Brown's juxtaposition of Toussaint and Christophe to Nat Turner suggested. When that spirit of revolt combined with the impulses from the American Revolution, Brown believed, "the revolution of St. Domingo will be reenacted in South Carolina and Louisiana."[74]

Thus, the cyclical notion of history again bequeathed a legacy to the Western hemisphere. But what traditions did the French and American Revolutions produce? Were they consistent with liberty or opposed to it? In Brown's analysis, both George Washington, the father of the American Revolution, and Napoleon Bonaparte, heir of French Republicanism, paled in comparison to Toussaint L'Ouverture. Napoleon and Toussaint were both of humble origins and ended their careers in exile. But the differences in how they achieved their fame seemed too striking to overlook: "Toussaint fought for liberty; Napoleon fought for himself. Toussaint gained fame by leading an oppressed and injured race to the successful vindication of their rights; Napoleon made himself a name and acquired a scepter by supplanting liberty and destroying nationalities, in order to substitute his own illegitimate despotism." George Washington, the legitimate heir of the American Republican tradition, fared no better than Napoleon when compared with Toussaint L'Ouverture, who, Brown concluded, was the true republican, for his government made "liberty his watchword, incorporated it in his constitution, abolished the slave trade and made freedom universal among his people." Brown argued that Washington's government took the opposite course and in doing so, perverted the true spirit of republicanism. Washington's government "incorporated slavery and the slave-trade, and enacted laws by which chains were fastened on the limbs of millions of people." Brown also explicitly inverted Washington's legacy by putting it in the context of the ideological contest of the 1850s: Washington gave "strength and vitality to an institution that would one day rend asunder the *Union* that he had helped to form." Despite the fact that a slave revolt did not ultimately occur in the South during the 1850s, Brown insisted that as a result of the failure to fulfill the revolutionary promise, the "slave in his chains in the rice swamps of Carolina and the cotton fields of Mississippi burns for revenge."[75]

It is ironic that in Holly's account, Toussaint and Washington were each cast as "the regenerator and savior of his country," individuals eminently suited to the exigencies of revolution and the demands of statecraft. Using Toussaint's success to make a case for blacks' capacity for self-government, Holly argued that the power of his government originated from his ability to impose strict regulation on land and quotas on sugar production in order to stabilize the island's commercial enterprises. Sensitive to the needs of the formerly enslaved population, he pursued a course of action that facilitated international commerce and paved the way for the enactment of the Rural Code, which helped the island return to the prosperity it had known prior to the Revolution. That code compelled the unemployed to seek a private employer and, if one could not be found, to seek employment by the government on sugar plantations in rural areas. In Holly's opinion, Toussaint's success proved more enduring than that of the British or the Americans. Haiti's labor regulations were fairer and did not resort to apprenticeship or encourage voluntary or forced immigration of Asians to meet the production goals of planters.[76] The fact that Haiti never resorted to an apprenticeship program and that Toussaint's plan of wealth distribution did not defraud the peasants in favor of the landed class boded well not only for claims of innate ability for self-government but in the assurance of democratic forms of government which treated all citizens fairly regardless of race or class.[77]

When Holly turned to Toussaint L'Ouverture's successors, he found that they possessed the sophisticated qualities of statesmanship exhibited by their predecessor. Similar to his presentation on Oge, Holly failed to mention the darker side of Dessalines's reign, such as the massacre of thousands of mulattoes in southern Haiti. He focused instead on Dessalines's ability to build a six-thousand-man army, and his attempt, albeit unsuccessful, to unite the French and Spanish portions of the island. Holly also glossed over the serious problems of class and caste in the regimes of Pétion and Christophe: despite their opposition to one another, here they appeared (at least symbolically) united against a common external enemy. In casting them this way, Holly obscured important internal problems of their rule. Although under Boyer, the divisions between the Spanish and French portions of the island were temporarily healed, civil war and disorder erupted. Holly attributed the chaos to "the animosities that the ancient regime of slavery had created among them." Of importance to Holly was his conclusion that the then-current leader Faustin I settled all dissension and discord.[78]

THE INTENSE POLITICAL DEBATES about the future of slavery in America, which proslavery forces at times seemed to be winning, presented a major challenge for African American writers during the late antebellum period. The continuing spread of slavery across the country made it clear that action was absolutely necessary. Unable to take up arms, these writers took up their pens, and they created narratives that aimed to intervene in the politics of the day and make the strongest case possible for the abolition of slavery and the extension of freedom, democracy, and citizenship to all Americans. Better educated than their predecessors had been, less steeped in clerical traditions, and with powerful examples in the American and Haitian Revolutions, they used their pens and their voices to great effect.

The American Revolution, with all its promises, and the Haitian example, with all of its, allowed these writers to move beyond but not totally transcend their reliance on ancient, biblical, and classical evidence in their effort to make the case for black humanity. But the powerful literary devices of heroism, vindication, and even examples of representative men and women continued to prove useful. In fact, they assisted in making a compelling case for black inclusion into ideas regarding republicanism and democracy.

"Liberty and justice for all" were among the ideals for which the colonists fought the American Revolution. Its participants purchased their freedom through their sacrifices of blood, sweat, and tears. Framed as a justifiable revolt against a tyrannical mother country, England, the American Revolution not only heralded the birth of a new nation, but also a uniquely new historical reality in which, *supposedly*, "all men are created equal." Unfortunately, these words did not apply to blacks or Native Americans or women. More than eighty years after the Revolution, blacks still were not able to participate fully in its promise of independence. African Americans vehemently argued that the participation of blacks in the American Revolution not only deserved recognition and respect but constituted an essential service to the nation that should have guaranteed the benefits of citizenship, but did not.

Haiti, like the United States, had experienced discovery, exploration, and exploitation. The island's rapid rise as the crown jewel in the French colonial empire because of its sugar production occasioned serious problems for its slave population. The tremendous need for labor to maintain and increase production levels encouraged the continuous importation of slaves, which, combined with the brutal conditions under which they worked, the denial of rights to free blacks, and the expectations created by the French Revolution created the perfect conditions for revolt. While African Americans never mounted a comparable revolt in the United States, Haiti's success buoyed their hopes of participating in a free republic as fully free and equal citizens. Moreover, the Haitian Revolution was more than a spontaneous outburst of slave fury, a charge these writers constantly rebuffed in the United States. It represented the legitimate desire of these individuals of color to achieve the much-vaunted "Rights of Man." The Haitian Revolution, if carefully assessed, provided a template, or an incendiary warning, for what could happen in the United States if the antislavery war was lost. And Haitian independence, despite its contentious and problematic history, proved, once and for all, that black people were capable of governing themselves.

Black intellectuals like William C. Nell, James McCune Smith, George Vashon, James Theodore Holly, and William Wells Brown used the spoken and written word to reread black participation in the American Revolution and to read the Haitian Revolution as a legitimate revolutionary construct. Like other historical writers of the nineteenth century, these writers deployed historical knowledge in highly subjective and didactic ways. But to argue that their works were naïve, simplistic, or narrow and uniform would be a mistake. Closely wedded to cyclical and teleological understandings of history, they were less concerned with linear presentations of the facts than with presenting a narrative that used the past, whose legitimacy had been denied in the mainstream, to intervene in the realities of the present, a present that seemed particularly contested and uncertain. This process created some demands that resulted in their work appearing similar. That is, they used the American Revolution in similar ways, and they saw the goal of freedom in the Haitian Revolution in the highest possible terms. But given the desire to provide a more forcefully historical narrative that tangibly connected the past and present, black historical writers, in some ways echoing the work of earlier writers, offered sophisticated interpretations of the past rather than simply reporting what had happened. In short, these works linked the common desire shared by early republic and antebellum writers to present a nuanced portrait of black humanity with the added urgency of the nation's antislavery war. More than the precursor to a fierce military contest between pro- and antislavery forces, these works provided intellectual signposts that aimed to demonstrate black patriotism, argue for black citizenship, and prove the capacity of black people to govern themselves.

The pre- and post–Revolutionary War history of America and Haiti, despite America's failed and empty promises and Haiti's turbulent history, offered tangible examples for African Americans of the possibilities of a world of their own making. They envisioned the American Revolution through the lens of the antislavery war and sought to legitimize black contributions to it. Linking Haiti's revolutionary past to the annals of the larger Western revolutionary tradition, they sought to carve out a space for the recognition of their own efforts to destroy the institution of slavery forever. In many ways, these writers believed that through their efforts, "the destiny of the colored race" might ultimately be fulfilled. For many during this time period, black destiny remained uncertain and unfulfilled. Did destiny represent the possibilities of independence offered by the success of the Haitian Revolution? In the case of Haiti, the revolution's aftermath proved extremely problematic. Discord, anarchy, and civil war characterized the nation, so black writers could only point to the revolutionary story and the possibilities that freedom and independence presented for a bright future. This was also true in the American case. Uncertain of whether the slave power or antislavery forces would win the antislavery war, black historians looked to the past as a guidepost for the possibilities of the future. Haiti became both sign and symbol of freedom denied and freedom won. If blacks could win the antislavery war, then they were determined to make the most of independence. They were assured that their historical writing would present the race as fully capable of assuming the mantle of humanity. It was impossible to know at the time that freedom's advent would usher in a new age of social, economic, and political possibility that would allow them to present the United States rather than Haiti as the best example of the benefits and blessings of freedom.

CHAPTER 4

The Historical Mind of Emancipation

Writing African American History at the Dawn of Freedom, 1863–1882

> Whenever emancipation shall take place, immediate though it may be,
> the subjects of it, like many who now make up the so-called free population,
> will be in what Geologists call, the "Transition State." The prejudice now felt
> against them for bearing on their persons the brand of slaves, cannot die out
> immediately. Severe trials will still be their portion—the curse of a "taunted
> race" must be expiated by almost miraculous proofs of advancement; and
> some of these miracles must be antecedent to the great day of Jubilee.
> —CHARLES L. REASON, "Introduction: The Colored People's
> Industrial College," 1854

BETWEEN 1863, which marked the passage of the Emancipation Proclamation, the publication of William Wells Brown's *The Black Man*, and the decisive Union victory at Gettysburg, and 1882, the year of the publication of Joseph Wilson's *Emancipation: Its Course and Progress*, there occurred a decisive shift in the style and content of historical writing among African Americans. Between Brown's and Wilson's work, William Still's *The Underground Railroad* represents a tangible example of the method by which black scholars wrote and disseminated African American history. Still, head of Philadelphia's Vigilance Committee from 1850 to 1861, reconstructed the harrowing tales and escapes of fugitive slaves and printed them in a massive tome, which he subtitled, "A Record of Facts, Authentic Narratives, Letters &c., Narrating the Hardships, Hair-breadth Escapes and Death Struggles of the Slaves in Their Efforts for Freedom, as Related by Themselves, and Others, or Witnessed by the Author."[1] Still's innovations in publishing and dissemination laid the groundwork for the subsequent explosion in the production of and market for black historical texts in the 1880s and 1890s.[2]

Momentous changes in book production and distribution occurred against the backdrop of the Civil War—the most cataclysmic event of the nineteenth century in America and a harbinger of change in the culture. The historian

Robert Wiebe has characterized this period as one in which the United States "searched for order." The nation moved from an insular, disconnected, autonomous set of "island communities" to a more cosmopolitan, connected, and bureaucratized set of interlocking spheres. These changes affected the intellectual community in significantly different ways than other sectors of society. An insular, elitist, and regionally oriented intellectual class gradually evolved into a more pluralistic, scientific, and nationally oriented intelligentsia. As Dorothy Ross has noted, the intellectual crisis of the Gilded Age (1865–96) involved diminishing the power of the antebellum clerical elite, which had held the social sciences in colleges hostage to religious concerns and moral philosophy. With the gradual transference and eventual adoption of German models of scientism and objectivity in American institutions of higher learning as the period progressed, the clerical leadership of the nation's intellectual life increasingly came under scrutiny.[3]

The formation of educational institutions throughout the South during the postbellum years led to the establishment of the black academy. But unlike for the white population, this period did not see a substantial departure from the clerically oriented model of the antebellum period in these new institutions.[4] As Johns Hopkins, Cornell, and Stanford, and graduate departments at Columbia and Harvard enthroned scientism and objectivity, a substantial number of the new black normal schools and colleges, still dominated by clerical elite and missionaries, emphasized religion and moral philosophy. Their purpose was to enhance conditions for the group, to be sure, but also, significantly, to act as a mechanism of social control and, in some instances, as a means of discouraging significant agitation for civil and political rights. Consequently, the emergence of a black, university-trained elite with graduate degrees in the newly constituted social sciences was in the offing, but not a tangible reality in the years between 1863 and 1882.[5]

Located outside of the nascent black academy, giving them some degree of autonomy from the clerical elite who dominated the educational institutions for some years to come, "older" black intellectuals, especially historical writers like William Wells Brown and William Still used the status garnered from the antebellum period to promote their racial agenda and lend their experience to a race just emerging from slavery. Frederick Douglass, the representative man of the race until his death in 1895, used the pen as a weapon to end slavery and to define freedom. And the critical markers for all these writers were the Emancipation Proclamation and the Thirteenth Amendment. These intellectuals used the postbellum period to outline and sketch the "historical mind of emancipation." Using antebellum historical formations—the focus on black achievements in classical antiquity and, now, post-slave-trade Africa; black participation in the nation's founding dramas; and, most important, biographical sketches of representative men and women—these writers provided even more tangible evidence of black participation in the nation's unfolding story. Unlike the writers during the period between 1850 and 1860, who could only envision freedom and independence as a possibility rather than as a certainty, black intellectuals writing after the Civil War lived and wrote in a nation where slavery no longer legally existed. A characteristic distinguishing these histories from earlier ones involved their Januslike quality—their ability to look backward and forward in ways that their antebellum predecessors could never do. Black intellectuals constructed narratives that not only concerned the future possibilities of the race but also hearkened back to the courageous role played by African Americans in the antebellum period to end the horrid institution of slavery.

Narratives that reflected the past heroism and the future prospects of the race required an outlet for distribution. Because the Gilded Age offered unparalleled opportunities for the publication and dissemination of books, local and regional networks gave way to national ones. The 1860s witnessed the convergence of a number of older forms of literary production such as sampling books, trade papers, and literary and book agents, with a virtual explosion in the production of books and magazines wrought by changes in the organization of labor within the larger publishing houses, which began in the 1850s. Rather than an occasional review in the black press and publication in one or two editions, historical works increasingly appeared in numerous editions and with sample books and aggressive advertising strategies making them more visible than ever. The story of the race became inextricably linked to the commercial demands of the marketplace. And some, more than others, utilized these approaches extensively—with outstanding results.[6]

This chapter examines the work of William Wells Brown and William Still, two prominent writers whose work reflected many of these trends. Continuing to build upon the traditions established by antebellum writers, Brown produced three seminal works on the black experience in the early postbellum period: *The Black Man, His Antecedents, His Genius, and His Achievements* (1863), *The Negro in the American Rebellion: His Heroism and His Fidelity* (1867), and *The Rising Son: The Antecedents and Achievements of the Colored Race* (1874). Not only did these works represent three specific types of historical production—the biographical catalog, military history, and race history—but they offer critical insights into Brown's hemispheric and diasporic visions at midcentury.

William Still, head of Philadelphia's Vigilance Committee from 1850 to 1861, played an important role in the Underground Railroad during the antebellum period and compiled these experiences in a massive book titled *The Underground Railroad* (1872), which he reprinted and for which he developed a nationwide network of salesmen. Examining the work of these African American intellectuals provides critical insights into the world of black writers just after midcentury, their writing strategies, their use of commercial distribution outlets for their historical production, and their attempt to merge antebellum sensibilities and postbellum realities to provide a "faithful account of the race."

Brown's *The Black Man,* the first work under consideration here, is a carefully constructed biographical catalog of representative men and women. He included information on prominent black abolitionists and their exploits and devoted a substantial portion of the text to discussions of the intellectual achievements of African Americans in the antebellum period. In the book's introduction, Brown made clear that his antebellum experiences significantly shaped his historical writing. His "long sojourn in Europe," and the opportunity to research "amid the archives of England and France and in the West Indies," provided him with "information respecting the blacks seldom acquired."[7]

Williams Farrison, Brown's principal biographer, has characterized Brown's project as a miscellany of random facts. But we should rather see, first, that the volume suggests the importance of the earlier writers themselves and the subjects of their publications. Brown's work featured sketches of scholars, poets, writers, scientists, abolitionists, and others. They included James McCune Smith, James W. C. Pennington, Henry Highland Garnet, Charles Reason, George Vashon, William Nell, Henry Bibb, Frederick Douglass, William Still, Charles Lenox Remond, Charlotte Forten, Samuel Ringgold Ward, Ira Aldridge, Alexander Dumas, James Whitfield, François-Dominique Toussaint L'Ouverture, Jean-Jacques Dessalines, and Henri Christophe of Haiti, and President Joseph Jenkins Roberts of Liberia, Crispus Attucks, Nat Turner, Denmark Vesey, Joseph Cinque, and Benjamin Banneker. Second, Brown structured the narrative in such a way as to denote the relative importance of the person and his or her contribution. And third, the volume was a clear attempt to define freedom through a project of racial vindication, showing achievement at the height of slavery as well as after freedom. But fourth, despite the postbellum publication, the work is also an extension of the abolitionist crusade.[8] If slavery had a detrimental impact on African American moral, mental, social, political, and economic advancement, which all the opponents of the institution believed, surely with the fetters of slavery sundered, African Americans would demonstrate to the world their ability to rise rapidly and assume their rightful place in American society.[9]

As an effort to normalize African Americans as fit subjects for emancipation, Brown's sketches, in ways similar to others of his day, used the romantic device of representative men and women to characterize individuals by physical appearance, intellectual accomplishment, and moral standing in the black community. His sketch of Henry Highland Garnet is instructive in this regard. Brown described Garnet as "forty-five years of age, unadulterated in race, tall; and commanding of appearance, . . . [with] an eye that looks through you and a clear and ringing voice." He described Charles Reason, a professor of belles lettres at New York Central College, as a "man of fine education, superior intelligence, gentlemanly in every sense of the term, and one of the best of students." George Vashon was "a poetic genius far superior to many who have written and published volumes." And Brown praised the intellectual accomplishments of James McCune Smith by noting that his essays on the comparative anatomy and physiology of the races "completely vindicated the Negro, and place that author among the most logical and scientific writers of the country." Rather than a random assortment of details and people, these and other entries in Brown's catalog suggest his interest in documenting an antebellum tradition of accomplishment. It was one that simultaneously suggested what could yet be accomplished now that slavery had been abolished.

Brown also praised individuals for their service to particular causes, especially abolition. It was not simply an attempt to be laudatory. Brown was, after all, involved in the movement; he was a living witness. And so it was also important for him to keep the memory of the struggle alive in the mind of a race on the threshold of freedom. In that regard, Brown highlighted the work of William C. Nell, about whom he ventured that "No man in New England has performed more uncompensated labor for humanity, and especially for his own race, than William C. Nell." He also praised Nell's contributions to textual historical discourse. Brown described Nell's seminal work, *Colored Patriots of the American Revolution*, as a book "filled with interesting incidents connected with the history of this country, past and present." Brown's high praise also extended to the abolitionist clergy, most notably James W. C. Pennington. Brown and Pennington had much in common. Both had experienced slavery, escaped, and established themselves as prominent abolitionists. Deeply appreciative of their similar experiences, Brown praised Pennington's efforts to acquire basic literacy and study theology.[10]

Also suggesting the thought that went into the volume, Brown included, but only had disdain for, the emigrationists. Martin Delany and James Theodore Holly bore the brunt of this rebuke. Although Brown provides a fairly thorough overview of Delany's varied career as an emigrationist, especially his 1858–61 exploration of the Niger Valley (in present-day Nigeria) with Afro-Jamaican Robert Campbell, Brown criticized Delany throughout. He characterized Delany's oratorical style as "somewhat violent in his gestures and paying but little regard to the rule of oratory." He also derided Delany's strong sense of what he labeled "Negro Nationality," a term Brown defined as an uncritical alliance to Africa or other diasporic locations. Brown viewed Holly's emigrationist, civilizationist, and Negro nationalist ideology as folly and a dangerous "infatuation." Holly's personal sacrifice, which included the death of several members of his family within the first six months of their settlement in Haiti, did not seem to justify his continued commitments to emigration.[11]

Brown's harsh critique of Delany and Holly provides an interesting lesson in the politics of historical writing. Although Brown himself advocated emigration in the 1850s and early 1860s, as the tide turned in favor of the Union troops during the Civil War, he gradually abandoned these interests and turned to discussing how blacks might adapt to freedom in America. Delany, however, only temporarily abandoned his emigration interests. He returned to the United States from the Niger Valley by way of England in 1861. In 1863, Delany received a commission as major in the Union Army, but after the collapse of Reconstruction in the 1870s, he turned again to emigration as a strategy for the race. Holly, on the other hand, never wavered from his belief in emigration and continued to promote immigration to Haiti. While Brown appreciated the seminal role the diaspora played in African American life, when he promoted emigration, he saw it as a means of accomplishing black equality in the United States, not as an end in itself. Emancipation and the Thirteenth Amendment made emigration seem no longer necessary.[12]

Brown's concern with the African diaspora, in *The Black Man*, principally revolved around Haiti. As already noted, Brown held a great deal of pride and admiration for the Haitian struggle. Although marginal and unrecognized as a sovereign republic during the antebellum period, its official recognition by the United States in 1862 instantly transformed Haiti into an even larger symbol of black possibility; possibility that seemed fully obtainable in the postbellum period. Thus, sketches of postindependence Haitian leaders dominate Brown's study. In addition to the portraits of Toussaint L'Ouverture, Dessalines (1804–6), and Christophe (1807–10, 1811–20), he included sketches of Andre Rigaud (1810–11), Alexandre Pétion (1806–18), Jean Paul Boyer (1818–43), and President Fabre Geffrard (1859–67). Rulers in office for only two or three years sometimes received several times the space of those who served for decades. This, too, on the surface, makes Brown's construction seem odd, random. But there was a logic to Brown's biographies. He suggested the importance of each of these leaders in part by the number of pages he devoted to them, and his ranking of their importance was related to when they served. Those who held office during the revolutionary period were clearly the most important to Brown. And so his sketch of Toussaint L'Ouverture, taken verbatim from his antebellum treatise *St. Domingo: Its Revolution and Its Patriots* (1855), is more than twelve pages in length. Toussaint's successor, Dessalines, received eight pages, and Henri Christophe, six. Post-revolutionary rulers received fewer than three pages each. Brown's sketches followed the traditional antebellum approach to Haiti's glory. Although most historians now agree that both Dessalines and Christophe were tragically flawed as leaders, Brown considered those who took an active part in the revolution and ruled the country during the first days of independence to be the greatest Haitian leaders.[13]

Brown's diasporic preoccupations continued in *The Rising Son*. Despite the fact that less that half of the text focused on Africa and the diaspora and that its assessments of Haitian and black American antebellum life were taken from earlier works, the book contributed a highly original perspective on African history.[14] Its greatest strength is the assessment of Africa during the era of free trade (1830–80), a historical moment characterized by the European rush for commercial expansion, the civilizing mission, and the desire for worldwide domination.

The British and the French, the two most powerful colonial operatives in Africa at the time, moved aggressively to acquire territory. The British military extended its influence throughout western Africa, penetrating from the Gulf of Benin into the hinterland of the Asante, one of the most highly organized kingdoms in West Africa. By 1882, British and French capital had crippled the Egyptian state, and British occupation became necessary to stabilize the situation. The French did much the same in Algeria, where in 1830 they garrisoned forces in order to combat a Muslim jihad—a religiously inspired war to rid the territory of infidel invaders. The French also penetrated Senegal and Mali, territories in what later became known as French West Africa.[15]

Like western Africa, southern Africa incurred the full brunt of the imperial onslaught. The Boers, a mixture of French, German, and Dutch peoples from the lower classes, had settled at the Cape in South Africa in the seventeenth century and established a town. British arrival at the Cape and their imposition of restrictive laws on the Boers led to the first of several *trekboers*—movements by small groups of Boers into the hinterland. Once in the hinterland, Boers came into conflict with the indigenous Nguni peoples. These interactions led to a series of conflicts lasting through the mid-nineteenth century. The discovery of diamonds and gold in the Orange Free State and Witwatersrand permanently altered the South African landscape. Aggressive British settlement and the influx of British capital left the Boers at a distinct disadvantage and displaced virtually all the Nguni people in the area.[16]

It is in this moment of imperial expansion, which worked to destroy African societies, that Brown placed his narrative. Like his predecessors, he addressed Africa's ancient glories but placed more emphasis on contemporary achievements to make a case for both its historical importance and current relevance. He described typical African cultural practices, such as the making of pottery, but more important, he highlighted the achievements of specific African empires. In this case, he looked *not* to the Ethiopia of classical antiquity but that of the nineteenth century. Despite its feudal traditions, he praised the organization of the state and devoted a portion of his discussion to the reign of Theodore I. He also pointed out that Ethiopia, long impregnable to the onslaught of Islam and the machinations of European colonizers, had a distinguished biblical tradition. The rulers claimed direct descent from King Solomon as a result of a sexual liaison between Makeda, the queen of Sheba, and Solomon, the king of Israel.[17] Moving from northeast to sub-Saharan Africa, from one region to the next, like the nineteenth-century travel narratives that provided a model for Brown's work, the reader sees eastern and central Africa through Brown's reconstruction and refashioning of missionary accounts. In one instance, Brown described Segu, the capital of the Bambara in eastern Africa, using information from Mungo Park, a British missionary who explored the region and left extensive travel records. Brown described Segu as a thriving city of thirty thousand with mosques and two-story houses. In central Africa, he praised the Mandingo and Fulbe as strong proponents of Islam.[18]

Brown's examination of west Africa focusing on slavery and his presentation of civilizationist discourse are particularly intriguing. Looking primarily at Sierra Leone, Dahomey (a creation of the slave trade), and Gabon, Brown examined some of the social patterns common to the area, such as polygamy and polytheism. Particularly incensed about the continuance of slavery in Dahomey, Brown portrayed the society in the most lurid terms possible, accusing Dahomean soldiers, for example, of having been little more than hunters of slaves for two centuries. As if hunting slaves were not problematic enough, he claimed the Dahomeans practiced human sacrifice and kept reptiles in storage pens in the center of town for elaborate ceremonies to elicit confessions from criminals.[19]

· As critical as Brown was of the Dahomeans, his larger point was that slavery debauched African society, but the civilizing influence of the West, especially Great Britain, would go far to correct this unfortunate situation. This view was no doubt an outgrowth of Brown's participation in the transatlantic abolitionist community. For abolitionists, slavery represented a regressive practice fueled by the greed of Africans and Europeans alike. The fact that the British became the first European power to abolish the slave trade gave them an honorific place in the narratives of many prominent black abolitionists. No exception to this general rule, Brown heralded the British role in trying to eradicate slavery from west Africa.[20]

While Brown uncritically praised the role of the British in eradicating slavery, he said little about Britain's growing imperial power. His praise instead revolved around his belief in the power of capitalist acquisition and mid-nineteenth-century notions of civilizationism. In a chapter titled "Progress of Civilization," Brown wrote, "To the English first and the Liberians next, the praise must be given for the suppression of this inhuman and unchristian traffic. Too much, however, cannot be said in favor of the missionaries, men and women, who, forgetting native land and home comforts, have given themselves to the work of teaching these people, and thereby carrying civilization to a country where each went with his life in his hands."[21]

Given his former status, worldly attainments, and burgeoning literary career, Brown could also appropriate the role of "carrier of civilization" for himself. He also connected himself tangibly to African American uplift, even as he praised the so-called agents of culture in Africa. "Education is what we now need," wrote Brown, and blacks must achieve it "at all hazards." He viewed the liberal arts schools such as Howard, Atlanta, and Fisk Universities as "harbingers of light to our people." African Americans, like Africans, were also in need of an educated ministry—a tactful admission of both of that need but also of the power of clerical elites in the black community. Blacks were also in need of "Temperance, that John the Baptist of reforms." Temperance, "along with every other method resorted to by the whites for their elevation," urged Brown, "should be used by the colored men."[22]

Brown did not selectively apply his program of civilization. The need for civilization in Africa, although not as great as Europeans portrayed it, depended on training natives in the rudiments of Christian theology and culture, especially in those areas where the slave trade had the greatest impact. Brown's discussion of Samuel A. J. Crowther, an ex-slave member of the Church Missionary Society and later bishop, who played an important role in opening the lower Niger Valley to British trade and Christianity, provides an example of the ultimate civilizationist argument, lifting Africans from the blindness of witchcraft and superstition to the light of civilization.[23]

Brown did not see European civilization as the only carrier of culture. Like his contemporary Edward Blyden, he recognized the positive impact of Islam in Africa. Here, Brown wanted to show the relative sophistication of non-Western religious and cultural value systems in relation to those in the Western world. His point is not only about the high level of civilization in the non-Western world but also about the capabilities of African Americans in freedom. Brown viewed Islam as an important stabilizer of polytheistic African societies rather than a disruptive force as it is seen in many Western accounts. Brown also rejected the contention that Arabs imposed Islam on Africa by force. Rather, he recognized that traders and clergymen had spread the religion to various parts of Africa, and Africans had modified the religion to suit their own needs.[24]

Brown's discussion of Islam in Africa also relates to other aspects of African culture. While the inhabitants of Guinea, the Congo, and the Western Cape bordered on barbarism, other groups such as the black South Africans, he wrote, "inhabit towns and cities, have made progress in the arts of industry, cultivate vast fields of sugar and tobacco, and manufacture various kinds of cutlery." Along with his praise of other African groups such as the Mandingo and the Fulani for their industry in agricultural arts, he acknowledged that some African groups were in need of civilization. But he did not view the entire continent as stereotypically languishing in total darkness.[25]

In Brown's selective, Januslike assessment of mid-nineteenth-century history, the race could look back to the glories of ancient antiquity but should also understand the dynamics of changing perceptions of Africa during a moment of capitalistic acquisition and imperial expansion. Understanding the present meant discussing Africa's future, which, in Brown's mind, was tethered to how closely African traditions, customs, and social mores approximated those in the West. Rather than the vacuous space presented by fifteenth- and sixteenth-century explorers of Africa, late eighteenth- and nineteenth-century writers described an Africa that was abundant in natural resources and possessed fairly sophisticated social and economic structures. These civilizationist projects not only pertained to Africa, but extended to African American reality as well.

In the African American historical experience, the Civil War understandably became a defining event. As such, discussions of it consumed a significant amount of space in historical narratives of the period. It became for these writers another vantage point from which they could provide a faithful account of the race. Brown wrote one of the earliest monographs on the Civil War, *The Negro in the American Rebellion*. He made extensive use of the reports and records of newspaper correspondents, battlefield officers, and actual participants in the "colored" regiments. He also used a number of secondary historical sources in his narrative, including Bancroft's multivolume *History of the United States*, Frank Moore's *Diary of the American Revolution*, and Arnold's *History of Rhode Island*. One of the most important of these early texts was George Livermore's *An Historical Research* published in 1863. Livermore initially presented his findings on the role of blacks "as citizens and soldiers" in the *Proceedings of the Massachusetts Historical Society*, 1862–63. The work focused primarily on black participation in the Revolutionary War and the War of 1812. However, the book's balanced treatment of the black experience, pioneering methodology, and lucid presentation made it one of the most important documentary texts of the period and a model for Brown and subsequent historical work.[26]

Brown's *Negro in the American Rebellion* examined black participation in the Revolutionary War and the fight for inclusion in the nation's body politic. Like William Nell before him, Brown re-created the revolutionary impetus provided by the Boston Massacre, detailed black heroism at Bunker Hill and Red Bank, and cited the grateful acknowledgment of black services to the nation in General Andrew Jackson's "Proclamation to the Free People of Color," a staple practice in antebellum histories. He also provided short accounts of the Denmark Vesey and Nat Turner revolts. But most important here, Brown located the origin of the Civil War in the passage of the infamous Fugitive Slave Law in 1850 and the intense contestation over slavery in the 1850s. One might recall that Brown, a fugitive slave himself, traveled abroad in the 1850s to avoid recapture. The hurt, anger, and betrayal Brown felt toward Northerners and Southerners over slavery resonated in the language of his text.[27]
Mentioning the Anthony Burns and David Simms cases in Boston, in which

the courts returned these two recaptured fugitive slaves to the South, Brown castigated the Northern supporters of the Fugitive Slave Law, exposing the gulf between the nation's ideals and its realities:

> On that occasion, the sons of free enlightened and Christian Massachu-setts, descendants of the Pilgrim Fathers, bowed submissively to the behests of tyranny more cruel than Austrian despotism; yielded up their dignity and self-respect; became the allies of slave catchers, the associates and companions of slave catchers and serviles, they seized the image of God, bound their fellow man with chains and consigned him to torture under the lash of a piratical overseer. God's law and man's rights were trampled upon; and the self-respect, the constitutional privileges of the free states were ignominiously surrendered.[28]

Brown described the Boston courthouse, the scene of numerous fugitive slave cases, as shrouded "in chains." According to Brown, the courthouse was also the place where "two hundred rowdies and thieves were sworn in as special policemen" and used to augment the traditional police force in the recapture of fugitive slaves. While the Fugitive Slave Act inflicted irreparable harm on the black communities throughout the nation, the *Dred Scott* Supreme Court decision represented the final straw. For Brown and fellow abolitionists, the "Dred Scott decision added fresh combustibles to the smoldering heap." While blacks were struggling to affirm their worth, the seeming success of proslavery forces emboldened slaveholders "whose wealth made them arrogant" and "in-dependent of the United States." According to Brown, this arrogance and in-dependence left no doubt in the minds of the "authors of the rebellion" of the "success of the attack on the Federal government."[29]

Upon the outbreak of hostilities, blacks were eager to join the Union ef-fort but were initially rebuffed by Northern authorities. Brown pointed out the problematic aspects of this policy: While Northern forces were returning blacks to their masters, "it was a notorious fact the enemy was using Negroes to build fortifications, drive teams and raise food for the army." In Montgomery, Alabama, the first capital of the Confederacy, "negroes were being drilled and armed for military duty." Meanwhile, in the North, General Lewis impressed the Black Brigade in Cincinnati to work on the fortifications in Covington and Lexington, Kentucky. Guarded by the police and forced to work at bayonet point, the impressed black soldiers worked without weapons from the third of September to the twentieth, 1862. Despite their being unarmed for a time, the city fathers heralded these African Americans for their important role in protecting the city.[30]

From proving their loyalty in support roles, African Americans soon found themselves on the front lines as combat soldiers. This change in policy was due, in no small part, to the issuance of the Emancipation Proclamation in 1863. Assumption of combat duties did not bring an end to black American's unequal treatment in pay, working conditions, and advancement as compared with Northerners or recrimination from Southerners. Brown cited the massacre of almost an entire black company that had surrendered to a Rebel army at Fort Pillow, Tennessee, in 1863, as a startling example of this treatment.[31]

Brown understood that the war's end brought even greater challenges to the nation than its commencement. While it was important to chronicle African American participation in the war, Brown also, in keeping with the intent of historians at midcentury, offered a prognosis for the future. What meanings did the war have for African Americans? How would they cope with freedom? How would they ensure their hard-won rights? These questions were of paramount importance. The assassination of Abraham Lincoln, "the Great Emancipator," and the ascension of the vice president and Southern sympathizer Andrew Johnson to the presidency caused great consternation among Radical Republicans and black civil rights advocates. While Reconstruction enjoyed the support of Congress between 1865 and 1870, signs of outright resistance to the process emerged as early as 1867. The formation of the Ku Klux Klan, a vigilante group including former planters who used intimidation and murder to thwart the plans of Reconstruction governments, and Andrew Johnson's blanket pardons of former Southern confederates and willingness to restore former Confederate states to the Union with minimal requirements, led to Johnson's impeachment and the gradual erosion of the Reconstruction experiment.[32]

From the vantage point of an intellectual, Brown, like Charles Reason, argued that the Civil War had created a great deal of animosity between Southerners and Northerners, blacks and whites, former masters and former slaves. The defeat of the Confederacy then left deep scars on the Southern psyche. According to Brown, these feelings intensified the white Southerners' sense of dominance and superiority over blacks rather than fostering feelings of defeat and despair. And these feelings of racial superiority emboldened white Southerners' desires to "reduce the Negro to serfdom." Meanwhile, the agencies and auxiliaries of the federal government, such as the Freedmen's Bureau and federal troops, were powerless to stop them. Brown also cited the 1865 riots in Memphis and New Orleans and the involvement of former confederates in outrages and violations of federal law as tangible manifestations of the hostile feelings of white Southerners toward blacks.[33]

As Benjamin Quarles has remarked, where Brown's history fails as a complete account of the Civil War, it succeeds in telling the human side of the story. Brown, in fact, produced as complete a discussion of the war and black participation in it as one possibly could, only two years after its conclusion. While antebellum writers could only make declarative statements to foster the abolition of slavery, postbellum writers had a more weighty charge: to provide guidance and informed assessments of African Americans' conditions in freedom. In response to Southern animosities, vigilantism, presidential pardons, and race riots, Brown asked, "Now, what shall be done to protect these people from the abuse of their former masters?" Brown's question was not rhetorical; rather, he sought to provide a tangible blueprint for how the race should adapt to freedom. Brown proposed granting blacks the franchise, which would soon become a reality with the passage of the Fifteenth Amendment in 1870. But ironically, acquisition of the vote was the only directive he provided. Brown viewed voting as a critical possession, a natural right, not a privilege. In fact, the vote was the very basis of a republican government: "Does anyone doubt this?" asked Brown. "Let him ask himself what constitutes a republican government, or government of the people, and what is implied by such a government, and he will soon see, that without the elective franchise, or right to choose rulers and law-makers, there can be no such governments." The vote, political enfranchisement, had important ramifications for newly freed African Americans. Its usage would give rise to substantial political empowerment during the Reconstruction era.[34]

The Negro in the American Rebellion is an interesting specimen of race history combined with racial prognosis from the early postbellum period. As historical text, it leaves much to be desired, but as a record of and reflection on the events of the period, it is invaluable. Brown melded lived experience from the antebellum period with the concerns and sensibilities of the early postbellum period. Better positioned than most historians to tell the story of the race, Brown tangibly tied together the agitation to end the peculiar institution in the antebellum era with the mapping and charting of race possibilities in the postbellum period.[35]

In three different but very related texts, Brown foreshadowed many of the issues that African American intellectuals would confront in the post-Reconstruction period. Although Brown focused on the black experience in the

United States, he was not unmindful of the African diaspora. Moreover, he understood the connection between historical, social, political, and economic issues as well as other concerns about what Michele Mitchell has termed "racial destiny." To this end, Brown also revealed the seminal role that black intellectuals played in presenting plans, blueprints, thoughts, and ruminations on race politics. Like his friend and confidant William Still, Brown worked to make tangible the connections between a recent African American history characterized by slavery and the new possibilities for the race engendered by freedom.[36]

William Still and the Selling of The Underground Railroad

William Still's *Underground Railroad* represents an important intervention in and continuation of the tradition of postbellum historical writing inaugurated by William Wells Brown. Like Brown, Still was largely self-made and pursued opportunities for book production and publication at a time of great fluidity in the African American and national communities. Capitalizing on the changed dynamics of the African American predicament, Still was poised to assume the mantle of race leadership in the arena of book production. His work skillfully bridged the divide between the black antebellum past of slavery and the postbellum realities of freedom and untold possibility, as he offered his readership an opportunity to retell and reenvision the past through the lens of present opportunities. At many levels ranging from historical memory to the economic practicalities of Gilded Age consumerism, Still's work played a foundational role in presenting one of the earliest paradigms for African American history in the postbellum period.

William Still, one of eighteen children, was born in Medford, New Jersey, in 1821 to Levin and Charity Still, who had escaped from slavery. With little formal education, Still left home at twenty and found work on neighboring farms. In 1844, he arrived in Philadelphia, where he found employment as a janitor and later as a clerical assistant in the office of the Pennsylvania Society for the Abolition of Slavery. The Philadelphia Vigilance Committee had begun assisting fugitive slaves in 1838, led by the militant Quaker Thomas Garrett, but was largely defunct by the late 1840s. In 1852, the Pennsylvania Society for the Abolition of Slavery convened a meeting to reorganize the Vigilance Committee.[37]

Inspired by the Compromise of 1850 and the Fugitive Slave Law, the new Vigilance Committee bolstered its effectiveness through centralized leadership. Still became the corresponding secretary and chairman.[38] Following the example of abolitionist William Whipper, Still even traveled to Canada in 1853 to assess free black communities. He subsequently used his findings about their condition to dispel the idea that former slaves were incapable of living satisfactorily as free persons.[39] All of his experiences deepened his resolve to pursue abolitionist activities. He championed the belief that African Americans, through both independent and interracial activity, could fundamentally alter their status in the United States and win the respect of their fellow citizens. Still's work with the Philadelphia Vigilance Committee and subsequent publication of The Underground Railroad in 1872 represented a significant role in the articulation of a postbellum historical voice among African Americans.

The Pennsylvania Abolition Society launched Still's writing career through a resolution in May 1871:

Whereas,

The position of William Still in the Vigilance Committee connected with the "Underground Railroad," as its corresponding secretary, and chairman of its acting subcommittee, gave him peculiar facilities for collecting interesting facts pertaining to this branch of the antislavery service.

Resolved,

That the Pennsylvania Anti-Slavery Society request him to compile and publish his personal reminiscences and experiences related to the "Underground Railroad.[40]

Given his extensive involvement in the abolitionist movement and his familiarity with all aspects of the Underground Railroad, Still was probably the best choice for this undertaking. For his own part, Still was also keenly aware of the importance of appealing to public sentiment regarding historical events. He merged this historical sense with shrewd business practices to generate high sales by exciting reader interest.

There were several factors that worked in Still's favor. First, prior to 1872, there were no expansive studies or accounts of the Underground Railroad. Second, Still understood that producing a solid book and generating sales of it depended upon the authenticity and credibility of the account as well as the dramatic retelling of incidents in the lives of fugitive slaves. As historian Phillip Lapansky has noted, "while other Underground Railroad histories focus mainly on the white agents and the remote country houses with secret cellars and attics, Still's work and his book underscore that in Philadelphia the muscle and backbone of the operation was the black community." Thus, at the heart of the issues of readability and marketability was the authenticity of the account. Still prefaced the text with his own experiences, both professional and personal, rather than following the practice commonly used in the antebellum slave narratives of prefacing a book with the remarks of prominent white abolitionists as proof of the validity and importance of the material. Given the sensational nature of some of the material, which was subject to charges of fabrication, Still informed readers that "the most scrupulous care has been taken to furnish articles, stories, simple facts — to resort to no coloring to make the book seem romantic," for he was "fully persuaded that any exaggerations or additions of his own could not possibly equal in surpassing interest, the original and natural tales given under circumstances, when life and death seemed about equally balanced in the scale, and fugitives in transit were making their way from Slavery to Freedom, with the horrors of the Fugitive Slave-law staring them in the face."[41]

Still's retelling of his personal experience with the horror wreaked by slavery on families rendered the narrative more authentic while providing a riveting example that appealed to readers. As a result of his work with the Philadelphia Vigilance Committee, Still reunited with his brother, Peter, from whom he had been separated shortly after birth. Still believed that his and others' personal stories helped to animate his efforts to render public what was heretofore private. Still's description of his reunion with his brother heightened the account's authenticity: "But after the restoration of Peter Still, [my] own brother (the kidnapped and the ransomed), after forty years' cruel separation from his mother, the wonderful discovery and joyful reunion, the idea forced itself upon [my] mind that all over this wide and extended country thousands of mothers and children, separated by slavery, were in a similar way, living without the slightest knowledge of each other's whereabouts, praying and weeping without ceasing, as did this mother and son."[42]

Still was also aware of the deeply emotional and harrowing toll that slavery took on fugitives, because he often interviewed them. And he took copious notes. Moreover, fugitives assisted by Still, once safe, wrote letters of praise and thanks to him. He never thought this information would be published; Still simply hoped to use it to help families reunite once freedom came. Especially after the passage of the Fugitive Slave Law, Still knew that both he and his records would be extremely valuable to proslavery elements who sought to disrupt the effectiveness of the Underground Railroad. According to Still, secrecy and privacy were uppermost in his mind. Unlike the dramatic slave narratives and autobiographies published as a means of heightening popular sentiment against slavery, Still's complex work in aiding fugitive slaves, although known in abolitionist circles, could not be made public. In order to preserve the secrecy of his operations, Still hid his records in the loft of a remote barn and in the Lebanon Cemetery. These actions ensured that the specifics of his operation remained private.[43]

Still also anchored his text in the experiences of slaves—old and young, men and women—and accounts from the letters of fugitives gave added poignancy to the narratives. One of the most gripping accounts was that of Romulus Hall, an elderly slave who lost his life trying to escape. His companion, a younger man, successfully negotiated the journey, but Hall succumbed to the cold and was left behind. He was eventually found, but not before suffering frostbite. Despite impending death, when questioned by the Vigilance Committee regarding the prudence of his escape, Hall replied, "I am glad I escaped." The Vigilance Committee provided medical services until he died and buried him in Lebanon Cemetery in Philadelphia.[44]

In other accounts, Still described how some fugitives had to resort to the threat of physical violence to affect their escape. One story he tells is about a group of slaves, three men and two women, who escaped from Loudon County, Virginia. At Cheat River, Maryland, slave catchers confronted them, demanding to know why such a large group of slaves was on the road without adequate documentation. The fugitives refused to answer, whereupon

> one of the white men raised his gun, pointing the muzzle directly towards one of the young women with the threat that he would shoot. "Shoot! Shoot! Shoot!" she exclaimed, with a double-barreled shot gun in her hand and a long dirk knife in the other, utterly unterrified and fully ready for a death struggle. The male leader of the fugitives by this time had pulled back the hammers of his pistols and was about to fire. Seeing the determination of the party, the slave catchers retreated, and the party proceeded north.[45]

Still's concern for the authenticity of the text, his personal engagement with the slavery community, and his dramatic public rendering of harrowing tales of escape from bondage, which heretofore had been private, combined to make *The Underground Railroad* a very marketable product indeed. Still's "postbellum slave narrative," a term popularized by literary historian William Andrews, contained all of the elements necessary to breathe life into a bygone era, and in doing so, offer insight into the abolitionist movement and the meaning of free-dom in the postbellum era. Still's marketing and selling of the book brought these dynamics into bold relief.

Still was a man of his time, fully aware of contemporary trends and very much involved in them, and in an age that ushered in aggressive marketing techniques, Still's distribution of *The Underground Railroad* took advantage of the new milieu. Technological advancements in the printing industry, many of which took place in the late antebellum period, allowed the prolifera-tion of book and magazine publication in the postbellum period. One of the most important of these advancements was the reorganization of the printing industry.

In the early antebellum period, it was necessary for printers to master a wide variety of skills ranging from operating the printing press to selling books and stationery. Printers conveyed this information to a host of journeymen and apprentices, whom they supervised from sunup to sundown. By the 1840s and 1850s, the creation of publishing houses had streamlined the process and al-lowed book production to take place in one factory. The steam-driven flatbed press made it easier to produce more books at a cheaper cost. These innova-tions radically altered the nature of book publication and consumption. Now, historical works by African Americans could easily be published in numerous editions, accompanied by sample books and aggressive advertising in other publications. Still took advantage of this, aggressively marketing his book in a number of ways including the active solicitation of sketches and comments from Pennsylvania Abolition Society members and other notables. He also undertook an advertising campaign in the *Christian Recorder* and established a nationwide network of book agents.[46]

Many of the advertisements for his book included endorsements from nota-ble persons, such as James Miller McKim, corresponding secretary and general agent of the Pennsylvania Anti-Slavery Society; Reverend William H. Furness, a Harvard-trained Unitarian minister and fund-raiser for the Philadelphia Vigi-lance Committee; and Charles Sumner, U.S. senator from Massachusetts and prominent Radical Republican, whose African American advocacy straddled the antebellum and postbellum periods. Still's most notable supporter was Oli-ver Otis Howard, a Civil War general and commissioner of the Freedmen's Bu-reau.[47] Another important endorsement came from the dean of abolitionists, William Lloyd Garrison, who examined the book "with a deep and thrilling interest," concluding that Still's work was "voluminous and well-executed" and uncovered "a most important portion of Anti-slavery History, which, but for [Still's] industry, research, and personal experience and knowledge might nearly all have been lost to posterity." Garrison hoped the sale of the book would assist Still in covering his expenses. But more important, Garrison thought the message and the meaning of *The Underground Railroad* was "for the enlightenment of the rising generation as to the inherent cruelty of the defunct slave system, and to perpetuate such an abhorrence of it as to prevent all further injustice towards the colored population of our land."[48]

Still's work also received support from African Americans, most notably William Whipper and Frances Ellen Harper. Their individual testimonials helped to sell the book and at the same time showcased their role in the abolitionist movement. Whipper, the co-owner (with black merchant Stephen Smith) of lumberyards in Columbia and Philadelphia, Pennsylvania, was one of the wealthiest African Americans during the antebellum period and an important financier of the Underground Railroad. Between 1847 and 1860, he provided the then-enormous sum of one thousand dollars per year to aid fugitive slaves. During the Civil War, he provided roughly the same amount to the Union Army. Moreover, Whipper was an active participant in the conventions of free people of color between 1830 and 1835. In a letter to Still in 1871, he shared important information about his role in the Underground Railroad: "In a period of three years from 1847 to 1850," wrote Whipper, "I passed hundreds to the land of freedom, while others, induced by high wages, and the feeling they were safe in Columbia, worked in the lumber and coal yards of that place." Whipper concluded his letter by giving thanks for the privilege of "laboring with others for the redemption of my race from oppression and thralldom." He added, "I would prefer to-day to be penniless in the streets, rather than to have withheld a single hour's labor or a dollar from the sacred cause of liberty, justice and humanity."[49]

In highlighting the life of Frances Ellen Watkins Harper, Still was able to present an African American woman in a light similar to that used for men. Still felt that while the "narratives and labors of eminent colored men such as Banneker, Douglass, Brown and others have been written and sketched very fully for the public, and doubtless with advantage to the cause of freedom," he lamented that there was not to be found "in any written work portraying the Anti-slavery Struggle (except in the form of narratives) as we are aware of, a sketch of the labors of eminent colored women." Still was "glad of the opportunity to present a sketch not merely of the leading colored poet in the United States, but also of one of the most liberal contributors as well as one of the ablest advocates of the Underground Railroad and of the slave."[50]

The sophistication of Still's marketing plan for *The Underground Railroad* resulted in no small part from his previous business experience. Aside from his work in the antislavery office, Still owned a small but profitable coal and ice yard, and during the Civil War, he secured a contract from the federal government as a supplier for Camp William Penn, located outside of Philadelphia. Despite his business success, Still, a member of the Berean Presbyterian Church, was frugal rather than showy and a model of what historian Roger Lane termed the "Protestant bourgeois." Still's modest personal taste was partly influenced by the fact that he never reached the same level of business success as fellow abolitionists William Whipper and Stephen Smith. Rather, Still sold small quantities of coal and ice to grocers and served the needs of ordinary people in Philadelphia. However, his belief in the acquisition of capital by African Americans for the purpose of providing useful services to the black community served him well in the area of book publication.[51]

On January 29, 1872, Still entered into a formal agreement with Porter and Coates, a white-owned publishing house in Philadelphia, to publish ten thousand copies of *The Underground Railroad*. The agreement terms stipulated that the book would be published by subscription only, on good quality paper, and with a variety of bindings. Porter and Coates reserved the sole right to publish the book for one year and pledged to pay Still a royalty of 62 and 1/2 cents on each copy sold, based upon a monthly sales report, which they would provide. Still could purchase the books at the customary rate for agents. Porter and Coates kept insurance on the electrotype plates in the amount of $2,500. Still would later purchase these plates to continue publication of the book.[52]

Although advertisements for Still's *Underground Railroad* appeared in a number of papers during the 1870s, the advertising campaign in the *Christian Recorder* was the most extensive. The *Christian Recorder* was the official organ of the American Methodist Episcopal Church, with which Still was closely associated. Its readership included the most urbane and well educated among the race. Moreover, the *Christian Recorder* circulated widely in A.M.E. strongholds in the Northeast, South, and Midwest. Each of the five major advertisements used for the *Underground Railroad* emphasized the themes of intrigue, interracial cooperation, subversion of gender roles, and the impact of the peculiar institution (slavery) on families. Replicas of the illustrations featured in the text provided potential purchasers and readers of the book with a visual introduction to the dramatic stories of fugitive slaves on the Underground Railroad. The first advertisement for the book was an advance notice, which appeared in July 1871. A fairly simple ad, it noted that Still was a "well-known benefactor of the race" and predicted the contents of Still's book "will be devoured with avidity." By March 1873, a small advertisement announced the sale of the book and the need for agents. Just one month later, in April 1873, the first full-page advertisement appeared.[53]

Still's use of advertisements aimed to present the most dramatic and well-known incidents of the Underground Railroad history to excite reader interest in the book. Antebellum developments in electrotyping allowed an impressment of the set type, which could be fashioned into a relatively inexpensive permanent metal plate for subsequent printings. As book historian Robert Zboray has noted, publishers, as a result of this procedure, knew the exact size of the first edition and encouraged lengthy advertising campaigns designed to bolster sales of the book as well as the author's popularity. Moreover, if the book sold well, the continued use of similar advertisements and the quick production of a second edition would likely follow.[54]

The advertising campaign for Still followed this new formula. The book's title, *The Underground Railroad*, was emblazoned in bold letters across the top of the page. In the center of the page, one of the book's seventy illustrations, "Resurrection of Henry Box Brown," was prominently displayed. Brown's daring escape from slavery—he shipped himself in a crate to Philadelphia in 1848—had already captured the attention of antebellum readers. The advertisement probably also had special meaning for Still because he was one of several abolitionists who greeted Brown as he emerged from his crate. And, finally, also in the interest of market advertising, Still included a section titled "What Has Been Said about It by Prominent Abolitionists," featuring brief endorsements of the book.[55]

Perhaps the "Resurrection of Henry Box Brown" advertisement did not have the desired effect, for it appeared only once more, on April 24, 1873. By May 15, the featured illustration in the advertisements was "The Mayor of Norfolk Searching Captain Fountain's Vessel for Runaways," representing the great risk whites took and the role they played in helping fugitive slaves. It also illustrated Still's belief in interracial cooperation and its power in helping to undermine slavery. This illustration only appeared twice more, on May 22 and May 29, 1873. The next advertisement was captioned "The Death of Romulus Hall." A particularly striking image, suggesting the nobility and the tragedy in the struggle against slavery, it depicts Hall, an elderly slave, on his deathbed talking with a member of the Vigilance Committee. If Still wished to convey the horror of slavery, Hall's pleading yet tender and wise face succeeded. Still used this advertisement in thirteen consecutive issues, from June 5 to September 1, 1873.[56]

Presenting yet another facet of the slave experience is the illustration captioned "A Desperate Conflict on the Underground Railroad—Women Facing the Enemy with Revolvers and Bowie-Knives." Demonstrating Still's technique of manipulating certain images for the specific purpose of advertising, this illustration is labeled simply a "Bold Stroke for Freedom" where it appears in the book, and apparently the knives used by the men and women were dirks, swordlike daggers, and not bowie knives, with their large single-edged blades. In the advertisement, Still placed the women in the foreground, making the story seem even more sensational by accentuating the bravery of the women. It also forcefully represented the unusual dangers and hardships women had to endure and suggested that women defied gender roles to escape from slavery. Indeed, in both the book and the advertisement, the escape of these slaves was a "Bold Stroke for Freedom." Still used this ad in twenty-three consecutive issues, from September 18, 1873, to March 26, 1874.[57]

Another popular advertisement, which also featured the plight of black women, was captioned "The Father Died in the Poor House, a Raving Maniac, Caused by the Sale of Two of His Children. The Heroic Mother with the Balance, Sought Flight on the Underground Railroad." Again, the caption for this illustration in the book itself was less dramatic and simply listed the names of Anna Maria Jackson's seven children. This advertisement, which appeared on April 2, 1874, featured assessments from reviews printed in the *New York Daily Tribune*, *Friends Review*, *Lutheran Observer*, and the *Nation*. With the strong endorsements of the white press, Still was positioned to profit immensely. His use of the Anna Maria Jackson story demonstrated his recognition of the power of this subverted gender role, his commitment to black women, and his determination to show the devastating impact of the peculiar institution on the African American family. The ad appeared in more than forty consecutive issues.[58]

The details of Still's marketing strategy went beyond advertising and involved a nationwide network of agents. The details, however, are sketchy because his letterbook contains only his letters to the agents between 1873 and 1874. But since he was widely known in Philadelphia and various parts of the country, we can glean some of his marketing techniques through his correspondence with other individuals. Beginning in 1873, the year Still completed his one-year contract with Porter and Coates, he gained the exclusive right to print and distribute the book, and he began to create a network of agents facilitated by his contacts in the A.M.E. Church and the new black schools. Still also received help in promoting his book from such notables as Bishop Daniel Payne, president of Wilberforce University and later founder of the Bethel Literary and Historical Association; William and Ellen Craft, ex-slaves who escaped from slavery by passing for white; General Samuel Chapman Armstrong, president of Hampton Institute; and William Wells Brown, who often relied on Still for advice in selling his book, *The Black Man*.[59]

Still's approach to selling books was predicated on a practical understanding of the needs of both the agents and the subscribers. He employed both male and female agents and both African Americans and whites. While not discriminating on the basis of sex or race, Still did insist that agents meet certain standards. He sought to ensure that the agents he hired were college educated, had "some knowledge of canvassing and [the ability to] enter fully into the work, thoroughly canvassing one, two or three townships before stopping," and the ability to sell books to individuals of all classes. Once he identified a potential agent, Still wrote to the individual, inquiring, "Have you any experience as a book canvasser?" and "If you should be appointed, what amount of time could you devote to the agency?"[60]

Once Still recruited an agent, he offered very generous compensation. In his circular, "Terms for Agents," which he insisted agents keep confidential, he described his contract. For a minimal cost of $3.75, agents could purchase copies of the book, a dummy volume for orders, and one hundred circulars. Initially, Still offered 40 percent of the sale to agents. In 1872, he raised that to 50 percent, and for prepaid orders of at least one standard case of forty-eight books, he offered 60 percent. Despite these generous terms, Still also imposed a system of checks and balances on his agents. He maintained regular correspondence with them, preferring to send prepaid orders. If orders were not prepaid, Still usually sent them cash-on-delivery. As a testament to his success, within a few months, the number of agents for *The Underground Railroad* increased from thirty to more than one hundred.[61]

Still offered the book in several attractive covers at prices consistent with the market: Fine English Cloth, $4.50; Paneled Style, $5.00; Sheep Library Style, $5.50; and Half Turkey Morocco, $6.50. Still's ability to offer his book in a variety of bindings also related to technological innovations in bookbinding. Hand-operated stabbing machines (invented in the 1820s), folding machines, rounders and backers, and a number of other machines, created primarily during the 1840s, assisted in marbling, cutting, and trimming the bindings.[62]

Good agents often guaranteed timely delivery of the book, increasing confidence in the overall efficiency of the business and bolstering sales. At its height in 1874, Still's sales network included agents in California, Indiana, Illinois, Iowa, Georgia, Massachusetts, Missouri, Nebraska, New York, North Carolina, South Carolina, Pennsylvania, Tennessee, and Texas. He encouraged his agents to be responsible and to take advantage of every opportunity to sell *books*. He believed that "Agents who hold themselves prepared to deliver to all who will take their books immediately succeed best. Strike when the iron is hot."[63] He discouraged agents from canvassing large areas. He thought it was preferable to canvass a small area thoroughly before moving to a larger field because "canvassing is no holiday play. . . . It requires] learning and much perseverance."[64]

Still clearly practiced what he preached. In addition to recruiting professional men such as W. H. Stanton, publisher of the *Freedom's Journal* in Clinton, Missouri, G. L. Smith, superintendent of schools in Bolivar County, Mississippi, and Marshall Taylor, the first black editor of the *Southwestern Christian Advocate*, the official organ of the Methodist Episcopal Church, Still also used family members. His niece, Mrs. Catherine Still, the daughter of his brother, Peter Still, canvassed in Syracuse, New York. His son-in-law, Edward A. Wiley, a partner in several of the business interests, became an agent for the book in 1873. Wiley controlled several agencies in Harrisburg and Pittsburgh, Pennsylvania. In Pittsburgh, he sold more than four hundred books in six months and earned more than $1,500. He had similar successes elsewhere. Wiley died of a brain hemorrhage on a trip to promote *The Underground Railroad* in Baltimore during 1874.[65]

Another component of Still's business strategy included appealing to race pride to bolster the confidence of agents in their product. Although it is easy to see this characteristic of Still's sales method as nascent "black nationalism," his correspondence suggests that his interest was in promoting economic self-sufficiency and the Protestant work ethic.[66] He made this explicit in an 1873 letter to an agent in Lawrence, Kansas, in which he connected race pride to economic advantage. "This book needs to be presented by a man who appreciates and comprehends the value of having our heroes and our martyrs under slavery well represented in the history of our times — to make the work take exceedingly well," he insisted.[67] In a letter to an agent in Columbia, South Carolina, Still used the book's success among whites as a means of embarrassing African Americans into supporting it: "I can not say the UGRR is being appreciated by our people as well as by the whites for wherever it has been pushed among them, it has been well received. When we consider that we have no books or history produced by colored men (except now & then one few and far between)[and] that our enlightened age is demanding of us now greater show of ability than we have hitherto had the opportunity to evince, it seems to me that such work would be heartily sought after."[68]

Despite his tremendous success—estimates indicate that Still had sold between five and ten thousand copies of his book by the late 1870s, and he proudly displayed the book at the Philadelphia Centennial in 1876—he, like other businessmen, encountered problems. Some agents did not fulfill their obligations, forcing Still to sever his relations with them. One of the most highly publicized cases was that of Felton Jones, a reliable agent in Kent County, Delaware. In a deviation from his standard practice, Still sent thirteen books to Jones in June 1873 prior to their being paid for. Jones did not respond, nor did Still receive any money for the shipment. After hearing nothing for several months, Still wrote a harsh note to Jones, relieving him of his duties and threatening to "publish him" and to "take legal action to have this matter lifted." In another case of fraud, William Perry, an agent also in Delaware, after failing to pay for several shipments of books, wrote to Still and stated that his trunk was open, and he suspected robbery. Still also dismissed Perry and warned him not to engage in any further sales of the book.[69]

Despite the unscrupulous behavior of a few agents, Still's work sold extremely well, and agents throughout the country prospered. Hence, in 1883, he followed up with another edition of the volume titled *Underground Railroad Records: With a Life of the Author.* Whether intentionally or not, the publication of this work coincided with the publication of George Washington Williams's *History of the Negro Race, 1619–1880.* Still's advertisement included a sample book, which was a replica of the actual book and a standard marketing tool for booksellers. It included a lengthy introduction to the issues raised in the book, endorsements from prominent abolitionists, reviews, and excerpts from the work itself. In a summary of the work's import, Still boldly proclaimed, "For the colored man no history can be more instructive than this, of his own making, and written by one of his own race. The generations are growing in light. Not to know of those who were stronger than shackles, who were pioneers in the grand advance toward freedom; not to know of what characters the race could produce when straightened by circumstances, nor of those small beginnings which ended in triumphant emancipation, will, in a short time, be a reproach." Thus, Still was as aggressive in promoting the revised edition as he had been the first. With his added personal biography, the new edition was twenty pages longer than the original study. He sent it to President Grover Cleveland in 1886, and until his death in 1902, he promoted it on the lecture circuit.[70]

While promoting his book, Still continued to render valuable service to Philadelphia's black community. He served as president of the Berean Building and Loan Association in 1888. An extension of his church, this organization helped people purchase homes. Still used his extensive contacts with white philanthropists to raise the seed money for the initial loans. In 1889, Still served as a Pennsylvania delegate to the Nashville Convention of Colored Men. He also served as the hub of the black abolitionist networks. As president of the Home for Aged and Infirm Persons in Philadelphia, he assisted in providing care for residents over sixty years old. Sojourner Truth, sickly, nearly destitute, and in need of funds to stave off eviction from her home, asked Still about the possibility of procuring lodging for her in Philadelphia in order to sell copies of her book. Another correspondent inquired about the welfare of Harriet Tubman, "the Moses of her people." Still thought she was living in Albany, New York, and promised to look for her. Others wrote to ask Still to make recommendations for various remembrances of the abolitionist movement.[71]

When Still died in 1902, he had fully emerged from the shadowy world of the Underground Railroad. His book about it, *The Underground Railroad*, recommended him as a respectable and honorable gentleman and endeared him to abolitionists and race men and women alike. Not only had he preserved the memory of a bygone area, but he had merged an engaged account of the African American experience in slavery and freedom with emerging national book distribution processes to market the first comprehensive history of the Underground Railroad throughout the country. Still's approach to issues of economic self-sufficiency and the Protestant work ethic led to the creation of his own well-organized sales network to fulfill his vision of American and African American possibility. It was an equal opportunity operation, with agents given wide latitude to canvass areas in the way they felt was best. He rewarded hard work and perseverance with a generous profit percentage while relieving unreliable agents of their positions. Most important, Still believed that race pride was predicated on reconstructing accurate and reliable histories of African Americans and presenting them in sophisticated ways that included considerations of book design and marketing as well as content.

THE WORK OF WILLIAM WELLS BROWN and William Still represented the Januslike sensibilities of the years following the Emancipation Proclamation.

Not only did these authors offer complex portraits of a world that began to diverge sharply from that of the antebellum period, but they began to chart the prospects of the race in this new era. Brown continued antebellum traditions by chronicling black participation in the nation's wars. He also used the concept of representative men and women in his biographical compilation, *The Black Man*, and built on the antebellum tradition by producing a lengthy race history, *The Rising Son*. Much the same can be said of William Still's *The Underground Railroad*, which chronicled the heroic efforts of slaves to sunder their bonds and boldly strike for liberty. The newness of this work, however, also embraced the postbellum period. With a combination of tutelary examples and practical advice, both Brown and Still wrote about heroism, self-sacrifice, and historical precedent to demonstrate what the race had achieved during its darkest hour as an indicator of what it could accomplish in freedom.

More important, the shifting nature of book production made it possible for Still's and Brown's works to appear in more than one edition. In Still's case, the self-published aspect of his work, and his success in constructing a nationwide network of agents, bolstered the effort. Still integrated an older story about race heroism into a new set of market-related forces that allowed this story to reach a much wider audience. The wider circulation of historical writing exemplified by Still's and Brown's works set the stage for subsequent developments in historical understanding among blacks. The years between 1883 and 1915 would not only witness the crystallization of these market-driven forces but would lead to an outpouring of race literature that the nation had not previously seen.

CHAPTER 5

Advancement in Numbers, Knowledge, and Power

African American History in Post-Reconstruction America, 1883–1915

> By far the most important and interesting period in the history of this people, is that which followed emancipation and witnessed their struggle for existence, their establishment as citizens of the United States, and their advancement in numbers, knowledge, and power. — WILLIAM ALEXANDER, *History of the Colored Race in America*, 1887

THE 1880S MARKED a complete break with antebellum modes of historical discourse. First, the post-Reconstruction period witnessed the intellectual maturation of several constituencies in the African American community. Although ministers, journalists, and educators — representative men and women of the race — assumed responsibility for presenting the race in the most favorable light, as they always had, their level of education and increasing sophistication separated them from their antebellum predecessors. Second, while early postbellum writers, primarily abolitionists, looked to the future by analyzing the past, historical writers of the new period firmly situated their historical discourse in the postbellum period as many of the luminaries of the antebellum and early postbellum period passed from the scene. The years between the publication of Joseph Wilson's *Emancipation: Its Course and Progress* in 1882 and the formation of the Association for the Study of Negro Life and History (ASNLH) in 1915 also witnessed an explosion in the number of what historian Kevin Gaines has termed "uplift" texts. Gaines argues that the catalyst for the rise of uplift texts included external and internal issues and events impacting the black community. Externally, the foreclosure of politics as a viable option for the amelioration of African American grievances occasioned the rise of what Dewey Grantham called a *herrenvolk* democracy, democracy for whites only. By century's end, the institutionalization of segregation in *Plessy v. Ferguson* officially circumscribed African Americans in the public sphere. Internally, African Americans, like any recently enfranchised group, sought to prove their worth in a society convinced of the race's inferiority and inability to adapt to freedom. This internal need promoted adherence to uplift ideology, especially among the middle and upper classes. Finally, African Americans combined the values of the Victorian period—sexual prudery, social and civic pride, and strong belief in the invincibility of the nation-state—with the idea of the race as a nation within a nation.[1]

This chapter views historical representations of African Americans during this period as something more substantial than celebratory and contributionist texts. Here they are the pretext for the rise of a critical African American historical voice. Representation, an idea embodied in what Henry Louis Gates has described as a "reconstruction of the image of the black," is of seminal importance in understanding the historical constructions of African Americans in this era. According to Gates, the intention of black intellectuals was to "restructure the race's image of itself." This reconstructed self, which presented the race in middle- and upper-class terms, was at sharp variance with, and sought to subvert, the social and intellectual stereotypes found in plantation fictions, blackface minstrelsy, vaudeville, pseudoscience, and social Darwinism.[2] Although Gates's construction of the meanings of these histories is essentially correct, race histories served an even larger purpose when viewed with an eye towards disciplinary coherence: they provided the catalyst for the growth and maturation of a more sophisticated historical discourse demarcated and defined by disciplinary boundaries. During the gradual process of the professionalization of African American history, the writings of black intellectuals amplified the importance of the discipline in the public sphere, aided in part by the fact that a number of the writers were affiliated with the nascent black academy. Actively involved in presenting useful information on race achievements for purposes of vindication, involved with mutual aid societies or historical and literary societies, some of which were the precursors of the ASNLH, these contributionist histories were very much part of their early professionalization process. Representation and progress, two dominant ideological and philosophical constructs of the late nineteenth century, are explicit in all of the works under consideration here. These works were the most frequently advertised in the leading African American periodicals of the time, such as the *A.M.E. Church Review*, *Voice of the Negro*, *Colored American*, and *Southern Workman*.[3]

History as Representation and Progress

For African American intellectuals, emancipation, dated either to Lincoln's promulgation of the preliminary Emancipation Proclamation on September 22, 1862, or to December 18, 1865, when the Thirteenth Amendment was ratified, became the starting point for measuring the progress of the race as it emerged from the "dark night of slavery into freedom." Emancipation was the culmination of a long struggle for slavery's abolition, beginning with the advent of the British abolition movement in the eighteenth century. The British, French, and Dutch abolished the slave trade and slavery prior to 1850. And like their international counterparts, African Americans and their allies waged an unrelenting war to end the peculiar institution in the United States. The success of the movement did not, however, lead to the granting of unfettered freedom. As historian Thomas Holt has shown, "slavery defined the outer boundaries of freedom." Freedom's inauguration, however, its inner boundaries—citizenship, including suffrage and civil rights—represented the contested terrain on which this concept rested. While the rights of citizenship were included in the Constitution, the maintenance of these rights proved much more difficult.[4]

Resolving the problematic of freedom occupied the thought and writings of a wide variety of African American intellectuals throughout the post-Reconstruction period. But in that earlier period, they provided only tentative outlines and programs for how the race should adapt to freedom. An acute rise in extralegal means of black proscription, often tethered to pseudoscientific constructions of race, spawned the belief that African Americans could not adapt to the conditions created by freedom and would thus become extinct.[5]

Widespread belief in African Americans' retrogression and degeneracy and its endorsement in the nation's scientific circles added scholarly legitimacy to racist conclusions about the "Negro Question," as both white and black Americans styled the issue in the post-Reconstruction period. According to George Frederickson, as early as 1874, articles began appearing in respectable intellectual journals suggesting the inevitable extinction of African Americans if they continued to press for basic civil and political rights, an issue in most instances equated with challenging the domination of Southern whites. In an atmosphere informed by social Darwinism and its variants—Anglo-Saxonism and Negrophobia—the size of the African American population was believed by some to prove, and by others to disprove, African American retrogression and degeneracy.[6]

By the 1880s, predictions regarding the future of the African American population swung back and forth like a pendulum. The census of 1880 contributed to the controversy by flatly contradicting the doomsayers. Instead of decline, the census showed that the African American population had increased so substantially that whites would have to use drastic measures to subdue it. In 1890, however, the census showed a relative decline in the black population.

Encouraged by these results, Frederick Hoffman, an insurance statistician, published *Race Traits and Tendencies of the American Negro* in 1896. Hoffman's study had the effect of reducing the availability of insurance to African Americans based on the prediction of the impending extinction of the race. Moreover, Hoffman argued that high crime rates among African Americans could be attributed to innate inferiority rather than environmental conditions. Influenced by Hoffman's study and an atmosphere of antipathy toward African American possibility, other studies such as Charles A. Carroll's *The Negro: A Beast* (1900), Joseph Tillinghast's *The Negro in Africa and America* (1902), and R. W. Shufeldt's *The Negro: A Menace to White Civilization* (1907) continued to perpetuate the idea of African American inferiority.[7]

In response both to the externally manufactured atmosphere of racial and cultural repression by white Americans and to the internally imposed interest in uplift and regeneration counseled by middle- and upper-class African American elites, the idea of collective progress, presented through the medium of representation, took hold among African Americans. This approach proved a necessity, given the complex interplay between competing visions of freedom espoused by different segments of the national population. Bourbon planters tended to think in terms of maintaining what little power they had and restoring the vestiges of the plantation system. Freed men and women focused on altering the relationship between themselves and their former masters. And Northern industrial capitalists, along with progressive Southern merchants, fought to make the South more cosmopolitan and promoted the region through aggressive booster campaigns designed to attract capital to their respective cities.[8]

To understand the internal motivations of African Americans they must be balanced against the restrictive atmosphere in which they lived. For instance, one effect of the Redemption of the South, a period described by Rayford Logan as the "nadir" (1877–1908), when African Americans witnessed the total erosion of the rights and guarantees of Reconstruction, was to motivate some African Americans to advocate an uplift philosophy out of the desire to conform to American mores and prove their worth as citizens in a "new nation." "New nation" here refers to the fact that African Americans as well as white Americans constructed themselves as new people in a nation baptized by the fire of the Civil War and the destruction of slavery's scourge on the land. The rise of new social arrangements throughout the nation, but especially in the South, forced a realignment of American society.[9]

Given the fluidity of these new social arrangements, the black middle and upper classes assumed both a paternalistic position in regard to the lower classes and a representative position in regard to white Americans. Their visions of the New South, the location of over 90 percent of the black population prior to 1915, and of the nation attempted to reconcile seemingly irreconcilable visions of black personhood and progress with white supremacy. In their historical writings, African American intellectuals deployed a number of strategies to demonstrate the compatibility of African Americans with the dominant strands of American social and political thought. Most importantly, black intellectuals informed their claims for unfettered citizenship by appealing to the late nineteenth-century ideas of progress, civilization, and the rhetoric of the New South.[10]

Progress, an important component of civilizationist theory, was premised on traditional beliefs in American exceptionalism and providential destiny. Despite increasing interest in other causal factors in historical events, these concepts remained at the heart of the historical enterprise into the early twentieth century. African American intellectuals, caught between contributionism and scientism, viewed progress as the solution to racial discrimination. If African Americans could prove they were a progressive race, it would be impossible to deny them full entry to the body politic.[11]

Civilization was the antithesis of Christian egalitarianism— a belief in the capacity of all human beings, without regard to race. Civilization as a "braided concept," to use Linda Kerber's term, contained, as Gail Bederman explained, components of race, sexual differentiation, and Anglo-Saxon dominance. Fused with concepts of social Darwinism, civilizationists argued, Anglo-Saxon (white American) civilization represented the apex of human achievement. They also believed that Western European societies were more advanced in terms of social, political, and economic structures than primitive or darker societies. Civilization also required socially demarcated spaces for men and women. Men emulated the masculine ideal; they were strong, rugged, and the primary supporters and protectors of women. Women conformed to notions of genteel womanhood; they were soft, feminine, and protectors and nurturers of children. The hegemonic functions of white male dominance precluded access to these traits by groups defined as less developed when compared to advanced white civilizations.[12]

African American intellectuals both supported and challenged the construct of civilization. As Claudia Tate has shown, many African Americans accepted the idea that men and women had prescribed roles. They sought to appropriate traditional notions of manhood and womanhood predicated on

Victorian conceptualizations of this idea and trumpeted the importance of developing civilization. Many, however, simultaneously rejected the idea of African Americans' innate inferiority that relegated them to the peripheries of the nation's promise, while at the same time Euro-Americans were entitled to the benefits of full citizenship. Black intellectuals challenged these ideas by using history to incorporate themselves into the New South paradigm and by appropriating Christian millennialism to argue for the eventual ascension of an infant race to the heights of power and prestige in America.[13] Unlike their use of the jeremiad, Providence, and destiny in the early nineteenth century, blacks no longer needed to look to the fulfillment of racial possibility in the distant and unknown future. Instead, as they began to do in the late antebellum period, they connected themselves in powerful and compelling ways with contemporary politics, national and regional, to make a case for black humanity in a new historical moment framed by freedom and the tangible benefits of citizenship.

Situating African Americans as progressive people required an intense engagement with New South philosophy of modernization, urbanization, and industrialization. Doing so would guarantee, so they believed, unfettered access to the social, political, and economic benefits of the region. Newness, now at the heart of the African American intellectual endeavors and also an integral part of New South rhetoric, symbolized the desire of the region to disconnect itself from the legacy of the antebellum period, in short, to transcend the old by amplifying the new. African Americans appropriated much of the imagery of Southern rebirth. Some advocates of this position even went so far as to suggest that African Americans, as a race, were in their infancy. Rather than reflecting an infantile regression, the inability to negotiate the terrain of black proscription, or a tacit acceptance of inherent inferiority as posited by social Darwinists, advocates of this approach believed it necessary to dislodge or disconnect the current condition of the race from the dehumanizing condition of slavery by treating it as a state of being that was temporary—infancy.[14]

Social Darwinist theory posited the notion that inferior races needed tutelage by stronger and more advanced groups in order to attain civilization. This idea often manifested itself in what, for lack of a better term, was a race-infancy theory in the writings of black intellectuals. This theory played on the notion of rebirth and newness and posited that since the race was in its infancy it needed protection. Like infants, the race required training by those more experienced—older and wiser—in the basic skills of life. The South, the baby's crib, was the site with which the race was most familiar. Advocates of this position counseled patience with the region's barriers to progress—lynching, sharecropping, and black codes—and urged African Americans to remain there, for the South was one of the few places where the race could learn to crawl, coast, and eventually walk. Training, tutelage, and progress figured prominently in developing a race "worthy of emulation." This adherence to civilizationist theory affirmed the importance of African Americans to the creation of a New South and new nation. It also incorporated the race into the dominant constructs of the period, demonstrating that African American elites, like other Southern and Northern counterparts, intended to encourage the development of civilization among the masses. Thus, it is not surprising that many black intellectuals measured the race's progress by the amount of time that had elapsed since Emancipation, almost in the same way one measures the progress of a child since its birth.[15]

The emphasis on progress and newness informed the race's approach to the meanings of slavery in the post-Reconstruction period. Although a great deal of attention has been accorded the argument of Booker T. Washington that the period of slavery taught the race much about freedom and was a necessary precursor to it, many African American intellectuals opposed this position, especially those who were active in the abolitionist struggle. Frances Ellen Harper, Alexander Crummell, Frederick Douglass, and others counseled a complete break with the legacy of the past, separating the memory of slavery from the present strivings of African Americans. In the *A.M.E. Church Review*, one of the most important forums for black intellectuals between 1884 and 1910, Frances Harper chronicled the history of the race but, in doing so, emphatically stated that the future, not the past, should inform racial possibility. She saw in the past "a race who have behind them ages of heathenism, and the inferior civilization of slavery, the deliverance that came through the Civil War and failure and crimes of the Reconstruction." She was quick to add, however, "To some, the aspect may seem gloomy, but if we look beyond the present to the future possibilities of our race, we have no right to despair." Alexander Crummell, in a commencement address at Storer College in Harper's Ferry, West Virginia, more clearly espoused disconnecting the memory of slavery from the realities of freedom.

What I would fain have you guard against is not the memory of slavery, but the constant recollection of it, as the commanding thought of a new people, who should be marching onto the broadest freedom of thought, in a new and glorious present and a still more magnificent future. My desire is that we escape the limit and restraint of both the word and the thought of slavery. As a people we have made an exodus from it. The thought, the routine, the wages and calculations of that old system are dead things; absolutely alien from the conditions in which life presents itself to us in our disenthralled and uplifted state.

Frederick Douglass's remarks, although uncharacteristic of his usual pronouncements on the topic, also urged the race to disconnect itself completely from the history of slavery. He wrote, "Our past was slavery. We cannot recur to it with any sense of complacency or composure. The history of it is a record of stripes, a revelation of agony. It is written in characters of blood. Its breath is a sigh, its voice a groan, and we turn from it with a shudder." Rather than see slavery as the pragmatic school that outfitted the race for freedom, these intellectuals argued that freedom was the school that would inculcate in the race the requisite skills to assume their rightful place among the citizenry of the country.[16]

Belief in progress, civilization, and New South philosophy now shaped the efforts of African American writers to promote the advancement of the race. As Wilson Jeremiah Moses has shown, African Americans were no longer the happy-go-lucky or complacent slaves of the antebellum period (if they ever were). Nor were they the aggressive, murderous brutes or lascivious wenches depicted in postbellum lore. Instead they were a new people, in the New South and the new nation, intent upon developing their civilization. These concepts were prominent in the emancipation narratives.

Race Histories, Emancipation Narratives

Race histories, overviews of black history from Africa through the late nineteenth century, proliferated during the post-Reconstruction period. These histories, which might more appropriately be called emancipation narratives, a modification of literary historian William Andrews's term for autobiographical accounts written by African American leaders in the postbellum period, played an important role in fueling the black history movement. While the appeal of these texts emanated from their representative function and use, without fail, emancipation narratives (including race textbooks and biographical catalogs, which I shall discuss shortly) adhered to late nineteenth-century conceptions of history as progress and civilization. In the nineteenth century, history functioned as an important component of the liberal arts and provided a record of the progress of races and the lives of prominent men and women. In addition to these themes, works produced by African Americans combined contributionist functions with the tutelary and exhortatory functions required by uplift philosophy. By combining these functions in the historical narrative, African American intellectuals produced a voluminous record of black achievement in the years following emancipation to diminish the ability of whites to portray black people as a retrogressive race.[17]

Joseph Wilson's *Emancipation: Its Course and Progress*, published in 1882, was one work that attempted to represent the meaning of the post-Reconstruction period. Wilson, former slave, Civil War veteran, and author of *The Voice of a New Race*, a collection of poetry, and *Twenty-two Years of Freedom*, also published in 1882, demonstrated an intense interest in the meanings of freedom. *Emancipation: Its Course and Progress*, published by the Normal School Steam Print Press of Hampton Institute in Hampton, Virginia, provided a "codification of the several acts by which the institution of slavery, peonage, vassalage and serfdom, or what other name may be used to signify oppression has been abolished in the several countries of the civilized world." His choice of words—"peonage, vassalage and serfdom"—all evocative of feudalism and early modern forms of social organization, demonstrated the extent to which he (and many of his contemporaries) viewed slavery as the by-product of an uncivilized world.[18]

The work's central premise is freedom, interpreted here not only to mean the abolition of slavery but the dawn of new possibilities for the race.[19] For Wilson, as was the case with many of his contemporaries, emancipation had no tangible meaning if African Americans could not demonstrate progress as a result of its occurrence. Civilizationism, the idea that there are defined indicators of progress and advancement, served as the vehicle for the articulation of these concepts. For Wilson, freedom was not only contained in the act of emancipation, but resided in the tangible documents and instruments of government used to effect this process. Wilson reviewed the progress of the race from the passage of the Thirteenth Amendment to 1875. He portrayed African Americans as "eagerly drinking draughts from the once forbidden well of knowledge," improving their home life, strengthening morals, building churches, and engaging in other activities that were indisputable evidence of their advancing. He believed "the social problems of the Negro" were being alleviated when, for example, churches condemned the casual practice of men taking more than one wife. Wilson also noted the gradual increase in the number of African Americans entering the professions. Blacks studying to become lawyers, doctors, ministers, and teachers faced less competition from other blacks, compared to white graduates, who were obviously more numerous. Wilson urged black graduates to take advantage of the newly created opportunities to advance the race. Apparently not convinced that the South was completely new, but certain of the importance of the role of African Americans in its postwar rebuilding, Wilson wrote, "The newer South must owe her obligation for the advanced position occupied today, not only to the influx of Northern capital, but to the brawny arms from which the shackles of slavery so recently dropped."[20]

One of the cleverest ways to demonstrate black progress was through the new scientific method of measuring social phenomena. George Washington Williams, one of Wilson's contemporaries, devoted an extensive portion of *History of the Negro Race* (1883) to the period of life after emancipation in which his illustration of African American progress took the form of various graphs, charts, and tables. One such table titled "Comparative Statistics of Education at the South" contrasted the white and black school populations. Although the table showed the disparity in funding for black schools, Williams nonetheless stressed that his statistics "exhibit the wonderful progress the Colored people of the South have made during the brief period of their freedom in the department of education." Other charts addressed the proliferation of African American educational institutions, population changes since 1770, and black investment in savings in the first five years after emancipation.[21] William Henry Crogman, in an 1884 lecture before the National Teacher's Association in Madison, Wisconsin, similarly used statistics to prove the race's progress since emancipation. "The colored people have nearly 1,000,000 children in school; publish over 80 newspapers; furnish nearly 16,000 schoolteachers." He also pointed out the 68,000 acres of land owned by blacks in Georgia alone, and the 5 million acres owned by the race in the South. Demonstrating the race's progress since emancipation, the statistical data challenged the myth of black inferiority and further buttressed blacks' claims of adaptation to freedom.[22]

Claims of progress did not preclude the need for continuing uplift and tutelage. As William Alexander rightly characterized the former slaves, "Between four and five millions of people suddenly thrown upon the world, ignorant, poor, and without a foot of land to stand upon," they were people who would obviously need help. Compounding their problems, former slaveholders, embittered because of the loss of their assets (slaves), did little to help. And Northerners, who might mean well, had "little conception" of the freed people's "nature and needs." Alexander praised the North's *noblesse oblige* in sending missionaries to educate blacks. Some Northerners, whom he labeled "enthusiasts," encouraged agitation for political rights. He believed these pursuits distracted the race from more important goals, such as establishing an economic base as taxpaying citizens and instead promoted an irresponsible doctrine of acquisition of goods and services based on entitlement rather than hard work and perseverance. Alexander's *History of the Colored Race*, published in 1887, less than four years after the Supreme Court declared the Civil Rights Act of 1875 unconstitutional, demonstrated the tenuous nature of political and legal enactments. As T. Thomas Fortune also made clear in *Black and White* (1881), a focus on politics rather than political economy caused the race irreparable harm. Civilizationists argued for a more concerted emphasis on internal racial development, especially economic development, to offset the most pernicious effects of racism.[23]

One aspect of black writers' internalist approach to racial advancement related to the issue of migration. Many Southern newspapers of the era depicted the North, a region thought by some migrants to be a safe and supportive haven, as a place filled with vice, corruption, and poverty. And Alexander applauded African Americans who resisted the temptation to abandon rural areas and settle in cities. But the advocates of civilizationism and adherents to New South philosophy did not slavishly adhere to an antimigration agenda. Alexander realized that if African American leadership advocated that the race remain in the South, those who stayed must be guaranteed a fair and equal opportunity to prosper. This meant the curtailment of the discriminatory land leasing and credit systems, which reduced many sharecroppers to a condition reminiscent of slavery. Only through the elimination of unfair economic conditions would the South rather than North be the nineteenth-century Canaan. In the meanwhile, however, "tillers of the soil," the Southern maxim suggested, "eventually became proprietors of the soil." In keeping with the maxim, Alexander argued that farming was not a lowly and undistinguished occupation; it offered a variety of social and even political benefits. Moreover, farming helped to make men—"men of broad views and deep intellects, men capable of thinking for themselves, men of such stuff as our Statesmen and Presidents are made of."[24]

Although classically trained elites as a group have largely been neglected by today's historians of uplift philosophy, these particular scholars were as interested in the phenomenon as the civilizationists. William Henry Crogman functioned as one its the most visible promoters among postbellum black elites. Born on the Leeward Island of St. Martin, Crogman was a member of Atlanta University's first graduating class and later a member of its board of trustees, a professor of Latin and Greek, and later president of Clark College, an activist in the Methodist Episcopal Church, and chief commissioner of the Georgia Exhibition at the 1895 Atlanta Exposition. Edward Park, a minister and member of the Gammon Theological Seminary faculty, summed up Crogman's commitment to the race: "Professor Crogman has been a living teacher in no mere technical or narrow sense. In his class instruction, he has aimed to lead his pupils not only to accuracy of technical scholarship, but to culture, to true and broader ideas of life and to character. In his more public educational work, he has aimed to promote the welfare and advancement of his own people and of all peoples."[25]

Crogman compiled sixteen lectures that he delivered between 1884 and 1893 into a volume titled *Talks for the Times* (1896). The original lectures, given at events ranging from dedications of various sorts to emancipation celebrations, reflect interests in the uplift of the broader African American community and the concept of progress. Compared to his previously noted presentation on black education, these essays were not as confident; they were more defensive. In his 1884 speech, cited earlier, Crogman used statistics to show racial progress in an attempt to appeal to the better classes of whites, the white intelligentsia, whom he believed would counsel fair treatment for the race. By the next decade, he seemed less certain and ultimately counted on God—Providence.[26]

In the "Thirty-second Anniversary of the Emancipation Proclamation," delivered at the 1894 commencement exercises of Clafin College in Orangeburg, South Carolina, Crogman premiered some of his historical interest on progress as he meditated on the meanings of emancipation. For Crogman, an appreciation of history was closely connected to the race's attainment of civilization. Noting the importance of chronicling historical events in ancient civilizations, he urged African Americans to adopt this custom, "for only thoughtful and intelligent men have been accustomed to attach vital importance to historic events, and set them up as a silent monitor to the generations passing by." Crogman's reliance on Providence in this text did not necessarily reflect a lack of sophistication, as Dorothy Ross argued was the case for George Bancroft's and Henry Adams's investment in Providence as a causal explanation of historical events, which in her opinion delayed the adoption of the scientism and objectivity of the Rankean approach to historical studies until the late nineteenth and early twentieth centuries. Just as professional and amateur historians worked at the same time in Euro-American history, scientism and contributionism coexisted until the mid-1920s among African American historians. In any case, Crogman linked his belief in Providence and millennialism to the acquisition of an unfettered citizenship. Using language that would appeal to reformists in both the white and black communities, he proclaimed, "Beyond Lundy and

Garrison and Philips and Sumner and Lincoln, beyond federal armies and federal enactments, stands in the background of our history the awful form of almighty God." It was God, not humankind, argued Crogman, who "for four years, riding on the storm cloud of war, flashing from the cannon's mouth, whizzing in the rifle's bullet, roaring on the battle's din, with a strong hand and an outstretched arm, brought us out into a purer atmosphere, a larger liberty and the enjoyment of blessings innumerable." If God was an operative force in history, especially African American history, then freedom was ordained by Him.[27]

If God ordained freedom, it naturally followed that Crogman could use the prospect of divine intervention to deflate the position of those who advocated African American emigration. Along with diverse groups of whites, African Americans of all stripes, ranging from Southern sharecropper Pap Singleton to A.M.E. Church bishop Henry McNeal Turner, saw emigration as a reasonable response to the increased rigidity of the color line.[28] Crogman's consideration of the emigration question hinged on his belief in liberalism and individual rights. As if he doubted that an appeal to Providence would convince secular Southerners of the futility of emigration, he equated the support for emigration with a tacit acceptance of disunion: "The best that can be said for this proposition is, that it is entirely foreign to the genius and spirit of the American government. The interests of the people of this country must ever be common. Slavery once divided them, and was swept away. The American people will never again allow any wall to be erected on the continent around any particular people or particular institution. Henceforth, the union will be maintained in its integrity." Invoking disunion, the catalyst for the Civil War, would set off alarm signals in the minds of the region's progressive merchant class, which was increasingly dependent on Northern capital, and former bourbon planters, who needed a tractable work force. Race leaders argued that African American efforts could be more profitably expended by maintaining and expanding the guarantees of citizenship in the United States rather than by focusing on acquiring these rights elsewhere.[29]

Crogman also understood other ramifications of emigration in this late nineteenth-century social and political atmosphere in which social Darwinism and ideas about Anglo-Saxon superiority proliferated. Crogman believed that advocating emigration was a tacit acceptance of white superiority. In light of the rapid expansion of the United States and the defeat of the last remnants of Indian resistance at Wounded Knee in 1890, African Americans needed to demonstrate their fitness for incorporation into American society. Even though many believed that American Indian society was in decline and being pushed aside by the modernizing influences of Euro-American culture, it was unthinkable to Crogman that Euro-Americans had a monopoly on manhood and modernity. If they did, African Americans, some would say, in the nascent stages of civilization, could never attain the heights of civilization. Emigration, then, in the final analysis, forestalled the possibility of actual competition between the races by removing African Americans from the contest, which was anathema to Crogman, invested as he was in demonstrating the ability of African Americans to compete in American society. Competing, rather than fleeing, resonated in the rhetoric of many who opposed emigration and certainly was inferred in the public pronouncements of Alexander Crummell, Frances Ellen Harper, and Frederick Douglass.[30]

Crogman's most popular work, *Progress of the Race; or, The Remarkable Advancement of the Afro-American Negro*, appeared in numerous editions between 1897 and 1925. Coauthored with John Gibson and Henry F. Kletzing, also an advocate of civilization through racial advancement, the volume contained an introduction by Booker T. Washington, the principal of Tuskegee Institute, whose *Up from Slavery*, is perhaps the quintessential example of the progressive uplift emancipation narrative. Washington's remarks revealed the importance of historians, of history generally, and of both to his own project of industrial civilizationism. On the one hand, the historian had an obligation to provide an objective reconstruction of the past: "His work must be the result of careful thinking and an astonishing amount of finesse and diplomacy." But Washington made it clear that history also had a contributionist component. "The Negro historian," Washington wrote, "must be able to prophesize [*sic*] and foresee the days to come. The eyes of the prophet must discern whether this leads upward or downward."[31] In each of the many editions of Crogman's text, the scientific and contributionist methods of history cohabitated. In addition to contributionist information on Africa, slavery, and black participation in the nation's war, Crogman devoted the majority of each text to the racial progress since emancipation. He included chapters that measured in quantifiable terms the achievements of black women, industry, financial growth, educational advancements, and cultural achievements. And at end of the book, Crogman included a section titled "Statistics of the Colored Race," an exhaustive listing of statistical data on all facets of the black population drawn from the Census of 1890.[32]

Emancipation narratives served as an important component of historical writing. Rather than simple linear and chronological accounts of race progress, they reflected the ideological terrain African Americans were forced to negotiate. Not surprisingly, all of these works staked out positions on the dominant racial questions of the day. Many modified aspects of the social Darwinist and New South philosophies to make a place for African Americans within them. In doing so, African Americans used history to not only present a progressive story, but one which they played an active role in molding.

Race Textbooks

Black intellectuals writing race histories between 1890 and 1915 consciously viewed their historical production in relationship to its larger applicability and usability in the wider community. Since many members of the black elite were associated with higher education in some ways, it is not surprising that race history, presented in the form of primers or textbooks for primary, secondary, and collegiate institutions, became popular means of heightening interest in historical writing. History told the story of civilization and served as a "signboard" containing social, cultural, and intellectual lessons for future generations. The instructive nature of history discourse here mirrored the pedagogical goals of teachers.[33]

Race textbooks, more than any other form of race history, served as the base for the superstructure of more sophisticated presentations of African American history. Daniel Barclay Williams's *Freedom and Progress* (1890), Edward Johnson's *School History of the Negro Race* (1892, 1899), Lelia Amos Pendleton's *Narrative of the Negro* (1908), and John Cromwell's *The Negro in American History* (1914) became regular textbooks for students in the nascent black academy. Organized explicitly around the concept of providing knowledge for future generations, and framed in simplistic ways to elicit understanding and interest, these immensely popular textbooks, produced also for general audiences, provided the first detailed exposure to history for many African Americans.[34]

Daniel Barclay Williams, although an obscure figure today, played an important role in the movement to promote black history textbooks. A graduate of Brown University, Williams worked in a number of capacities as an educator in the mid-1880s. He was a teacher in the public schools of Henrico County, Virginia, and briefly as an administrator in the Moore Street Industrial School in Richmond, Virginia. Williams also opened a private school which provided classes in ancient and classical languages. In 1887, he was elected to a professorship of ancient languages and an instructor in methods of teaching and school management at Virginia Normal and Collegiate Institute in Petersburg, Virginia. In this capacity, Williams authored *The Negro Race: A Pioneer in Civilization* (1883), *The Theory of Reverend John Jasper Concerning the Sun* (1884), *Science, Art and Methods of Teaching* (1887), and *Freedom and Progress* (1890). In these works Williams expounded on his beliefs in African American civilization, Americanism, and New South ideology.[35]

Williams's *Freedom and Progress* began with the race's condition in slavery in order to facilitate a better understanding of the progress of the race since the Emancipation. Like Joseph Wilson before him, Williams pointed to the sundering of domestic bonds, the tenuous nature of the marital union, and the lack of access to religious expression under slavery as major problems. Freedom altered these conditions, facilitating the preservation of domestic bonds, the restoration of the sanctity of marriage, and unfettered access to religious worship, often in churches controlled exclusively by African Americans. But Williams believed literature played an important role in the intellectual life of African Americans, demonstrating the race's possibility and adding "to the material, intellectual, and moral elevation of our race." Exposure to literature and developing a love of great authors and books served as the base of Williams's program of knowledge acquisition and production. "Good books," in Williams's estimation, gave the race a collective sense of its progress since the end of slavery.[36]

As a classicist, Williams was no doubt familiar with the Western conceptions of history. Located at the center of civilization in the biblical and classical periods, literature, a corpus of scholarly material, whether religious or secular, bequeathed a powerful legacy to future civilizations. But Africa was largely excluded from the well-known Hegelian construct of history at the time. Africa, according to Hegel, was part of the "Unhistorical, Undeveloped spirit." The aspersion of "unhistorical" caused alarm and outrage among African American elites.[37] Demonstrating movement and an engagement with history, especially a corpus of scholarly production, in an atmosphere which depicted the ancestral home of African Americans as uncivilized, took on added importance. Williams applauded the sizable race literature produced by African Americans since emancipation. Authors, primarily men, including William Wells Brown, William Still, Peter Clarke, Frederick Douglass, John Mercer Langston, George Washington Williams, Joseph Wilson, and T. Thomas Fortune, Williams believed, brought credit to the race. Alluding to the idea of race infancy, but clearly demonstrating growth and development, Williams asked, "What nation or race of mankind can point to a literature, so elegant, so profound, produced in the brief period of twenty-five years? None."[38]

Other components of Williams's civilizationist program also emerged in his text. Although very much a classicist, like many of his contemporaries he embraced industrialism. "Intelligence, Industry, Education and Morality," were the "sources and conservators of civilization," wrote Williams. Industrial education strengthened these qualities by promoting the ideas of self-help and the desire for higher education. He also believed that it served as a bulwark against crime. This reconciliation of the classical and industrial forms of education endeared Williams to Southern educators. Classical knowledge was necessary in promoting civilization, but industrial knowledge fueled the pragmatic needs of the race, building dignity and character.[39]

Edward Johnson's *School History of the Negro Race*, published one year after the Williams text, also reflected concerns with civilization and manhood. In the preface to his work, Johnson, a former slave, teacher, lawyer, historian, businessman, and politician, argued the importance of school children's studying the history of the race. Johnson gave "noble deeds" and "valor" special emphasis. "I have often felt that the children of the race ought to study some work that would give them a little information on the many brave deeds and noble characters of their own race," Johnson wrote. "It must, indeed, be a stimulus to any people to be able to refer to their ancestors as distinguished in deeds of valor, and peculiarly so to the colored people." He related different portrayals of African Americans to true and false history. True history, in Johnson's work, recorded the patriotism and valor of black soldiers in the nation's wars and the faithfulness of the black population to American values, and it offered an impartial assessment of African Americans' experience. False history emphasized the inferiority of African Americans, omitted the contributions of African Americans to the nation, and was biased and uncritical in its presentation.[40] Johnson sought to correct the omissions of false history by encouraging teachers "to teach from the truth of history that complexions do not govern patriotism, valor and sterling integrity." He also emphasized capitalizing the word "Negro." "It deserves to be enlarged," wrote Johnson, "and will help, perhaps, to magnify the race it stands for in the minds of those who see it." Johnson devoted his text to acts of heroism and valor within the African American population. He discussed black participation in the nation's wars, antislavery rebellions, and agitation, the African American role in Reconstruction, and the race's progress since freedom. In the 1911 edition, Johnson published the work with his popular *History of the Negro Solider in the Spanish American War*, a further testament to the history's heroic focus.[41]

Although most of those who produced race textbooks were classically trained and affiliated with the university, there were important historical traditions simultaneously operating outside of the nascent black academy that supported the growth of the academy. As archivists and historians Elinor Des Verney Sinnette, W. Paul Coates, and Tony Martin have shown, a loosely connected set of historical and literary societies and a closely connected set of authors and bibliophiles made important contributions to this enterprise. In addition to the Washington-based societies such as the Bethel Literary and Historical Society and the Mu-So-Lit Club, several influential societies existed in Philadelphia and New York. With the formation of the Afro-American Historical Society of Philadelphia in 1897, the black bibliophile tradition was born. Bibliophiles such as William Carl Bolivar, Robert Mara Adger, and Leon Gardiner collected important pamphlets, books, and articles related to the African American tradition. Each of these men also published significant bibliographies. In New York City, this tradition flourished through the work of the Negro Society for Historical Research led by Arturo Alonso Schomburg, a Puerto Rican bibliophile, and John Bruce, a journalist. Schomburg not only collected rare artifacts but was instrumental in promoting the inclusion of African American history in the curriculum of secondary schools and colleges.[42]

It was in this tradition of collection and preservation that John Cromwell produced *The Negro in American History*. Cromwell's interest in joining the academic to the communal was not serendipitous. He had spent most of his adult life living the example. A lawyer, historian, and newspaper editor, Cromwell was born a slave in Portsmouth, Virginia, and earned a law degree from Howard University in 1874. He secured an appointment in the Treasury Department and later became the first African American to argue a case before the Interstate Commerce Commission. Cromwell was also active in uplift work in various parts of the black community. He founded the Virginia Educational Organization, an advocacy group for black teachers in Virginia, and a newspaper, the *People's Advocate* (1876). During the 1890s, in Washington, D.C., he cofounded with A.M.E. Church bishop Daniel Payne the Bethel Literary and Historical Association, a showcase for black intellectual concerns, and became an active member of the American Negro Academy (1897), a group of African American men and one woman, Anna Julia Cooper, founded by Alexander Crummell, the Cambridge-educated Episcopalian minister and classical scholar. The academy sought to promote scholarship, educate youth, establish an archive to document the work of black authors, and foster increased intellectual production by black scholars. In short, it promoted a more enlightened African American in the public sphere.[43]

Many of the prominent bibliophiles active in the Negro history movement—Schomburg, Adger, and Daniel Murray, assistant librarian at the Library of Congress—were all contributors to Cromwell's book. He wrote the
book in response to a formal survey by a Mrs. Dykes, a former instructor at
Leland Stanford Jr. University (Stanford University) and a summer instructor
at Hampton Institute. Dykes surveyed more than six hundred black schoolchildren and found that the overwhelming majority of these students felt they
would never achieve wealth or become famous. Dykes concluded that these
low aspirations resulted from the Southern educational system which placed
little or no emphasis on the contributions of African Americans to American
society. Cromwell concluded that Dykes's formal survey affirmed his informal
sense of the needs of black schoolchildren: "This necessity [to teach race his-
tory] formally set forth by Mrs. Dykes, confirmed by my own experience in the
classroom covering twenty years, leads me to attempt the publication of a book
which shall give to teachers and secondary pupils especially the salient points in
the history of the American Negro, the story of their most eminent men and
a bibliography that will guide those desirous of making further study."[44]

With these guidelines in mind, Cromwell's work anticipated the more
scholarly contributionist work of the Woodson School, inaugurated just one
year after the publication of Cromwell's study. Cromwell's focus was on the
most recognizable aspects of black history, eminent personalities. Less than a
third of the book is devoted to the antebellum period. He did not spend an
inordinate amount of time justifying African American existence or discussing slavery or colonization. Cromwell covered slave insurrections, but only
briefly. He did, however, devote significant attention to the early convention
movement, which he viewed as the practical training ground for future African
American politicians. The demonstration of political interest, a characteristic
decried by industrial civilizationists as premature for a race in its infancy, justified some of Cromwell's affiliations. In 1865, Cromwell opened a school in
Portsmouth, Virginia, but his teaching career was cut short when he was shot
and his school was burned to the ground. After briefly returning to Philadelphia, Cromwell, who recognized the futility of educational initiatives without
political enfranchisement, embarked on a political career, during which he
served as a delegate to the first Republican convention in Richmond, Virginia,
in 1867.[45]

In Cromwell's book, the postbellum period provided the backdrop for an
extensive introduction to representative men and women from the antebellum
and postbellum periods—individuals such as Sojourner Truth, Henry Highland

Garnet, Frederick Douglass, Fanny Jackson Coppin, Henry Ossawa Turner, Booker T. Washington, and Edward Wilmot Blyden. His book also contained a number of modern features, including an appendix with information on several important antebellum phenomena such as the *Amistad* slave mutiny and the Underground Railroad as well as postbellum institutions like the Freedmen's Bureau and Bank. The book also featured a bibliography and a chronology of the black experience.[46]

Race textbooks, like emancipation narratives, offered a means to integrate black history into the embryonic black academy. Although lay and amateur historians wrote many of these books, their interest in history was closely connected to the burgeoning "Negro history" movement which found outlets in literary and historical societies, black colleges and universities, and numerous black churches around the country. History required a number of creative outlets in the black community and in the wider social, political, and economic spheres of the nation. In order to train race conscious leaders, it was necessary to instill pride and hope, but more important, to provide detailed and reliable ways to disseminate history. The race textbook offered a more reliable way of accomplishing these goals because of its close connection with the black academy.

Collective Biographies

The concept of representativeness was most prominent in the biographical catalogs and race uplift manuals. Although recent scholars have characterized these works as showy, gaudy, and miscellaneous catalogs of racial achievement, they also provided tangible meanings within the black community. In direct contradistinction to the images of black depravity rampant in popular and scholarly magazines of the day, African Americans in their collective biographies presented themselves as refined, bourgeois, and cultured. Some of the representations included stately portraits of African Americans dressed in the formal styles of the late nineteenth century. They included a large number of ministers, teachers, doctors, and lawyers from Northern and Southern cities that were considered to be meccas of African American achievement. Rather than a mimicking or accommodationist act, representation was an attempt to empower by presenting powerful views of racial possibility.[47]

The late nineteenth century saw the production of many biographical catalogs. Closely connected to biographical genres and perhaps the antebellum romantic concept of representative men and women, biographical catalogs functioned as sites for the edification of the race. Often compiled by a single author, they included pictures of eminent African American men and women and featured lengthy reprints of articles, speeches, and various commentaries designed to provide guidance or instruction for the race. Obviously, this form of representation stood in stark contrast to mainstream portrayals of African Americans as degenerate buffoons who were unable to manifest the higher virtues of civilization.[48]

One of the largest biographical catalogs published during this period was William J. Simmons's *Men of Mark*, a volume of more than one thousand pages. With the exception of Frank Lincoln Mather's *Who's Who of the Colored Race* (1915), this work is the most comprehensive biographical catalog published during this period. Simmons's position as a minister, educator, and journalist allowed him entree to diverse constituencies. And partly as a result of his connections, his book garnered more attention than other race catalogs published during this period.[49]

William Simmons (1849–90) was born a slave in Charleston, South Carolina. He served in the Union Army, and following the war, he studied at Colgate and Rochester Universities in upstate New York. He completed his undergraduate and graduate training at Howard University in 1881, and in 1883 he received the D.D. degree from Wilberforce University. Afterwards, he assumed the leadership of the Normal and Theological Institute in Louisville, Kentucky. His able management and leadership transformed the institution into the State University of Kentucky at Louisville.[50]

Simmons's *Men of Mark*, which he dedicated to African American women, began with an introduction by Henry McNeal Turner, a controversial A.M.E. bishop and ardent nationalist who structured the civilizationist approach of the study. The last part of the framing is the text itself.[51] Turner's introduction fulfilled his reputation. Simmons choice of Turner (rather than a white patron) to write the introduction was meant to eliminate the common criticism that works like this were imitative: few whites would have held up Turner as a role model for other black people. Turner castigated black scholars who after distinguishing themselves forgot "the rock from whence they were hewn, and waste their time in endeavoring to be white, or expend it in worshipping white Gods." Simmons, according to Turner, should be compared to "Herodotus, Josephus, Pliny and Plutarch and other historians enshrined in the gratitude of the world," because he was a true race man, upholding the highest ideals of the race. Simmons, of course, did not fit the negative caricature that Turner had just laid out, nor did the men in his biographical catalog. And so Turner's remark reads like a criticism of other, unnamed, persons, while also suggesting to readers paths they should or should not follow.[52]

At the center of Turner's discussion was a millennial aspect of civilization coupled with a belief in the manhood of the race. In Turner's estimation, future members of the race, the true beneficiaries of the current work of race leaders, would bring racial deliverance, ascension, and triumph. He couched his millennial visions in classical, national, and racial imagery:

> [From the] Negro giants now sleeping in the womb of the future will
> come forth an Armada that will defy the powers of the earth, trample
> color prejudice in the dust, write glory, honor and immortality itself upon
> the brow of the black; frown thunders at race distinctions, fire the citadels
> of manhood discrimination and burn them to the ground; hurl defiance
> in the face of defamers and condemnators, and with pens of lightning
> write up the history of our ancestry and present them before earth and
> heaven as no one now ever dream[t].[53]

Turner's millennial and national imagery challenged "the abominable heresies set adrift by pseudo-philosophers, and other figureheads as ignorant as they are mean and low, that the Negro race was naturally inferior and nothing great could ever be evolved from them."[54]

Despite the various modes of civilizationist evidence, black leaders such as Turner were deeply ambivalent about the possibilities of the race in the postbellum period. This ambivalence and endorsement of the civilizationist projects at times left leaders no choice but to embrace doctrines of Anglo-Saxon superiority to advance their own race claims. Turner, for example, presented the relationship between the three "races" in curious terms. In comparing the ability of these races to master the continent, he wrote, the "Indian is old, decayed and worn out." Native American inability to resist the onslaught of white settlement in the West meant that they had lost their manhood and were thus destined to disappear from the world stage. Reflecting contemporary notions of Anglo-Saxon superiority, "The whites," according to Turner, were "in the prime of life and vigor." Turner's moving from that position to one arguing that African Americans were equal to whites, appears, on the surface, to be incongruous. His belief in civilizationist discourse ought to have rendered this option meritless. To resolve this quandary, he enlisted race infancy and cyclical theories of history. "The Negro is a boy, a mere apprentice learning his trade," wrote Turner. "When the white race reaches decrepitude, as races are periodical as well as worlds, the Negro will have reached his own genius and industry to manufacture more and lift him to higher civilization, and he will stand out as the wonder of the world." The elaborate invocation of civilizationist theories and ideologies of manhood was a perfect preface for Simmons's book.[55]

The text chronicled the achievements of African American men, like Simmons, who had negotiated the contested terrain of slavery and emerged victorious. The overwhelming majority of these sketches were postbellum figures and part of an educated elite of clergymen (36 percent of 172) and academics (11.6 percent of the total), the embodiment of Simmons's ideal of social and intellectual responsibility in uplifting the race. In many ways, Simmons's text, which also included politicians, lawyers, artists, and others, is an extension of his own story, an attempt to make his life and the lives of those he chronicled what Henry Louis Gates has termed the "mean and norm" of the race. Citing a woeful state of ignorance among "that class of rising men and women" regarding the accomplishments of the race, Simmons hoped his book would end up in the hands of young people to inspire them to lofty pursuits.[56]

The attainment of lofty goals required reconciling the current possibilities of the race with its previous condition of slavery. Cognizant of the role slavery played in the dehumanization of the race, which Simmons termed "a sum of human villainies," he maintained that slavery did not crush out "the life and manhood of the race." Rather, he argued, the race's deep sense of spirituality sustained it throughout slavery. Portraying the race as degraded but God-fearing was another means of interjecting providential designs into black history. African Americans, Simmons maintained, waited patiently until God "broke their chains." But the idea of the faithful and contented slave was only half true. The more important point was African Americans possessed great patience and fortitude and were thinking and rational beings. Black people had built churches and schools and had educated ministers and children. Simmons wanted these examples "snatched from obscurity to become household matter for conversation."[57]

Like other forms of historical production in the nineteenth century, Simmons's biographical catalog uses representation as the dominant mode for disseminating acceptable and appropriate images of the race to the larger population. These images contained both literal and figurative power. Their literal power emanated from the fact that they served as both present and past examples of the race's achievement. The individual lives reflected examples of the values and beliefs that had sustained African Americans during slavery and propelled them forward in the postbellum period. Their figurative power emanated from their almost supernatural or metaphysical representativeness;

that is to say, their connection with the national and millennial imagery which their lives and associations represented. These images were more than gaudy displays of ostentation, but represented the racial—black—potential.

DEEPLY EMBEDDED IN THE social, political and intellectual realities of the period, black elites used historical writing not only to provide a heroic portrait of a race moving from slavery to manhood and womanhood, but more important, to reflect upon and engage the most pressing issues of their day. These issues included violence and social repression, black degeneracy, social Darwinism, and intellectual lampooning of black ability. Like the antilynching movement, the women's club movement, or the rise of educational institutions in the aftermath of the Civil War, the writing of historical texts served as a major intellectual landmark in the struggle to define the mean and the norm of the race. Moreover, their writing represented the beginnings of a scholarly discourse informed by the discursive strategies of representation and progress.

Rather than uncritical or unsophisticated texts of black achievement wholly unrelated to the social realties of the time, race histories, textbooks, and collective biographies embodied the complex realities faced by a rising race. At the center of these texts lies a critical engagement with the changing internal and external realities faced by African Americans. The shifting realities of African American life included the transition from slavery to freedom, attempts to stave off the worst manifestations of social Darwinism, and the need to present the race in a progressive manner. All of these concerns played an important role in the production of race literature. While heroic, these publications used history in a tutelary manner to teach the race what it needed to know in order to negotiate the often hostile terrain of freedom.

Women of Mark: African American Women and Historical Writing

Like their male counterparts, African American women played a central role in historical production throughout the late nineteenth and early twentieth centuries. Deeply committed and actively engaged in the creation of a black public sphere that accentuated the private sphere, as the black club women's movement and the founding of the National Association of Colored Women (NACW) shows, African American women continued to use the "power of the pen" to actively shape the race's and the broader public's understanding of them. Much more than representatives of what clubwomen defined as "the women's era," as they have regularly been cast, black women challenged certain aspects of uplift philosophy while also engaging in what literary historian Claudia Tate describes as "revising the patriarchal texts."[58]

As one might expect, these women were speakers as often as (perhaps more often than) they were (published) writers. But interest in them as speakers (curiosities, perhaps), and sometimes real interest in what they had to say, regularly resulted in their speeches being printed. With the exception of the women's consistent and aggressive challenge to contemporary gender norms, their production was hardly different from that of the men of their time: representation and progress were important parts of their discourse. They were especially productive in the area of collective biographies; in short and long form, they also produced their share of race histories or emancipation narratives, and, like the men, they all were profoundly concerned with uplift, or civilization. Speaking before the Brooklyn Literary Union, early in 1892, S. Elizabeth Frazier offered a direct response to the masculine focus of William Simmons's *Men of Mark* in her address, "Some Afro-American Women of Mark." Frazier began her remarks by somewhat sarcastically pointing out, "We have heard and read much of Men of Mark of our race, but comparatively little is known of able Afro-American women."[59] At the center of her effort was an attempt to wrest the historical discussion of black progress and representation from the purview of patriarchal authority. And her speech, which included comments on the achievements of Phillis Wheatley, Frances E. W. Harper, Fannie Jackson Coppin, and others, succeeded in that regard. But two of Frazier's better-known contemporaries, Gertrude Mossell and Pauline Hopkins, met the challenge, many would argue, more profoundly.

Gertrude (N. F.) Mossell understood the importance of history and its role in racial advancement. Married and the mother of two children, she devoted much of her life to encouraging women to transcend the domestic sphere. Claudia Tate has shown that Mossell was not an opponent of domesticity. Instead, she wanted women to combine domestic duties with public sphere work. Although she was involved in various uplift activities until her death in 1948, Mossell's *Work of Afro-American Women*, published in 1894, combined the representative portrayal of middle-class and upper-class African Americans with a well-developed philosophy of history.[60]

Mossell made no attempt to appeal to subtlety or high-minded intellectualism. Literature, especially history, she argued, was closely connected to race, race pride, and advancement. An opening quote summarizes her position: "The value of any published work, especially if historical in character, must be largely inspirational; this fact grows out of the truth that race instinct, race experience lies behind it, national feeling, or race pride always having for its development a basis of self-respect." She was also clear about the implications of emancipation for black women. Quite simply, emancipation inaugurated the "women's century," especially the expansion of the suffrage and temperance movements. The increased opportunities provided by these movements created unique opportunities for women of the race whose lives her book chronicled.[61] Although Mossell's effort to catalog their achievements was not as grandiose as Simmons's effort on behalf of the men, her portrait is ultimately more holistic. She does not, for example, seem to privilege the members of one profession over any other. Among the teachers, journalists, physicians, and attorneys was the little-known, at the time, career of Deborah Gannett, who served in the Revolutionary War under the name of Robert Shertliffe.[62]

Mossell viewed the accomplishments of her women as an important component of the intellectual history of the race, a history she deemed "always of value in determining the past and future" of the race. Harboring many of the ambivalent feelings toward Africa common among African Americans of her period, she regarded the African "condition of life and climate [as] not conducive to intellectual development." But she divided the history of African Americans into three epochs: the slave trade and early arrival in the Americas, the period of slavery, and the era of freedom.[63] The past, in Mossell's construction, provided useful hints for racial possibility. And, for Mossell, the writers of race literature were the true historians of the race.[64]

In order to understand what the race was doing, Mossell argued, it was necessary to examine the literary and historical production of the race. "Yes, this race is making history, making literature," she wrote. "He who would know the Afro-American of this present day must read the books written by this people to know what message they bear to the race and to the nation." With this in mind, she included an extensive list of literary and historical works by David Walker, Robert Benjamin Lewis, Martin Delany, William Wells Brown, William Still, and none other than William Simmons.[65]

While Mossell's collective biography inclined toward a philosophical engagement with history, the need for a more faithful account of the race undoubtedly inspired Pauline Hopkins (1859–1930), coeditor of the *Colored American* magazine, to skillfully combine her literary and historical interests to delve into the issue of race relations. Perhaps better known for her fictional work — *Hagar's Daughters: A Story of Southern Caste Prejudice*; *Winona: A Tale of Negro Life in the South and Southwest*; and *Of One Blood; or, The Hidden Self* —Hopkins also produced a significant corpus of nonfiction, among which were the "Famous

Negro Men" and "Famous Negro Women" series in the *Colored American* in 1901 *Women*
and 1902. Although the stated objective of the series was to acquaint members of the race with history and biography, many intellectuals have argued
that her real intention was to present a new history. This history would draw
upon the antebellum and postbellum contexts of racial agitation to discuss
the potential of the race in the present and future. Hazel Carby writes that at
the center of Hopkins's historical writing were attempts to revive the activity
of New England antislavery societies, a deep belief in the efficacy and importance of New England radicalism, and the belief that African Americans, not
Euro-Americans, were the guardians of New England's abolitionist legacy.[66]
Rhetorician C. K. Dorieski describes Hopkins's intellectual affiliations in terms
of "inherited rhetoric and authentic history." Dorieski argues that Hopkins
worked to reconstruct the New England regional tradition of biography as
a spiritual or ideological rendering of extraordinary lives. But, in fact, Hopkins made exemplary lives of the past (representative men and women) part of
the "present tense" in order to dramatize narratives of "imperiled citizenship."
As Dorieski points out, Hopkins framed her male subjects as great individual
men whose deeds were representative of the greater possibilities of the race.
However, she framed the women differently, in clusters and groups, I believe,
because of the women's *collective* (rather than individual) contributions to the
black community.[67]

The best example of the collective portraits is that of the club women. Biographical details of the lives of the individual leaders and most of the women
were readily available, but rather than simple celebratory history, this interesting group sketch traced the origins of the club movement from the formation
of the *Women's Era Club* in Boston in 1873 through the founding of the National
Association of Colored Women in 1895 focusing on the struggle of black wom-
en's clubs for legitimacy and particularly the conflict over the race question at
the Sixth Biennial of the General Federation of Women's Clubs in Los Angeles
in 1902. The controversy, as it had at the organization's meeting in Milwaukee,
Wisconsin, in 1900, focused on admission of the Women's Era Club, a black
women's club founded by Josephine Pierre Ruffin, to the general federation.
Rebuffed in Milwaukee, Ruffin carried the fight on to Los Angeles. And even
though her efforts there received the hearty support of Kate Lyon Brown, a
white Massachusetts delegate who blamed the general federation for capitulat-
ing to the Southern federation and castigated the Massachusetts delegation for
their initial role in rebuffing the black women, this was not the final battle in
the protracted war between white and black women's clubs. Hopkins viewed

Brown's protest as representative of the spirit of equality that permeated New England, but the battle for representation, rather than the individuals, and the connecting of the present to the past, remained center stage in this sketch.[68]

"Famous Negro Men," however, did focus on individuals. Toussaint L'Ouverture, Frederick Douglass, William Wells Brown, Blanche Kelso Bruce, and Booker T. Washington, obvious choices, were among them. But Hopkins also included biographical sketches of Robert Browne Elliott, Lewis Hayden, William Carney, and others, less well known. Dorieski argues that Toussaint L'Ouverture, Douglass, and Washington provided the larger cultural matrix of Hopkins's study. But for significant reasons, Booker T. Washington does not clearly serve as part of the cultural matrix that Dorieski proposes. Ambivalence rather than certainty characterized Hopkins's sketch of him from the outset. In the first paragraph of the sketch, Hopkins pointed out, "The subject of this sketch is probably the most talked of Afro-American in the civilized world today, and the influence of his words and acts on the future history of the Negro race will be carefully scrutinized by future generations. When the happenings of the twentieth century have become matters of history, Dr. Washington's motives will be open to as many constructions and discussions as those of Napoleon today, or of any other men of extraordinary ability, who whether for good or evil, have extraordinary careers."[69] Hopkins, in effect, deflated Washington's importance also by comparing him to Napoleon, the bête noire of the African-American antislavery community for his role in attempting to reinstate slavery in Haiti. At the very least, she viewed Washington as a problematic figure. Like Napoleon, Washington came to power in the aftermath of a revolution. Napoleon pursued a reckless course of territorial acquisition, eventually crowned himself emperor, was defeated at Waterloo in 1815 and forced into exile. Thus, from Hopkins's vantage point, Washington's success was not guaranteed. Although he had garnered accolades from white industrialists and segments of the black community, his final legacy was yet to be determined. The final gesture towards distancing Washington from the pantheon of (other) great men was the placement of his sketch. The biographical sketches of Toussaint L'Ouverture, Douglass, and Brown appeared at the beginning of the series, between November 1900 and January 1901. The Washington sketch did not appear until October 1901.[70]

There was no ambivalence in Hopkins's sketches of Toussaint, Douglass, and Brown. Their sketches were central to demonstrating African American capacity for "intelligence, integrity, the capability of receiving culture and becoming useful members of society." The deeds of Toussaint in Haiti spoke to the race's ability to assume its civic duties. And of course Frederick Douglass was the representative man of the nineteenth century. From his providential birth to the inauguration of the *North Star* (1848), before which Hopkins suggested "the race had no literature," he stood as an example of the future possibilities of the race. Hopkins concluded that William Wells Brown needed no eulogy. By offering no eulogy, there would be no closure to Brown's life, and his deeds would live on in perpetuity. Hopkins concluded her sketches of these men by reminding the race to use them as examples for racial advancement: "It is well for us of this generation, removed thirty-seven years from the maelstrom of slavery . . . it is well for us to ponder the history of these self-made men of our race and mark the progress they have made with nothing but the husks of living to stimulate the soul thirsting for the springs of knowledge."[71]

Hopkins's volume included diverse other individuals. She portrayed Lewis Hayden, an antebellum legislator in Boston, as slave rescuer and financial supporter of John Brown's raid on Harpers Ferry. Charles Lenox Remond, despite never being formally recognized as an outstanding antislavery speaker in the United States, was important for having taken his antislavery message abroad and winning acclaim. Black political figures, such as John Mercer Langston, Blanche K. Bruce, and Robert Browne Elliott, who held important positions ranging from college president and dean of a law school to county sheriff, state legislator, minister to Haiti, and U.S. senator, represented the role African Americans played in shaping postbellum American history. Hopkins presented them as politically astute actors, currently making race history.[72] And in a final shot at Booker T. Washington, Hopkins praised Robert Browne Elliott's political ability and used him as an example of the heights African Americans could attain "if the desire for [their] industrial development does not blind his eyes to other advantages in life."[73]

Concomitant to the importance of African Americans taking a leading role in their own regeneration was demonstrating the manly qualities necessary to accomplish this task. By Hopkins's account, it was black participation that made the difference in the Civil War. Before African Americans joined the war effort, Hopkins opined, sorrow "sat enthroned in every household at the North. Despair stalked abroad." Even the government was "trembling on the edge of abyss, order fled, terror reigned." Given the trauma of the war's uncertainty, African Americans entered the fray and restored Northern confidence. The noble sacrifices of William Carney, who received four wounds while holding the Union flag aloft during the Battle of Fort Wagner after the color-sergeant was mortally wounded, redeemed the honor of the race and New England. As similar as Hopkins's narrative was to George Washington Williams's *History of the Negro Troops in the Rebellion* (1887) and Joseph Wilson's *Black Phalanx* (1890), both of which praised the heroic and manly qualities of African Americans that enabled them to make tangible contributions to the war effort, Hopkins's appropriation of manliness had additional meanings for the race. Manliness was an essential quality in shaping the race's destiny.[74]

Although she devoted the largest portion of her sketches to black women educators, Hopkins anchored her discussions of individual women with two notable antebellum figures: Sojourner Truth and Harriet Tubman. Both women represented the past condition of the race, and by extension, the former condition of black women. But they provided important examples for present and future race leaders: their heroism, public persona, and ascetic lifestyles meshed well with the civilizationist discourse of the post-Reconstruction period. Hopkins believed it was important that the race "not forget the rock from which they were hewn nor the pit from which they were digged [*sic*]." These women represented both the rock—fortitude, strength, and courage—and the pit—slavery, degradation, and bondage—which characterized the history of the race. The representative qualities of Sojourner Truth's and Harriet Tubman's struggle against the peculiar institution looking backward and forward, paved a path for subsequent progressive women of the race.[75]

Altogether, Hopkins used her sketches of black men and women to revive the spirit of New England abolitionism in order to inspire her contemporary readers. Because of her implicitly political agenda and belief in the regeneration of the race, Booker T. Washington received no pass here. While Hopkins herself did not judge his activities, she made clear that the jury was still out, and only history would tell. It was a brave position to take.

Black female intellectuals' production of race textbooks was equally sophisticated. Although Fanny Jackson Coppin's pedagogical guidebook for teachers, *Reminiscences of a School Life*, has traditionally received the most scholarly attention, Lelia Amos Pendleton's *Narrative of the Negro* preceded its publication by six years. Pendleton, active in Progressive era projects of municipal reform, was founder of the Alpha City Club (1898) and the Social Purity League (1907). While her text provided considerable information on Africa and the diaspora, Pendleton's work also focused on presenting a progressive portrait of African Americans, replete with millennial imagery. An important image in her book was "the light," as Pendleton termed it. "The light" represented enlightenment and progress, and it grew brighter in every century until it reached its apex in the mid- to late nineteenth century.[76]

Pendleton did not define progress exclusively through the literal assertion of manhood. Representations of women were critical to the execution of her study. Many writers of textbooks and emancipation narratives either excluded women altogether or relegated them to the domestic periphery—as developers of civilization through rearing and educating their children.[77] Pendleton's chapters, the "Dawning Light," which chronicled the achievements of African Americans in the latter half of the eighteenth century, and "Frederick Douglass and Other Notables," an extension of her chapter on African American history in the first half of the nineteenth century, challenged the limited ideas of women's representation contained in the masculinized presentations of her contemporaries. In the "Dawning Light," the chapter's frontispiece is Phillis Wheatley, the distinguished poetess whom Pendleton considered an outstanding example of the maturity of African American literature. In "Frederick Douglass and Other Notables," the image of Douglass provides the chapter's frontispiece, but the personalities Pendleton considered representative were all female: Sojourner Truth, Harriet Tubman, and Frances Harper comprised the "other notables."[78]

Anna Julia Cooper's *A Voice from the South by a Black Woman of the South* was not nearly as subtle in its presentation of women. Although not exclusively a work of history, Cooper's work bore all the hallmarks of almost a century of scholarly production, with even better results. In this race textbook, progress and regeneration were features of the volume's first chapter. And the themes of civilization and uplift traverse the whole volume. The book argued for higher education for women. It also presented a stunning reversal of traditional antiquarian portraits of Native Americans. Cooper also proffered solutions to the so-called race problem. Combining all the old tropes, biblical imagery, ancient and modern literature, old and new science, deep classical allusions, patriotism and citizenship, with direct challenges to widely hailed, contemporary mainstream literature (and writers) of the day, *Voice from the South* stood, head and shoulders, above *all the* other work of the period, whether by males or females.

Besides what might have been simple native intelligence, some of Cooper's accomplishment can be attributed to her education. Cooper graduated from St. Augustine's Normal School and Collegiate Institute in the mid-1870s. About five years later, she entered Oberlin College for the B.A. degree, completing it in 1884, and in 1887 she completed the M.A. degree there. Cooper attended both schools at a time when the proscribed course was classical, and ancient texts and languages were very much a part of the curriculum. But she continued to study, first at Columbia University and later at the University of Paris, and in 1925 she earned a doctorate from the Sorbonne. Her *Voice from the South*, published in 1892, was Cooper's only book and the most potent and trenchant set of observations on the condition of Southern women in the post-Reconstruction period. Although, as already noted, it treated a wide variety of issues, Cooper's historical observations are most evident in the essay "Womanhood: A Vital Element in the Progress and Regeneration of the Race."[79]

"Womanhood," first presented in 1886 before a group of male Episcopal clergy and later reprinted in *Voice from the South*, provided an overview of women's treatment throughout human history and a blueprint for the uplift of women and the race. Deeply committed to civilizationist ideas and the belief in the efficacy of Victorian moralism and Western progress, Cooper's "Womanhood" posited a reductionist binary between oriental and Western civilizations. Eastern societies (her examples were China and Saudi Arabia) were regressive partly because of the place of women in them. In these countries, Cooper contended, women have "been uniformly devoted to a life of ignorance, infamy, and complete stagnation." Linking cultural practices to nationality, she criticized the nomadic quality of these societies and the devotion of men to the harem. As Gail Bederman has shown, Victorian masculinity could only be expressed within the context of the marriage, and extramarital or adulterous or engagement in commercial sex was viewed as a sign of moral weakness. Cooper concluded that concubinage in some "oriental" societies rendered these civilizations "effete and immobile." The West, in Cooper's essay, was "fresh and vigorous," and synonymous with all "that is progressive, elevating, and inspiring." Cooper also attributed the West's superiority to Christianity. It was not, however, a xenophobic attribution. Instead, Christianity, which encouraged equal treatment of all without regard to race, color, or sex, and feudalism, which promoted chivalry and respect for the place of women in society, grounded her promotion of Western culture as the race's example of civilization.[80]

Another important strategy in Cooper's writing was to encode her strong appeals for feminist discourses of power in the passive language of pure womanhood common in the late nineteenth century. This approach to racial advancement was two-pronged. First, Cooper believed that black women deserved the same venerated status as white women. And, second, like other civilizationists, Cooper believed black women needed to demonstrate the best qualities of the Victorian ideal. To reorient the common, and often negative, perceptions of African American women, Cooper sought what literary historian Edith Alexander describes as an active incorporation of a female voice into a male-dominated discourse on racial advancement.[81] Describing herself in the title of the book as a female voice from the South not only authorized Cooper's presentation by implying special or unique knowledge of both Southern conditions and of the women themselves, but positioning herself as an authority fulfilled her role as a civilizationist elite and gave her model of regeneration more potency. Regeneration, embodied in contemporary concepts of the New Woman, New Negro Woman, and New South, meant lifting black women from the state of degradation imposed during slavery to the high plane of respectability and civilization. Achieving this goal required an appreciation of the historical development of Western civilization on the womanhood question, an amplification of the needs and concerns of black women, and the linkage of black women's regeneration to the advancement of the race.[82]

Cooper included her now famous line, "when and where I enter . . . the whole race enters with me." If, by inference, the women were the race and the race could only be measured by the civilization of its women, women's advancement, argued Cooper, should be foremost on the racial advancement agenda. It was illogical in her estimation "for black men to quote statistics showing the Negro's bank account and rent rolls, to point to the hundreds of newspapers edited by colored men and lists of lawyers, doctors and professors, D.D.'s, LL.D.'s, while the source from which the lifeblood of the race is to flow is subject to taint and corruption in the enemies' camp." Rendering assistance to women required an appreciation of the condition of women in the South on the part of enlightened Northerners and Southerners. It also meant bringing to bear upon the situation of black women, especially in rural areas, the full power of representative institutions—the home, press, and most importantly, the church.[83]

The church, whose leadership was dominated by men, was both a bastion of culture and civilization and an influential forum for the discussion of racial advancement. Cooper's talk with Episcopal clergy simultaneously articulated a woman's viewpoint on the race issue, critiqued the masculine bias in uplift philosophy, and demonstrated her affinity with Victorian ideals. Cooper suggested that the Episcopal Church (a church she deemed more suited to the task of promoting civilization than the African Methodist Episcopal and Baptist churches) needed to play a more aggressive role in proselytizing throughout the South. To Cooper, it was unthinkable that the Methodist and Baptist churches would be in the forefront of directing religious life when most Northern clergy felt the Episcopal Church was better suited to the task.

But the Episcopal Church, Cooper opined, had done little to attract African American congregants. Rather, they were content to believe African Americans were too unsophisticated to adhere to the church's doxology. The same belief in racial proclivities characterized the church's position on attracting black ministers. In response to the church's failure, Cooper pointed out that African American clergy were not taken seriously in the church. Rather than being used to proselytize among Southern blacks, they were used as "manikins" and "machines," as figureheads and compliant followers. Moreover, at recent conferences of Episcopal clergy on promoting the welfare and advancement of African Americans in the church, the denomination failed to invite African American race leaders or clergy to address the group. For Cooper these meetings were little more than "remedial contrivances," were "purely theoretical," and demonstrated that the whole machinery of the church was "devoid of soul." To invest the machinery, the inner workings of the church, with soul, Cooper suggested a more humanistic approach to recruiting black congregants and clergy: active involvement in African American communities, sympathy and love, not mere abstractions, and as the congregationists had done throughout the South, schools, which would connect the church to youths.[84]

Cooper's major concern, however, was the training of women. Like her contemporary and fellow Episcopalian, Dr. Alexander Crummell, Cooper argued that the church should provide more training for women, citing Crummell's "The Black Woman of the South: Her Neglects and Her Needs," an address delivered before the Freedmen's Aid Society of the Methodist Episcopal Church in Ocean Grove, New Jersey, in 1883. Crummell, a consummate civilizationist, had argued that because of the history of enslavement, African American women were in need of protection and civilization. Rather than detailing the condition of African American women as Crummell did, however, Cooper pointed out that the Episcopal clergy was responsible for some of these circumstances, and she prescribed remedies, ranging from the creation of sisterhoods, which Crummell had proposed, to tutelage for poor girls by the middle and upper classes.[85]

The idea of regeneration permeated Cooper's speeches throughout the 1890s. One year following the publication of *Voice from the South*, in response to a lengthy address by Fannie Barrier Williams, prominent clubwoman and protégé of Booker T. Washington, Cooper chronicled the struggle for advancement among African American women in reminding the audience that the "fruits of civilization" could not be developed in the short space of thirty years, but "requires the long and painful growth of generations."[86] In 1902, she spoke before the General Society of Friends in Asbury, New Jersey, where she grounded her discourse in the historical circumstances of the post-Reconstruction period, which she correctly labeled as a time of "trial and bondage." She lamented the fact that the nation seemed intent on subjugating African Americans despite their contributions to the nation's progress in slavery and their loss of citizenship functions during the postbellum period. Despite a social atmosphere that she characterized as a "saturnalia of blood and savagery," Cooper hoped the nation would acknowledge its ethical obligations to the "Negro's uplift and amelioration."[87] She constantly evoked the historical record of African American progress and loyalty through the rhetorics of nation, patriotism, and character to reduce the distance between them and the benefits of American citizenship.[88]

Cooper was uncharacteristically conservative on the labor question, one of the most volatile issues in late nineteenth- and early twentieth-century American history. Still, she connected her ideas to historical circumstances and ethics.[89] An increase of immigrants from eastern and southern Europe, coupled with the rise of more radical options for societal reform promoted by anarchists, socialists, and communists, caused great concern among Progressive era reformers. African Americans, long considered a menace to American society, were often lumped together with immigrants as undesirable elements. Cooper's goal, then, was simply to use history to disassociate African Americans from immigrants. She hoped to demonstrate conclusively that immigrants and African Americans embraced different historical experiences and were subject to different historical influences.[90] "The Negro," proclaimed Cooper, "is the most stable and reliable factor today in American industry. Patient and docile as a laborer, conservative, law-abiding, totally ignorant of the anarchistic, socialistic radicalism and nihilism of other lands," she explained further, in an attempt to shift American perceptions of African Americans from something of a beast to a loyal, capable, and reliable citizen. She assured her white counterparts that "no dynamite plots are hatching amongst us, no vengeful uprising brewing." Rather, Cooper argued, Americans must recognize the fact that African Americans were part and parcel of the American republic and treat them as such. America's greatness, Cooper believed, should be predicated on more than "her expanse of territory, her gilded domes, and her paving stones of silver dollars," but on the nation's moral and ethical foundations.[91]

African American history in the post-Reconstruction period laid the groundwork for professionalization of the discipline. Rather than a conglomeration of lay historians and amateurs devoted only to contributionist and celebratory history, the postbellum writers produced a variety of historical representations—the emancipation narrative, race textbook, and collective biography. Many of these individuals such as Daniel Barclay Williams, John Cromwell, Lelia Amos Pendleton, William Henry Crogman, and Anna Julia Cooper were connected either to the nascent black academy, primary and secondary schools, or the fledgling Negro history movement. They were also likely to be associated with a plethora of historical and literary societies, including the Bethel Literary and Historical Association and the American Negro Academy. The works produced by these individuals served as the first models for more specialized historical production by better-trained historians in the early twentieth century. However, the historical productions of the preprofessional historians continued to coexist with the more professionalized production until the early 1920s.

The historical production of black intellectuals in this period was less objective than subsequent studies. This was undoubtedly related to the fact that these individuals linked the production of race literature to racial vindication. The partisan or subjective tone of this work would automatically relegate it to an inferior or substandard status when juxtaposed with subsequent work. But many of these writers consciously used their historical work to address concerns of importance to the black community such as the quest for progress and civilization, the development of the New South, a new Negro, and a new Woman. Historical production, then, for many of the individuals under discussion was not simply a matter of producing an objective and disinterested study, but an active affirmation of the success and failures of the race coupled with an attempt to change its present and impact its future.

Rather than a simplistic or linear drive toward professionalization, black historical writing throughout the nineteenth century continued to embody the aspirations of a people that understood the importance of giving their own faithful account of the race. Appropriating the recognizable forms of the nineteenth-century writing, namely the emancipation narrative, collective biography (biographical catalog), and race textbook, these writers refashioned the complex narratives of black life. In a moment framed by tales of black degeneracy and possible extinction, black writers used history to tell and shape an alternative textual record of racial possibility. Rather than degenerate, blacks in these narratives appeared as able contributors to their own and the nation's wellbeing, especially as citizens and soldiers. Furthermore, the story of the race since emancipation was not one of failure and inability to cope with the momentous change wrought by freedom, but adaptation, adjustment, and careful and critical negotiation of the myriad obstacles faced by what black writers termed "a rapidly rising race." Rather than a race on the verge of extinction, the narratives produced by black historical writers demonstrated, using the increasingly popular social science language of the day, the acquisition of property, the growing number of high school and college educated blacks, and the rapid formation of educational and religious institutions that facilitated their movement from chattel to respectable men and women "advancing in numbers, knowledge and power." The struggle to build educational institutions to serve, as literary and historical societies did in the colonial era and early republic, as sites of intellectual engagement for expanding historical knowledge in the late nineteenth and early twentieth centuries was their next logical step.

CHAPTER 6

To Smite the Rock of Knowledge

The Black Academy and the Professionalization of History

> Bear my congratulations to the brother race that has now been led out of Egypt and now finds the rock of knowledge smitten for them. It shall flow in full abundance for every thirsty soul. —HENRY WARREN *to* PRESIDENT THIRKIELD *of* G\AMMON THEOLOGICAL SEMINARY, December 10, 1888

BY THE TURN OF THE TWENTIETH CENTURY, two important efforts began to come together to allow an important shift in the production and promotion of African American history. First, black intellectuals of all stripes had over the previous century produced volumes of black history. Recalling the presence of black people in the Bible and ancient history, their contributions not only to all the nation's wars beginning with the American Revolution, but to the national economy, to independence movements in America and abroad, and to the general life of the country, the writers of history had established a published record of black participation. Second, black institutions of higher education, by now more than a generation old, not only began employing black scholars but producing them. The intersection of these two conditions created prime circumstances for establishing a national organization of scholars interested in the study of the African American experience. The creation of that organization signaled the completion of a process culminating in true professional status for African American history. Indeed, Henry Warren's appropriation of the biblical metaphor of smiting (striking) the rock of knowledge had come to fruition.

Anna Julia Cooper's *A Voice from the South*, published in the 1890s, symbolizes an important part of the shift from race studies written primarily by lay people, those who earned their living in other ways, as ministers, attorneys, laborers, and business people, or who relied on their spouse's income, to those written by professional scholars (including Crogman, Williams, Cromwell, Simmons, and others) who made their living as academics. In this gradual post–Civil War transfer of historical authority from avocational and lay historians to professional historians, historical organizations began to replace literary societies as the sites for presentations and public debates about history, and colleges and universities replaced churches and clubs as institutional homes for the history of African Americans. Although it was a fairly small, loosely connected group of avocational and amateur historians in the first portion of the period under examination here (beginning about 1900), they had, by 1915, the year of the founding of the Association for the Study of Negro Life and History, become a much better-defined professional group. That process cannot be separated from developments within the nascent black academy.

In order to chart the trajectory of professionalization, it is necessary to understand the respective visions of avocational and professional historians in the late nineteenth and early twentieth centuries. As John Higham has shown, avocational and professional historians viewed the historical enterprise in different ways. Avocational historians stressed independence; they believed that historical work should be judged on its individual merits; they possessed no collective identity; they worked for personal satisfaction; and most had little or no appreciation of technique. On the other hand, professional historians stressed the coordination of individual efforts; they emphasized interdependence among historians; they promoted authority; and they sought to consolidate their professional efforts around established historical societies and the university.[1]

The formation of the American Historical Association (AHA) in 1884 led to a tenuous alliance between avocational and professional historians in the mainstream. Ambivalent about the professional role of the organization and unresolved differences within it, Henry Baxter Adams, the AHA's first secretary and a patrician historian, began to devote much of his time to shoring up the weak alliance between the amateurs (who at first were the majority of the members) and the professionals. He hoped that the national organization would decrease tensions between these groups and secure the patronage of the federal government. By the mid-1890s, it became increasingly clear that the avocational vision of the profession, which included government patronage, was incompatible with the professional vision, which favored a relationship less dependent on the public sphere than on the emergent disciplinary structures located within the university.[2]

By 1895, tensions between the lay and professional historians reached such a pitch that George Burton Adams of Yale University, William A. Dunning of Columbia University, and Albert Bushnell Hart of Harvard University took decisive action to set the new organization on a course towards professionalization. They inaugurated the *American Historical Review*, a scholarly journal devoted to publishing historical research. James Franklin Jameson, a professor of history at Brown University and later director of the Carnegie Institute in Washington, D.C., became managing editor. With trained historians in the driver's seat, the field began to move aggressively toward professionalization. In short order, lay historians no longer dominated in the published work. With the rise of viable graduate history programs, the number of American students who made the annual pilgrimage to German graduate schools to study history also began to decline. And professionalization culminated in two seminal events in 1907: the formation of the Mississippi Valley Historical Association (precursor of the Organization of American Historians) which was, according to John Higham, a product of history's popularity among regional constituencies, and the installation of Jameson as the first president of the AHA. Jameson was not a German-trained scholar but rather graduated from Johns Hopkins University in 1882.[3]

The twentieth century furthered the process of specialization among American historians. This trend took the form of a wider range of course offerings in American rather than European history, and it clearly defined the parameters of historical inquiry; professional programs promoted the concept of scientism, the application of the exacting standards of the natural sciences to historical work. Two schools of thought developed on the increasing importance of scientism, or objectivity, in history. One school argued that history, like any other science, contained certain generalizations or laws akin to those in the natural sciences, like biology. A more extreme component of this belief was that history, if it was truly to be considered scientific, must be, first and foremost, a search for truth.[4]

By 1915, although the total membership of the AHA remained below four thousand, history was a thriving discipline. Changes in cataloging, book acquisition, and lending policies at the Library of Congress, which became an increasingly important site for research and writing, contributed to the process of professionalization. Moreover, many leading universities in the Northeast and Midwest significantly augmented their research libraries, allowing an increase in scholarly production by historians on faculty. The augmentation of research libraries led to the growth of university presses, beginning with the founding of Yale University Press in 1908, and the proliferation of specialized journals in subspecialties of American history.[5]

For black intellectuals, the course of professionalization was somewhat different. Although this process also involved postsecondary educational institutions, unlike their white counterparts, in the black institutions, by and large, the administration and faculty were dominated by clerics (most likely, white clerics) and missionaries and, in some instances, classically trained elites who were slow to incorporate the social sciences into the curriculum. Only a few of these institutions had adequate resources for the systematic study and promotion of African American history. And compounding these problems was the small number of African Americans with doctorates. Between 1875 and 1914, only fourteen African Americans received doctoral degrees in all of the social sciences; only three—W. E. B. Du Bois, Carter G. Woodson, and Richard Wright Jr.—held doctoral degrees in history prior to 1915. Until the turn of the century, history teachers in the black academy still tended to be white ministers and schoolteachers from New England or black graduates of prestigious Northern institutions with master's degrees.[6] Around 1900, black schools began to undergo a shift from the avocational practitioners of history of the previous generations to more professionally trained historians. Despite awareness of the importance of scientism and objectivity, black scholars and schools continued, for a time, to emphasize the contributionist and missionary aspects of black history. But the visibility and scholarly production of individuals such as Du Bois, Woodson, Wright, and Benjamin Brawley at that time was distinctly different from the avocational work of the earlier black intellectuals.

The clearest indication of change in the production of black history occurred in 1915 when Carter G. Woodson, the second African American to graduate from Harvard with a doctoral degree in history, founded the Association for the Study of Negro Life and History (ASNLH). Specialization and the formation of (black) academic presses would also begin in 1916 with the creation of Associated Publishers and the *Journal of Negro History*. Bereft of and sometimes excluded from white organizations (through lack of invitation rather than formal prohibition), black scholars continued to operate in conjunction with the plethora of antiquarian and contributionist literary and historical societies discussed in previous chapters. Individually, however, and within various institutional spaces, black historians published more scholarly work, offered a greater diversity of courses, and developed new repositories and collections, all of which demonstrated the importance of history within the black academic community and furthered the process of professsionalization.[7]

To make sense of the shift in historical production and the meanings of professionalization among African American scholars and within the black community, this chapter focuses on developments within the black academy, especially the different types of schools: classically oriented schools such as Howard and Atlanta Universities; missionary and clerical training grounds such as Clark and Morris Brown Colleges and Gammon Theological Seminary; and industrial and normal (that is, teacher training) schools such as Hampton and Tuskegee. Located in both urban and rural communities and reflecting different educational missions, these schools epitomized the contested trajectory of African American education during the period. Examining the role of history within these institutions sheds light on its importance to the development of the discipline in the diversity of the black academy.

Professionalization in classically oriented colleges and industrial schools was similar to the patterns in mainstream majority institutions, which served as the models for some of the black institutions and the training grounds for the majority of their faculty. There are, however, discernible differences in the processes that took place between the different types of schools under consideration here, and, perhaps more important, the three types of schools also promoted the use of history differently. Ironically, as James Anderson has shown in regards to their missions, and as this chapter will show, both Hampton and Tuskegee had significant avocational historical traditions, while the classical colleges did not institute historical courses until some years later.[8]

History and the Classical Colleges

In the late nineteenth century, few institutions, white or African American, had departments of history. Virginia Union, a leading school, founded in 1865 as Wayland Seminary, offered only four history courses between 1906 and 1915: Constitutional History of the United States, Modern Europe, Modern Era (1453–1900), and Biblical History. The structure of the history curriculum at Virginia Union differed little from other colleges and universities of its type. In the late nineteenth century, history had not completely emerged from the thicket of other classical disciplines. Most telling at Virginia Union, faculty who taught history could also be found teaching Latin or science. At Howard University, for example, Reverend Charles H. A. Bulkey, a white Presbyterian minister (pastor of the Fifteenth Street Presbyterian Church) and an early member of the AHA, also taught a variety of subjects, beginning in 1882, and served as the university's librarian. In 1889, his title became "Professor of English Literature, History, Rhetoric and Logic, and Elocution." Bulkey's successor, William Victor Tunnell, held the title "Professor of History and Literature, Logic, Rhetoric, and Elocution."[9]

The influence of higher education strongly grounded in classical forms began to wane in the 1890s. As classicism gave way to the scientism and objectivity of the late nineteenth and early twentieth centuries, discipline-based departments began to gain an identity of their own.[10] By 1905, a new crop of historians trained in the social sciences emerged and redirected the focus of the department at Howard. During Tunnell's absence from the college department, Charles Chaveau Cook, who held undergraduate and graduate degrees in literature from Cornell University, filled the position of chair of English Literature, History, Rhetoric, Logic, and Elocution and began to move the department in a progressive direction. Between 1892 and his untimely death in 1910, Cook introduced the first courses devoted exclusively to history: The History of Continental Europe from the Eighth to the Middle of the Eighteenth Century, and English History. During his tenure at Howard, Cook traveled abroad, studying at the universities of Heidelberg in Germany, Edinburgh in Scotland, and Oxford in England. He was an active member of the American Negro Academy and is best known for his occasional paper, "A Comparative Study of the Negro Problem" (1899), an assessment of English, Japanese, and American civilization designed to determine how these nations evolved from primarily agricultural societies to industrial powers. Several years later, in 1905, Cook participated in a symposium titled "The Negro and the Elective Franchise" in which he delivered a paper titled, "The Penning of the Negro," which discussed the systematic disenfranchisement of blacks in the South. Although Cook's death left a void in the maturation of historical studies at Howard, his work signaled the end of the classical era there.[11]

William Tunnell, who reassumed his duties as professor of history in 1906, became the leading light in Howard's history department after Cook's death in 1910. In addition to establishing a seminar titled "History of the Reconstruction Period," he also established a lecture series in 1911. The first speaker, John W. Cromwell, gave an address titled "Some Rich but Unworked Veins of Negro History," which emphasized the achievements of African Americans in the military, in secret societies, and in the black church. He also urged students to engage in collecting primary information on the Civil War and Reconstruction.[12] There were other important changes underway in the composition of Howard's faculty that also helped to effect the move away from a strictly classical/liberal curriculum focused on math, science, and the history and literature of classical antiquity.[13]

Scientifically trained historians had begun to take a more active role on Howard's faculty. This was one of the many changes that were directly related to the rise of graduate programs at leading institutions in the late nineteenth and early twentieth centuries. Whereas Tunnell and Cook trained under the classical curriculum, younger faculty members like Walter Dyson and Charles Wesley received advanced degrees in history. Dyson, who became an instructor at Howard in 1905, graduated from Fisk and Yale. In 1911, he studied history under Dana C. Munro at the University of Pennsylvania, and in 1913 completed an M.A. in history at the University of Chicago. The following academic year, he pursued additional studies in economics and history at Columbia University. In 1916, he became one of three associate editors of the *Journal of Negro History*. Charles Wesley was also a graduate of Fisk University. He pursued advanced study in economics and history at Yale and received an M.A. in 1913. Recruited to Howard's faculty by Dean Lewis Moore of the Teachers College, Wesley took an appointment as an instructor of history and modern languages, teaching courses in pedagogy and history. Wesley completed an important doctoral dissertation at Harvard University in 1927 titled "Negro Labor in the United States." And he also became an active force in the Association for the Study of Negro Life and History.[14]

The presence of these scholars undoubtedly strengthened the reputation of the Howard University Department of History, but the growing reputation also resulted from the administrative foresight of the university's officers, particularly Jesse Moorland, an alumnus and trustee, and Kelly Miller, dean of the College of Arts and Sciences. Through their influence, by 1915, Howard became a key repository for materials related to the study of African American history. The university had not only acquired the papers of the famous antislavery advocate Lewis Tappan, the "Catchart Clippings" of materials related to black participation in the Civil War and Reconstruction, but a sizable cache of manuscripts and other rare materials from Jesse Moorland (international secretary of the Young Men's Christian Association) helped to form the foundation of a major archive in black history on the campus, not far from the nation's most important archive, the Library of Congress. The university also pledged to establish a chair of sociology who would be responsible for "research in the field of Negro development, as well as to practical remedial endeavor."[15]

This pattern of developing a comprehensive set of courses in history and a research center for African American history was duplicated at other institutions, each in its own way. Atlanta University, from its 1869 inception, was a proponent of classical liberal education, and the university's first three presidents, Edmund Asa Ware (1869–85), Horace Bumstead (1888–1907), and Edmund Trichell Ware (1907–19), laid the groundwork for Atlanta's prominent classical curriculum. But Bumstead's interest in social problems and history, an extension of his belief in liberal education, resulted in his appointing John D.

Hincks as professor of history and social science. Hincks's administrative duties left him little time to promote historical studies, but in 1897, Bumstead, who also inaugurated the Atlanta University conferences, hired W. E. B. Du Bois as professor of economics and history. With his scholarly credentials already established by the publication of his doctoral dissertation, *Suppression of the African Slave Trade*, which became the first volume of the Harvard Historical Series, and his social study of African Americans in Philadelphia's Seventh Ward, *The Philadelphia Negro* (1898), Du Bois became the director of the Atlanta University Conferences, which focused on the African American experience in America. The Atlanta conferences, like most academic institutions at the time, blended history, economics, and sociology. In fact, history and sociology were housed together during much of Du Bois's tenure at the university.[16]

Atlanta University, however, offered the first scientific discussions of the African American culture in various phases and walks of life. The Atlanta conferences covered a wide range of issues from African American mortality to economic cooperation. As a result of the empirical work conducted for the conferences, courses in sociology, economics, and history became part of the curriculum, and courses in methodological training in teaching history were added in the pedagogy department. One of the strongest indicators that history, especially black history, had gained an important place in the black academy is that as early as 1910 the university began to include among its entrance requirements courses in or equivalent to United States history and the history of the Negro.[17]

The Atlanta University conferences and the intellectual enterprises of classically oriented colleges and universities benefited greatly from the reconstruction of the meanings of race in the early twentieth century. Prior to 1910, sociologists and anthropologists were the arbiters of racial science—people like Franklin H. Giddings, professor of sociology at Columbia University; Lester F. Ward, chief paleontologist of the U.S. Geological Survey; William Sumner, professor of political and social science at Yale University; Edward Ross, professor of sociology at the University of Wisconsin; Albion W. Small, president of Colby University; and Charlotte Perkins Gilman, one of the first female sociologists—who believed that race undergirded generalizations about human capacity. Even anthropologist Daniel Garrison Brinton, president of the American Association of Science, promoted ethnocentric constructions of race capacity. But cultural anthropologist Franz Boas, a native of Minden, Westphalia, attacked the comparative method in anthropology that established the European type as normative and compared other races to it. Rejecting the evolutionist framework, Boas believed that cultural determinants played a paramount role in racial development and that the evolutionists' method of comparing Europeans with other races without examining the differences in development was biased. In 1899, Boas became a professor of anthropology at Columbia University. From this position he attacked the central claims of racial determinist theories that blacks were congenitally, intellectually, and psychologically inferior. By 1911, the Boasian critique had infused a new approach into the University of Chicago's Department of Sociology and Anthropology. The adoption of naturalism and an empirical worldview also aided the move away from determinist and essentialist constructions of race. Robert Park, ghostwriter for Booker T. Washington and later a prominent member of Chicago's sociology department, would play an important role in training a number of leading black sociologists, including E. Franklin Frazier, Charles S. Johnson, Oliver C. Cox, and Bertram Doyle. Park also explicitly linked segregationist policies to sociological and not biological antecedents, and he moved away from essentialist constructions of race by pointing out that blacks displayed cultural heterogeneity. Some of these ideas found their way into the Atlanta University conferences and into the institution's sociological and historical courses instituted between the 1898 and the 1902 school years.[18]

Between 1897 and 1915, Atlanta's sociology and history department offered a number of courses on various aspects of the black experience, updating and augmenting its course offerings along the way. In the late 1890s, the department offered a course titled "Citizenship, Wealth, Work, and Wages and Social Reform." In conjunction with the Atlanta University conferences, the department also offered graduate-level study on the problems faced by African Americans in the South. During the 1902–3 school year, a sociological laboratory class was added specifically for seniors in the department. The course laboratory "consisted of a special library of books on statistics, economics, sociology and history, with duplicate copies of standard works; and of maps, charts, and collections illustrating social and historic conditions." And the senior class spent a full year on "the study of social conditions and methods of reform with especial reference to the American Negro."[19]

Additional changes came in a flurry, at least by Atlanta's standards. In 1903–4, the department added a course encompassing economic theory and history. In 1904–5, a new course offered in the pedagogy department stressed "analytical methods and discussions of methods of teaching." In 1905–6, there was a new course on the history of Africa. By 1909–10, the department instituted a clearly defined set of courses geared specifically to augmenting knowledge of African

American contributions to history. At the high school or college preparatory level, there was a half-year course on the history of the Negro in America. At the college level, courses included a junior-level one on the history of Africa, another on the economic history of African Americans, and a sociology course on the social conditions of African Americans. These courses represented an important effort by one black school to serve as the site for the intensive study of the African American condition.[20]

Critical to advancing the study of African Americans in the university was the creation of adequate libraries. During the administration of Edward Twichell Ware (1907–19), Atlanta University significantly augmented its library collections and began a transformation from one designed primarily to support a classical education to one also able to offer quality instruction to its students in the social sciences, particularly in history, sociology, and economics. The library's initial support came through the generous donations of R. R. Graves, a New York lawyer who provided a permanent endowment of $5,000. In 1906, a gift of more than $25,000 from Andrew Carnegie funded a new library building. The Carnegie Library contained all of the amenities of the modern library — a fireproof stack room, large reading and reference rooms, and a large storage area in the basement that was ideal for unpacking and processing new acquisitions. In 1908, the university partnered with the Marblehead Libraries, a system of traveling libraries (of fifty books at a time) inaugurated by James J. H. Gregory of Marblehead, Massachusetts. Atlanta's location at the point of major railroad connections and its reputation as a gateway to the South made it an ideal location. And, as pointed out by G. S. Dickerman of the John T. Slater Board, one of several agencies that supported black education in the South, Atlanta University also had a competent staff and a cooperative president in Ware.[21]

Much of the literature in the Marblehead collection reinforced the acculturating ideas of Progressive-era America and the celebratory themes of narrative history. Several books chronicled the lives of great men and women: P. C. Headley's *The Life of Mary Queen of Scots*, J. T. Headley's *Washington and His Generals*, Thomas Hughes's *The Life of David Livingstone*, Sarah K. Bolton's *Girls Who Became Famous*, Francis Lynee's *Empire Builders*, Thomas Arnold's *The Life of Hannibal*, and Louise Putnam's *The Children's Life of Abraham Lincoln*. The books in the collection ranged from great literature, such as Charles Dickens's *A Christmas Carol*, *Aesop's Fables*, John Bunyan's *Pilgrim's Progress*, Ralph Waldo Emerson's *Representative Men*, Jack London's *Call of the Wild*, and Rudyard Kipling's *The Jungle Book*, to historical and race uplift texts such as Charles Chesnutt's *Frederick Douglass* and Booker T. Washington's *The Negro in Business.*[22] With a new library, support of the Marblehead program, and a committed faculty and staff, by 1915, the university could boast one of the best libraries of modern and African American history among classically oriented black schools.[23]

The changes taking place at Howard and Atlanta were not isolated. Around this time, one of Atlanta University's much smaller neighbor schools, Morehouse College, had also hired a professionally trained historian. Benjamin Brawley, who had graduated from Atlanta Baptist (renamed Morehouse College in 1913) with a B.A. degree in 1901, received his first M.A. from the University of Chicago in 1907 and a second M.A. from Harvard University in 1908 and was a faculty member from 1902 to 1911. In 1911, Brawley joined a faculty committee at Howard University to oversee the work of master's candidates. In 1912, he returned to Morehouse College as a professor of English and dean of the college. Assisted by his teacher and mentor at the University of Chicago, William E. Dodd, Brawley published *A Short History of the American Negro* (1910), which consisted of fifteen chapters surveying the history of African Americans from the inception of slavery. Suggesting the more progressive nature of his study, Brawley's text was half the length of earlier race histories, and although the content of the book leaned toward moral suasion, the text, nevertheless, presented a logically organized and factual history with footnotes and a bibliography.[24]

These changes in facilities, faculty credentials, libraries, courses, and research agenda prepared the formerly classically oriented schools to produce a new generation of discipline-based scholars, and in doing so they made an emphatic statement about the importance of history, especially black history, in the educational process. They also contributed immensely to the production of historical texts that privileged scientism and objectivity over the older classically and clerically based forms. The process was a gradual one that moved at a different pace and took different forms at various schools. But once the changes were under way, they would transform even those schools with other missions.

Theological Schools and the Practice of History

The most important of the theological schools was Gammon Theological Seminary, also located in Atlanta. Associated with Clark University until 1889, Gammon was established in 1883 through a gift of $500,000 by Reverend Elijah

Gammon. Conceived as a training ground for ministers and missionaries, Gammon was a leading proponent of the missionary approach to the proselytization of Africa and the promotion of African and African American history in the United States.[25] But from the outset, Gammon was beset by problems similar to those of other institutions of its type. Inadequate housing, especially for married students, lack of proper library facilities, and a lack of publicity were some of the most pressing issues. The seminary's first dean and later president, Wilbur Thirkield, later president of Howard University, integrated the college's curriculum with the collegiate courses at Clark University, built housing for married students, and worked for the passage and implementation of the "New England Conference Alcove," which facilitated the collection of books from active ministers, the donation of libraries from deceased and retired ministers, and a donation of at least two books from each member of the Methodist Conference. Thirkield also embarked on an aggressive campaign to publicize and promote the school.[26] His most important accomplishments, however, especially as they relate to the historical programs promoted by the school, include establishing a division of historical theology, organizing a historical society, and, most important, founding the Stewart Missionary Foundation for Africa.

Establishing the department of historical theology was an important component in promoting the school's history program. The institution's rapid growth necessitated the expansion of the school's offerings. W. H. Crawford, a member of the Rock River Conference of the Methodist Episcopalian Church and a graduate of Garrett Biblical Institute and Northwestern University, became a full-time professor, and courses he instituted fostered the systematic study of the books of the Bible.[27] In 1890, Crawford became the seminary's librarian. In 1891, like many of his colleagues in liberal arts colleges, he traveled to Europe to deepen his knowledge of modern church history. Upon returning from his trip, Crawford embarked on his most important historical enterprise: he established a historical society, which aimed "to build up, in connection with the Seminary library, a complete and trustworthy historical department upon the various movements that relate to the Negro and the South."

> The historical society proposes to extend its conference and local
> branches and by individual effort throughout the Nation. It is collecting
> books, pamphlets, addresses, articles, biographical and descriptive, upon
> the origin, ethnology, and history of the Negro; upon the rise, develop-
> ment, and destruction of Negro slavery; upon the origin and work of the

abolition movement; and is also preserving the literary productions of Negroes. In addition to this, it proposes to collect the history of the ecclesiastical and educational movements of the churches among the colored people, and to compile a statistical record of the progress of the Negroes in wealth, learning, industry, inventions, mechanical art, and ecclesiology, and to preserve on file for future study whatever shall illustrate the history and promote the interest of the colored people.[28]

While records related to the specific operations of the historical society are scant, it is clear that the school's faculty and administration, though very much absorbed in the school's mission of training ministers and missionaries, had similar interests to those in the universities in the process of creating history departments.

At Gammon, the Stewart Missionary Society, founded in 1895 by W. H. Stewart of the Rock River Conference to prepare missionaries to "teach the gospel to every creature," launched some of the same processes that were taking place in other universities in and around history departments. The missionary society sponsored lecture series and literary and oratorical prizes for students in all levels of the school. Stewart donated more than $400 for the purchase of books, curios, stereopticon slides, and other materials focusing on the products, industries, and life of Africa and also for the use of the students. The missionary society provided funds that enabled President Thirkield to travel in Europe, where he conducted research at the British Museum in London and the Bodleian Library in Oxford, England. He compiled a list of 900 volumes that provided accounts of early African history through the era of free trade and purchased 350 books from this list. By 1895, the seminary had made considerable progress in establishing an African museum and supplying it with specimens of African artwork and handicrafts in wood, brass, and cloth. In addition, they procured more than 200 stereopticon slides for schools and churches to illustrate the products and industries of Africa. The promoters of the Stewart Missionary Foundation felt their efforts were "only the beginning of the collection of illustrated material on Africa and its peoples, which it is hoped will be made one of the greatest of its kind in this country."[29]

The foundation's most ambitious project involved sponsoring a national conference, Africa and the American Negro, in 1895. Designed to further the work of the foundation at home and abroad and to assemble the brightest minds in the country for work on and in Africa, the conference was an unparalleled success. The timing, however, could not have been more ironic. By 1900,

European countries had colonized most of the African continent (excepting Ethiopia and Liberia), and an important component of the missionary fervor was the belief that European culture, especially the culture of Western Europe and America, offered redemption for the "Dark Continent." Even black leaders and missionaries wholeheartedly participated in the civilization project. E. L. Parks, a professor at Gammon, spoke for many blacks and whites when he noted, "The industrial, intellectual, moral and spiritual progress of the colored people in America is a prophecy, both of what they will become and will do for the redemption of their fatherland and also of what the native African is capable of becoming." Still, the Stewart Missionary Foundation was genuine in its offer of aid and assistance to various African countries and territories. Many of these missionaries thought the colonial project of land acquisition and the theft of Africa's resources were as morally reprehensible and as problematic as the slave trade. Thirkield, who presided over the 1895 conference, proclaimed in his opening remarks at the meeting, "In other centuries the curse was the '*stealing of Africans from Africa.*' Now, it is the game among European nations of 'shut your eyes and grab' in their efforts to '*steal Africa from the Africans.*' But God is yet in the world. Not in vain has its two hundred millions stretched forth their hands to him. He causeth the wrath of man to praise Him. Even through the greed and wars of nations in their selfish partition of Africa, he shall yet 'save many of the people alive.'"[30]

The conference sponsored by the Stewart Missionary Foundation for Africa was held in conjunction with the December 1895 Cotton States and Industrial Exposition that launched Booker T. Washington's fame. Whereas the Atlanta exposition focused on showcasing the social, political, and economic advancements of the South, Gammon's Africa and the American Negro conference offered a way for delegates to conceptualize the connection between the plight of Africa and the condition of African Americans. Ironically, rather than the symbolic politics of caste and race and compromise of the Atlanta exposition, the Africa conference offered a program of genuine understanding and cooperation between American missionaries and Africans, based on mutual respect. The organizers facilitated this respect by including the participation of a cross-section of delegates—black diplomats and white missionaries, Africans and African Americans.

The conference was divided into two parts. The first part, "Africa: The Continent, Peoples, Their Civilization, and Evangelization," produced insightful comments on the relationship between African Americans and missionary work in Africa. John Smyth, an African American who served for several years as minister to Liberia, went farther than most. Like his contemporary, Alexander Crummell, Smyth was intimately acquainted with the complexities of the relationship between Africa and the United States and found the constant assault by the American press on the efficacy of the Liberian experiment to be discouraging. Representing the Republic of Liberia, Smyth called for an enlightened approach to missionary work and for building long-term institutions in Liberia and throughout Africa that would maintain the sovereignty and dignity of the African peoples. Quoting extensively from the work of Edward Wilmot Blyden, the author of *Christianity, Islam, and the Negro Race* and former president of Liberia College, Smyth affirmed the purposes of the conference by pointing out the differences between ineffective missionary work that failed to appreciate indigenous cultures and practices, and effective missionary work. Smyth illustrated the former with the example of the early Portuguese missions in the Congo, which brought priests and took slaves. Effective missionary work, then, depended less on the establishment of Christian missionaries than on the development of indigenous religious organizations responsible for converting members of various African societies to Christianity. The success of these projects required fostering an attitude of understanding and respect for African cultures, their complexity, and the potential of their societies on the part of missionaries.[31]

Part two of the conference was "The American Negro: His Relation to the Civilization and Redemption of Africa." The speeches presented in this section accentuated the civilizationist discourse that was prevalent among white and African American elites in the late nineteenth century. J. W. E. Bowen, a formidable African American intellectual, stressed the importance of gathering information on various facets of the African experience and lauded the achievements of African Americans since the abolition of slavery. Henry McNeal Turner, the emigrationist A.M.E. Church minister, castigated the lamentable position of African Americans vis-à-vis whites in the United States, and he advocated the construction of conditions favorable to African Americans and Africans on the African continent. T. Thomas Fortune favored the nationalization of the continent under the auspices of the English.[32]

In the years following the conference, the foundation continued to augment its collections in African history, sending the first library of duplicate books to several schools and libraries in 1896. In 1898, the seminary sponsored an "Africa Day" five-day mini-conference on various aspects of the ministry in Africa and America. The conference also held discussions titled "The Church and the Ministry," "The Church and the People," and "The Seminary and Its Alumni."[33]

The fruit of the foundation's work was especially evident after the turn of the century. By the 1904–5 academic year, at least five members of the seminary and their families were actively involved in missionary work in Africa. By 1909, the Stewart Missionary Foundation in conjunction with the seminary's historical society inaugurated a course of studies and lectures on a wide range of topics related to African history, literature, and geography. The president of Gammon, J. W. E. Bowen, conducted the Stewart Mission seminar once a week. In 1910, the secretary of the Stewart Mission Association, became a regular professor in the Department of Missions, responsible for arranging a regular curriculum of mission study, which began in 1911. The courses included "Africa: Its History and Geography," "Africa: Its People and Religions," and "Africa: Its Mission and the Influence of Christianity."[34]

Despite the different mission of the theological seminary compared to the university, teaching history, especially by experts, and developing history programs, libraries, and conferences aimed at passing on important information were equally important. While in the seminary the courses often concerned historical theology, the concerns for more accurate knowledge were just as strong. Because many of Gammon's students were planning for a life of missionary work in Africa, administrators there were also more concerned with courses in African life and history than those at many of the other universities. In order to accomplish Gammon's local and international missions effectively, students not only needed basic theological information but also the historical context into which they could insert this information.

History and the Industrial Model: Hampton and Tuskegee

Because both Hampton and Tuskegee received much of their early funding from industrial philanthropists, people commonly mistake their primary mission as the training of black manual laborers. More accurately, the industrial school mission concerned instilling a work ethic rather than job training, even though manual training was an important part of the curriculum, especially at Hampton. The industrial model was meant to teach regularity, discipline, and punctuality. And the Hampton program, which emphasized hard physical labor, mental conformity, and moral improvement, developed around a rigorous daily schedule, sometimes seventeen hours long, helping to ensure the realization of training.[35]

Educators at both Hampton and Tuskegee were preeminently concerned with producing teachers, especially for the rural South. And both schools had uplift missions. The ideological programs of African American uplift subscribed to by the leaders of these schools, however, were different. Samuel Armstrong's philosophy at Hampton was based on the idea that African American character was fixed and incapable of reformation except through the industrial and normal projects of Hampton Institute. By contrast, Booker T. Washington, who was trained at Hampton and founded the Tuskegee Institute, offered industrial civilizationism as the paradigm for African American uplift from the debilitating practices of slavery. This paradigm stressed frugality, social and moral responsibility, and a focus on issues internal to the community, such as land and business ownership.[36]

The obvious difference between these two schools and the liberal/classical schools or the seminaries was their missions. But more important for our purposes was the difference in their deployment and teaching of history. The industrial schools developed a committed, consistent history curriculum much more quickly than the other types of schools, largely because they wanted to produce effective teachers. As a 1915 Hampton catalog put it:

> Hampton does not prepare men and women for professions. While a number of its graduates have fitted themselves for professional life after leaving school, the majority have devoted themselves to "helping the common people do common things in an uncommon way." Hampton is endeavoring to meet certain great needs of the masses of the Negro and Indian races. The first of these is for efficient teachers.

To produce well-trained teachers, the schools could not neglect teaching history.[37]

But even among the industrial schools there were profound differences. Hampton's history curriculum during much of the period under discussion remained mired in the insipid paternalism of the time and the civilizationist mission of the school. Tuskegee, however, developed a richer, more nuanced historical curriculum based on practical knowledge and the belief that African Americans could contribute important information and knowledge to the changing South.

Within four years of its 1867 opening, Hampton Institute began to offer courses in history as a part of its three-year normal curriculum. The primary purpose of the enlarged curriculum was to qualify students to receive a basic teaching certificate. In the program's first year, referred to as the junior year, students studied early U.S. and British history; in the middle year, students completed instruction in American history; and in the senior year, students studied universal (world) history. Not surprisingly, Tuskegee's curriculum was similar. During the first (junior) year, when there was some concentration on basic courses in reading, spelling, grammar, and elocution (along with math, geometry, geography, and writing), students had only one history course, "History of the United States." Universal history and English history, with some emphasis on connections to American history, were the courses of the middle year. Students had no history requirement during the senior year.[38]

The very *basic* nature of these history courses probably had much to do with their teachers. Most of the early history classes in the normal school were taught by unmarried white women graduates of New England schools who also had some prior teaching experience in Northern academies. Often these teachers were deeply influenced by an explicit belief in civilizationist ideology and possessed an elevated missionary zeal toward recently freed African Americans in the South, and Hampton's mission of improving the character of presumably morally deficient people appealed to them. In their writings and public pronouncements, these teachers promoted an evolutionary paradigm for black growth and advancement. Hampton's program, they believed, was simply an extension of the missions of social uplift emanating from the New England rhetoric about the industrial civilizationism of the South.[39]

One of the most influential early history teachers at Hampton was Mary Dibble (Smith), a native of Seymour, Connecticut, and graduate of Smith College. Dibble taught history and reading from 1881 to 1884. In the reports produced by her division, Dibble often focused on the practical impact of historical studies on the students. A general consensus existed among the teachers that African American students were "wholly ignorant" of American history, and so teachers often grappled with how best to present it. They used supplementary readings, mostly reference books, in conjunction with the main text, especially in the junior and middle classes. The teachers also employed additional exercises, especially games, to stimulate student interest. For upper-level students, teachers focused on the lives of notable personalities in history. Probably because of the minimal background of their students, the teachers' general aim was "not to teach history but rather to teach *how to study history.*"

Dibble was frank about her expectations and the shortcomings of the program. After posing a quasi-rhetorical question, "What does the study of history amount to, in practical value to these students?" she answered that "We [Hampton's teachers] do not look for great results," adding, "Expecting little, we are not discouraged by the results." According to Dibble, the senior-level students achieved the greatest results in the ancient history class, which remained important as a part of universal history. Hampton's curriculum echoed the sentiments of many industrialists and classicists who believed that ancient history served as the primary introduction to the Judeo-Christian ethic, the ideological and theological bedrock of the Western tradition. Dibble felt that exposure to the Western tradition was not only a means of increasing students' understanding of the Bible and books in general but also helped to foster a "better understanding and appreciation of our own times."[40]

Anne Scoville, another prominent Hampton teacher, was the granddaughter of Reverend Henry Ward Beecher and the great-niece of Harriet Beecher Stowe. Educated at Dana Hall in Wellesley, Massachusetts, Wellesley College, and in Oxford, England, she taught history at Hampton from 1891 to 1897. Her work focused primarily on Indian folklore, but she also wrote several articles in the *Southern Workman* on various aspects of the African American historical experience. A notable piece was "The Negro and the Bible," in which Scoville combined her interests in Indian folklore and artifacts with an assessment of the ritualistic aspects of the African American church. Given her abolitionist family heritage and their missionary tradition, Scoville's presentation of the meanings of religion to African Americans is not surprising. In the article's first paragraph, however, she stereotypically proclaimed: "To the Negro belongs the tropic fervor, the religious passion, the power of song, and the past of bondage and release. He can sit down to his Old Testament with a sense of ownership which no one else but the Jew can claim."[41] In a linear and civilizationist assessment of African history and African American possibility, Scoville concluded that African Americans adopted many practices of the Christian church but often diluted or compromised the integrity of these ceremonies by employing "the witch-doctor, the hag, the conjuror, and the voodoo dance." Ultimately, Scoville's article offered more insights into Hampton's (Armstrong's) and her civilizing mission than African American religious history. The Bible, rather than classical literature, was more suitable to missionary civilizationists such as Scoville. And the effects of biblical training were duly noted: "Truly the student who has found spiritual ideals, learned Christian virtues, conquered superstition, gained sympathy with other races, and mastered the English language in his Bible studies has a liberal education."[42]

The civilizationists undoubtedly employed the Bible to improve the mental and moral character of African Americans and further the school's industrial agenda. This agenda (and Scoville's low estimation of her students) was made explicitly clear when Scoville discussed how Hampton instructed African Americans to interpret certain biblical passages:

When the apostle said, "steal no more, but rather let him labor," Hampton says, "That means teach him a trade." And when, again, the mandate comes, "Pure religion and undefiled before the Father is this, to visit the widows and the fatherless," Hampton says, "That means for you boys to mend Aunt Marthy's roof and chop wood for old Pete." And when they read, "Go ye into the world and teach the Gospel to every creature," Hampton says, "You may go to Africa by-and-by, but this morning that means to go out and teach Sunday school, sing in the jail, and read to the old people in the cabins."[43]

Hampton required all of its students to take courses on the Old and New Testaments. The Bible demonstrated the factors that led to the rise and fall of kingdoms (Israel), recounted the lives of notable personalities (Moses), and affirmed the belief that every group of people endured a period of suffering and wandering prior to achieving some degree of stability and permanence. These were important life and history lessons.[44]

Of all the teachers of history on Hampton's faculty, none was more prolific than Helen Ludlow, a graduate of Springler Institute, a precursor of Vassar College. Ludlow taught at Hampton from 1872 to 1893. She served on the *Southern Workman* staff from 1893 to 1895 and as editor of the magazine from 1895 to 1910. Also known as Armstrong's assistant in fund-raising in the North, she managed the Hampton Singers (modeled on the Fisk Jubilee Singers) during the mid-1870s and was responsible for teaching the group while they were on the road. She also wrote about various aspects of the Hampton program, including *Twenty-two Years: Works, Records of Negro and Indian Graduates* (1893) and *From the Beginning* (n.d.). Her articles in *the Southern Workman* ranged from an assessment of the philosophy of Ralph Waldo Emerson to an examination of the abolition of slavery in Brazil from 1872 until the early 1900s.[45] Although Hampton did not teach African American history during the early years, *Southern Workman* and other Hampton periodicals partially filled the void by publishing short historical articles, reviewing works of history, and generally promoting black history. Other institutional activities, including the Hampton Negro Conference, also provided important opportunities to present new research.[46]

By the 1890s, the history curriculum at Hampton began to change. In addition to adding civics and economics to the curriculum, U.S. history moved from the junior year to the middle year, and the course added sections on the Declaration of Independence and the Constitution, focusing on the study of its amendments. Although the course catalog emphasized the failures of the government to apply the principles of the Declaration and the Constitution fairly. Hampton had other, more mundane, though intimately related goals, such as promotion of the concept of intelligent citizenship. By 1892, instruction in history and geography were combined, which furthered another change taking place in the published literature; that is, an environmental focus on world history and the development of civilizations and the progress of races.[47]

Despite important changes in individual courses, Hampton never really modernized its history curriculum during the years under consideration here. In the twentieth century, Hampton continued to pursue its industrial civilizationist goals even as the school turned slightly more attention to African Americans in the historical curriculum. In the 1904–5 catalog, Hampton's graduate history curriculum included "The Status of the Negro and [the] Indian" as the topic of a course aimed particularly at future schoolteachers. Catalogs between 1908 and 1915 focused almost exclusively on history's role in uplifting African Americans. A major source for the lessons in uplift remained the Bible. In 1908, the study of the Old Testament was explicitly listed as a junior-year history course.[48]

Tuskegee Institute, although similar in its mission to Hampton, was very different from its parent school in its teaching of history. Although Booker T. Washington may justly be criticized for his 1895 "Atlanta Compromise" speech at the Atlanta Cotton States and Industrial Exposition, in which he emphasized acquiescence and accommodation, as well as self-help, by amplifying the core values of the New South ideology and the Progressive era, he placated Southern politicians, won the admiration of Northern industrialists, consolidated his leadership among many African Americans, and consequently received the kind of support that allowed for extensive internal development at Tuskegee Institute. Some of the most far-reaching changes at Tuskegee after 1895 related to the history curriculum.[49]

In its early years, the Tuskegee curriculum's emphasis on teacher education, the dignity of hard work, division into junior, middle, and senior classes, and a three-semester academic year resembled that of Hampton Institute. The two schools were also similar in their early offerings in American, European, and universal history.[50] But during the 1899–1900 academic year, probably in anticipation of the erection of a new library, administrators announced their intention to make Tuskegee "a center of information regarding all matters bearing upon Negro literature." This project encompassed every division's collecting "every pamphlet and book of value whether fiction, autobiography, or history, written by a Negro author." By 1904, Charles Winter Wood, a graduate of Beloit College, the University of Chicago, and Columbia University, served as head of the library. In addition to his duties as university librarian, Wood introduced Shakespeare and other classics to the Tuskegee students and faculty. After the erection of the Carnegie Library in the 1901–2 academic year and the receipt of a $60,000 contribution from Andrew Carnegie in 1903, the institute was better positioned to achieve its goals regarding the collection of literature.[51]

An especially important change took place in the faculty. Dramatically distinguishing it from Hampton, prefiguring further distinctions in the two schools' history curriculum, and, ultimately, also reflecting a true difference in the ideologies of the founders and presidents of the two schools, Tuskegee, soon after its 1881 opening, began to hire classically trained black teachers in the history department. In 1888, upon the recommendation of T. Thomas Fortune, editor of the *New York Age*, Edna Hawley came to teach geography and history courses. Ethel Chesnutt, the daughter of Charles Chesnutt and a 1901 graduate of Smith College, began teaching during the 1901–2 academic year. And John Mercer Langston Jr., son of the renowned orator, lawyer, and activist, taught history and geography between 1902 and 1904. Although it is not clear whether the hiring of these well-trained teachers resulted in changes in the curriculum or whether Washington planned changes in the curriculum and hired these teachers in order to facilitate them, what is clear is that Tuskegee's history curriculum embraced the African American experience and was broader and deeper in coverage than any other school at the time, including the elite, liberal/classical universities.[52]

Working from the premise, commonly applied at Hampton, that history was essentially the study of great men, officials at Tuskegee came to believe that history could assist in race development and should not be limited to the study of great white men—Washington, Adams, and Jefferson. Tuskegee's American history courses focused on the "peculiar position of the Negro in American history from the time of Narváez and Desoto through the wars with England and the civil war, to the present time." Thus, at Tuskegee, according to the school's catalog, African American history is "given due importance, not by isolating it, but introducing it in its proper place along with other events."[53] Whether the course was on the state history of Alabama, the United States under the Constitution in the early republic, or the United States since the Civil War, history courses at each level included African Americans, from slavery to freedom. By 1905, Tuskegee offered a course on slavery and the Civil War. And in 1910, the institute devoted a significant portion of the senior class to a course titled

"The Negro in America." The implementation of this course coincided with the publication of Booker T. Washington's quasi-historical study, *The Story of the Negro*.[54]

Historical courses on the African American experience were an important component of instilling pride and confidence in a people recently emancipated from slavery. With this objective in mind, while Hampton's curriculum for the senior class concentrated on providing potential graduates with important civics lessons, Tuskegee's curriculum focused, among other things, on the "Negro's life as a freeman, and his place in American life; his achievements, his mistakes, and his service to his country." The organization of the course and topics covered in it evoke the emancipation narratives and biographical catalogs common in the period. By the 1913–14 academic year, in addition to the *Census Reports*, the course texts included Booker T. Washington's *Story of the Negro*, Benjamin Brawley's *Social History of the American Negro*, and John Cromwell's *The Negro in American History*, all leading race textbooks of the period.[55]

Tuskegee added courses in African history and geography in 1910.[56] Washington's interest in Africa and the African diaspora was political, economic, and intellectual. His relationship to Africa began in 1908, when he played an important role in renegotiating Liberia's debt payments to various European powers and secured an American protectorate over the country. Moreover, as Louis Harlan has suggested, Washington's program of industrial education attracted many Africans, especially from colonies with a strong missionary presence. His interest in the affairs of people of African descent and Africans led to his sponsorship of the International Conference of the Negro held at Tuskegee from April 17 to 19, 1912. The conference featured representatives from several Caribbean, South American, and African countries. Rather than focusing on issues of race and nationalism, the topic of earlier race conferences, Washington limited the conference's purview to education: in particular, he was concerned with "the solution of some of these new and difficult problems, which have sprung up in different parts of the world, as the result of the closer contacts of the white and colored races." Using this approach, the conference was divided into three parts: conditions, missions, and methods.[57]

The interest of this conference seemed to be in harnessing the power of the West to assist developing nations. This evolutionist approach, combined with Washington's belief in industrial civilizationism, meshed well with the interests of big business and the Republican Party, which supported his work. While some conference attendees such as W. I. Thomas, professor of sociology at the University of Chicago, felt that more effort should be devoted to studying African peoples, other participants advocated different approaches. Robert Park, a former secretary of the Congo Reform Association of America, located in Boston, used his speech to provide an overview of the colonization process in Africa and to suggest that Africa could benefit from the Tuskegee model. Washington's interest in and promotion of Africa and other international sites mirrored his concerns for the study of African American history.[58]

It is possible that no one was more capable of, or more successful at, promoting the scholarly study of history than Booker T. Washington. First, as important as black history was to scholars like W. E. B. Du Bois, who produced his very important *The Souls of Black Folk* in 1903, few of these scholars had the personal networks or the institutional control that Washington had, which were very important to the success of any effort. In fact, few white schools manifested any real interest in black history to this point, and most black schools were still directed (controlled) by white men, whose interests, however noble, simply did not result in a broad and deep incorporation of black history into their curricula. Washington, a staunch supporter of the "Negro History Movement," used his considerable political and economic influence to promote and produce works that celebrated various facets of the African American experience, and he recruited capable individuals to assist in providing the American public with accurate information regarding African American history.[59]

One of Washington's political forays, the Committee of Twelve, had important implications for the production of historical work. Having designed it primarily as an advocacy group, Washington envisioned that its members would "represent the race's leading achievements in all directions" and "seek through free and frank discussion, to devise, if possible, such measures as would possibly improve conditions among our people." He informed the invitees that "the present condition as a race in this country demands we should make every sacrifice and put forth every effort to attend this conference. The matters to be considered are of the greatest importance to our future. I do not believe that there has ever been a race meeting so fraught with value and seriousness as this one will be concerning which I am writing." While some historians have dismissed the committee as a "paper committee" run from Hugh Browne's office at Lincoln University in Pennsylvania, the work of the committee demonstrates the keen interest of Washington and among black elites in the production of reliable and accurate facts on the African American experience.[60]

The Committee of Twelve originated in a conference in New York City on January 6–8, 1904, consisting of eighteen to twenty of the leading citizens of the race. Washington chaired the committee, Hugh Browne served as secretary, and Archibald Grimké was treasurer.[61] A primary objective of the committee was to emphasize the progressive effort within the race and to amplify the achievements of African Americans in all areas. The committee was also charged with tabulating "data bearing upon the condition and progress of the race, as well as the relation of other races to our own."[62] Despite the political and even partisan nature of some of the material produced by the committee, some of it had historical value; for instance, Richard Robert Wright Jr.'s pamphlet, *Self Help in Negro Education*. Wright later became a research fellow in sociology at the University of Pennsylvania and author of *Economic History of the Negro in Pennsylvania* (1911). D. W. Woodward's *Study of the Conditions of the Negroes in Jackson* offered a sociological overview of one black community. Although the Committee of Twelve was a short-lived organization and most of its work was political in nature, it did provide an outlet for disseminating important historical information to the wider American public.[63]

Washington's own historical production had a much longer-lasting impact. The publication of *Story of the Negro* not only represented his interest in promoting Tuskegee Institute but also his understanding of the importance of disseminating accurate and reliable facts on the African American experience. His engagement with history was an outgrowth of his autobiographical musings in *Up from Slavery*. In this seminal work, Washington had not only presented a blueprint for racial advancement but used his own history as representative of racial possibility and demonstrated the importance of history in general as a roadmap for human possibility. The race's rise from slavery required an appreciation of the history of the public and personal habits necessary to accomplish stature and respectability in the world. Washington's goal was to write himself and, by extension, the race, into the human record. Although he used ghostwriters for this book, including Robert E. Park, Monroe Nathan Work, and Alphonsus Orenzo Stafford, it is clear that he wanted his historical work to reflect his self-help agenda at Tuskegee and to present the historic personalities of the race in a realistic but uplifting manner. In addition to having Park and Work produce the index and edit the book to ensure its accuracy, Washington suggested to Stafford, the principal ghostwriter of the work, to "have a chapter showing what the Negroes themselves did to bring about freedom. We could use in this chapter such persons as Douglass, Harriet Tubman, Judge Gibbs and other strong characters that are little known about. Of course, you have already treated this subject under another head, but I think you could make a *real romantic chapter* under this head" (emphasis mine).[64]

Washington's most substantial contribution to the study of African American history probably relates to his hiring Monroe Nathan Work as the director of Records and Research at Tuskegee. Work, who held a B.A. in philosophy and an M.A. in sociology from the University of Chicago, began his educational career with the intention of becoming a minister. While enrolled at the Chicago Theological Seminary, Work embarked on a study of African American crime in the city of Chicago, which appeared in the *Journal of Sociology* in 1900. After completing his studies at Chicago, Work secured a position, with the assistance of his friend Richard R. Wright Jr., teaching education and history at Georgia State Industrial College in Savannah.[65] While there, Work became actively associated with W. E. B. Du Bois and the Niagara movement, a short-lived protest movement (precursor to the NAACP) that included some of the most notable black intellectuals of the turn of the century. Work served as the group's secretary of the Committee on Crime beginning in 1905. In 1908, Du Bois asked Work to go to Lowndes County, Alabama, to study conditions for African American people there. Work produced a pamphlet titled "Self Help among Negroes," which *Survey* magazine published.[66]

Work's primary biographer, Linda O. McMurry, traces his transformation from a progressive liberal to a firm believer in industrial civilizationism because of the deteriorating condition of African Americans in the South. Race riots in Wilmington, North Carolina, in 1898 and Atlanta in 1906, as well as disturbances in Brownsville, Texas, all heightened racial tensions throughout the South and indicated that circumstances were not getting any better. Moreover, the meager facilities for research and writing at Georgia State Industrial College were discouraging for Work. Consequently, when he received Washington's offer to join the faculty at Tuskegee Institute, an affirmative answer was not long in coming. Work recalled his conversation with Washington and Emmett Scott: "I told him he did not want a History Department of the Negro but I thought what he wanted was information about what is taking place at present with reference to the Negro." Work's self-created position came with a salary of $1,200 for a twelve-month period and one month's vacation with pay.[67]

Work established and took charge of Tuskegee Institute's Department of Records and Research, where he handled the graduate reports for the school and pursued an aggressive research agenda. As he outlined in his "Plans for Making Tuskegee a Greater Center for Information Relating to the Negro," Work continued to build a library of materials on various aspects of the African American experience and to produce a bibliography of publications on African Americans. Especially important to the study of history, Work focused on making the material currently at Tuskegee more available through indexes and special card catalogs, further dividing them into historical materials (documents, books, pamphlets, and articles) and sociological materials (statistics, press clippings, studies of various sorts, and public opinion materials). He created a newspaper and magazine clipping file, indispensable to scholars today, reflecting his search of more than one hundred newspapers and periodicals, domestic and foreign, mainstream and African American. He also collected press clippings and government reports. Additionally, Work established personal contacts with several important organizations, including the National Urban League, National Negro Business League, and the National Association of Teachers in Colored Schools. As Work implied in one comment on his efforts, the collection of this material would make it possible for scholars of all stripes "to measure and evaluate what is taking place with respect to all phases of Negro life, first in the United States and second throughout the world."[68]

In publishing *The Negro Yearbook* in 1913, Work became one of the first scholars to benefit from these collections. Although initially envisioned by Washington as a one-time pamphlet to celebrate the fiftieth anniversary of African American emancipation, the project gained firmer footing through the establishment of the Negro Yearbook Publishing Company, suggested by Robert E. Park and owned by Work, Park, and Tuskegee. Work handled the book editing, Park handled the publishing, printing, and advertising, and Emmett Scott handled the finances.[69] The purpose of the yearbook was to present a combination of statistical and historical information on various aspects of the black experience. According to Work, the project served an important educational function:

> The notion of placing education within the reach of the masses is carried out in the publication of the *Negro Yearbook*. Information on both the common and the uncommon things of Negro life and history have been placed within the reach of all. This information thus becomes both a defensive and offensive mechanism, which on the one hand gives strength, courage, inspiration and hope to the Negro and on the other hand, presents to the white world a convincing argument concerning the Negro's capabilities.

The production numbers of the early volumes of the *Yearbook* suggest its success. In 1912, Work printed 5,000 copies, and 10,000 copies in 1913.[70]

Very few institutions could boast the changes achieved by Tuskegee between

1900 and 1915. The expansion of the library facilities, the hiring and retention of a highly skilled, black, liberal arts faculty, the addition of extensive course offerings on the African and African American experience, the establishment of a Department of Records and Research, and the publication of the *Negro Yearbook* made Tuskegee a leading institution in the promotion of black history. Perceived by many historians as backward and backward-looking almost from its founding, Tuskegee Institute certainly contributed as much to the preservation and promotion of African American history as any other institution in its day. And on a day-to-day basis, Tuskegee's students had a greater opportunity for exposure to this history than students in any other school.

But it was work going on in all the schools that helped to institutionalize African American history and enhance the professionalization of the discipline. Black schools, like their white counterparts, responded to the shift from religion-based notions of education to more scientific and objective pedagogical ideas. Hampton's inability to move forward undoubtedly relates to the hold of white civilizationist clergy and missionaries on its administration. But as scientism and modernism began to take hold among African American intellectuals, social scientists like W. E. B. Du Bois, liberal clergymen such as J. W. E. Bowen, and even college presidents, especially Booker T. Washington, designed innovative programs and conferences to study systematically various aspects of African American life and history. Schools developed their libraries to support these changes, and they developed various collections—manuscript, print, and artifact—to facilitate the study of history, often in the context of the missions of their schools. But each school viewed its historical programs as important not only within the academy but also in the larger African American community. For instance, Du Bois's Atlanta University Studies were intended to provide reliable information on African Americans for use by local, state, and federal governments as well as colleges and universities. The Stewart Missionary Association at Gammon Theological Seminary was designed to foster a more complete understanding of the relationship between Africans and African Americans. And although Hampton did not go nearly as far as its sister institution in terms of its history curriculum, the school's press, the Normal Steam Printing Press, printed Joseph Wilson's *Emancipation: Its Course and Progress* (1882) and the *Southern Workman*, which published the work of black intellectuals ranging from Du Bois to Work. With a sizable body of historical scholarship in place, schools committed to the research, and libraries and archives able to support it, the professionalization of African American history was imminent.

*The Creation of the Association for the Study of Negro Life and
History and the Beginnings of Professionalization*

The institutionalization of African American history in the black academy
provided an encouraging environment for the further development of the
field. The subsequent formation of the Association for the Study of Negro
Life and History (ASNLH) heralded the culmination of a century-long effort to
legitimize the study of the African American experience. Founded by Carter
G. Woodson in 1915, ASNLH represented the maturation of efforts of individual
writers and scattered historical and literary societies to find, collect, present,
and promote the history of black people. ASNLH, however, differed from all
those earlier efforts because of its permanence, its publication of a scholarly
journal, and its avoidance of direct advocacy. Much more than a repository
of information, ASNLH, as Woodson envisioned it, would be a disseminator
of truth through scientific investigation of the African and African American
past.[71]

ASNLH's founding meeting especially distinguishes it from the founding of
the AHA and the Mississippi Valley Historical Association. The initial meeting
to organize the association convened in Chicago on September 9, 1915, in the
offices of A. L. Jackson, executive secretary of the Wabash Avenue branch of
the Chicago Young Men's Christian Association (YMCA). Rather than an exclusive meeting of professional historians, the attendees included a variety of
people—George Cleveland Hall, a prominent Chicago surgeon; W. B. Hartgrove, a teacher in the Washington, D.C., public schools; businessman James
E. Stamps; and Carter G. Woodson. Hall, Jesse E. Moorland, and Woodson became president, secretary-treasurer, and director of research and editor, respectively. Woodson's selection of executives, an executive council, organizational
leaders, and teachers to serve in elective and appointive capacities, was not
coincidental. He understood that a fledgling organization such as the ASNLH
needed more than historical expertise to survive; it also needed broad-based
support and financial backing. The organizational structure, the inclusion of
people from diverse professional backgrounds, Woodson's control of scholarly
production, and the fact that both Hall and Moorland had fund-raising experience with the YMCA addressed all the major concerns—professional and
practical.[72]

As was the case for the mainstream historical organizations, ASNLH quickly
established a scholarly journal. In 1916, Woodson borrowed $400 against a
$2,000 life insurance policy with New England Mutual to publish the *Journal of*

Negro History (*JNH*). In the first year of the *JNH*'s operation, Woodson produced three separate issues, and between 1916 and 1919, he concentrated on developing the journal's reputation. In publishing a journal, Woodson continued an earlier tradition of using the written word as a weapon to combat racism and stimulate pride among African Americans. Early issues of the *JNH* began several traditions for combating stereotypical and misleading portrayals of African Americans: the use of primary documents in historical analysis; a "Notes" section to announce important publications and events in African American and American history; and the encouragement of revisionist historical treatments by black scholars. W. E. B. Du Bois once remarked that, "Woodson's greatest contribution to history was not his books but his editorship of the *Journal* which brought into print some of the best scholars in that branch of history."[73]

The collection and printing of primary documents relevant to African American history proved one of the crowning achievements of the ASNLH and the *JNH*. From the earliest issues, the wide-ranging and diverse primary-source documents suggested the kinds of investigations Woodson hoped to conduct in African American history: the history of persons of African descent in foreign countries, important black institutions, major events, and traditions in African American life. Altogether, the documents in the *JNH* served the dual purpose of exposing the public to the history of African Americans in documentary (primary source) form and providing a forum related to the production of factual histories of the race in every facet of American life.[74]

The "Notes" section of the *JNH* provided useful discussions of various publications and events relevant to African American and American history. Most history journals included "calendars" of important upcoming events. But the *JNH* was the only historical journal to offer an up-to-date listing of publications in African American history. In 1917, Woodson announced the publication of Arthur Schomburg's *Biographical Checklist of American Negro Poetry*. In 1918, an announcement promoted the publication of Benjamin Brawley's *The Negro in American Literature and Art*. In 1919, Woodson announced that the association itself would publish a scientific history of African American participation in "the Great War" just ended (World War I).[75]

It is, however, possible that the most important aspect of Woodson's promotion of African American history involved the production of revisionist history. Although Woodson considered the work of the *JNH* as a search for truth, he also understood that the racist nature of scholarly inquiry into issues concerning blacks led to biased interpretations by white scholars. One of the earliest examples of revisionist work to appear in the journal was that of John Lynch's 1917 article, "Some Historical Errors of James Ford Rhodes," which he augmented with another article in 1918, "More about the Historical Errors of James Ford Rhodes." In these articles, Lynch, a Reconstruction-era Mississippi legislator, analyzed the work of Rhodes, an important amateur historian who published the influential *History of the United States from the Compromise of 1850*, which Lynch found incredibly baised.[76]

Both black and white scholars and laypersons critically acclaimed early issues of the JNH. In response to the first issue, Edward Channing, who "liked the looks of the thing—the page, the print," became a subscriber and requested Harvard's Widener Library to subscribe as well. George Cable, author of *The Negro Question*, pledged his support for the JNH and offered assistance in obtaining subscribers. Casely Hayford, a Gold Coast activist, expressed deep gratitude for ASNLH's work, especially the JNH. Hayford wrote, "The get-up is excellent and highly credible to our race in America." Dada Adeshigbin, a Nigerian businessperson, wrote of the JNH, "I am pleased to know that it was edited and published by my own color. I am impressed by the excellent form in which the publication was got up."[77]

Despite these favorable evaluations, Woodson found it difficult to raise the necessary funds to publish the JNH and to maintain the association. In 1916 alone, he sent out more than two hundred letters to philanthropists. The mailing generated only $14. By the end of the year, both J. N. Grisham and S. P. Breckinridge had resigned from ASNLH's executive council. In an advertisement titled "A Neglected Work," Woodson outlined the goals of the association and defined the urgency of the situation. Reminiscent of earlier calls for "a faithful account of the race" and of the calls for African Americans to produce their own historians, Woodson wrote:

> Excepting what can be learned from current controversial literature, which either portrays the Negro as a persecuted saint or brands him as a leper of society, the people of the age are getting no information to show what the Negro has thought and felt and done. The Negro, therefore, is in danger of becoming a negligible factor in the thought of the world. In centuries to come when white scholars after forgetting the prejudices of this age will begin to make researches for truth, they will have only one side of the question if the Negro does not leave something to tell his own story.[78]

Woodson listed five ways the public could assist the association in raising money and promoting the collection and preservation of black history: "1) subscribe to the *Journal*; 2) become a member of the Association; 3) contribute to our research fund; 4) collect and send us historical material bearing on the Negroes of your community; 5) urge every Negro to write us all he knows about his family history." Subscriptions to the *JNH* cost $1 in 1916, comparable to the price of other historical magazines of the day. But because of the small number of trained black historians, Woodson's appeal to a lay audience was essential to the survival of the association. The public was not only a source of monetary support but also a rich resource of information for the emerging specialty of African American history. At that point, however, public support was not sufficient to sustain a comprehensive historical association; thus Woodson turned his attention to cultivating the support of the large philanthropic organizations.[79]

Jesse Moorland took the lead in raising funds for the ASNLH and the *JNH*. In October 1916, Moorland persuaded Julius Rosenwald to support the association. Rosenwald pledged $100 quarterly to the Research Fund, which was to "employ investigators to carry out the designs of the Association." Robert E. Park donated $30; and Margaret Murray Washington donated $15. Continuing the tradition of self-sacrifice and expressing his own confidence in the *JNH*, Woodson donated another $30. The establishment of the Research Fund and the subsequent contributions did little to relieve the association's debt. At the end of 1916, the ASNLH's debt averaged between $1,200 and $1,500.[80] Circumstances seemed desperate enough that in 1917 (and again in 1920), Du Bois was "twice alarmed" because of "Woodson's meager income and his overwork" and offered to incorporate the *JNH* into the NAACP's Department of Research and Publications. Woodson apparently preferred to maintain the journal independently, even at great sacrifice to himself.[81]

The association's prospects did, however, look brighter in 1917 with the receipt of several important endorsements and invitations. The noted author Charles Chesnutt praised Woodson's work, writing, "It is customary to assume that the Negro has contributed nothing noteworthy to civilization; that a magazine, which in the interest of truth will call attention to the other side of the ledger will supply a distinct need and ought to be cordially and adequately supported." Chesnutt also became a subscriber to the *JNH*. Walter H. Brooks, pastor of the Nineteenth Street Baptist Church in Washington, D.C., commended the association's work. He wrote, "You are rendering the race and humanity a service in your publications. Your journal exists to tell the story of the race in all lines of worthy endeavor. May you have readers in every family in the country." Mary Talbert, president of the National Association of Colored Women, invited Woodson to speak at the group's convention in Denver, Colorado, in December 1918. Talbert felt that Woodson could "with telling effect impress the women teachers and mothers with the necessity of our beginning to know something about their history."[82]

Woodson used the association's first biennial meeting on August 27, 1917, to stress the beneficial aspects of black history as well as appeal to the philanthropists for financial assistance for the association. Thus, not surprisingly, this meeting featured a who's who of white and black notables and, particularly, representation from all of the major philanthropic organizations. Mrs. Alice Thatcher Post, wife of the assistant secretary of labor; Dr. James H. Dillard, director of the John P. Slater Fund; George Foster Peabody, a New York banker and head of the Peabody Fund; Dr. Thomas Jesse Jones from the U.S. Bureau of Education; and Julius Rosenwald, among others. Black notables included Monroe N. Work; George E. Haynes, social scientist and cofounder of the Urban League; Dr. C. V. Roman, medical doctor and author of *American Civilization and the Negro* (1916); Channing Tobias, Moorland's assistant for youth work; Benjamin Brawley; and A. L. Jackson.[83]

The speakers at the meeting addressed the organization's diverse needs. Woodson took this opportunity to discuss the importance of the association's work and the need to raise money to employ investigators to collect and process valuable documents relevant to African American history. Julius Rosenwald, who also addressed the meeting, approved of the association's work and praised the scholarly standards of the *JNH*. James Dillard stressed the importance of studying Africa. The meeting also showcased scholarly work, including Monroe Work's paper on black involvement in the Great War. And the business meeting formalized the association's existence by ratifying its constitution.[84]

The most important aspect of the meeting was the nomination of new officers and members of the executive council. Woodson skillfully reshuffled the council to reflect the priorities of the association in achieving its most pressing goal, the acquisition of sufficient funding from the philanthropic organizations. Thus, the new members of the executive council featured influential and conservative African Americans as well as representatives of the major philanthropies. Robert R. Moton, principal of Tuskegee Institute, declined the invitation to serve on the council but pledged his support for the cause. Julius Rosenwald consented to serve on the executive council with the stipulation that he not be obligated to take part in the organization's work. James Dillard and J. G. Phelps Stokes rounded out the list of philanthropists. Other influential black leaders who became council members included John R. Hawkins, banker and financial secretary of the A.M.E. Church, and Robert E. Jones, editor and clergyman. Other prominent whites including L. Hollingsworth Wood, Urban League chairman, and Moorfield Storey, national president of the NAACP, joined them. With Robert E. Park as president of the ASNLH, Woodson prepared to launch a major drive to raise $10,000.[85]

Despite financial difficulties, Woodson worked hard to create an agenda for African American research. After completing a study titled *A Century of Negro Migration* in 1918, he initiated the first of a series of new historical investigations. The areas of inquiry included studies titled "The Negro in Africa," "The Enslavement of the Negro," "Slavery and the Rights of Man," "The Reaction against Slavery as an Economic Institution," "The Free Negro in the United States," "The Abolition Movement," "The Colonization Project," "Slavery and the Constitution," "The Negro in the Civil War," "The Reconstruction of the Southern States," "The Negro in Freedom," and "The Negro and Social Justice." Although Woodson predicted the completion of his work in February 1918, its magnitude was such that this series of projects would engage the work of the association for the next thirty years.[86]

Woodson continued to receive support and encouragement for the ASNLH's work from prominent individuals.[87] This support allowed it to pay many of its debts, and upon the elimination of those debts, Woodson hired a field agent, J. E. Ormes of the business department of Wilberforce University, to sell books and solicit subscriptions for the *JNH*. Ormes also had the responsibility for organizing clubs to study black history. Finally, Woodson announced another ambitious project: preparation of a textbook of African American history titled *The Negro in Our History*. Woodson conceived of the text to provide the historical profession with fundamental facts, suggestions, and references for a more intensive study of black history by high school seniors and first-year college students. He also obtained suggestions from the public on extending the scope of the study.[88]

Besides the presentation of important scholarly papers at the 1919 meeting, the "Report of the Director" indicated that the period from 1917 to 1919 had been successful years. The number of subscriptions to the *JNH* reached four thousand. Additionally, Woodson supplemented the income of the association by selling books on African and African American history. Woodson believed that these efforts indicated "that the Association will soon develop into a nucleus of workers known throughout the world as publishers of authoritative and scientific books bearing on Negro life and history." Moreover, Woodson thought this early success, especially the increased production of scholarly studies, would result in more support from philanthropists.[89]

In 1919, Woodson became the dean of the College of Liberal Arts and head of the graduate faculty at Howard University. Although he held the latter position for only one year (1919–20), Woodson was clearly an innovator. He conducted one of the first graduate seminars at Howard incorporating the study of black history. One of Woodson's students, Arnett Lindsay, recalled some of his methods. Woodson did not use a textbook; rather he prepared an extensive outline of materials to supplement his lectures. He encouraged his students to conduct primary research for the M.A. thesis in the Library of Congress. And Lindsay also recalled that Woodson's "retentive memory enabled him to cite sources accurately and quote verbatim from documents, narratives, and other historical materials."[90]

Despite his superior teaching abilities, Woodson's tenure at Howard was short-lived. He resented the patronizing style of Howard's white president, J. Stanley Durkee, and Durkee's attempts to reduce him to simply a dean of the college. Looking back on the incident years later, Woodson noted, "The President began to hit me like this, and I began to hit him like that." This dispute led Woodson to criticize Jesse Moorland's unwillingness to come to his aid. Woodson wrote to Moorland, "You have a weakness for good-for-nothing white people because of your broken down theory that in the Negro schools the best of the two races may be united. This has never been true, and it will never be until the Negroes have made such progress as to be recognized as the equal of whites." Woodson concluded by noting, "it is all but criminal to impose such medieval misfits [Durkee] on Negro institutions when these positions can be admirably filled by scientifically trained Negroes."[91]

In May 1920, Woodson resigned from Howard. Because of his intemperate remarks, he had also alienated his most ardent supporter, Jesse E. Moorland. But it was during this period that Woodson began working with J. Franklin Jameson, editor of the *American Historical Review* and director of the Department of Historical Research at the Carnegie Institution of Washington. Jameson had taken an interest in the ASNLH's work from its inception. Impressed by Woodson's work and convinced that a subsidy from a large foundation would further the association's efforts to conduct scientific studies of blacks, Jameson assisted Woodson in initiating a grant proposal to the Carnegie Foundation of New York. The process was successful. With firmer and more substantial funding in place, the 1920s ushered in a period of great growth and expansion for the ASNLH and positioned the organization to make even greater contributions to the study of African American life and history. Building on a strong tradition of lay and avocational interest in historical representation and production that extended back to the early republic, black historians by 1920 entered into professionalized spaces for the study of history.[92]

Professionalization of black history did not automatically usher in historical studies written in the form and style we are accustomed to today. For the first fifteen to twenty years after its establishment, black scholars were dependent on the scholarly work of scholars from the nineteenth century as a basis for their scholarly production. The two best examples of the difference in professionalism between the nineteenth-century and twentieth-century historical work are Carter G. Woodson's *The Negro in Our History*, the first textbook of African American history, published in 1922, and W. E. B. Du Bois's *Black Reconstruction: An Essay toward a History of the Part Black People Played in the Attempt to Reconstruct Democracy, 1860–1880*, published in 1935.

Woodson's *The Negro in Our History* represented the culmination of a six-year effort to set the ASNLH on a sound financial and intellectual footing. Although Woodson firmly situated his study in the scientific world of professional history and objectivity as it manifested itself in the early twentieth century, it is clear that the work owed much to the earlier nineteenth-century writers. In his chapter "A Declining Anti-slavery Movement," which charts the rise of abolitionism, Woodson discussed the impact of David Walker's *Appeal to the Coloured Citizens of the World*. Woodson presented the document as the first "systematic address to the slaves [that] appealed to them to rise against their masters." Even Woodson's discussion of economic slavery and the plight of free blacks relied in part on the work of nineteenth-century writers. His discussion of the rise of the plantation system and the development of an internal slave trade after the official closure of the external slave trade in 1808 referenced William Wells Brown's *Rising Son*, and George Washington Williams's *History of the Negro Race in America*. In discussing the success of blacks in founding newspapers such as *Freedom's Journal*, the accomplishments of lumber merchants Joseph C. Cassey and William Platt, the famous caterer Thomas Downing, or the sailmaker James Forten, Woodson referenced William Wells Brown's *The Black Man*, Martin Delany's emigration manifesto *The Condition, Elevation, Emigration and Destiny of the Colored People of the United States*, and William Simmons's extensive biographical catalog, *Men of Mark*.[93]

Woodson's discussion of free blacks extended to their active role in overturning the system of slavery. In a chapter titled "Blazing the Way," Woodson discussed the role African Americans played in obtaining their own freedom.

Despite the publication of Wilbur Siebert's *The Underground Railroad*, which Woodson cites in his text, he was more interested in discussing the role that blacks played in securing their own freedom. For this he turned to an exploration of the work of black abolitionists such as William Whipper and Levi Coffin. Although he did not explicitly mention William Still's *The Underground Railroad* or Levi Coffin's 1879 book of the same title, he referred to Still and his work in the text. The fact that so many references to nineteenth-century secondary sources appeared in Woodson's work is not coincidental. The presence of a large, intellectual lay community in the absence of a professionally trained one demonstrates the extent to which, as Peter Novick has shown, professionalization relied on preprofessional scholarship and documentation. Woodson relied heavily on the work of his nineteenth-century predecessors to provide the foundational material upon which he built a viable professional historical project.[94]

Although published in 1935, W. E. B. Du Bois's *Black Reconstruction*, like Woodson's *Negro in Our History*, is a contributionist study designed to examine the central role blacks played in the reconstruction of democracy. Not unlike writers of the nineteenth century, Du Bois was highly trained in and conversant with contemporary theoretical and methodological constructs. In fact, numerous literary scholars have suggested, Du Bois's lyrical style in *Black Reconstruction* is reminiscent of his *Souls of Black Folk*, which has a definite nineteenth-century literary sensibility about it. His skillful conceptualization of recently emancipated freedpeople as a proletariat fighting against a landed bourgeoisie represented a creative use of Marxist ideology and its application to a moment of tremendous upheaval in American history. Although Du Bois's use of Marxist ideology to conceptualize Reconstruction was novel, his recognition that economics lay at the base of racial destiny was not. The fiery orator and editor of the *New York Age*, T. Thomas Fortune, suggested the economic basis of Reconstruction and its impact on freedpeople in his *Black and White: Land, Labor and Politics in the South* (1884). Clearly drawing on the contemporary crisis in the United States in the 1930s, the Great Depression, as his guide, Du Bois sought to humanize the goals of African Americans in their quest to become citizens and subjects, acquire education, and obtain the basic economic necessities of life.[95]

Another important goal of the study was to rethink the shortcomings of earlier histories, which portrayed Reconstruction as a tragic era. The "Tragic Era" legend was fueled by the endemic belief that the political and legislative policies of Reconstruction far overreached their bounds. As the legend went, lazy, improvident, and illiterate African Americans were handed the reins of government in the war-ravaged South. Unable to think or act for themselves, African Americans were aided and abetted in their quest for "Negro Domination" by unscrupulous carpetbaggers, opportunists from the North who had come South looking for quick riches, and by scalawags, Southern sympathizers with Northern interests. Blacks, carpetbaggers, and scalawags immediately set about instituting policies to ensure black domination of the South. While Du Bois's *Black Reconstruction* is largely credited with delegitimizing the Tragic Era view, it is clear that his work relied on the that of early lay historians as well as Woodson's cadre of associate investigators in the ASNLH. John Cromwell, John Lynch, and William Sinclair had also offered assessments of the period, challenging the idea of Reconstruction as a moment of general lawlessness in the South and an undeserved moment of black empowerment. Lynch's *The Facts of Reconstruction* and Sinclair's *The Aftermath of Slavery* presented African Americans as competent stewards of the reins of government throughout the Reconstruction period. They pointed to the fact that although blacks held high elective offices in numerous states, few sustainable charges of fraud were leveled against them. They also, like Du Bois would later do, pointed to the ways in which black governance benefited the larger body politic, providing better roads, schools, and job opportunities for all.[96]

Du Bois's work was also informed by the contributionist work of early twentieth-century scholars such as Alrutheus Ambush Taylor. Taylor, the first associate investigator for the ASNLH, like his nineteenth-century predecessors, was not initially trained in history; his bachelor's degree was actually in mathematics from the University of Michigan. Recruited by Woodson to the ASNLH while an instructor at West Virginia Collegiate Institute, where both men taught in the early twentieth century, Taylor went on to write at least two pathbreaking state studies on Reconstruction, *The Negro in the Reconstruction of South Carolina* (1924) and *The Negro in the Reconstruction of Virginia* (1926). In these studies Taylor not only stridently challenged the Dunning and Burgess school but pointed out many of the shortcomings in their method and errors in their content. Taylor also championed the use of James Harvey Robinson's *New History*, which promoted social history rather than an exclusive focus on political and legislative history. Social, intellectual, and economic aspects of history, Taylor argued, deserved attention in these studies. This approach to dissecting the limitations of the Tragic Era school became an important part of Du Bois's *Black Reconstruction* a decade later.[97]

The march to professionalization for black scholars was not a linear process.

Professionalization was informed as much by the new scientific orientation of Rankean objectivity as it was by the work of lay intellectuals in the black community who continued to contribute to, undergird, and add their own uniqueness to the nature of the professional project. From the mid-nineteenth century onward, black lay intellectuals tried to forge a relationship with the nascent academy. Starting out as a small set of schools loosely divided into those based on classical, theological models and industrial (and normal) models, the black academy worked in tandem with lay intellectuals to support and extend the intellectual space to construct a professional black history discipline. As history became increasingly located in institutional spaces, independent and autonomous spaces such as Woodson's ASNLH continued to exist because of the persistent efforts of a small number of professionally trained black historians and many more lay historians to identify, collect, and preserve sources in African American history. Because of the collective efforts of these historians using a wide variety of theoretical, methodological, and ideological tools combined with a strong communal desire to present complex and nuanced portrayals of African Americans in all facets of history, they provided a "faithful account of the race."

Conclusion

AS A HISTORIAN INTERESTED IN HISTORIOGRAPHY, I constantly look for ways to interject into conversations some discussion of the origins and evolution of African American history as a discipline. Most often, however, conversations of this type occur in class or among colleagues and friends. Despite an outpouring of pathbreaking work in African American history and the common belief that more opportunities to engage African American history exist than ever before, our ideas about the field's origins, especially textual writing, remain fairly underdeveloped and static. When people are asked what they know about the field's origins, it is not uncommon for history students, academics, or laypersons to voice some version of the two dominant narratives that continue to inform our perceptions. The first and most obvious narrative, especially at a moment informed by the culture wars, describes African American history emerging as part of the protest culture of the civil rights movement and its turbulent aftermath, the black power movement. Black history is presented as an angry intruder in the midst of a placid (and even staid) academic field marked by order, discipline, and rigor. In this narrative, black history barges onto the field in an undisciplined and chaotic manner and forces recognition from the history establishment. Compared to other areas of scholarly inquiry, its methods are less rigorous, its scope less encompassing, and the important sources are largely confined to the twentieth century, perhaps with the exception of material on slavery. For most people, this history thrives on white guilt and feeds on black anger. The second narrative, although more nuanced than the first, is still largely situated in the twentieth century. In this narrative, W. E. B. Du Bois and Carter G. Woodson emerge as the "fathers of black history." Nothing of substantial scholarly weight preceded their work, so the narrative goes, and everything that came after was profoundly influenced by that work. Although both of these narratives possess kernels of truth, they ultimately leave African American history truncated and blunt any attempts to frame a more holistic and complex portrait of its actual origins and evolution.[1]

One can only subscribe to these narratives if one refuses to consider the long history of black historical writing, a history with roots much deeper than the twentieth century. The positioning of African American historians as recognizable professionals by the 1920s was the result of a development that took place over more than a hundred years of historical writing. Because the work of nineteenth-century writers regularly falls outside the pale of "sophisticated" or academically acceptable scholarly writing, we miss the many nuances in early historical writing and begin the discussion of the field's origin, ironically, just at the point where an important aspect of it—its professionalization—logically ends, namely the founding of the Association for the Study of Negro Life and History in 1915. A number of literary scholars and historians have confronted the challenges presented by the two dominant narratives of African American history, and on the foundation of their pioneering work I have attempted to build a more complete interpretation of the origins and evolution of African American history.

The basic intellectual trends that predominate today in African American history and literature, ranging from skillful critiques of American race relations designed to accentuate black humanity, to an engagement with Africa and the wider world, are rooted in the complex realities of the social, political, and economic conditions of the nineteenth century. Nineteenth-century black writers, as I have shown, were far more sophisticated in their presentations of history than even some scholars who recognize the importance of their work generally acknowledge. Determined to present an accurate and detailed history of their origins, these early black writers created historical narratives that engaged the current conditions of the race—the hard realities that black people faced on a day-to-day basis—and in doing so they also depended upon and deeply reflected nineteenth-century historical forms and ideas circulating in the national and international mainstreams. Borrowing from Puritanism and essentialism, from scientism and objectivity, they demonstrated a high level of intellectual engagement with the large and dynamic world of ideas. Often melding oratorical, rhetorical, and textual forms, black writers looked to history—just as other nineteenth-century writers did—to make sense of the past, explain the present, and predict the future. By doing so, these writers located themselves squarely in the longer trajectory of American historical writing and, perhaps more important, provided the outlines for a discernible African American historical tradition.

The outline of that tradition begins with African American writers' engagement with the biblical and classical sources during the years of the early republic. One could easily treat their use of theology as evidence of the customary religiosity of African American writers or even reduce it further, to an inherent personality trait of African Americans (superstition, voodoo). The black engagement with the ancient world has likewise appeared fanciful (that is, not serious) or as an example of Afrocentricism. I would argue, however, that when black writers draw on biblical and classical sources, that is rather evidence of their appropriating the tools of the larger intellectual culture with which they were intimately familiar. These ancient ideas and revered symbols defined the rise of Western civilization, and they defined African and African American history as well.

The early black historical tradition not only drew upon the same sites of authority, namely the Bible and works of classical antiquity, but it was also part of the same intellectual movements, such as classicism, Romanticism, realism, and scientism, that are evident in mainstream history disciplines. This allowed black writers to make a case for the centrality of the black subject in the nation's past, present, and future. While undoubtedly operating out of a desire to liberate the race and prove their humanity, black writers also clearly understood that history was an important intellectual endeavor that linked them to other educated communities.

The first years covered in this study witnessed the early wrangling of Americans to define themselves. Although they had recently won a war for independence, the meaning of patriotism and republicanism was not yet settled. African American writers integrated themselves into this debate by questioning the nation's revolutionary heritage not only because it failed to live up to its creed of freedom and liberty for every man but also because it failed even to acknowledge (and in some instances erased) black contributions to this history. Thus, much of the history writing of the nineteenth century was, indeed, political and even somewhat reactionary. The antislavery war began almost as soon as the Revolutionary War ended, and during the antebellum period, the proslavery factions were, if not winning, at least undaunted. Still, antislavery writing represented much more than political polemics: it reflected the development of a historical methodology that utilized the best sources available in the mainstream culture, in order to make the best possible case for black freedom—a freedom that remained unrealized until the antislavery war melded into the Civil War, and the antislavery factions finally won.

As important as mass cultural events—parades, commemorative and memorial ceremonies, and diverse forms of public demonstrations—were to the creation (and reflection) of African American history, the context of black intellectual and historical production was much more stable than these spontaneous situations suggest; and the results were the product of conscious, long-term intellectual objectives and efforts; moreover, they were intended to live long after their creation not only as the evidence of black thought but as the documented, unequivocal history of the black contribution to the development of the American nation (and even the history of the world). These works were not "hidden transcripts."[2] They represented concerted, organized efforts both to participate fully in the life of the nation and to develop and sustain the institutions within the community that had supported and promoted the work. Black writers, for obvious reasons, were at first concentrated in the North—in the states where slavery ended (at different times) after the American Revolution. And the context in which black writers worked included a whole host of black institutions, such as churches, literary and historical societies, the press, conventions, and a nascent academy.

Across the time period under discussion in this volume, the purposes to which the history is put are just as important as the production of it. Black writers used history not just to report, or even to challenge, but also to define the very contested terrain they encountered. When popular culture defined black people as inferior and most black people remained enslaved, these writers turned to Haiti not simply to celebrate black freedom, but to demonstrate black potential, to write black people into the history of world revolutions, and to warn America of its grave mistake in holding onto a tradition that the "civilized" world had long abandoned. When, after the Civil War, the "New South" ideology did little to incorporate them into the life of the nation, they became a "new" race, with slavery behind them and a future filled with nothing but potential. And as the nineteenth century gave way to the twentieth, professionally trained historians continued the work of their predecessors, collecting the raw data and shaping the new and emerging forms of history informed by scientism and objectivity. By the time Carter G. Woodson formed the Association for the Study of Negro Life and History, African American history had easily fulfilled David Walker's admonition to "trouble the pages of historians."

Heeding Walker's admonition proved challenging for African American historians in the nineteenth century. Fettered by the bonds of slavery in the South and a limited freedom in the North, these intellectuals also suffered from sociocultural prohibitions and proscriptions that limited their access to the full range of educational opportunities and relegated them to the margins of American society. Illiteracy rates for African Americans loomed at more than 90 percent for much of the early republic and antebellum periods. On the other hand, white historians operated in an entirely different sphere. Trained at the nation's leading theological schools or at German universities, they produced histories that emphasized a progressive and expanding republic founded on Providence, progress, and patriotism. This was certainly the case for George Bancroft, the dominant American historian of the nineteenth century. Narratives like Bancroft's *History of the United States*, published from the 1830s up through the 1890s, although broad in scope, had little to say about African Americans or Native Americans. Such histories promulgated a vision of what Alexander Saxton has termed "the white republic," a sociocultural formation that largely excluded African Americans and Native Americans from the progressive and teleological story of American advancement. Despite these difficulties, black writers produced a plethora of historical works, formed literary and historical associations, acquired advanced graduate training, instituted departments of history in black colleges and universities, and by 1915, formed one of the most enduring professional organizations for the study of African American history, the ASNLH.

Historians have been slow to label much of the work discussed in this book as historical, which can be attributed largely to contemporary, modernist ideas of what constitutes history. These critiques involve issues of writing style, sources (documentation), citation forms, and general presentation. Lectures, pamphlets, textbooks, and histories produced by African Americans, especially prior to the late nineteenth century are, to be sure, missing some of the stylistic markers of contemporary histories grounded in rigorous documentation, careful and consistent citations, and authorial detachment. Black writers, however, clearly understood the importance of history and of historians. In fact, we only need look at Walker's *Appeal* and its Enlightenment-driven intention to uncover the facts of history by "troubling the pages of historians." But just as histories of our own day reflect the cultural and ideological realities of the world we inhabit, these nineteenth-century histories produced by black thinkers were grounded in the recognizable scholarly and intellectual constructs of their own time.

While mainstream historians have been slow to recognize the richness of African American historical and intellectual production, literary scholars and literary historians have paved the way in uncovering the complex genealogy of African American writing. Over the past decade, scholars including Henry Louis Gates, the late Nellie McKay, Jean Fagan Yellin, Nina Baym, Frances Smith Foster, Rafia Zafar, Deborah McDowell, Vincent Carretta, Elizabeth McHenry, and John Ernest, among many others, not only recognized the diversity of black writing but have explored the varied ways in which it accentuated

African, African American, and European sensibilities. By engaging with a broad range of European and American intellectual movements, these scholars have recovered the work of little-known authors and explored the myriad ways that this work demonstrates the depth and scope of the scholarly imagination. Black literary figures ranging from Phillis Wheatley to Ann Plato, Frances Ellen Harper to Pauline Hopkins, remind us of the legacy of black intellectuals and recover what Elizabeth McHenry terms "forgotten readers." These scholars have asked readers to think more critically and concretely about African Americans as thinking and rational beings dedicated to upward mobility and the art of high literature.[3]

Historians, largely following the lead of literary scholars, have also contributed immensely to our knowledge of African American and American culture. Julie Winch, John Saillant, Patrick Rael, Bruce Dain, Richard Newman, Peter Hinks, Elizabeth Bethel, Mitch Kachun, John Stauffer, and others have been central to the reconstruction of an African American connection to the broader streams of American culture. Julie Winch's biographical treatment of James Forten and Richard Newman's examination of the life of Richard Allen skillfully link the lives of these two towering figures in African American political, community, and religious life to the founding traditions of the early republic. Peter Hinks's biographical examination of David Walker expands our understanding of his *Appeal* beyond the narrow purview of a nationalist document. Elizabeth Bethel's work on the construction of black identity and memory and Mitch Kachun's thorough examination of commemorative parades and celebrations during the nineteenth century provide us with more nuanced ways to think about the meanings of African American culture, life, and history. In many ways, this work has forced us to think beyond the narrow binaries of an essentialist African or American identity. It has also helped us to think in more dynamic ways about the complex cross-fertilizations of African- and European-centered cultures and allowed us to uncover and recover the myriad ways African Americans contributed to and constructed what we consider mainstream culture.[4]

Despite the pioneering work of literary scholars and historians, much remains to be done. In many ways, African American historiography is viewed as the stepchild of African American history. More fruitful investigations of African American historiography can point us more constructively towards a fuller understanding of the twentieth-century world that emerged after 1915 that provided the "groundwork" for the Harlem Renaissance, the growth of black educational and cultural institutions, and the advent of the modern civil rights movement. Such investigations may even shed light on our contemporary engagements with Afrocentrism, with the "history standards" that have become such a central issue in the culture wars, and with the relevance of history programs in our increasingly multicultural and multiethnic public schools. Despite the attention that has been given to Carter G. Woodson and the ASNLH (now called the Association for the Study of African American Life and History), we do not have a full-length study of this organization's evolution. More important, Woodson, as Pero Dagbovie has recently reminded us, did not create the conditions for the professionalization of African American history alone. We lack studies of a large number of these individuals who worked directly with Woodson: James Hugo Johnston, Alrutheus Ambush Taylor, Lorenzo Greene, Luther Porter Jackson, William Sherman Savage, Charles Wesley, Frenise Logan, L. D. Reddick, and Merl Eppse. Black women, until recently, have been largely absent from discussions of the historical profession. Deborah Gray White's recent work on black women historians, *Telling Histories*, is an important intervention. With the exception of a few, more famous individuals, little is known about the lives of numerous black female historians such as Ruth Anna Fisher, Youra T. Qualls, Letitia W. Brown, Elvena Bage Tillman, Margaret Nelson Rowley, and Elise Lewis. Uncovering all of these stories would provide important insights into the wealth of black historical research and its meanings for the larger American historical profession.[5]

That African American history is an integral part of a larger American historical story is more than a cliché; and we should not allow reductionist binaries to negate the innumerable ways in which the mainstream of history is really an amalgamation of the different cultural and contextual stories shaped and reshaped by all groups. Nineteenth-century writers clearly saw themselves as something more than members of disconnected and scattered groups, helpless chattel, or brute, subhuman creatures. They viewed themselves as men, and women of intelligence and erudition and as active shapers of the world they inhabited. Their visions of the past history and present possibilities of the race shaped the remarkable narratives they composed and inspired them to see themselves as participants in a human drama that stretched back to the "first ages of humankind."

To tell and appreciate the full story of the origins and meanings of African American history requires a broadening of our traditional vision of the evolution of this field; it requires our entering a world very unlike our own. In this world, despite limited resources and lack of access to seats of power, African Americans carved out intellectual spaces to present a more intricate and nu-

anced worldview about what Cornel West has famously described as "race matters." They turned to cultural survivals and to black protest culture, but they
also took up the intellectual weaponry of the nineteenth century: the jeremiad,
the Bible, classicism, Romanticism, realism, and scientism and objectivity; and
with such weapons they waged an unrelenting war on stereotypes and misperceptions about the race. In combating these obstructions, African American
intellectuals demonstrated how conversant they were with the wellsprings of
American intellectual culture. Their writings also make clear the impact of the
broader intellectual culture, especially print culture, in disseminating information to black people.

For these writers, the past was not, as one author has suggested, "a foreign
country."[6] Instead, it represented a living and breathing part of the present and
a hope for the future. For the orators and writers discussed here, history was a
tangible reality that they recited, discussed, debated, and actively reframed as
text. Only by reframing the original story, these authors believed, could one
truly understand the past and the role that all people, especially African Americans, played in the nation's history. Despite some shortcomings and mistakes,
their work serves as an enduring testament to their determination to provide
a faithful account of the race, informed by the raw material of the past, shaped
by the objective and subjective realities of the present, and infused with the
hope and possibility of the future.

Notes

Introduction

1   Blackett, *Building an Antislavery Wall.*

2   W. W. Brown, *Rising Son*, v–ix.

3   Bethel, *Roots of African American Identity*; Fabre and O'Meally, *History and Memory*; Kachun, *Festivals of Freedom*; and K. Savage, *Standing Soldiers, Kneeling Slaves.*

4   Literary scholars and historians active in the recovery of African American literary production have been especially adept in recognizing the importance and prevalence of textual production among early African American intellectuals. See Foster, *Written by Herself*, 1–2.

5   Ernest, *Liberation Historiography.*

6   Black engagement with texts is discussed in Porter, *Early Negro Writing*; Bruce, *Origins of African American Literature*; Peterson, *Doers of the Word;* and McHenry, *Forgotten Readers.* Issues regarding the importance of literacy are explored in Cornelius, *"When I Can Read"*; and H. A. Williams, *Self-Taught.*

7   Zafar, *We Wear the Mask*, 3.

8   McHenry, *"'Dreaded Eloquence,'"* 32–56, and *Forgotten Readers.*

9   R. Brown, *Knowledge Is Power*; Davidson, *Revolution and the Word.*

10 See Ronnick, *First Three*, "Latin Quotations," "Racial Ideology," and "Twelve Black Classicists." Also see Fikes, "It Was Never Greek," and "African American Scholars."

11 On the construction of history in the early republic and antebellum periods, see Gay, *Loss of Mastery*, 3–22; Calcott, *History in the United States*; Kraus and Joyce, *Writing of American History.* Interpretations of the jeremiad include Perry Miller, *New England Mind;* and Bercovitch, *American Jeremiad*, introduction. The jeremiad's impact on black thought is discussed in Moses, *Black Messiahs and Uncle Toms*, 30–48; and Howard-Pitney, *Afro-American Jeremiad.* Classicism's influence on nineteenth-century education is ably explored in Winterer, *Culture of Classicism*, 10–43. African American opposition to the Great Books, or "canon," is featured in the following studies: Bloom, *Closing of the American Mind*; Casement, *Great Canon Controversy*, 40–83; and Denby, *Great Books*, 89–91.

12 Bender, *Intellect and the Public Life.* Information on the meanings of history among African Americans is explored in Moses, *Afrotopia*, 1–43; and McHenry, *"'Dreaded Eloquence.'"* The building of an intellectual and institutional infrastructure in the African American community is discussed in H. Reed, *Platform for Change.* Discussion of various themes and issues in antebellum newspapers, especially *Freedom's Journal*, is featured in Penn, *Afro-American Press and Its Editors*, 25–70; Dann, *Black Press, 1827–1890*; Bacon, *Freedom's Journal;* and Hutton, *Early Black Press in America*, 3–6.

13 For a good introduction to the development of intellectual life in the United States from 1760 to 1800, see Shalhope, *Roots of Democracy*. My definition of Romanticism is based on Susan Conrad's work on the impact of Romanticism on female intellectuals. Conrad uses Morse Peckham's classic work, *Romanticism*. Peckham dates Romanticism from the late eighteenth century and suggests it promoted a "new formula for the universe, an organic interpretation of nature, the cosmos and humanity." Conrad, *Perish the Thought*, 9. It was a self-conscious worldview. However, *I wish to distinguish between the rationalism and empiricism of the Enlightenment view of the world (older view) versus the romantic view, which was rooted more in the senses or an organic interpretation of reality.* The relationship between history and Romanticism is explored in Levin, *History as Romantic Art*, 3–7. For information on the relationship between Romanticism and race, see Freimarck and Rosenthal, *Race and the American Romantics*. For another good discussion of Romanticism during the period, see Reynolds, *Walt Whitman's America*.

14 See Blight, *Frederick Douglass' Civil War*, 148–88.

15 The late-nineteenth-century shift to scientism is chronicled in a number of studies; see Cotkin, *Reluctant Modernism*, 51–73; and Ross, *Origins of the Social Sciences*, 53–76. Thomas Bender has done the most substantial work on the intellectual community in the antebellum period; see *Intellect and Public Life*. The development and transcendence of prehistoricist methodologies is discussed in Mandelbaum, *History, Man, and Reason*; Ross, "Historical Consciousness in Nineteenth-Century America"; Iggers and Powell, *Leopold von Ranke;* and Novick, *That Noble Dream*, 21–31. Examinations of the development of historicism include Breisach, *Historiography*; and Appleby et al., *Telling the Truth about History*, 52–90. For information on Northern intellectuals and the Civil War's impact in converting a class-conscious Boston Brahmin elite into proponents of Gilded Age ideology, see Frederickson, *Inner Civil War*.

16 Historian William Banks views the Civil War and its aftermath as fostering the rise of a black intellectual infrastructure; see *Black Intellectuals*, 33–47. For other important treatments of black intellectual life during the Emancipation, Reconstruction, and Gilded Age, see Maffly-Kipp, "Mapping the World." Maffly-Kipp relies heavily on "the trope of reconstruction," as a central factor in the emergence of race history in the late nineteenth century. This idea is borrowed from Gates in "Trope of the New Negro." Gates's work on canon formation within the African American literary tradition also has meaning for the efforts of early African American history; see "Master's Pieces." The invidious opposition to the acquisition of black literacy as well as the intense quest for intellectual respectability is chronicled in Dalton, "Alphabet Is an Abolitionist." Histories of African American women which explore educational advancement and general uplift include Neverdon-Morton's *Afro-American Women of the South*; Lerner, *Black Women in White America*; and Giddings, *When and Where I Enter*. Also see Margaret Murray Washington, "The Advancement of Colored Women," 183–89. The definitive discussion of socialization and professionalization among African American women is Shaw, *What a Woman Ought*. Other works include Lemert and Bhan, *Voice of Anna Julia Cooper*; Mossell, *Work of the Afro-American Woman*; Gruesser, *Unruly Voice;* and Jones, *All Bound Up*, 119–204.

17 See J. W. Cromwell, "History," in Bethel Literary and Historical Association Pa-

pers, Moorland-Springarn Research Center, Howard University; and Meier, *Negro Thought in America*, 33, 45, 48, 50, 53, 55, 178. The history of the American Negro Academy is explored in Moss, *American Negro Academy*. There are a number of studies on the development the black bibliophile tradition in Philadelphia and New York; see Wayman, "American Negro Historical Society of Philadelphia and Its Officers," 287–94; Spady, "Afro-American Historical Society"; and two essays, Martin, "Bibliophiles, Activists and Race Men," and "Arthur Alonso Schomburg, (1874–1936), Black Bibliophile and Collector," both in Sinnette, Coates, and Battle, *Black Bibliophiles and Collectors*. For a listing of black bibliophiles, see Gubert, *Early Black Bibliophiles*. Crowder's *John Edward Bruce* is a useful study of a black bibliophile.

18 Correspondence with Daniel Payne and William Wells Brown can be found in William Wells Brown to William Still, February 2, 1865, in reel 6, American Negro Historical Society Collection, 1790–1905, Historical Society of Pennsylvania, Philadelphia (hereafter ANHSC). See Wilson, *Emancipation*. Mention of J. W. Cromwell's and Benjamin Brawley's histories appears in *Thirty-first Annual Catalogue of the Tuskegee Normal and Industrial Institute, 1911–1912*, 32; and *Thirty-third Annual Catalogue . . . 1913–1914)*, 33. Edward A. Johnson to Booker T. Washington, January 12, 1891, in *Booker T. Washington Papers*, 3:121. On Washington's writing, see the introduction to Kletzing and Crogman, *Progress of a Race*.

19 See Reuben, *Making of the Modern University*.

20 My thinking on the modernist approach has been shaped by examinations of the literary and historical literature on the development of black historicism. Most writers on black historiography share the view that antebellum historical discourse was less sophisticated than work produced in the late-nineteenth and early twentieth centuries. This lack of sophistication is usually based on methodological considerations (use of sources, footnotes, style of writing, and training). Vernon Loggins's *Negro Author*, an influential book in the canon of African American literary history, argues that historians writing between 1865 and 1900 were more sophisticated and "began to discard the old manner of spreading propaganda and to adapt the usages of scientific investigation." Loggins is also very critical of many of the writers of the latter period (1865–83). He, like John Hope Franklin, viewed George Washington Williams, author of the *History of the Negro Race* in 1883, in a more favorable light because of the similarities in method and style to scholarly work based on twentieth-century historical approaches. See Loggins, *Negro Author*, 177–211. Earl Thorpe's *Black Historians: A Critique*, widely viewed as one of the earliest assessments of black historiography, assessed early black historical production using modernist standards. Thorpe assessed this production based on "quality, historical methodology, thoroughness in the use of sources, objectivity, soundness of interpretation and philosophy of history." After subjecting these works to the previously stated criteria, Thorpe stated that "none of the authors were employed in teaching history. They usually had no formal training in historical methodology and did superficial research." See Thorpe, *Black Historians*, v–vi, 29–45. Benjamin Quarles, despite his recognition that a tradition of historical writing existed in the antebellum period, remained critical of the historical production of antebellum black intellectuals. Quarles wrote, "In summary, the history propounded by antebellum blacks was open to question in its

documentation and tone. Their concept of history strong on the theoretically infer-able, these black chroniclers did not, in general, deem it necessary to furnish their sources. Such as cavalier attitude toward documentation inevitably led to some un-supportable claims. In addition these black writers and speakers reflected the spread-eagle period in which they lived, with bombastic language the vogue. Chroniclers of the black past shared in this widespread penchant for overstatement, especially since they viewed Afro-American history as a form of shock therapy." See Quarles, "Black History's Antebellum Origins," 133–34. Jacqueline Goggin's work on black historiography and her biography on Woodson, although much more respectful of African American historical methods that preceded Woodson, clearly viewed Wood-son's work as a more sophisticated and systematic scholarly endeavor than that earlier work. See J. Goggin, "Carter G. Woodson," 18–49, and *Carter G. Woodson*, 32–66. John Hope Franklin began his generational approach to the evolution of black his-torical scholarship with George Washington Williams's *History of the Negro Race*. Franklin's designation of Williams as a the inaugurator of an African American scholarly historical tradition is clearly based on the fact that his methodology and writing style—and his publisher—mirrored those of twentieth-century historians. Franklin remarked that Williams's *History of the Negro Race* "was published in 1882 by a reputable publisher, G. P. Putnam and Sons, was about one thousand pages long . . . [and] I saw that it was carefully researched—with plenty of footnotes—logically organized and well written." *George Washington Williams*, xv. See also Franklin, "On the Evolution of Scholarship," 13–22. August Meier and Elliott Rudwick offer a similar modernist approach to early black writing: "Their books and pamphlets, largely informed by biblical arguments and celebrating black contributions to an-cient civilizations and more recent individual accomplishments, had been infused with the purposes of stimulating racial self-esteem and pride among blacks and of educating whites regarding Negro achievements. . . . Most of the work came from the pens of popularizers rather than scholars." *Black History and the Historical Profession*, 2. Some of the work on commemorative culture also seems to replicate the modern-ist approach. Blyden Jackson is critical of most nineteenth-century historians, with the exception of George Washington Williams. His criticisms focus on the areas of methodology, arguments, and sources. Writing black history was reduced to "an easily understandable reflex action on their part against the contemptible position in the American social order of blacks, of all of whom, collectively, it was customary for other Americans to say they were so inferior among the races of mankind as to have no history." Jackson's *History of Afro-American Literature* continues in the mod-ernist vein by applying current historical approaches to the past. This approach is clear in Jackson's assessment of Robert Benjamin Lewis, William Nell, William Still, and George Washington Williams. Jackson characterized Lewis as "part Indian and part Negro" and claimed that he "very vastly resented white characterizations of the Negro as a man without an honorific past." Going further, Jackson suggests Lewis's enlarged, 1844 edition of *Light and Truth* served to justify his subtitle: "Containing the Universal History of the Colored and the Indian Race, from the Creation of the World to the Present Time." Jackson completely overlooks arguments regarding consanguinity and suggests instead that the starting point for Lewis's study of "the two American minorities [blacks and Native Americans] is the Creation as given in Genesis in the Holy Bible, where neither blacks nor American Indians, except for a conjectural reading of an exasperated outburst by Noah, manifest any vestige of the slightest appearance. As a matter of fact, Lewis relies on the Bible plus hearsay as the main authority for his history throughout a far and near antiquity in which he identifies as Negroes Solon, Plato, Hannibal, Pompey, Epictetus, and even Homer and Euclid. Documentation of any of his many flat assertions is no problem for Lewis. He simply makes his case and lets them stand." Jackson is also critical of Lewis's discussion of the similarities between Native Americans and the Lost Tribes of Israel, despite the fact that this was a legitimate intellectual discussion and speculation in the nineteenth century. Jackson takes much the same approach in assessing James W. C. Pennington's *Textbook*, which he viewed as having been written largely for children. He concluded that Pennington's work is "not respectable history." William Nell is also criticized for his *Colored Patriots*. Jackson is critical of the work's organization and Nell's use of records. He lamented that Nell used records too indiscriminately and even went so far as to "incorporate whole a vexing number of the pages of a direct quotation, with no deletions or condensations at all, into his text." In an extended reference to method, Jackson notes that Nell's history is amorphous. He goes on to say that it "lacks, in the first place, the coherence and firm inner structure present in the work of historians who, as historians should, see in their mind patterns for the pasts they are presenting and are guided by those patterns as they compose their histories. The formlessness of the documentation in *Colored Patriots* but duplicates, therefore, and so increases, the formlessness of the book's total conception and execution." He concluded by praising some aspects of the book but suggested that "only embryonically is Nell a historian." Jackson applies many of the same criticisms of form, style, and methodology to William Still's *Underground Railroad*. He suggested that Still was "woefully without any conception of how a history should be organized, and so, the *Underground Railroad* is nearly eight hundred pages of memorabilia of various kinds, a miscellany of containing, although in no manner generating from them a coherent work of art or of history, letters (too often quoted at exorbitant length) from slaves, fugitives, abolitionists, excerpts from newspapers, legal documents, tales, biographical sketches and reminiscences from Still himself." In Jackson's presentation, George Washington Williams, however, is viewed as "generally the first black American to write history at a level of competence [that] entitled him to serious designation as a genuine forerunner of such black historians as John Hope Franklin and Benjamin Quarles." See Jackson, *History of Afro-American Literature*, 200–218. Clarence Walker offers a similarly dismissive assessment of nineteenth-century historians in "American Negro as Historical Outsider." Elizabeth Raul Bethel's approach to the development of African American historical memory privileges the trajectory of African American consciousness "from a focus on personal experiences recounted in real time through autobiographical memory to an emphasis on collective experience recalled through cultural memory and reconstructed in historical time." See Bethel, *Roots of African American Identity*, 1–4, 194.

21 John Ernest's work represents a substantial engagement with postmodern ways of framing history; see *Liberation Historiography*, 1–38. For good introductions to post-

modern theory and history, see Breisach, *On the Future of History*, 1–6; Berkhofer, *Beyond the Great Story*, 1–5; Jenkins, *Re-Thinking History*, 5–6; and White, *Metahistory*, 1–132, and *Content and Form*. Works that explore nontextual manifestations of black history include Bethel, *Roots of African American Identity;* Fabre and O'Meally, *History and Memory*; and Kachun, *Festivals of Freedom*. Although his work is not directly commenting on history, Kirk Savage is deeply interested in issues of representation of the black past in public space, see K. Savage, *Standing Soldiers, Kneeling Slaves*. The relationship between ethnology and history is explored in Bay, *White Image in the Black Mind*. One of the most sophisticated discussions of the textual meanings of the early period is in Ernest, *Liberation Historiography*.

22 Notions of the public sphere are articulated in Habermas, *Structural Transformation of the Public Sphere*. On the black public sphere in the eighteenth and nineteenth centuries, see J. Brooks, "Early American Public Sphere"; and Martha Jones, *All Bound Up*, 1–2. For the application of this concept to aspects of late nineteenth- and twentieth-century African American history, see Higginbotham, *Righteous Discontent*; and the Black Public Sphere Collective, *Black Public Sphere*.

23 Thorpe, *Negro Historians in the United States*. For an earlier critique of the contributionist model of black history, see Reddick, "New Interpretation of Negro History"; and Quarles, "Black History's Antebellum Origins."

24 Thorpe, review of *Black History and the Historical Profession*, by August Meier and Elliott Rudwick, 123–27.

25 The periodization for this chapter is also influenced by the work of the literary scholar Dorothy Porter Wesley; see *Early Negro Writing*, 1. Wesley ends her examination of early African American literary production in 1837, due to the fact that African Americans were engaged locally and nationally in efforts to improve their condition. She also notes that the 1840s witnessed the rise of more capable writers. Also see Calcott, *History in the United States*; Sweet, *Black Images in White America*; Banks, *Black Intellectuals*; Bay, *White Image in the Black Mind*; Kachun, *Festivals of Freedom*; Ernest, *Liberation Historiography*; and Joan Bryant, *Reluctant Race Men*, forthcoming.

26 This work builds upon and modifies Earl Thorpe's periodization of African American history first presented in several seminal works that include his dissertation and two subsequent studies. See "Negro Historiography in the United States," *Negro Historians in the United States*, and *Black Historians*.

27 Franklin, "On the Evolution of Scholarship," 13–22.

Chapter One

1 For information on how African Americans engaged print culture, see McHenry, *Forgotten Readers*, 1–21.

2 For information on commemorative culture, see Bethel, *Roots of African American Identity*; Fabre and O'Meally, *History and Memory*; Kachun, *Festivals of Freedom*; and K. Savage, *Standing Soldiers, Kneeling Slaves*.

3 See Hinks, *To Awaken My Afflicted Brethren*; and McHenry, *Forgotten Readers*.

4 For information on the engagement of African Americans with intellectual issues,

see Banks, *Black Intellectuals*, 1–48; Swift, *Black Prophets of Justice*; and Peterson, *Doers of the Word*, 3–23. The institutional and communal challenges faced by black intellectuals are chronicled in Horton and Horton, *In Hope of Liberty*; H. Reed, *Platform for Change*; and Rael, *Black Identity and Black Protest*, 12–53.

5 One of the best discussions of George Bancroft's engagements with Providence and its extension to Teutonic germ theory is found in Levin, *History as Romantic Art*, 78–91. The jeremiad is explored in Bercovitch, *American Jeremiad*; and Howard-Pitney, *Afro-American Jeremiad*, 3–16; and more recently in Saillant, *Black Puritan, Black Republican*.

6 Historical conventions in the nineteenth century are examined in Calcott, *History in the United States*. Discussions of classical culture in America are found in Reinhold, *Classica Americana*; and Winterer, *Culture of Classicism*.

7 On Progress, see Calcott, *History in the United States*, 3–6; and Ferguson, *American Enlightenment*, 22–23. The idea of progress in American social and intellectual life is discussed generally in May, *Enlightenment in America*, 26–41, 153–306; Landsman, *From Colonials to Provincials*; Matthews, *Toward a New Society*; and Shalhope, *Roots of Democracy*.

8 These two approaches (modernist and postmodernist) are represented in the work of Wilson Jeremiah Moses and John Ernest. See Moses, *Afrotopia*, 1–43; and Ernest, *Liberation Historiography*, 1–37. Both of these approaches tend to limit the perspectives from which we can comprehend the complexity of the African American historical enterprise. Moses talks about forms of historicism in the nineteenth century but frames these approaches as precursors of Afrocentric thought as opposed to serious framing for black history. Here, I build on Moses's engagement with eighteenth- and nineteenth-century historicism as an important means of excavating the meanings of black historicism. Ernest, on the other hand, utilizes a postmodern approach to frame nineteenth-century black history, which looks to contemporary understandings of history through his privileging of the politicized aspects of this history as well as the liberationist construct, which is drawn from the 1960s articulation of liberation theology contained in the work of black theologian James Cone.

9 Information on black engagement with print culture is contained in McHenry, *Forgotten Readers*; and Andrews, *To Tell a Free Story*. Also see J. Brooks, "Early American Public Sphere."

10 Black historical presentations in the public sphere are addressed in several studies; see Bethel, *Roots of African American Identity*, 29–84; Kachun, *Festivals of Freedom*, 16–53; K. Savage, *Standing Soldiers, Kneeling Slaves*, 21–51; and Rael, *Black Identity and Black Protest*, 54–81. Examples of early black pamphlets and literature include Jupiter Hammon, *An Address to the Negroes in the State of New York* (1787); Prince Hall, *A Charge Delivered to the Brethren of the African Lodge on the 25th of June, 1792* (1792); Jones and Allen, *Narrative of the Proceedings* (1794); Hall and Schomburg, *Charge Delivered to the African Lodge* (1797); Coker, *Dialogue* (1810); Cuffee, *Brief Account of the Settlement* (1812); Forten, *Letters by a Man of Colour* (1813); Forten and Parrot, *To the Humane and Benevolent Inhabitants* (1817); Saunders, *Address Delivered at Bethel Church* (1818); and Young, *Ethiopian Manifesto* (1829). Black literature played an important part in the

African American intellectual scene during this period; see, Potkay and Burr, *Black Atlantic Writers*; Brooks and Saillant, *"Face Zion Forward"*; and Equiano, *Interesting Narrative of the Life of Olaudah Equiano*.

11   See Newman, Rael, and Lapansky, *Pamphlets of Protest*, 1–7. Commemorative celebrations in the African American community in the nineteenth century are discussed in Bethel, *Roots of African American Identity*; and Kachun, *Festivals of Freedom*.

12   The books that utilize these approaches include the following: On vindicationism and contributionism, see Drake, *Black Folk Here and There*, preface, 121, 130–32; and Moses, *Afrotopia*, 21–23. On Afrocentricism, see Moses, Afrotopia; Lefkowitz, *Not Out of Africa*; Howe, *Afrocentricism*; Berlinerblau, *Heresy in the University*; Shamit, *History in Black*; and C. Walker, *We Can't Go Home Again*. On Masonry, see J. Brooks, *American Lazarus*, 115–50; and Wallace, *Constructing the Black Masculine*, 53–81. Here I concur with John Ernest's concern with history as a matter of argument and record. Ernest's argument appears in the introduction to his book, *Liberation Historiography*, 1–37. Moses in *Afrotopia* does a wonderful job of contextualizing black historicism in the nineteenth century, but he does so in an attempt to provide a genealogy for Afrocentricism. Many of the ideas discussed in the book treat early black historicism as myth, popular history, and legend. Moses does not believe that early black historicism can serve as a viable precursor for serious historical interrogation of the black past. I argue, however, that the modernist and postmodernist paradigms, in terms of interpreting the literature on black writing, focus less on the contextual ground of eighteenth- and nineteenth-century historical practice. Modernist assumptions locate historical coherence in the late nineteenth and twentieth centuries, whereas postmodern concerns essentially represent a reaction to the limitations or shortsightedness of modernists regarding a fixed and objective historical record. While Ernest urges serious attention be given to the writing of nineteenth-century intellectuals, he does so for the ways these narratives transcend the limitations of a deeply contentious historical moment and represent more contemporary notions of history as fluid, political, decentered, and open to multiple interpretations and casual explanations. In this way, we can easily explain why and how this history differs from our current perceptions of history, while at the same time embracing its politicized and activist elements, which affirm a post-1960s understanding of race and foreground liberation as the casual explanation for why blacks engaged in writing history. This approach, while extremely useful in deepening our understanding of communal and activist sentiments in the nineteenth century and framing black history as an activist and interventionist discourse, would also benefit from a deeper contextualization within the eighteenth and nineteenth centuries.

13   For information on early American historicism, see Gay, *Loss of Mastery*, 3–22; Calcott, *History in the United States*; Kraus and Joyce, *Writing of American History*. The best study of the impact of eighteenth- and nineteenth-century historicism on popular black historicism is Moses, *Afrotopia*. A good study of prominent eighteenth-century historians is J. B. Black, *Art of History*. Montesquieu is known for his *Spirit of Laws* (1748); David Hume, for his *History of Great Britain* (1754–62*)*, *Treatise on Human Nature* (1739–40), and *Philosophical Works* (4 vols., 1826); Gibbon, for *The Decline and Fall of*

the Roman Empire (1776); and Robertson, for *History of Scotland* (1787) and *History of the Americas (1792)*. Examinations of history in the eighteenth century cannot overlook the impact of race. While most historians of race recognize the impact of the shift from natural to scientific explanations of race by the late eighteenth century, it is still the case that despite the popularity of Linnaeus, Hume, and others, as George Mosse has noted, moralistic and pietistic beliefs about race were still common in the literature. The trajectory from natural history to the hard scientific racial theory of the nineteenth century was a gradual process. See Mosse, "Eighteenth Century Foundations," in Bulmer and Solomos, *Racism*, 40–45. Also see Dain, *Hideous Monster*, 1–40. Uncertainty about the meanings of race and its relationship to degeneration and to blacks turning white is discussed in ibid., 19–26; and Sweet, *Bodies Politic*, 142–44, 275–86. See also Morrison and Stewart, *Race and the Early Republic*.

14 Most writers, like Wilson Moses and Bruce Dain, discuss interest among African Americans in Africa, especially as it relates to Egyptomania, as a form of Afrocentricism, or black Egypt interest. See Moses, *Afrotopia*; Dain, *Hideous Monster;* and Bernal, *Black Athena*. More nuanced approaches can be found in the work of Trafton, *Egypt Land*; and Keita, *Race and the Writing of History*.

15 My reading of the Western canon and black engagement with it differs from John Ernest's assessment that the "racial state" that informed black history and existence in the nineteenth century precluded serious use of "white nationalist historiography" and by extension the Western canon, especially that which arose during the Enlightenment. See Ernest, *Liberation Historiography*, 2–9. Enlightenment understandings of blacks and the African past were extremely varied and included both positive and negative portrayals. Moreover, depending on the context in which they appeared, they continued to utilize classical and universal notions of history. See Eze, *Race and the Enlightenment*, 1–8. African American engagement with the classics in the nineteenth century is discussed Fikes, "It Was Never Greek to Them," 3–12, and "African American Scholars." Also see Ronnick, "A Pick instead of Greek and Latin," 60–61; and the reprint of *The Autobiography of William Saunders Scarborough*, a noted nineteenth-century black classicist, which Ronnick edited. Also see Moses, *Alexander Crummell*, 67–88. More general examples of the role of classicism in nineteenth-century life include Wills, *Cincinnatus, George Washington and the Enlightenment*, and *Lincoln at Gettysburg*. Complex presentations of blackness in the ancient world abound, some positive and others negative. It is clear, however, that black writers used these images selectively. Using the classical approach as an example, for an assessment of negative and positive Greek descriptions of various parts of the African continent (Libya, Egypt and Ethiopia), see Mudimbe, *Idea of Africa*, 71–104. For a discussion of the varied portrayals of blacks in the ancient world, see Keita, "Deconstructing the Classical Age." American engagement with Egypt is another important component of this argument and central in historicizing the projects of nineteenth-century historical writers. See Irwin, *American Hieroglyphics*; J. Davis, *Landscape of Belief*; Obenzinger, *American Palestine*; and Harvey, *American Geographics*. The best contemporary study of Egyptomania is Trafton's *Egypt Land*.

16 The importance of oratory in the colonial era and the early republic is explored in

Gustafson, *Eloquence Is Power*. Brief discussions of the work of John Marrant, Peter Williams, and William Hamilton appear in Bruce, *Origins of African American Literature*, 90–91, 107–9, 123–24; and Kachun, *Festivals of Freedom*, 324–25.

17   See Marrant, "You Stand on the Level." Also see Marrant's narrative reprinted in Carretta, *Unchained Voices*, 110–34. A recent discussion of Masonry that situates Marrant's work in this tradition is J. Brooks, "Prince Hall." Discussions of black masonry are included in Crawford, *Prince Hall and His Followers*; Muraskin, *Middle-Class Blacks in a White Society*; and Williams, *Black Freemasonry*. Maurice Wallace offers a useful critique of the representational practices of black freemasons and argues that Martin Delany's "Objects and Aims of Freemasonry," is one of the first documents to make an Afrocentric case for Africa; see *Constructing the Black Masculine*, 53–81.

18   Marrant, "You Stand on the Level," 30–31. Marrant's religious views are discussed at length in Saillant, "'Wipe Away All Tears from Their Eyes,'" http://www.mille.org/publications/winter98/journvol1issue1.html. For the location of Paradise, see Josephus, *Antiquities*, 1:3, 15:11. Assessments of the attitude of the early church are explored in Logan's classic article, "Attitude of the Church."

19   Marrant, "You Stand on the Level," 36. Dickson Bruce makes the point that Marrant's scholarship, especially his assessment that ancient white civilizations also previously existed in a state of slavery, was drawn from earlier debates over civilization and savagery in European culture. Moreover, these sentiments appeared in Equiano's *Interesting Narrative*. See Bruce, *Origins of African American Literature*, 90. For information on various manifestations of slavery prior to the rise of the Western hemisphere, see Blackburn, "Old World Background."

20   Peter Williams, *Abolition of the Slave Trade*. Readings of Africa as the Garden of Eden are also found in Equiano's *Interesting Narrative*. Historian Bruce Dain argues that Equiano's presentation represents the "preliterate self as innocent and Africa as Eden." *Hideous Monster*, 50.

21   P. Williams, *Abolition of the Slave Trade*," 68. For information on seventeenth-century views of the New World, see MacCormack, "Limits of Understanding." An assessment of Robertson's critique of Amerindian societies is contained in Brading, *First America*, 432–41; and Canizares-Esguerra, *How to Write the History*, 120–24, 178–82, and "Entangled Histories." Information on William Robertson is located in Black, *Art of History*, 117–43; Smitten, "Impartiality"; Francesconi, "William Robertson"; and S. Brown, *William Robertson*. Information on Spanish (imperial) histories of the Spanish conquest is contained in Brading, *First America*. One of the most famous of these histories of conquest is Diaz, *Conquest of New Spain*. Sources on the Black Legend include Las Casas, *Devastation of the Indies*; and C. Gibson, *Black Legend*. While subsequent orations link Spanish, English, Dutch, and French involvement in the slave trade, it is clear that the Portuguese and the Spanish, given their early involvement, remain central to the story of the Atlantic slave trade.

22   Hamilton, *O' Africa*. Dickson Bruce provides a useful discussion of the influences on Hamilton's work, in *Origins of African American Literature*, 110–11. His assessment of *O' Africa* appears on 124–25.

23   Hamilton, *O' Africa*, 96. The assumption of Spanish barbarism is discussed in the work of Charles Gibson and Lewis Hanke. The use of the Black Legend in William

Robertson's work is discussed in Smitten, "Impartiality," 62–65. For information on the Black Legend in British circles, see Maltby, *Black Legend in England*. Information on Vico is found in Breisach, *Historiography*, 210–14.

24 This approach is most evident in William Robertson's work; see Phillipson, "Providence and Progress." For the dynamics of the correlation between the human condition and commerce in eighteenth-century historical thought, see Breisach, *Historiography*, 199–214. Some of this interest in commercialism was also connected to the publication of Adam Smith's *Wealth of Nations*, the primary promoter of mercantilism in the eighteenth century. Russell Parrott's oration on the slave trade uses language similar to that found in Hamilton's oration. He pointed to "the infamous barbarities committed by the Spaniards in their newly discovered possessions upon the offending inhabitants, caused some pious men, who migrated for the purpose of promulgating the Christian religion, to lay their sufferings before the government, to save the aborigines from slavery cast the shackles upon the African." In another instance Parrott wrote, the "piratical Portuguese . . . were the first violators of the rights of the African." Parrott, *Oration on the Abolition*, quoted in Porter, *Early Negro Writing*, 384.

25 Peter Williams used the same terminology in his 1807 oration *Abolition of the Slave Trade*, regarding "ancient" and "learned" observers. This language suggests a common intellectual culture knowledge base among African American intellectuals. Ancient accounts of Africa included Herodotus, *Histories*, 2:90–95; Strabo, *Geography*, book 17; Pliny the Elder, *Natural History*, 54–62. Eighteenth-century sources with information about Africa include Buffon, *Natural History* (1748, 1804); Hume, "Of Natural Characters," (1748, 1758); Beattie, *Essay on the Nature and Immutability of Truth* (1770); Kant, "On the Different Races of Man" (1775); Herder, *Ideas for a Philosophy of History for Mankind* (1784–91). Other sources for African Americans' engagement with Africa drawn from Greek and Roman sources are cited in Keita, "Deconstructing the Classical Age." Information on classical culture in the nineteenth century is found in Reinhold, *Classica Americana*, 23–93.

26 For a discussion of the humanistic nature of black historiography in the early nineteenth century, see Handlin, "Search for Truth."

27 Oson, *Search for Truth*, 1.

28 Randall Burkett quotes a portion from Frank Croswell's diaries indicating that Oson, despite limited knowledge, collected materials on Africa and managed them quite well for an autodidact. Burkett also discusses Croswell's diaries and provides biographical information about Oson. See "Reverend Henry Croswell." See also Bragg, *History of the Afro-American Group*.

29 Piersen, *Black Yankees*, 15–16. For additional information on black intellectual life in Connecticut in the colonial and early republic periods, see Saillant, *Black Puritan, Black Republican*, 9–47. Dickson Bruce briefly mentions Oson's work in *Origins of African American Literature*, 124–25.

30 Shepard, *History of St. Mark's Church*, 101; "Ordination," *Freedom's Journal*, March 14, 1828. Information about Oson's impending missionary service is featured in the *African Repository* 3, no. 9 November 1827): 270–71, quoted in Burkett, "Reverend Henry Croswell," 11n. Oson's death notices appear in *Episcopal Watchman*, September 20,

1828, 214; and *African Repository* 4, no. 9 (November 1828): 283–84. Additional death notices include *Freedom's Journal*, September 26 and October 3, 1828.

31 Oson, *Search for Truth*, 4–5.

32 Ibid., 4, 5, 10. One of the best recent treatments of the Curse of Ham is Goldenberg, *Curse of Ham*. Nineteenth-century racial theory is discussed in George Frederickson, *Black Image in the White Mind*; Goldberg, *Racist Culture*; and Dain, *Hideous Monster*.

33 For Oson's statement on consanguinity, see *Search for Truth*, 6. For information about the argument of consanguinity, see Bay, *White Image in the Black Mind*, 13–37.

34 Oson's use of biblical sources is not surprising given his involvement with the Episcopal Church; see *Search for Truth*, 6–7. For information on African involvement in the early Christian church, see Isichei, *History of Christianity in Africa*, 1–44. Discussions of the black public sphere tend to locate black interest in ancient Africa as related to Masonry. See J. Brooks, "Early American Public Sphere," and *American Lazarus*, 115–59. A more recent discussion of the centrality of Masonry among blacks is Wallace, *Constructing the Black Masculine*, 53–81.

35 General information on Egypt's symbolic presence and importance in nineteenth-century culture is explored in Irwin, *American Hieroglyphics*; and Trafton, *Egypt Land*.

36 Oson, *Search for Truth*, 8

37 Ibid., 10

38 Ibid., 12

39 Moses suggests that heroic monumentalism is an essential component of popular nineteenth-century black historicism; see *Afrotopia*, 23–25.

40 An assessment of the role of the *African Repository* on historical presentations of Africa is contained in Hinks, *To Awaken My Afflicted Brethren*, 181–95.

41 For assessments of Africa in the Western mind, see Curtin, *Image of Africa*; Nederveen Pieterse, *White on Black*, 18–51; and Sanneh, *Abolitionists Abroad*, 166.

42 See Reinhold, *Classica America*, 142–49; and Winterer, *Culture of Classicism*, 10–43.

43 The best recent study on *Freedom's Journal* is Bacon, *Freedom's Journal*. See "Africa," *Freedom's Journal*, February 7, 1829. DeVastey's editorials were excerpted in large part from the *London Weekly Register* and the *African Repository*, which were featured in two subsequent issues on February 14 and 21, 1829. Other articles devoted exclusively to history include "History of Slavery," *Freedom's Journal*, July 20, 1827; and "Extracts from an Enquiry concerning the Intellectual and Moral Faculties and Literature of Negroes, by Henri Abbé Grégoire," *Freedom's Journal*, November 14, 1828.

44 Volney's work includes "Observations on the Negro-Race," *Freedom's Journal*, December 12, 1828, and "Memoranda in the History of the Slave Trade and Slavery," *Freedom's Journal*, January 24, 1829.

45 The best discussion of Russwurm's "Mutability of Human Affairs" (*Freedom's Journal*, April 6, 1827) is found in Moses, *Afrotopia*, 51–55.

46 My approach builds on Wilson Moses's assessment of eighteenth-century historiography, which recognizes the importance of historiographies of decline in eighteenth- and nineteenth-century thought. See Moses, *Afrotopia*, 44–56. Dain examines mutability through the lens of racial theory and black interest in Egypt and redemptive Christianity; see *Hideous Monster*, 112–48; and Russwurm, "Mutability of Human Affairs."

47   "The Scrapbooks of Africanus" appear in *Freedom's Journal*: "Hayti, No. 1," April 20, 1827; "Hayti, No. 2," April 27, 1827; "Hayti, No. 3," May 4, 1829; "Hayti, No. 4," June 15, 1827; "Hayti, No. 5," June 29, 1827; and "Hayti, No. 6," October 12, 1827. They are discussed in Bethel, *Roots of African American Identity*, 155–56. The lack of public celebrations relating to the Haitian Revolution is discussed in Kachun, *Festivals of Freedom*, 57, and "African Americans, Public Commemorations and the Haitian Revolution."

48   *Freedom's Journal*, May 11 and 14, 1827. Also see John Russwurm, "Conditions and Prospects of Haiti" (1826).

49   Numerous articles on classical studies appeared in the *North American Review* leading up to the inauguration of the black press: "On the Priority of Greek Studies," July 1820, 209–18; "Study of the Classics," October 1820, 415–23; and Review of *The Latin Reader*, by Frederick Jacobs, July 1825, 246–48.

50   The best study of Walker's *Appeal to the Coloured Citizens of the World* is Hinks, *To Awaken My Afflicted Brethren*.

51   Garnet, *Walker's Appeal*, v–vii; Stuckey, *Slave Culture*, 98–120, and *Ideological Origins*, 9–13; Franklin, *Free Negro in North Carolina*, 64–75; Hinks, *To Awaken My Afflicted Brethren*, 70–71.

52   Responses to Walker's *Appeal* include "Walker's Pamphlet," *Liberator*, January 29, 1831; and "Walker's *Appeal* No. 3," *Liberator*, May 28, 1831. An intriguing contemporary reading of the *Appeal* is R. Levine, "Circulating the Nation."

53   A study that exposes some of the limitations and failings of the American Enlightenment in relation to African Americans, women, and Native Americans is Ferguson, *American Enlightenment*, 150–91.

54   Bailyn, *To Begin the World Anew*; Ball, *Hamilton, Madison, and Jay*. For an examination of dissent in relation to federalism, see Cornell, *Other Founders*. See also D. Walker, *Appeal*, 15. McHenry offers a close textual reading of Walker's *Appeal*, which discusses his belief in the Declaration of Independence and the Constitution as foundational documents; see *Forgotten Readers*, 23–42.

55   Frederickson, *Black Image in the White Mind*; Banton, *Racial Theories*, 17–43; Bay, *White Image in the Black Mind*; Dain, *Hideous Monster*; Jefferson, *Notes on the State of Virginia*, 140–43. Boulton, "The American Paradox: Jeffersonian Equality and Racial Science," 467–93.

56   The importance of the Enlightenment and its impact on intellectual production is discussed in Gay, *Enlightenment*, 56–84; Perry, *Intellectual Life in America*, 95–158; and May, *Enlightenment in America*. For specific discussions of black engagement with Enlightenment thought, see Hinks, *To Awaken My Afflicted Brethren*, 211; and Gilroy, *Black Atlantic*, 44–45.

57   D. Walker, *Appeal*, 3, 6. Walker's *Appeal* is a more sophisticated take on Robert Alexander Young's "Ethiopian Manifesto," also published in 1829, which is reprinted in Stuckey, *Ideological Origins of Black Nationalism*, 30–38.

58   D. Walker, *Appeal*, 9. Information on Josephus is found in Feldman and Huta, *Josephus, the Bible, and History*; and Feldman, *Josephus and Modern Scholarship*, 75–117.

59   D. Walker, *Appeal*, 10, 12. Information on the uses of Haiti and Egypt in African American antebellum discourse is included in Dain, "Haiti and Egypt," and *Hideous Monster*, 1–39; and Trafton, *Egypt Land*.

60 D. Walker, *Appeal*, 16.

61 Ibid., 19–20. The importance of national history in the nineteenth century is discussed in Calcott, *History in the United States*.

62 D. Walker, *Appeal*, 20. Walker's remarks could easily have come from an 1808 work of Prince Saunders in which he offered a similar assessment of the place of Africa in the creation of Western civilization: "If by investigating the historic page of antiquity, we take a retrospective view of the numerous votaries of literature and the useful arts who flourished at those early periods when the improving influences of knowledge and civilization were wholly confined to the oriental regions, we shall then discover some traces of their views of the intrinsic utility of mutually associating, to aid the progress of those who were aspiring to taste the Castilian spring, while ascending the towering heights of Parnassus, that there they might behold the magnificent temple of the Ruler of the Muses and hear its venerated oracle." Saunders, "Address Delivered at Bethel Church," 89. See Bethel, *Roots of African American Identity*, 147–49; and D. Walker, *Appeal*, 22. Discussions of the ancient glories of Africa were quite extensive in the black press. Some of the best discussions appear in the *African Repository*, the official organ of the American Colonization Society. See Bowdich, "Interesting Extracts from 'An Essay on the Superstitions, Customs and Arts Common to the Ancient Egyptians,'" August 1825; "Africa," December 1825; and "Africa," December 1826. Also see Dain, "Haiti and Egypt." The role of black antislavery proponents in shaping perceptions of Africa is explored in Sanneh, *Abolitionists Abroad*.

63 D. Walker, *Appeal*, 37. The jeremiad qualities of the *Appeal* are discussed in Moses, *Black Messiahs and Uncle Toms*, 38–39. For Las Casas's description of the Spanish conquest, see *Devastation of the Indies*. Although an acceptable source for the nineteenth century, Butler's work was criticized for its excessive references to Divine Providence and spirituality. See Review of *Complete History of the United States*.

64 D. Walker, *Appeal*, 59–61. The classic study on the colonization movement is Staundenraus, *American Colonization Movement*. A more recent study of the black role in colonization is Clegg, *Price of Liberty*.

65 D. Walker, *Appeal*, 62.

66 The intellectual context of the *Appeal* is explored in Hinks, *To Awaken My Afflicted Brethren*, 173–95.

67 See A. Smith, *Autobiography*; Peterson, *Doers of the Word*; Moody, *Sentimental Confessions*; and Painter, *Sojourner Truth*.

68 Haywood, "Prophesying Daughters."

69 The reference to David Walker is found in Stewart, "Religion and the Pure Principles of Morality: The Sure Foundation on Which We Must Build," *Liberator*, October 8, 1831. Richardson, *Maria W. Stewart*, 3–7; Foster, *Written by Herself*, 46–53; Bacon, *Humblest May Stand Forth*; Moody, *Sentimental Confessions*; Martha Jones, *All Bound Up*, 23–26.

70 Maria Stewart, "Maria Stewart's Farewell Address to Her Friends in the City of Boston," *Liberator*, September 1833. For her most historical oration, see Stewart, "An Address Delivered at the African Masonic Hall," *Liberator*, March 2, 1837.

71 Stewart, "Address at the African Masonic Hall."

72 Ibid. Discussion of the millennial aspects of Stewart's work appears in S. Logan, *"We Are Coming,"* 23–43.

73 See R. B. Lewis, *Light and Truth* (1844 ed.), 330–34. Marilyn Richardson, Stewart's principal biographer, suggests Stewart was highly regarded in both the antebellum and postbellum periods. This is demonstrated by the fact that all of her original orations were printed in William Lloyd Garrison's *Liberator* and this work was subsequently reprinted in 1879 with an endorsement from the noted black intellectual Alexander Crummell, whose church, St Luke's, Stewart was a member of. See Richardson, *Maria W. Stewart*, 10–12, 93–95. For a description of Crummell's association with Stewart, see Moses, *Alexander Crummell*, 199.

74 Bay, *White Image in the Black Mind*, 13–38.

Chapter Two

1 For Pennington's comments on the meaning of history, see the introduction to *Textbook*. General studies of the 1830s and 1840s include Freehling, *Road to Disunion*, 289–453; W. L. Miller, *Arguing about Slavery*; and Johannsen, *To the Halls of the Montezumas*. The murder of Elijah Lovejoy, the larger context of the period, and the meaning of history were discussed in several issues of the *Colored American*: See Icluis, "What Colored People Have Suffered," October 6, 1838; "An American Citizen Murdered! The Press Destroyed! Slavery Triumphant!," November 25, 1837; and "Education of the Youth," November 11, 1837. Changes in American historical practice are chronicled in Calcott, *History in the United States*, 67–72; Casper, *Constructing American Lives*, 135–52; and Lowenberg, *American History in American Thought*, 221–38.

2 Conrad, *Perish the Thought*, 9. For definitions of Romanticism, see Peckham, *Romanticism*, 15–33. Examples of celebratory Western history include William H. Prescott, *History of the Reign of Ferdinand and Isabella* (1839) and *History of the Conquest of Mexico and Peru* (1843), and John Lothrop Motley, *Rise of the Dutch Empire* (1855), which posited the rise of the Spanish Empire in the fifteenth and sixteenth centuries and the Dutch Empire in the sixteenth and seventeenth as the dawn of civilization in the Western hemisphere. The meanings of Romanticism are explored in Levin, *History as Romantic Art*, 3–7. On the centrality of the meanings of the West, see Wertheimer, *Imagined Empires*. Interest in American antiquities included a substantial engagement with Native American history. See Konkle, *Writing Indian Nations*, 1–41. Closely related to the antiquity of America is Mormon cosmology, which, among other things, suggests that Christ brought the gospels to the Native Americans after his resurrection. On Mormon cosmology, see Brooke, *Refiner's Fire*; and Persuitte, *Joseph Smith*.

3 A good example of how romantic historians envisioned history is found in the work of George Bancroft. While I agree with historian John Ernest that Bancroft's vision of providential history played a role as the context for nineteenth-century African American historical production, it is also clear that Bancroft's vision limited the scope of American history to the rise of the West: "The three races, the Caucasian, the Ethiopian, and the American, were in presence of one another on our soil. Would the red man disappear entirely from the forests, which for thousands of years had sheltered him safely? Would the black man, in the end, be benefited by

the crimes of mercantile avarice? At the close of the middle age, the Caucasian race was in nearly exclusive possession of the elements of civilization while the Ethiopian remained in insulated barbarism. No commerce connected it with Europe; no intercourse existed by travel, by letters, or by war; it was too feeble to attempt an invasion of a Christian prince or an Arab dynasty. The slave trade united the races by an indissoluble bond; the first ship that brought Africans to America was a sure pledge that, in due time, ships from the New World would carry the equal blessings of Christianity to the burning plains of Nigrita, that the descendants of Africans would toil for the benefits of European civilization." *History of the United States*, 2:464–65. Black historians have seriously contested this limited vision of Africa's role in world history. Also see Ernest, *Liberation Historiography*, 98–99. Other biographical assessments of Bancroft's work include L. Sweet, *Black Images of America*, 7–22. A good biographical treatment of George Bancroft is Handlin, *George Bancroft*.

4 For biographical information on Hosea Easton, see Nell, *Colored Patriots*, 33, 345–47. For Easton's activism in Massachusetts and Connecticut, see Easton, *Appeal to the Christian Public*. For biographical information on James W. C Pennington see, *Fugitive Blacksmith*; Thomas, *James W. C Pennington*; Swift, *Black Prophets of Justice*, 204–43; and Blackett, *Beating against the Barriers*, 1–86. Pennington's activism is explored in Warner, *New Haven Negroes*, 36–97. Pennington published a column in the *Colored American* titled "Common School Review" in 1840 and 1841. Pennington's role in the *Amistad* mutiny is explored in James W. C. Pennington to Lewis Tappan, October 9, 1841, Pennington to A. F. Williams, November 1, 1841, and Pennington to Tappan, 5 November 1841, in American Missionary Association Archives, Amistad Research Center, Tulane University, New Orleans, La. Additional information on the *Amistad* issue is found in "The Amistad Case," *Colored American*, December 26, 1840; and "Amistad Captives," *Colored American*, March 13, 1841. Biographical information on Henry Highland Garnet is found in Simmons, *Men of Mark*, 656–66; Stuckey, "Last Stern Struggle"; and Schorr, *Henry Highland Garnet*, 1–24. Biographical information on Ann Plato and James W. C. Pennington's comments are found in Plato, *Essays*, introduction. Additional information on Plato's writing style is found in Bassard, *Spiritual Interrogations*, 71–86, and Bacon, *The Humblest May Stand Forth*, 53–55. *The most comprehensive biographical information on Robert Lewis is located in Mary Augusta Lewis Johnson to Daniel Murray, May 11, 1900, in reel 1, Daniel Murray Pamphlet Collection, Library of Congress.*

5 On the Bible as an incubator for leadership see Swift, *Black Prophets of Justice*. On the Bible as a paradigm for black life see Glaude, *Exodus!* Discussions of major theoretical and methodological issues in black religion include Wimbush, *African Americans and the Bible*; Wilmore, *Black Religion, Black Protest*; Felder, *Stony the Road We Trod*; and Bailey, *Yet With a Steady Beat*.

6 "The Literature of the Bible," *Pennsylvania Freeman*, April 1838; Tytler and Nares, *Universal History*, 21. Tytler developed his academic reputation as a historian in the eighteenth century. His *Elements of General History*, first published in 1801, covered human history up to the eighteenth century. See Pennington, *Textbook*, 19.

7 James Ussher was widely known for his chronology of humankind, which appeared in *Annales veteris testamenti, a prima mundi origine deducti* (Annals of the Old Testament

Deduced from the First Origins of the World), which appeared in the seventeenth century and is sometimes referred to as the Ussher-Lightfoot chronology. Good discussions of the chronology include Barr, "Pre-Scientific Chronology"; and Gould, *Eight Little Piggies*, 181–97. Gould's reflection on Ussher's establishment of a chronology posits that scholars must appreciate the intellectual project of the seventeenth century to provide a usable chronology for humankind. For information on the decline of Ussher's chronology as a means of determining the date of creation, see Numbers, "Most Important Biblical Discovery."

8   Tytler, *Elements of General History*, 461. Also see Rollin, *Ancient History* (1808), 232–314, and *Ancient History* (1829), 151–80.

9   Chronological tables are included in Pennington's *Textbook*, but they are not complete or systematic. He discusses the great empires or divisions of ancient history, which is an important chronological division in universal histories. See *Textbook*, 19–20. Hosea Easton provides a lengthy chronology comparing the black and white races. See *Treatise*, 74–80. Robert Benjamin Lewis also included a chronological table in his study. See *Light and Truth* (1844 ed.), 336–46. (Except where noted otherwise, all citations are to the 1844 edition.) Lewis also devoted a small chapter to a discussion of the major periods of biblical and historical chronology; see 369–70. Also in Barr, "Pre-Scientific Chronology," 380–82.

10   Critical treatments of Lewis's work include Howe's *Afrocentricism*, 37–38, 56n5. Howe labels Lewis "the true father of Afrocentricism's wilder theories," according to whom "practically every figure of Antiquity from Euclid to Jesus Christ was of African descent." Howe's assessment of Lewis is based not on an actual reading of his text, but on a 1974 summary by Immanuel Geiss. Howe states that he "could not locate a copy of Lewis' work." Mia Bay situates Lewis in an ethnological tradition. She asserts that *Light and Truth* provides an early example of how easily African American efforts to rebut white racial doctrine could shade into a black chauvinism that mirrored the very racist logic it opposed. She cites Martin Delany's assessment of Lewis's work to make her broader claim. See *White Image in the Black Mind*, 45. John Ernest offers the most extended treatment of Lewis but largely concludes that Lewis's work represents both racism and anti-Semitism. See *Liberation Historiography*, 101–13. He, too, cites Delany's criticism of Lewis's work. It is clear, however, even from Delany's comments, that Lewis's work is deeply indebted to the work of eighteenth-century historians. Delany writes: "This book is nothing more than a compilation of selected portions of Rollin's, Goldsmith's, Ferguson's, Hume's and other ancient histories; added to which is a tissue of historical absurdities and literary blunders." Delany, *Condition*, 128. Moreover, Delany's criticisms, while contextually important, represent opposition to an older form of historical methodology, which he considered dated. Delany's focus on political economy, emigration, and the possibilities of the African diaspora represent a very different approach to national and hemispheric concerns than Lewis's attempt to write a universal history, which was heavily dependent on eighteenth-century historical styles.

11   R. B. Lewis, *Light and Truth*, 10.

12   Ibid.

13   Other popular biblical dictionaries included Edward Robinson's and Richard

Watson's. Both of these studies associate Adam with the color of the earth, which, probably following Josephus, is red. See Robinson, *Dictionary of the Holy Bible*, 6; and Watson, *Biblical Dictionary*, 18. For the use of biblical genealogy in R. B. Lewis, see *Light and Truth*, 1–40. For Pennington's engagement with genealogy, see *Textbook*, 10–11. Lewis also provides a detailed chronology of human history beginning with 4004 B.C. and ending with the crowning of Charlemagne in Rome in A.D. 800. This periodization encompasses fourteen periods of history. See Lewis, *Light and Truth*, 369–70.

14 See Oson, *Search for Truth*, 12. A useful examination of Africa and the Bible is Isichei, *History of Christianity*, 13–44. Specific discussion of important references to events in Africa in either the Old and New Testaments are included in Yamauchi, *Africa and the Bible*. Also see Adamo, *Africa . . . in the Old Testament*, and *Africa . . . in the New Testament*. Good interpretive discussions of Africa's presentation in patristic literature, especially Ethiopia and Ethiopians, appear in Courtes, "Theme of Ethiopia." Also see Copher, "Black Presence in the Old Testament."

15 Garnet, *Past and Present Condition*, 9–10. Assessments of the relationship between the Queen of Sheba and Solomon and his international marriages are in Yamauchi, *Africa and the Bible*, 80, 91–101. Also see Adamo, *Africa . . . in the Old Testament*, 87–93. Another detailed discussion of the ethnicity of Sheba and the location of her kingdom, which analyzes the various versions of the story from the Old and New Testaments, as well as Jewish, ancient and modern Christian traditions, and Ethiopian religious and popular traditions, is found in Adamo, *Africa . . . in the New Testament*, 60–65. Also see Lavik, "African Texts"; Habtu, "Images of Egypt"; Adamo, "Image of Cush"; and Holter, *Old Testament Research*.

16 Howard-Pitney, *Afro-American Jeremiad*, 3–13; Moses, *Black Messiahs and Uncle Toms*. The term "righteous discontent" is the title of one of Higginbotham's works.

17 Garnet, *Past and Present Condition*, 6, 21.

18 Easton, *Treatise*, 20.

19 Pennington, *Textbook*, 43.

20 "Our Claims on the Church," *Colored American*, May 6, 1837. Other articles in the *Colored American* which address the African role in the church and issues of justice include "Facts for Colored Americans" (editorial), May 6, 1837, and "Africa Has Claims Upon Us," April 29, 1837. For a concise discussion of the use of the jeremiad in black oratory and print, see Howard-Pitney, *Afro-American Jeremiad*, 3–13.

21 Pennington, *Textbook*, 37–38. For information on the fortunate fall, see Moses, "African Redemptionism and the Decline of the Fortunate Fall Doctrine," in *Wings of Ethiopia*, 141–58.

22 Books on the proslavery question include Sollors, *Neither Black nor White*, 78–111; and Stringfellow, "Brief Examination." Assessments of the varied meanings of the Curse of Ham are in Goldenberg, *Curse of Ham*; and Braude, "Sons of Noah."

23 Pennington, *Textbook*, 7–8, 13. Assessments of the meaning of *aithiops* or *aethiops* can be found in Thompson, *Romans and Blacks*, 57–85.

24 Pennington, *Textbook*, 15–18. The curse of Ham is presented in different ways in various religious traditions. In the Babylonian Talmud, the dog, the raven, and Ham copulated in the Ark. As punishment the dog was tied, the raven is forced to ex-

pectorate its seed into its mate's mouth, and Ham was smitten in the skin. In the Christian tradition, God's anger at Cain caused him to be "smitten by God and his face was turned to coal." In Europe, the preadamite view postulated that the Hamites were white. Cain, and by extension blacks, originated prior to Adam. Cain found a black wife and procreated. Copher, "Black Presence in the Old Testament." See also Goldenberg, *Curse of Ham*.

25 Garnet, *Past and Present Condition*, 11.

26 See Tytler, *Elements of General History*, 3.

27 Garnet, *Past and Present Condition*, 11. Some Christian scholars debate whether or not the Ethiopian eunuch was from Ethiopia. However, the Ethiopian Orthodox Church views the conversion as the foundation of their church. This episode is described in the *Kebra Nagast*, The Glory of the Kings, written in the fourteenth century. See Yamauchi, *Africa and the Bible*, 161–63.

28 My reading of the use of the Bible by black Christians in the nineteenth century views it as less a manipulation than a conscious attempt to enact its liberatory meanings. Black writers responded to the Bible's use as either a justification for proslavery doctrine or a nationalist reading of national possibility. They sought to subvert the nationalist typology of whites. Black writers enacted what Vincent Wimbush terms a "third reading of the Bible entailing the establishment of a canon and a hermeneutic principle." Wimbush, "The Bible and African Americans: An Outline of Interpretative History," in Felder, *Stony the Road*, 81–84, 89–93. See also Mark Noll, "The Image of the United States as a Biblical Nation," in Hatch and Noll, *Bible in America*, 39–57. For a discussion of the uses of the Bible on racial questions see Kidd, *Forging of Races*.

29 Winterer, *Culture of Classicism*, 1–77. For information on women and classicism, see Winterer, *Mirror of Antiquity*. Calhoun quoted in Moses, *Alexander Crummell*, 20. For information on the influence of classical literature in the eighteenth and nineteenth centuries, also see Reinhold, *Classica Americana*, 250–61.

30 Representative examples of classicism in this period are drawn from the *Colored American*. "Intellect of Negroes," May 13, 1837; "Lecture IV: Mr. Buckingham's Lectures," December 2, 1837; "Lecture VI: Mr. Buckingham's Lectures," December 16, 1837; "The Husbandman," May 3, 1838; "Letter V," June 16, 1838, "Ancient Carthage," October 20, 1838; "Our Heroic Age," June 15, 1839; "Address to the Colored People of the United States," March 2, 1839; "Wedding Letters of the Lower Classes in Augusta and Messina," October 5, 1839. Among the best discussions of African American engagement with the classics are Moses, *Alexander Crummell*; and Ronnick, *Autobiography of William Sanders Scarborough*. For good discussions of black intellectuals and their engagement with mainstream intellectual trends, see Saillant, *Black Puritan, Black Republican*; Blight, "In Search of Learning"; Martin, *Mind of Frederick Douglass*; and Stauffer, *Black Hearts of Men*, 144–55.

31 R. B. Lewis, *Light and Truth* (1836), preface, 83–86. Lewis also listed a number of ancient histories translated by English authors. They included Herodotus, translated by Belocin in four volumes; Sallust, translated by Murphy; Justin's *History*, translated by Turnbull; Xenophon's *History of Greece*, translated by Smith; Livy, translated by Baker; *History of Arrian*, translated by Rook; and Tacitus, translated by Murphy.

Examples of eighteenth-century reading matter in the classics appear in Reinhold, *Classick Pages*.

32   R. B. Lewis, *Light and Truth* (1836), 58, 60, 65, 67, 83.

33   William Leo Hansberry and Frank Snowden argue that complex relationships existed between Africans and the societies of classical antiquity that were totally non-racialized. See Harris, *Pillars in Ethiopian History*, vol. 1, and *Africa and Africans*, vol. 2. Also see Snowden, *Blacks in Antiquity*, 1–101. A recent work that poses a counterargument to the Snowden thesis (that racial prejudice was nonexistent in the ancient world) is Issac, *Invention of Racism in Classical Antiquity*, 1–53. Another traditional, but useful, assessment of the relationship between the Ethiopians and Egyptians is Redford, *From Slave to Pharaoh*, 1–4, 19–57, 80–145. For a contemporary assessment of African American scholarly writing on ancient Africa, see Keita, *Race and the Writing of History*, 15–41.

34   Studies that present diasporic writing among black intellectuals in the eighteenth, nineteenth, and twentieth centuries as either Afrocentric or a precursor of Afrocentricism include Shamit, *History in Black*; and Howe, *Afrocentricism*. Shamit suggests that some of these writers were attempting to frame an Afrocentric universal history. The components of this history included the centrality of Egypt and the Nile Valley, the presence of the black race on various continents, Africa as a historical and ontological construct, race and racial distinctions as central to world history. Shamit suggests that "the founding books of radical Afrocentricist theory were pseudo-scholarly books and sermons (by both black and white writers)." He includes the work of Hosea Easton and James W. C. Pennington in this group and argues that these works planted the seeds for the work of Cheikh Anta Diop and Ivan Van Sertima. As my work shows, the writings of Easton and Pennington were not Afrocentric and did not subscribe to the components of an Afrocentric world history that Shamit describes, which seems driven by presentist understandings of Afrocentricism rather than a contextualization of the past. See Shamit, *History in Black*, ix–x, 7–9. He discusses aspects of Afrocentric universal history on 16–35. Stephen Howe, in a chapter titled "Diasporic Images of Africa before Afrocentricism," lists a number of nineteenth- and twentieth-century works by black authors on Africa. Compared with Shamit, Howe is more nuanced. He briefly discusses the work of Hosea Easton, David Walker, James W. C. Pennington, and Henry Highland Garnet. Although he places too much emphasis on Egypt, he does suggest that black writers were balanced in their presentation of blacks in the ancient world. He points to the fact that Pennington avoids creating a one-dimensional portrait of Africans or claiming the ancient Egyptians were black. This is a point made also by Wilson Jeremiah Moses. Howe is less convincing in his discussion of Robert Benjamin Lewis (whose treatment is discussed in an earlier note), and he goes on to discuss Blyden and Brown as if their approaches directly mirrored those of earlier writers. . Blyden, as a native of the Danish West Indies, resident of Liberia, and admirer of Islam, and Brown, as a member of the transatlantic community and a postbellum writer of black history, represent very different facets of diaspora understanding. Brown wrote histories in the middle of the era of free trade and just before the advent of the colonization of Africa by European powers in the late nineteenth century. Howe is strongest in his

presentation of contemporary Afrocentric thought. See Howe, *Afrocentricism*, 35–59; and Moses, *Afrotopia*, 60.

35 Books that have come to define the Afrocentric controversy include Asante, *Afrocentricity*, and *Kemet, Afrocentricity, and Knowledge*; Lefkowitz, *Not Out of Africa*; and Bernal, *Black Athena*, vol 1. Lefkowitz's work was written as a response to what she considered the excesses of the Afrocentric movement, especially the work of Asante and Bernal. Martin Bernal's response to his many critics is contained in *Black Athena Writes Back*. One of the more nuanced assessments of Afrocentricism is Stephen Howe, *Afrocentricism*. As I suggest in the text, it is also important to distinguish subsequent twentieth-century Afrocentric work from the production of nineteenth-century writers, who in many instances, especially in the case of most of the writers I consider in the antebellum period, were operating from a very different set of priorities grounded in biblical authority and classical, ancient, and modern history. Good examples of work that subscribes to the twentieth-century ideas presented in the studies of Lefkowitz, Howe, and Shamit include Rogers, *World's Greatest Men of Color*, vols. 1 and 2; G. G. M. James, *Stolen Legacy*; Ben-Jochannan, *African Origins*, *Africa*, and *Black Man of the Nile and His Family*; J. G. Jackson, *Introduction to African Civilizations*, and *Man, God, and Civilization*; C. Williams, *Destruction of Black Civilization*; and Person-Lynn, *First Word*.

36 See Winterer, *Culture of Classicism*, 10–43. Books on the canon wars and the implications of Afrocentricism on academic disciplines include Bloom, *Closing of the American Mind*; Casement, *Great Canon Controversy*, 40–83; Arthur and Shapiro, *Campus Wars*; Denby, *Great Books*, 89–91; Schlesinger, *Disuniting of America*; Berlinerblau, *Heresy in the University*; Shamit, *History in Black*; and C. Walker, *We Can't Go Home Again*.

37 George Price and James Brewer Stewart assert that Easton's understanding of race is rooted in Christian environmentalism and the nonacceptance of African Americans by whites who prevented their best efforts to assimilate into the larger culture; see Price and Stewart, *To Heal the Scourge*, 1–47.

38 The development of race theory in the nineteenth century is explored in George Frederickson, *Black Image in the White Mind*, 1–42; Banton, *Racial Theories*, 17–43; Smedley, *Race in North America*, 226–49; and Dain, *Hideous Monster*.

39 Banton, *Racial Theories*, 50–62. Other important texts on race in the nineteenth century include Allen, *Invention of the White Race*, 27–51; Horsman, *Race and Manifest Destiny*, 79–186; and Takaki, *Iron Cages*, 108–46.

40 Baker, *From Savage to Negro*, 14–17; Josiah C. Nott, "Two Lectures on the Natural History of the Caucasian and Negro Race," in Faust, *Ideology of Slavery*, 206–38.

41 Pennington, *Textbook*, 7; Easton, *Treatise*, 67.

42 Pennington, *Textbook*, 91–96.

43 Easton, *Treatise*, 69–70. For a more traditional reading of Hosea Easton, see Price and Stewart, *To Heal the Scourge*, 1–47. For a discussion that situates Easton's work within the context of white racial thought in the eighteenth and nineteenth centuries and presents him as one of the first black racial theorists, see Dain, *Hideous Monster*, 170–96.

44 Easton, *Treatise*, 69–70.

45 R. B. Lewis, *Light and Truth* (1836), 40–41.

46 "Egypt" meant many different things in the eighteenth and nineteenth centuries than it does today. For African Americans, Egypt was a site of pride and oppression. It was a site of pride because of its historic association with the dissemination of knowledge, an idea embedded in Masonic ritual. It was linked with oppression because of its association with the enslavement of the Israelites, who were considered in the Jewish and Christian traditions as God's chosen people. This is clear when one looks at popular literature, orations, poetry, and other textual evidence. Black writers who focused on history, however, tended to follow mainstream historical thinking. Egypt became more racialized after the Napoleonic occupation in the late eighteenth and early nineteenth centuries. As I have noted, black intellectuals who wrote history utilized older conceptualizations of Egypt's place in relationship to the rise of Western civilization. For information on the varied uses of Egypt, see Glaude, *Exodus!*; Smith, *Conjuring Culture*; Wallace, *Constructing the Black Masculine*; and Moses, *Afrotopia*.

47 Rollin, *Ancient History*, 135–36.

48 Ibid., 8; Webster, *Elements of Useful Knowledge*, 55.

49 "Africa," in Anthon, *Classical Dictionary*, 78–82. Also see Pratt, *Imperial Eyes*, 38–107.

50 Anthon, *Classical Dictionary*, 78–82.

51 Webster, *Elements of Useful Knowledge* (1806), 3:246; "Egypt," in Anthon, *Classical Dictionary*, 34–54. In his discussion of the "complexion and physical structure of the Egyptians," Anthon, after reviewing the descriptions provided by Herodotus, which suggest that the Egyptians are black, wrote, "The Hebrews were a fair people, fairer at least than the Arabs. Yet, in all the intercourse they had with Egypt, we never find in the sacred history the least intimation that the Egyptians were Negroes; not even on the remarkable occasion of the marriage of Solomon with the daughter of Pharaoh." In a pseudoscientific turn, Anthon also considered paintings and "scull" measurements. In each instance he concluded that the Egyptians were probably of Arabic or Berber origin; see ibid., 38–40. Discussions of blacks in antiquity can be found in Bernal, *Black Athena*, vol. 1; Snowden, *Blacks in Antiquity*, and *Before Color Prejudice*; and Drake, *Black Folk*.

52 Easton, *Treatise*, 76. More caustic interpretations of Easton's work appear in Dain, *Hideous Monster*, 170–96.

53 Easton, *Treatise*, 71.

54 Ibid., 70–72.

55 Rollin, *Ancient History*, preface. Wilson Jeremiah Moses reads this tendency as African Americans engaging in a historiography of decline. Moses, *Afrotopia*, 44–95.

56 Webster, *Elements of Useful Knowledge*, 247. Pennington, *Textbook*, 21–22.

57 Pennington, *Textbook*, 22–28. Frank Snowden cites Herodotus's assessment of the Persian delegation and the Ethiopians. The Macrobian Ethiopians, who defeated the Persians, were characterized as "the tallest, and most handsome men on earth and had a high regard for justice." Snowden, *Before Color Prejudice*, 46–47.

58 Pennington, *Textbook*, 27–9. Information can also be found in the entry on "Carthage," *Anthon's Classical Dictionary*, 302–9.

59 Pennington, *Textbook*, 30–31. Moses also recognizes the complexity inherent in

Pennington's characterization of the Carthaginians as Africans but not blacks. See Moses, *Afrotopia*, 60.

60 R. B. Lewis, *Light and Truth* (1844), introduction. Other editions appeared in 1843 and 1851. Thomas Dalton and James Scott are discussed in ibid., 101; Horton and Horton, *Black Bostonians*, 88; and Cromwell, "The Black Presence in the West End of Boston, 1800–1864," in Jacobs, ed., *Courage and Conscience*, 160. Black elites in Boston are discussed in Adelaide Cromwell, *The Other Brahmins*. The most comprehensive biographical information on Robert Lewis is located in Mary Augusta Lewis Johnson to Daniel Murray, May 11, 1900, in reel 1, Daniel Murray Pamphlet Collection, Library of Congress.

61 R. B. Lewis, *Light and Truth*, 47. Other works by prominent nineteenth-century writers of this period included Lord Woodhouselee, *Tytler's Elements of General History*; Grégoire, *Enquiry*; and Child, *Appeal*.

62 R. B. Lewis, *Light and Truth*, 49, 103–7.

63 Entries on Strabo and Euclid are found in Hornblower and Spatworth, *Oxford Classical Dictionary*, 564, 1447. The claims regarding Homer and Plato are included in the quotes previously cited from Easton, R. B. Lewis, and Rollin.

64 Discussions of the shifting importance of Egypt is discussed in Trafton, *Egypt Land*. Shifting notions of race are explored in Horsman, *Race and Manifest Destiny*.

65 Tacitus, *Agricola and Germania*. More nuanced evaluations of the roles of the Germanic peoples in the making and unmaking of the Roman Empire are explored in P. S. Wells, *Barbarians Speak*; and Burns, *Rome and the Barbarians*. A particularly good discussion of how notions of the romantic or noble savage figured into African American historical thinking is contained in Moses, *Afrotopia*, 149–68.

66 Gibbon, *Decline and Fall*, 714–16; Easton, *Treatise*, 73.

67 Easton, *Treatise*, 74.

68 Ibid., 74.

69 Ibid., 81.

70 Garnet, *Past and Present Condition*, 11.

71 Pennington, *Textbook*, 39–43.

72 Ibid., 48.

73 Biographical treatments of notable personages were common in nineteenth-century America. Many believed that biography had the power to shape and mold human characteristics and define the national spirit. Literary historian Scott Casper calls this phenomenon "biographical mania." See *Constructing American Lives*.

74 Levin, *History as Romantic Art*, introduction; Bancroft, *History of the United States*, 402–13. Although the universal notion of progress was central to Bancroft's framing of history, Africa engaged the West through the institutions of the slave trade and slavery. In fact, Africans are viewed as possessing an incomplete or unformed consciousness. According to Bancroft, "they came with the limited faculties of the uncivilized man" and brought with them to the Americas no language, no abiding usages, no worship, no nationality. They were also "destitute of common traditions, customs and laws." Improvement for Africans could only occur through exposure to American social, political, and economic institutions. This vision of the modern world differed substantially from that of many black writers who continued to look

to biblical and ancient history while turning selectively to the modern record to refute the many problematic presentations of African American reality.

75 Biographical information on Anthony Amo is contained in Hountondji, "An African Philosopher in Germany in the Eighteenth Century," in *African Philosophy*. Biographical information on Thomas Fuller can be found in Nash, *Forging Freedom*, 107. Biographical information on Jacobus Eliza Capitein can be found in Prah, *Jacobus Eliza Johannes Capitein*.

76 Garnet, *Past and Present Condition*, 10–12.

77 Pennington, *Textbook*, 54–74.

78 Ibid., 53.

79 Plato, *Essays*, 30–31, 77, 80–89; Baym, *American Women Writers*.

80 R. B. Lewis, *Light and Truth*, 304–35. The importance of the Alexandrian libraries to the ancient world is discussed in Delia, "Alexandrian Library."

81 Grafton, *New Worlds, Ancient Texts*, 11–58; Wickett, *Contested Territory*, 1–41. Also see Remini, *Andrew Jackson*; and Conn, *History's Shadow*.

82 *National Anti-Slavery Standard*, February 1, 1849; review of *Biography of the Indians*. John Ernest views Robert Benjamin Lewis's assertion that Native Americans were possibly the descendants of the Hebrews as outlandish, yet Lewis, like Bancroft, cites many of the same nineteenth-century scholars who believed this was possible. In fact Bancroft states: "It is chiefly on supposed analogies of customs and language, that the lost tribes of Israel, who took counsel to go forth into a farther country where mankind dwelt, are discovered now in the bark cabins of North America, now in the secluded valleys of the Tennessee, and again, as the culture, on the plains of the Cordilleras." Bancroft disputed these claims, but this issue was very much in debate during the period. Bancroft cited Du Pratz, Gallatin, Clavigero, Boudinot, and Agilo's *Antiquities of Mexico* as well as Schoolcraft and Von Humboldt, among others, as authorities on the issue. See Bancroft, *History of the United States*, 2:501–2. Information on nineteenth-century scholars and the Hebrew origins of Native Americans can be found in Ethan Smith, *View of the Hebrews*; and Perdue, *Cherokee Editor*. For more contemporary understandings of the origins of this thought in Puritan circles, see Hertzeberg, *Jews in America*, 32–45. Locating the lost tribes also seemed to be of some interest in the antislavery press. An article titled "The Missing Tribes" notes that the subject was always one of deep interest and has occupied the attention and research of eminent divines and historians. M. M. Noah, "The Missing Tribes," *National Anti-Slavery Standard*, February 1, 1849. R. B. Lewis, *Light and Truth*, 273.

83 One of the best-known Native Americans who worked simultaneously within constructs of assimilation and autonomy is Elias Boudinot. Information on Boudinot is found in Perdue, *Cherokee Editor*.

84 Historical studies in the *Weekly Advocate* include "Useful Knowledge: A Brief Description of the United States," January 1, 1837; "A Brief Description of the United States—Continued," January 14, 1837; Robert Sears, "A Brief Description of the United States Carefully Compiled by Robert Sears," January 7, 1837; "Using Knowledge: Selected Life of Franklin," January 28, 1837; "Principal Features of the Various Nations of the Earth—Continued," February 4, 1837; "Miscellaneous: Ancient

Names of Countries and Places," February 18, 1837; "On Knowledge," February 25, 1837; "Tables of Population," and "Prejudice against Color in Light of History," March 18, 1837; "Intellect of Negroes," May 13, 1837; and "Historical Evidence concerning the Efforts of Emancipation," June 3, 1837.

85 Installments in the series "Sacred Geography and Antiquities" are found in *Colored American*, May 9, June 6 (subtitled "Assyria Situation and Extent"), and June 13 (subtitled "Assyria"), 1840.

86 Specific information about exploration and the veneration of ancient sites, especially biblical cities, is found in Larsen, *Conquest of Assyria*, 1–13; and Kuklick, *Puritans in Babylon*, 1–9, 19–25.

87 One can argue that Holy Land mania contained jeremiad qualities about it. Certainly, as Albert Raboteau noted earlier and as Eddie Glaude has recently observed, African Americans identified with the Exodus narrative and tended to focus on Egypt as opposed to Israel, as an ancient example of liberation from bondage. Here I want to stress that the examinations of these kingdoms are related to traditional understandings of these issues, but the broad interest of African American intellectuals in antiquities and in Holy Land mania suggests a wider set of influences on black historical writing. See J. Davis, *Landscape of Belief*, 22–23.

88 Interest in the Holy Land among American missionaries, explorers, and artists is examined in ibid., 1–101,; and Obenzinger, *American Palestine*, 1–13.

89 See MacFarlane, *Seven Apocalyptic Churches*.

90 The Seven Apocalyptic Churches appeared in the *Colored American*. See "Pictorial Illustration of the Bible—Ephesus," June 19, 1841; "Pictorial Illustration of the Bible—Smyrna," June 26, 1841; "Pictorial Illustration of the Bible—Thyatira," July 3, 1841; "Pictorial Illustration of the Bible—Laodicean," July 10, 1841; "Pictorial Illustration of the Bible—Sardis," July 31, 1841; "Pictorial Illustration of the Bible—Philadelphia," August 7, 1841; "Pictorial Illustration of the Bible—Patmos," August 14, 1841. For information on American travelers to and perspectives on the Holy Land, see J. Davis, *Landscape of Belief*, 27–52. Also in *Colored American*, see "Pictorial Illustrations of the Bible and Views in Palestine," June 12, 1841, and "Two Hundred Pictorial Illustrations of the Bible, Consisting of Views of the Holy Land, by Robert Sears," October 17, 1840. Sears also produced a comprehensive biblical history. See *New and Complete History*, 13–16. Also see R. B. Lewis, *Light and Truth*, 210–12.

Chapter Three

1 E. Foner, *Free Soil, Free Labor*; B. Levine, *Half Slave, Half Free*; Freehling, *Road to Disunion*; Anbinder, *Nativism and Slavery*.

2 Morgan, *American Slavery, American Freedom*. Also see D. B. Davis, *Problem of Slavery*.

3 My thinking on the themes of African American history in the 1850s has been influenced by the work of literary historian Eric Sundquist, who views the literature of the period as enacting the disequilibrium between slavery and freedom in the Western hemisphere. This is certainly true in the United States, where free states outpaced slave states and gave rise to expansionist plans to annex Cuba. Moreover, given the ongoing contestation over slavery's role in American life, the literature,

most notably Herman Melville's *Benito Cereno* and Martin Delany's *Blake; or, The Huts of America*, highlights the unfinished work of the American Revolution to extend the benefits of life, liberty, and the pursuit of happiness to all. Although the Civil War settled questions of annexation and expansionism, the volatility and uncertainty of the period is reflected in the literature. See Sundquist, *To Wake the Nations*, 135–39. Delany's book was first serialized in the *Weekly Anglo-African* in 1861 and 1862.

4   The classic surveys of the period include Potter, *Impending Crisis*; and Sewell, *Ballots for Freedom*. Information on the slave power is found in Collins, "Ideologies"; Gerteis, "Slave Power"; and May, " Slave Conspiracy Revisited."

5   Assessments of Delany's work include Levine, *Martin Delany*, 8–11, 63–71; Adeleke, *Without Regard to Race*, 158–59; and Ernest, *Liberation Historiography*, 113–32. See also Delany, *Condition*, 51. According to one of Delany's earlier biographers, Victor Ullman, when Delany was exposed to classical antiquity, he was fascinated how the Greeks and Romans were influenced by earlier civilizations. He later established the Theban Literary Society. See Ullman, *Martin Delany*, 24–25.

6   See Delany, *Condition*, 53. For a description of West Africa and the Lander Expedition to discover the Niger, see Lander and Lander, *Journal of an Expedition*.

7   Delany, *Condition*, 56. One of the most popular travel journals of the period was Barth's *Travels and Discoveries*. For information on the uses of travel literature in the nineteenth century, see Pratt, *Imperial Eyes*.

8   Delany, *Condition*, 62.

9   Ibid., 162.

10   See Delany, *Origins and Objects*, 10–13.

11   St. Cyprian Lodge was formed by Richard Cleaves of Philadelphia after he became the deputy grand master of the Independent Grand Lodge in 1846. For a brief discussion of Cleaves's work, see Curry, *Free Black in Urban America*. My discussion differs from Robert Levine's, which focuses on *Origins and Objects* as essentially a discussion of ancient African culture. See Levine, introduction to *Martin Delany*. A speech that contained much of the same historical discussion as Delany's is Ward's "Origin, History and Hopes."

12   Delany, *Origins and Objects*, 14–16.

13   For information on the Prince Hall Masons, see Grimshaw, *Official History of Freemasonry*; Muraskin, *Middle-Class Blacks*, 31; and Williams, *Black Freemasonry*, 16–17. See Delany, *Origins and Objects*, 26–28.

14   Delany, *Origins and Objects*, 32–33. For information on the Allen incident, see Winch, *Philadelphia's Black Elite*, 12–15.

15   Delany, *Origins and Objects*, 36–37. Louis (Lajos) Kossuth was a leader in the Hungarian revolt against Austrian rule. He was eventually named governor-general of the Hungarian state, but the uprising was short-lived. He was widely viewed as a freedom fighter by antislavery advocates in the United States. Information on Kossuth can be found in "Kossuth on Bunker Hill," and "Kossuth at Faneuil Hall and on Bunker Hill," *Liberator*, May 7, 1852. Delany was not the only abolitionist who used the fugitive, or slave, analogy to refer to Louis Kossuth. In a well-publicized letter to Kossuth, William Lloyd Garrison noted that Kossuth was "a liberated captive, the victim of European absolutism, an exile from your native country, and asking

sympathy and aid in the spirit of universal liberty." In another section of the letter, Garrison referred to Kossuth as "a fugitive from Austrian vengeance, as a rebel, as the leader in a formidable insurrectionary movement." See R. B. Lewis, *Letter to Louis Kossuth*, 6–8.

16 Nell, preface, in *Colored Patriots*, and *Services of Colored Americans*.

17 Yates, *Rights of Colored Men*, iii–iv.

18 Ibid., 278. Day's speech was printed in Day, *Loyalty and Devotion*, 1.

19 See Weems, *The Life of George Washington* (1809); and Sparks, *The Diplomatic Correspondence of the American Revolution*. For information on David Ramsay, see Schaffer, *To Be an American*.

20 See Lossing, *Pictorial History of the Civil War*; and Sims, *Life of Francis Marion*. An assessment of historical writing in the decades leading up to the Civil War is contained in Mahan, *Benson Lossing*.

21 Easton, *Treatise*, 27–34.

22 O'Leary, *To Die For*, 3–8.

23 William C. Nell to Maria Weston Chapman, August 24, 1863, in reel 3, Black Abolitionist Papers, 1830–1865, University of Detroit (hereafter cited as BAP); Adelphic Union Library Association, *Liberator*, October 27, 1843; and William Wells Brown to Charles Sumner, December 29, 1845, in reel 4, BAP; "Western Anti-Slavery Society," *North Star*, January 7, 1848. Biographical information on Nell is located in Robert P. Smith, "William Cooper Nell"; "William C. Nell," in Winston and Logan, *Dictionary of Negro Biography*, 472–73; and Horton and Horton, *Black Bostonians*. Nell's involvement in integrating Boston Public Schools and with the Adelphic Union, the Western Anti-Slavery Society, and the *North Star* is chronicled in Mabee, " Negro Boycott."

24 Nell to Phillips, April 15, 1841, in reel 3, BAP; Botta, *History of the War*. Information on George Twelve Hewes can be found in Young, *Shoemaker and the Tea Party*. See the extensive collection of Nell's correspondence in Wesley and Uzelac, *William Cooper Nell*.

25 Nell, *Services of the Colored Americans*, 16.

26 Ibid., 15–18.

27 Ibid., 34–40. Less than a year after the publication of the first edition, in a letter to Wendell Phillips, Nell wrote: "I am preparing for a second edition of my pamphlet. Having some additional facts, I expect to receive from a few friends the means to pay costs at once and thus relieve me of future anxiety." Nell to Phillips, October 5, 1852, in reel 7, BAP. Nell detailed his expenses regarding the publication of the second edition in a letter to Phillips, October 27, 1852, in ibid.

28 Reviews of Nell's second edition appeared in "New Books," *Aliened American*, April 19, 1853. See also "Merited Testimonials," *Liberator*, December 17, 1852; "New Books," *Aliened American*, April 10, 1853; "Publications," *Frederick Douglass' Paper*, February 17, 1860; and Nell, "Colored Patriots of the American Revolution," *Anti-Slavery Bugle*, May 26, 1855.

29 Nell, *Colored Patriots*, 236–37, 244.

30 Ibid., 136, 161. See Kaplan, *Black Presence*, 20–21, 55–56.

31 Nell, *Colored Patriots*, 162. On Forten, see Robert Purvis, "Remarks on the Life and

Character of James Forten," delivered at Bethel Church, March 30, 1842, in reel 4, BAP; and Gloucester, *Discourse.* The idea of republican mothers is discussed in Norton, *Founding Mothers and Fathers.*

32 Nell, *Colored Patriots,* 380–81.

33 "John G. Whittier to William C. Nell," *Liberator,* March 12, 1858.

34 Review of *Colored Patriots of the American Revolution,* by William C. Nell, *Liberator,* October 26, 1855; "Books for the Times," Review of *Colored Patriots of the American Revolution, Radical Abolitionist* (Supplement), November 1, 1856; and William Howard Day, Review of *Colored Patriots of the American Revolution, Provincial Freeman,* January 19, 1856.

35 Delany, *Condition,* 67–85; Watkins, *Our Rights as Men,* 13–17; "John Langston," *Frederick Douglass' Paper,* September 22, 1854; *Memorial of Thirty Thousand,* 14–17; Langston, "Legal Disabilities of Colored People in Ohio," *Antislavery Bugle,* January 19, 1856.

36 Geneviève Fabre, "African American Commemorative Celebrations in the Nineteenth Century," in Fabre and O'Meally, *History and Memory,* 72–91. Nell's commemorative celebrations are discussed in Bethel, *Roots of African American Identity,* 1–8.

37 Advertisements for commemorative celebrations written by Nell include "Commemorative Meeting in Faneuil Hall," and "Items," *Liberator,* February 19, 1858; and "Program of the Boston Massacre Commemoration Festival," in reel 10, BAP. The most comprehensive recent study of black commemorative culture is Kachun, *Festivals of Freedom.* Also see Rael, *Black Identity and Black Protest,* 54–81. For examinations of black expressive culture, see White and White, *Stylin.*

38 Nell, "Program of Boston Massacre," in BAP, and "Crispus Attucks, Once a Slave in Massachusetts," *Liberator,* August 5, 1859.

39 Nell, "Program of Boston Massacre," in BAP.

40 "Address of William Nell," *Liberator,* March 12, 1858. Nell's remarks were reprinted in "Colored American Patriots," *Anglo-African Magazine,* January 1859. The festival is discussed in Nell to Garrison, February 2, 1859, in reel 11, BAP, and "Remarks of William C. Nell," *Liberator,* April 1, 1859. Nell's work continued to receive notice during the Civil War. "Advertisement: *Colored Patriots of the American Revolution,*" *Frederick Douglass' Paper,* February 17, 1860; "Interesting Facts — Colored Soldiers in the Revolution," *Douglass Monthly,* August 1862. Articles about the Revolution also continued to appear in black newspapers, possibly inspired by Nell's work: "The Mother of Washington," and "General Braddock's Expedition," *Christian Recorder,* July 20, 1861; "Washington: His Life, Character and Opinions: With Special Reference to Our Times," *Christian Recorder,* March 1, 1862; "Colored Men in the Revolution and the War of 1812," *Christian Recorder,* May 10, 1862. Information on the Crispus Attucks Memorial is contained in *Memorial of Crispus Attucks.*

41 Haiti's role as a site for emigration and the general relationship between the state and society in the nineteenth century are discussed in Plummer, *Haiti and the Great Powers,* 15–40. Also see Plummer, *Haiti and the United States,* 26–31.

42 See Hunt, *Haiti's Influence on Antebellum America,* 1–106. The noted African American historian Benjamin Quarles argued that African Americans were "keepers of the Revolutionary flame." See "Revolutionary War."

43 The transatlantic community is discussed in Blackett, *Building an Antislavery Wall.*

Discussion of the antislavery war and black destiny is in Nell, *Colored Patriots*; and Delany, *Condition*.

44 As Plummer has observed, the outcome of both the Haitian Revolution and the French Revolution concerned American republicans. Social leveling, radical and violent overthrow of the monarchy in France, and the ascendancy of former slaves to power in Haiti through an armed uprising raised alarms. These fears were compounded by the Denmark Vesey revolt in Charleston in 1822. Plummer, *Haiti and the United States*, 34–49.

45 The literature on the Haitian Revolution is extensive. Works central to this study include C. L. R. James, *Black Jacobins*; Genovese, *From Rebellion to Revolution*; Ott, *Haitian Revolution*; Nicholls, *From Dessalines to Duvalier*; Laurent Dubois, *Avengers of the New World* and the related study of emancipation in Guadeloupe around the same time as the Haitian Revolution, *A Colony of Citizens*. The most thorough discussion of Haiti and its relationship to the United States and African Americans is in Plummer, *Haiti and the Great Powers* and *Haiti and the United States*, 21–50. Also see Frick, *Making of Haiti*; and Trouillot, *Silencing the Past*.

46 In addition to the material that appeared in *Freedom's Journal* and *Rights of All*, Haiti was an active topic of discussion in the black press prior to 1850, especially in the *Colored American*. See "Hayti," *Liberator*, August 6, 1831; "The Republic of Haiti," *Weekly Advocate*, March 11, 1837; "A Colored Community Taking Care of Themselves," *Colored American*, July 1, 1837; Robert Douglass, "Haiti," *Colored American*, March 3, 1838; and "The Hour and the Man: Toussaint L'Ouverture," *National Anti-Slavery Standard*, February 11, 1841. For an examination of Haiti's place in the Pan-African lenses of African Americans, see Bethel, *Roots of African American Identity*, 149–54.

47 For announcement of Smith's lecture, see "Notices: Lectures in Clinton Hall by James McCune Smith, M.D.," *National Anti-Slavery Standard*, February 11, 1841. Smith's lecture was delivered as part of an institute lecture series for free blacks. See James McCune Smith, *Lecture on the Haytien Revolutions*.

48 J. M. Smith, *Lecture on the Haytien Revolution*, 11–15. Smith's engagement with the larger issues of the period are more clearly discussed in *Destiny of the People of Color*.

49 J. M. Smith, *Lecture on the Haytien Revolution*, 11–15. Ott, *Haitian Revolution*, 34–35.

50 Information on the Proclamation of March 8, 1790, can be found in D. B. Davis, *Problem of Slavery*, 139–40; and C. L. R. James, *Black Jacobins*, 70–73.

51 J. M. Smith, *Lecture on the Haytien Revolution*, 15–18.

52 Dessalines, the black general of the South, played a seminal role in the War of the Knives against mulattoes in the South. Rigaud eventually defected to the French and returned with the invasion forces in 1800 to subdue the island. Christophe crowned himself emperor of the South and eventually committed suicide.

53 The literature on Toussaint L'Ouverture is extensive. I have focused on the major works published in English. They include Martineau, *Hour and the Man*; Beard, *Life of Toussaint L'Ouverture*; and Redpath, *Toussaint L'Ouverture*.

54 J. M. Smith, *Lecture on the Haytien Revolution*, 19–27. The best scholarly discussion of the Haitian Revolution is C. L. R. James, *Black Jacobins*. For information on Toussaint L'Ouverture's portrayal in intellectual circles, see Hunt, *Haiti's Influence on Antebellum America*, 84–106.

55 For biographical information on George Boyer Vashon, see Nell, *Colored Patriots*, 328; and Hatchett, "George Boyer Vashon." Vashon later assumed a professorship at Central College in McGrawville, New York.

56 Biographical information on William Wells Brown is found in Farrison, *William Wells Brown*; and Whelchel, *My Chains Fell Off*.

57 Biographical information on Holly is found in Dean, *Defender of the Race*. Some of Holly's thoughts on colonization are included in a series of articles in the *Voice of the Fugitive* titled "Canadian Colonization," published April 12 and 21, 1848; and July 16 and 30, 1851.

58 Nicholls, *From Dessalines to Duvalier*, 82–84; and Trouillot, *Haiti: State against Nation*, 35–58.

59 Vashon's visit to Haiti is discussed in Hatchett, "George Boyer Vashon," 208–9. His letters were published in the *North Star* April 21, June 9, August 8 and 21, 1848; April 7 and September 28, 1849. Holly's journey to Haiti is discussed in Dean, *Defender of the Race*, 22–24. Brown's intellectual development is explored in Farrison, *William Wells Brown*, 255–58.

60 Griffiths, *Autographs for Freedom*. Also see Sherman, *African American Poetry*, 153–54.

61 Vashon, "Vincent Oge," 50 and 51.

62 Ibid., 53–54.

63 Ibid.

64 C. L. R. James, *Black Jacobins*, 70–73.

65 Vashon, "Vincent Oge," 53–54. The Spartan defense of the Pass of Thermopylae during the Persian War is discussed in Herodotus, *Histories*, book 7, 586–601.

66 Oge's trial and torture are described in C. L. R. James, *Black Jacobins*, 74–75. The state's ability to torture and execute Oge and his brother demonstrates its sheer power to destroy the revolt. This was not the case for Leonidas, the leader of the Spartans. The Persians inability to possess the body of the enemy lessened their stature and heightened the heroism of the Spartans.

67 For the best literary discussion of Brown's "St. Domingo," see Sundquist, *To Wake the Nations*, 31–36.

68 Brenda Gayle Plummer notes that the "American Revolution offered inspiration to the Haitians, but the revolutionary generation in the United States feared Caribbean upheaval. Eighteenth-century conservatives perceived Haiti as a source of subversion and a threat to slaveholding societies." Plummer, *Haiti and the United States*, 4–5.

69 Holly, *Vindication of the Capacity*, 30–35.

70 Ibid., 30–31.

71 Ibid., 25.

72 Ibid., 36–39.

73 W. W. Brown, "St. Domingo," 6–8; Holly, *Vindication of the Capacity*, 41–42.

74 W. W. Brown, "St. Domingo," 22–23.

75 Ibid., 22–23, 35–37. According to William Farrison, Brown's principal biographer, Brown's characterization of L'Ouverture borrowed heavily from the work of John Beard, a minister who wrote *Toussaint L'Ouverture: Biography and Autobiography* (1863).

76 Holly, "Vindication of the Capacity," 45–46. The British colony that imposed the most extensive apprenticeship program was Jamaica. Information can be found in T. Holt, *Problem of Freedom*, 55–114.

77 Holly, "Vindication of the Capacity," 47–49. This criticism regarding the extension of rights to all the people also pertained to the British during the Revolutionary War. Holly pointed out that William Pitt the Younger, the prime minister of England during the Revolutionary War, satisfied the needs of the wealthy in the policies he pursued, but failed to meet the needs of the common people.

78 Holly, *Vindication of the Capacity*, 55.

Chapter Four

1 Still, *Underground Railroad*, title page.

2 Hall, "To Render the Private Public."

3 Wiebe, *Search for Order*. The late nineteenth-century shift to scientism is chronicled in a number of studies; see Cotkin, *Reluctant Modernism*, 51–73; Ross, *Origins of the Social Sciences*, 53–76; Bender, *Intellect and Public Life*; Mandelbaum, *History, Man, and Reason*; Iggers and Powell, *Leopold von Ranke*; Novick, *That Noble Dream*, 21–31; and Frederickson, *Inner Civil War*.

4 Anderson, *Education of Blacks*; and Sernett, *Abolition's Axe*. The Philadelphia Institute for Colored Youth was founded in 1837. The best overviews of the school's history and its leadership are Coppin, *Reminiscences of School Life*; and Perkins, *Fanny J. Coppin*. An overview of black education prior to the Civil War is Woodson, *Education of the Negro*.

5 Gaines, *Uplifting the Race*.

6 Arbour, *Canvassing Books*, xi–xxiv.

7 W. W. Brown, *Black Man*, 1–50; Farrison, *William Wells Brown*.

8 William Farrison, Brown's chief biographer, offers a fairly harsh assessment of Brown's biographical sketches in *Black Man*, calling them a "miscellany of random facts." See Farrison, introduction to *William Wells Brown*; and W. W. Brown, *Black Man*, 138–42, 160–62, 190–98. Some of the sketches in the book first appeared in *Pine and Palm*, an emigrationist paper founded by James Redpath. They include "Celebrated Colored Americans: Madison Washington," August 17, 1861, and "Celebrated Colored Americans: Nat Turner," August 3, 1861.

9 Brown's alternative vision of America is explored in Mulvey, "Fugitive Self."

10 W. W. Brown, *Black Man*, 149–51, 187–89, 223–26, 238–40.

11 Brown's assessment of Delany is based on Delany's *Official Report*. Delany's expedition to Africa is discussed in Ullman, *Martin Delany*, 211–46. Also see Levine, *Martin R. Delany*, 315–76. On the emigration question, see Holly, "Vindication of the Capacity."

12 Thomas Hamilton's *Weekly Anglo-African* supported the emigrationist cause by printing articles about it and promoting the sale of Delany's *Official Report*, 1861 and 1862. For a typical example of Redpath's interest in Haiti, see "Notes of the Movement: Haitian Bureau of Emigration," "Letters from Hayti," "History of the Haytian Press," and "Haytian Advertisements," in *Pine and Palm*, August 24, 1861. In 1861, Redpath

also authored a guide for emigrants from America, *Guide to Haiti*. Also see Horner, *Life of James Redpath*.

13 Brown lectured in upstate New York on the benefits of Haitian emigration. "Advertisements of Hayti: Lecture by William Wells Brown Delivered in Troy, New York," *Pine and Palm*, August 17 and 24, 1861.

14 W. W. Brown, *Rising Son*, 362–64.

15 Freund, *Making of Contemporary Africa*, 83–91.

16 W. W. Brown, *Rising Son*, 76–77; Wood, *History of South Africa*.

17 W. W. Brown, *Rising Son*, 98–100; D. L. Lewis, *Race to Fashoda*, 99–136.

18 W. W. Brown, *Rising Son*, 65–77. On East Africa, see July, *History of the African People*, 57–182.

19 W. W. Brown, *Rising Son*, 104–6. Dahomean society was built on the slave trade, and its decline was directly related to a decrease in European demand for slaves. According to Robert July, Dahomeans practiced human sacrifice, and bloodletting was a staple part of the culture. In most cases, Dahomeans performed these ceremonies to prove their ferocity to Europeans and improve their position in the slave trade. See July, *History of the African People*, 143.

20 W. W. Brown, *Rising Son*, 111–12.

21 Ibid., 143.

22 Ibid., 417.

23 Biographical information on Samuel A. J. Crowther is contained in Ayayi, "Samuel Ayayi Crowther of Oyo," in Curtin, ed., *Africa Remembered*.

24 W. W. Brown, *Rising Son*, 90. Islam in Africa is discussed in Hrbek, *General History of Africa*, 3:16–62. For shifting perceptions of the Prophet Muhammad and Islam, see Almond, *Heretic and Hero*; and Sha'ban, *Islam and the Arabs*.

25 W. W. Brown, *Rising Son*, 60–70.

26 Livermore, *Historical Research*; Lossing, *Pictorial History of the Civil War*.

27 W. W. Brown, *Negro in the American Rebellion*, 1–36.

28 Ibid., 40. Sources on the Simms and Burns case include Toner, *Boston Slave Riot*; Parker, *Boston Kidnapping*; Stevens, *Anthony Burns*; and Collison, *Shadrach Minkins*.

29 W. W. Brown, *Negro in the American Rebellion*, 52.

30 Quarles, *Negro in the Civil War*; Cornish, *Sable Arm*; Glatthaar, *Forged in Battle*; Gladstone, *United States Colored Troops*; Jordan, *Black Confederates*, 201–51; McPherson, *Negro's Civil War*. Also see Clark, *Black Brigade of Cincinnati*; and C. Wesley, *Ohio Negroes in the Civil War*.

31 W. W. Brown, *Negro in the American Rebellion*, 54, 58–59, 235–54. Black intellectuals agitated to join the war; see Green, *Letters and Discussions*; and Cornish, *Sable Arm*, 173–79.

32 McKittrick, *Andrew Johnson and Reconstruction*; Benedict, *Impeachment and Trial*, and *Compromise of Principle*.

33 Brown's chapter that recited a litany of outrages committed against freed people was titled "Ill Treatment of Colored People South," in *Negro in the American Rebellion*, 345–54. The decline of black fortunes in the aftermath of Reconstruction is chronicled in R. Logan, *Betrayal of the Negro*.

34 For discussion of political solutions to black problems, see E. Foner, *Reconstruction*;

and Holt, *Black over White*. For alternatives to political solutions, see L. H. Putnam, *Review of the Revolutionary Elements*.

35 Benjamin Quarles viewed Brown's work as anecdotal, but Dudley Cornish saw it as an important aid in enhancing our understanding of the Civil War's meanings, despite the work's limitations. See Quarles, *Negro in the Civil War*, 350; and Cornish, *Sable Arm*, 316. *The Negro in the American Rebellion* was reprinted in 1880 and 1885.

36 Advertisements for *The Rising Son* appeared in *New National Era*, September 18 and 25, October 2 and 23, November 6, December 4 and 18, 1873, January 1 and 29, and February 12, 1874; and in *Christian Recorder*, September 25, October 2 and 23, 1873; January 8, April 30, June 4, 18, and 25, 1874. Also see "The Negro Again," *Christian Recorder*, September 25, 1873; and Review of *The Rising Son,* by William Wells Brown, in *Christian Recorder*, January 8, 1879. The book also appeared in numerous editions; see *Rising Son* (New York: A. G. Brown & Co., 1876, 1885).

37 "Organization of the Vigilance Committee," in Still, *Underground Railroad*, 635.

38 Gara, "William Still," 34.

39 P. Foner, "Battle to End Discrimination."

40 For the resolution from the Vigilance Committee, see Still, *Underground Railroad*, 1.

41 Lapansky, "Aboard William Still's Underground Railroad," 4. For nineteenth-century work on the Underground Railroad, see Coffin, *Reminiscences of Levi Coffin*; Siebert, *Underground Railroad*; W. M. Mitchell, *Underground Railroad*; Smedley, *Underground Railroad*; Pettit, *Sketches in the History of the Underground Railroad*; H. U. Johnson, *From Dixie to Canada*; and Hope, *Heroes in Homespun*. For more recent work, see Griffler, *Frontline of Freedom*; Clinton, *Harriet Tubman*; Blight, *Passages to Freedom*; Bordewich, *Bound for Canaan*; Still, *Underground Railroad*, 1–2; Ernest, *Narrative of the Life*; and Ruggles, *Unboxing of Henry Brown*.

42 Still, *Underground Railroad*, 2–4. The slave narrative of Peter Still and his wife Vina is titled *The Kidnapped and the Ransomed*. Still's brother was not kidnapped. Also see "Catalogue of Children of Children of Levin Still and Charity, his wife"; "William Still's Recollections of Being United with His Brother, Peter," 7 August 1850; William Still to Peter Still, May 10, October 12, and December 18, 1852; William Still to E. Gray Sonsing, April 29, 1853; and William Still to Peter Still, November 9, 1853, in the Peter Still Papers, Special Collections and University Archives, Archibald Stevens Alexander Library, Rutgers University.

43 Still, *Underground Railroad*, xiii.

44 Ibid., 51–54.

45 Ibid., 124–29, 281–84.

46 Zboray, *Fictive People*; Joyce, *Gatekeepers of Black Culture*.

47 Sketches of James Miller McKim and William Furness appear in Still, *Underground Railroad*, 654–55.

48 William Lloyd Garrison to William Still, April 7, 1872, in Still Papers, Rutgers University.

49 William Whipper to William Still, December 4, 1871, in Still, *Underground Railroad*, 762–67.

50 Still, *Underground Railroad*, 755. For Still, Harper was the quintessential woman. Like Phillis Wheatley, a slave who manifested literary talents, Harper was born of free

parentage in Baltimore and also demonstrated poetic talent at an early age. Her first publication, *Forest Leaves*, published during her teens, established her as a poet of some merit. In the 1850s, Harper became a teacher as well as an active participant in the antislavery movement. She served as a lecturer for the State Anti-Slavery Society of Maine, a job she began in 1854, and later worked as an antislavery speaker in Canada and the Great Lakes Region from 1856 to 1859. Despite her growing commitments, Harper often inquired about the status of the Underground Railroad. In characterizing her interest in antislavery work, Still noted that Harper was not "content to make speeches and receive plaudits, but was ever willing to do the rough work and to give material aid wherever needed." Demonstrating *noblesse oblige*, like Still, throughout the late nineteenth century, Harper, in the aftermath of the Civil War, traveled throughout the Southern states. She visited plantations, cities, and towns, giving addresses and lectures on the needs of African Americans as they adjusted to freedom. In keeping with his theme of Harper's devotion to the race, Still reprinted a series of Harper's reflections on freedwomen. These reflections mirrored Still's own beliefs about the needs of African Americans throughout the first half of the nineteenth century: "Desiring to speak to women who have been the objects of so much wrong and abuse under Slavery, and even since Emancipation, in a state of ignorance, not accessible always to those who would urge the proper kind of education respecting their morals and general improvement, Mrs. Harper has made it her duty not to overlook this all-important duty to her poor sisters." *Underground Railroad*, 755. Still's examination of Harper's life was unique for his day. A more contemporary take on Harper can be found in M. Jones, *All Bound Up*, 135–36.

51 Adjutant General's Office to William Still, Washington, D.C., February 4, 1864, in box 9G, folder 17, Leon Gardiner Collection, Historical Society of Pennsylvania, Philadelphia. An assessment of the life and accomplishments of William Still can be found in Lane, *William Dorsey's Philadelphia*, 104–6.

52 Agreement with Porter and Coates, January 1, 1872, and Supplemental Agreement, March 5, 1872, in Society Collection, Historical Society of Pennsylvania.

53 Early advertisements for Still's *Underground Railroad* appeared in the following issues of the *Christian Recorder*: July 8, 1871; March 28, April 18 and 25, and August 15 and 22, 1872; April 3 and 10, 1873. The impact of the *Christian Recorder* as an organ of the A.M.E. Church, is examined in Gilbert Anthony Williams, *Christian Recorder*.

54 Zboray, "Antebellum Reading."

55 For the Henry Box Brown advertisement, see the *Christian Recorder*, April 24 and May 15, 1873. Brown's involvement in Henry Box Brown's rescue is discussed in Switala, *The Underground Railroad*.

56 Advertisements in the *Christian Recorder* featuring Romulus Hall appeared on June 5, 12, 19, and 26; July 3, 10, 17, 24, and 31; August 7, 14, 21, and 28; and September 11, 1873.

57 For pictorial illustrations of "Bold Stroke for Freedom," see the *Christian Recorder*, September 18 and 25; October 2, 16, 23, and 30; November 6, 13, 20, and 27; December 4, 11, 18, and 25, 1873; January 8, 15, 22, and 29; February 5, 12, and 26; March 5, 12, and 26, 1874.

58 The Anna Maria Jackson advertisement appeared in the following issues of the *Chris-*

tian Recorder: April 2, 9, 23, and 30; May 7, 14, and 21; June 4, 18, and 25; July 4, 16, 23, and 30; August 6, 13, and 27; September 3 and 10; October 29; November 5, 12, 19, and 26, 1874.

59 For Still's correspondence with black notables, see William Wells Brown to William Still, February 2, 1865, and Ellen Craft to William Still, June 13, 1873, in reel 6, American Negro Historical Society Collection, 1790–1905, Historical Society of Pennsylvania, Philadelphia (hereafter ANHSC); William Still to G. L. Smith, May 19, 1874, in box 34, folder 7, Henry P. Slaughter Collection, Atlanta University Archives, Robert Woodruff Library, Clark Atlanta University (hereafter Slaughter Collection); T. F. B Marshall to William Still, April 30, 1874, and W. H. Stanton to William Still, January 15, 1872, in reel 6, ANHSC.

60 William Still to F. W. Lather, Fulton, Mo., August 13, 1873, in William Still Letterbook, 1873–1874, 331, Historical Society of Pennsylvania; William Still to W. H. Jones, June 3, 1873, in ibid., 4.

61 See Lapansky, "Aboard William Still's Underground Railroad," 14.

62 The styles of Still's book appear at the end of every advertisement for the book.

63 William Still to William McHenry, August 27, 1873, in Still Letterbook, 381.

64 William Still to James William, Bloomington, Ind., September 1, 1873, in Still Letterbook, 416.

65 William Still to John Green, January 15, 1874, in Still Letterbook, 724.

66 Assertions of William Still's nationalism are found in Blockson, *Underground Railroad*.

67 William Still to Rev. J. E. Embry, October 14, 1873, in Still Letterbook, 547.

68 William Still to W. D. Harris, June 5, 1873, in Still Letterbook, 13–14.

69 William Still to W. D. Jones, September 1, 1873, in Still Letterbook, 421–23.

70 Still's *Underground Railroad Records* (1883), sample book; B. W. Austin to William Still, August 13, 1892, and R. P. Hallowell to William Still, August 13, 1892, in box 34, folder 7, Slaughter Collection, Clark Atlanta University.

71 See Sojourner Truth to William Still, January 4, 1876, in reel 6, ANHSC; Austin to William Still, August 13, 1892, and Hallowell to William Still, August 13, 1892, Slaughter Collection.

Chapter Five

1 Gaines, *Uplifting the Race*. The shifting terrain of Southern life is discussed in Ayers, *Promise of the New South*; and Grantham, *Southern Progressivism*.

2 See Henry Louis Gates, "Trope of the New Negro." On black organizational issues, see Lee, "Negro Organizations." For the emerging philosophy of the "New Negro" in *Alexander's Magazine*, see S. Laing Williams, "The New Negro" (October 15, 1908), 17–23. Class formation among African Americans was a slow and gradual process with roots in the class stratification of the antebellum free black population. It was also clearly linked to issues of respectability and propriety. See "Class Distinctions among American Negroes"; Meier, "Negro Class Structure"; Landry, *New Black Middle Class*, 1–66; and Gatewood, "Aristocrats of Color."

3 The connections between professional black historians and the lay and amateur his-

torians are explored in several studies. One of the earliest expressions from a biblio-phile was Schomburg, "Negro Digs Up His Past." Also see Meier and Rudwick, *Black History*; J. Goggin, "Carter G. Woodson," 18–61; and Sinette, Coates, and Battle, *Black Bibliophiles and Collectors*, 3–58.

4 Numerous studies have explored the relationship between slavery and freedom. Classic studies include Morgan, *American Slavery, American Freedom*; and David Brion Davis, *Problem of Slavery*. See O. Patterson, *Freedom in the Making*, xiii; McGlynn and Drescher, *Meaning of Freedom*; T. Holt, *Problem of Freedom*, 3–12; and Oshinsky, "*Worse than Slavery.*" A postmodern reading of the problem of freedom is Hartman, *Scenes of Subjection*.

5 The theory of retrogression was an integral part of biological and essentialist con-ceptions of race; see Frederickson, *Black Image in the White Mind*. Important studies of lynching include Brundage, *Lynching in the New South*, and *Under Sentence of Death*; and Tolnay and Beck, *Festival of Violence*.

6 Frederickson, *Black Image in the White Mind*, 238–41.

7 Hoffman, "Vital Statistics of the Negro," and "Race Traits and Tendencies."

8 Analysis of shifting social, political, cultural, and intellectual trends in American life appears in E. Foner, *Reconstruction*; Jaynes, *Branches without Roots*; George Cotkin, *Reluctant Modernism*, 51–73; Lears, *No Place of Grace*; Doyle, *New Men, New Cities*; and Du Bois, *Black Reconstruction*.

9 Kevin Gaines makes a distinction between the connotations of uplift. There were clearly two visions. The first, "a broader vision of uplift signifying collective social aspiration, advancement, and struggle," had been the legacy of the Emancipation era. The second meaning, an elite appropriation of "class stratification as race progress," is linked to "bourgeoisie qualifications for rights and citizenship." Gaines, *Uplifting the Race*, xv. The representation of freedom and its contested meanings in the public sphere is addressed in K. Savage, *Standing Soldiers, Kneeling Slaves*.

10 Gaines, *Uplifting the Race*, 1–17; Greene and Woodson, *The Negro Wage Earner*, 19–74; Woodson, *Negro Professional Man*; Harris, *Negro as Capitalist*; Frazier, *Black Bourgeoisie*, 15–128.

11 Adolph Reed has identified the belief in progress as one of several characteristics of late nineteenth-century African American intellectuals; see *W. E. B. Du Bois*, 3–6. Also see Moses, *Golden Age of Black Nationalism*, 15–31.

12 Both Gail Bederman and Jackson Lears emphasize the correlations between race, gender, and class in the construction of masculine ideas of civilization. Lears, like George Cotkin, also situates these developments alongside other antimodernist im-pulses. See Bederman, *Manliness and Civilization*, 1–44; Lears, *No Place of Grace*, 107–16; and Cotkin, *Reluctant Modernism*.

13 Claudia Tate, examining the literature written by black women during the post-Reconstruction period, convincingly demonstrates that African American writers used their literary work to create domestic situations that reflected their political desires. See Tate, *Domestic Allegories and Political Desires*.

14 Crummell, *Civilization*, 5–6. Also see several earlier addresses by Crummell, "The Social Principle among a People" and "The Destined Superiority of the Negro," in Crummell, *Greatness of Christ*, 285–311, 332–52.

15 This idea draws upon the characterization of the race presented in the works of Adolph Reed, Wilson Jeremiah Moses, and Kevin Gaines. The sense of a rebirth is present in all of the historical works under examination. Black intellectuals usually employed this imagery not to suggest the race was uncivilized, but rather to argue for more ethical treatment of the race. An example of race progress writing is Willetts, "After Forty Years of Freedom," 11–18.

16 Crummell, "Need of New Ideas," 115–18. For a full explication of Crummell's civilizationist beliefs, see Moses, *Alexander Crummell*. Frederick Douglass's assessment of slavery differed little from that of Harper and Crummell. See "Future of the Race: As Carefully Reviewed by Mr. Douglass," 220. For a reprint of Harper's remarks, see "The Democratic Return to Power—Its Effects," 213–50. Also see, Moses, *Black Messiahs and Uncle Toms*, 86–107. A recent work that discusses the development of African American ideas about racial destiny is M. Mitchell, *Righteous Propagation*. A good discussion of the struggle to preserve memory of the abolitionist past is Jeffrey, *Abolitionists Remember*.

17 A definition of the postbellum slave narrative is included in Andrews, "Representation of Slavery." Examples of this type of work include Washington, *Up from Slavery*; and Pickens, *Heir of Slaves*, and *Bursting Bonds*.

18 For biographical information on Joseph Wilson, see Halley, *Afro-American Encyclopedia*, 80; see also Sara Dunlap's biographical sketch in the introduction to Wilson, *Black Phalanx*; Cornish, *Sable Arm*, 128–29; and Cornish's foreword to the 1994 Da Capo edition of Wilson's *Black Phalanx*. Advertisements for Wilson's book appeared in *Southern Workman*, November 1882, 116, and December 1882, 128. See also Joseph T. Wilson, "Some Negro Poets," 236–45.

19 Wilson, *Emancipation*. See Kachun, *Festivals of Freedom*.

20 Wilson, *Emancipation*, 142, 146–47.

21 G. W. Williams, *History of the Negro Race . . . 1800 to 1880*, 388. George Washington Williams's pioneering methodology is discussed in numerous articles and a book-length study by Franklin, *George Washington Williams*. See G. W. Williams, *History of the Negro Race . . . 1619 to 1800* and *History of the Negro Race . . . 1800 to 1880*. The management of the *Washington Bee* was particularly critical of Williams, both professionally and personally. "Our Review," *Washington Bee*, May 5, 1863; "On Williams' *History of the Negro Race in America*," *Washington Bee*, May 19, 1883; "The Colored Historian," *Washington Bee*, July 24, 1886.

22 The 1884 lecture before the Teacher's Association is cited in Crogman, *Talks for the Times*.

23 See Alexander, *History of the Colored Race*, 463–64. Discussions of the importance of labor in uplift philosophy are found in Gaines, *Uplifting the Race*. Also see Fortune, *Black and White*.

24 Alexander, *History of the Colored Race*, 469–70.

25 For biographical information on William Henry Crogman, see the sketch in Crogman, *Talks for the Times* , x–xxiii; Gibson and Crogman, *Colored American*, 505; and Winston and Logan, *Dictionary of American Negro Biography*, 140–41.

26 Crogman, "Thirty-second Anniversary of the Emancipation Proclamation," in *Talks for the Times*, 52–53.

27 Crogman, *Talks for the Times*, 315–18. Nineteenth-century, or prehistoricist, methodologies of history are discussed in Mandelbaum, *History, Man and Reason*; and Ross, "Historical Consciousness."

28 Redkey, *Black Exodus*; Painter, *Black Exodusters*.

29 Crogman, *Talks for the Times*, 320–323.

30 Harper's, Douglass's, and Crummell's remarks are cited in note 16 above. Crogman believed in the indomitable spirit of Anglo-Saxonism. He referred to the tendency of whites to explore in the following way: "He is scouring the seas, dredging the oceans, tunneling the mountains, boring his way into the frozen parts of the north, parceling out the continent of Africa, and giving civilization and laws to the tribes— It is not likely, I say, that this restless, energetic white brother will respect the boundary line of a state or territory at home; he has not done so with reference to the Indian; he would never do so with reference to us. Were it possible for us to go off to-morrow into some territory by ourselves, within a week the Connecticut Yankee would be there peddling his wooden nutmegs. The patent medicine man would be there selling his nostrums. The Georgia cracker and the Kentucky horsetrader would be there trading their horse and mules." Crogman, *Talks for the Times*, 321–22.

31 Kletzing and Crogman, *Progress of a Race*. Advertisements for the book in *New York Age* include "Books Make the Best Presents," January 1905; "Books of Race Value," June 29, 1905; and "Books of Real Value," November 20, 1905. Numerous advertisements for the book appeared in volumes 3–5 of *Voice of the Negro*: 3 (May 1906): front cover; 3 (July 1906): back page; 3 (September 1906): back page; 3 (November 1906): front page; 4 (March 1907): front page; 5 (May 1907): back page; 5 (June 1907): back page.

32 Kletzing and Crogman, *Progress of a Race*, 191–278, 299–446. The evolution of approaches to African American history is discussed in Franklin, "On the Evolution of Scholarship." Franklin also provides an excellent discussion of generational shifts in the writing of Afro-American history. Also see Franklin, "Dilemma."

33 Assessments of the importance of literature and history were featured in the *A.M.E. Church Review* in the post-Reconstruction period; see G. M. Elliott, "We Must Educate," 1 (April 1885): 330–44; T. B. Snowden, "Development," 2 (January 1886): 205; H. T Johnson, "Negro Literature and Book Making," 7 (October 1890): 192–201; and Archibald Johnson, "The Study of Universal History in Liberal Education," 12 (January 1896): 352–77. Also see Council, *Lamp of Wisdom*.

34 Daniel Barclay Williams, *Freedom and Progress*; Pendleton, *Narrative of the Negro*; and J. W. Cromwell, *Negro in American History*.

35 Biographical information on Daniel Barclay Williams is found in *Freedom and Progress*, 7–8. See ads for all three of his books in "Agents Wanted for Popular and Useful Books for the People," *A.M.E. Church Review* 7 (October 1889): back page; (July 1890): 129; (October 1890): back page. See also Daniel Barclay Williams, *Science, Art and Methods of Teaching*, 19–20, and *Freedom and Progress*, 102–29.

36 D. B. Williams, *Freedom and Progress*, 4–5. The following articles appeared in the *A.M.E. Church Review*: Reverend H. Edwards Bryant, "Our Duties, Responsibilities: Negro Literature," 1 (January 1885): 257–67; Daniel B. Williams, "The Colored American and Higher Education," 7 (April 1891): 392–412; Reverend W. L. Brown,

"The Value of a Classical Education," 8 (January 1892): 269–75; and L. J. Coppin, "The Negro in American Literature," 15 (October 1898): 628–88.

37 D. B. Williams, *Freedom and Progress*, 27–30; Hegel, *Philosophy of History*; Straker, "The Negro in Science, Art, and Literature," *A.M.E. Church Review* 1 (July 1884): 56–60.

38 D. B. Williams, *Freedom and Progress*, 29–30.

39 Ibid., 138.

40 Biographical information on Edward A. Johnson is contained in Fuller, *Pictorial History of the Negro*, 288; and Winston and Logan, *Dictionary of American Negro Biography*, 349–50. Also see E. Johnson, *School History of the Negro Race*, iii–v. Other books by Edward Johnson include *History of the Negro Soldiers in the Spanish American War* and *Light Ahead for the Negro*. Contemporaries felt that Johnson was a highly successful author who sold many books: "Professor Johnson has a wonderful record for selling books to members of his race. The secret of his success lies in the fact that whatever he writes is written from the Negro point of view and in an able and intelligent manner." "Professor Edward A. Johnson and His Books," *Alexander's Magazine*, August 15, 1905, 41–42. Johnson also emphasized the importance of history for African American youth in an address before the Association of Educators of Colored Youth in 1894: "The importance of instructing colored youth in Negro history is apparent to such minds as have given the future status of the race any consideration. But the first inquiry should be, 'Has the Negro any History worth teaching?' Our white friends who have written American histories, have evidently answered this question in the negative, for in making a careful examination of the various American white school histories, I find only one that has but a slight reference to the Negro and his doings in this country. . . . Even the Encyclopedia Britannica, a book of authority the world over, does more to our inquiry than condemn the race with silence — it publishes to the world the truth of history that NO genuine Negro has ever achieved greatness. The geographies print in cuts of the race a savage Negro for Americans to study as a model. But our inquiry is, has the Negro done any anything worthy of historical mention? If he has, the youth of the race ought to know it." "Importance of Instructing the Youth."

41 Johnson was closely associated with the black academy, received an LL.B. degree from Shaw University in Raleigh, North Carolina, in 1891, where he subsequently served as an instructor of law, typing, and stenography and as dean of the Law Department. E. Johnson, preface, *School History of the Negro Race*.

42 There are a number of studies on the development of the black bibliophile tradition in Philadelphia and New York. Among the most significant are Wayman, "The American Negro Historical Society of Philadelphia and Its Officers," 287–94; Spady, "Afro-American Historical Society"; Tony Martin, "Bibliophiles, Activists, and Race Men," and "Arthur Alonso Schomburg (1874–1936), Black Bibliophile and Collector," in Sinette, Coates, and Battle, *Black Bibliophiles and Collectors*, 23–34, 38–42. For a listing of black bibliophiles, see Gubert, *Early Black Bibliophiles*. Also see Crowder, *John Edward Bruce*, 207–335.

43 For biographical information on John W. Cromwell, see Culp, *Twentieth Century Negro Literature*, 291; and Winston and Logan, *Dictionary*, 141–42. The history of the Bethel Literary and Historical Association is explored in J. W. Cromwell, "History

of Bethel"; and Meier, *Negro Thought in America*, 45–50. The Virginia Educational Association is discussed in J. Goggin, "Carter G. Woodson," 22. The history of the American Negro Academy is explored in Moss, *American Negro Academy*; and Cromwell, "Our Colored Churches," 89–100.

44 J. W. Cromwell, *Negro in American History*, xi–xiii.

45 Ibid., 1–46; Winston and Logan, *Dictionary*, 141–42.

46 J. W. Cromwell, *Negro in American History*, 134–40, 255–59, 261–66.

47 For examples of the representative imagery of the "New Negro" man and woman, see "Rough Sketches: A Study of the New Negro Woman," *Voice of the Negro* 1 (July 1904): 323–26; "Rough Sketches: The New Negro Man," *Voice of the Negro* 1 (October 1904): 447–52; "Rough Sketches: William Edward Burghardt Du Bois," *Voice of the Negro* 2 (March 1905): 176–81. Outside of Boston, Philadelphia and Washington, D.C., had the most prominent black families prior to 1900. Both groups benefited from strong, free black populations prior to 1860. Philadelphia was not only the site of Mother Bethel, the first established church of the African Methodist Episcopal Church, but also the home of the Purvis and Forten families—two of the wealthiest black families prior to the Civil War—as well as the site of the prestigious Philadelphia Institute for Colored Youth. Free blacks in Washington, D.C., supported more private schools than any other urban community in the United States. The Civil War and Reconstruction experiment, which facilitated the building of Howard University, elevated this community to an enviable place among African American elites in the postbellum period. See Curry, *Free Black in Urban America*, 152–53, 159–60, 221–22. Postbellum assessments of these communities include Lane, *William Dorsey's Philadelphia*, 91–154; and C. M. Green, *Secret City*, 91–154. See Gatewood, *Aristocrats of Color*. This discussion of the meanings of representation and uplift is influenced by Henry Louis Gates. He was one of the first literary historians to discuss the rise of black literary production and its relationship to the creation of a "New Negro" in the late nineteenth and early twentieth centuries. He challenges the idea that representation is simply a function of bourgeois culture among African Americans or an attempt to accommodate the mainstream.

48 See Gates, "Trope of the New Negro." Wilson Jeremiah Moses has written critically about the flowering of New Negro literature in the late nineteenth century; see "The Lost World of the Negro," in Moses, *Wings of Ethiopia*, 201–22.

49 The importance of Simmons's text is discussed in Ernest Kaiser's foreword to the 1968 New York Times and Arno Press edition of *Men of Mark*. Advertisements for the book include *A.M.E. Church Review* 5 (April 1888): front cover.

50 For biographical information on Simmons, see Henry McNeal Turner, introduction to Simmons, *Men of Mark* (1887); "Reverend Wm. J. Simmons, D.D.," *Washington Bee*, March 16, 1889; Brawley, *Negro Builders and Heroes*, 200; and Winston and Logan, *Dictionary*, 556–57.

51 See Simmons, *Men of Mark*, 3–10, 39–63. Also see W. Bishop Johnson, "Eulogy on William J. Simmons, Delivered at the Memorial Exercises of the Sunday School Lyceum, Held December 7, 1890," in reel 3, Daniel Murray Pamphlet Collection, Library of Congress.

52 H. M. Turner, introduction to Simmons, *Men of Mark*. For biographical information

on Henry McNeal Turner, see Redkey, *Black Exodus*. Also see Angell, *Bishop Henry McNeal Turner*.

53 See Simmons, *Men of Mark*, 60–62.

54 Ibid. For a discussion of the different versions of millennial thought in the post-Reconstruction period, see Fulop, "Future Golden Day."

55 Simmons, *Men of Mark*, 61.

56 Ibid., 6–7. My own calculations reveal the following results: Ministers made up 36.0 percent, academics 11.6, politicians 7.5, lawyers 6.9, and artists 6.4.

57 Simmons, *Men of Mark*, 7–8.

58 Discussions of the stereotypes of black women include Morton, *Disfigured Images*; and White, *Ar'n't I A Woman*. The history of the National Association of Colored Women is discussed in Kendrick, "They Also Serve." Also see Carby, "On the Threshold," and *Reconstructing Womanhood*, 96–97. Early twentieth-century accounts of black women's involvement in the club movement and their positions on uplift provide critical insights into their work. All of the articles by black clubwomen that follow appeared in the *Voice of the Negro*. Fannie Barrier Williams, "The Club Movement among the Colored Women," 1 (March 1904): 99–102; Addie Hunton, "Negro Womanhood Defended," 1 (July 1904): 280–82; Josephine Silon Yates, "The National Association of Colored Women," 1 (July 1904): 283–87; Mrs. Booker T. Washington, "Social Improvement of the Plantation Woman," 1 (July 1904): 288–90; Mary Church Terrell, "The Progress of Colored Women," 1 (July 1904): 291–94; Josephine Bruce, "What Has Education Done for Colored Women," 1 (July 1904): 294–98; and Sylvanie Franciaz Williams, "The Social Status of the Negro Woman," 1 (July 1904): 298–300. For a discussion of black women on the suffrage question, see Jones, *All Bound Up*, 151–206.

59 Frazier, "Some Afro-American Women of Mark," 373–86. Also see Bentley, "The Women of Our Race Worthy of Imitation," 473–77. Early collective biographies of African American women include Shorter, *Heroines of African Methodism* (1891); Anna Amelia Smith, *Reminiscences of Colored People* (1913); Mossell-Griffin, *Afro-American Men and Women* (1900). Collective biographies of women by men include Scruggs, *Women of Distinction* (1893); and Majors, *Noted Negro Women* (1893).

60 For biographical information on Gertrude E. H. Bustill, who wrote under the name of her husband, Nathan Francis Mossell, see Mather, *Who's Who of the Colored Race*, 201; and Hine, Brown, and Terborg-Penn, *Black Women in America*, 820–21. Also see Tate, *Domestic Allegories*, 132–34, 154.

61 Mossell, *Work of the Afro-American Woman*, 9.

62 Ibid., 15–18; Hine, *Black Women in White*.

63 See Mossell, *Work of the Afro-American Woman*, 48–49.

64 Ibid., 54.

65 Ibid., 60.

66 Carby, *Reconstructing Womanhood*, 121–62.; Gruesser, *The Unruly Voice*, 1–20. Biographical information on Hopkins in found in Hine, Brown, and Terborg-Penn, *Black Women in America*. The 1990s witnessed a renewed interest in the work of Pauline Hopkins. A number of important dissertations have been produced in literary studies which examine the historical implications of her fictional works: T. C.

Reed, "Subjects of Consumption"; K. M. Brooks, "Transgressing the Boundaries of Identity"; M. H. Patterson, "'Survival of the Best Fitted.'" Also see the following books and articles on Hopkins: Allen, *Black Women Intellectuals*; Shockley, "Pauline Elizabeth Hopkins"; Otten, "Pauline Hopkins"; and Gilman, "Pauline Hopkins and the Occult." Also see a recent study, L. Brown, *Pauline Elizabeth Hopkins*.

67 Dorieski, "Inherited Rhetoric and Authentic History," 71–75.

68 Pauline Hopkins, "Famous Women of the Negro Race: Club Life among Colored Women," *Colored American*, August 1902, 273–77.

69 Pauline Hopkins, "Booker T. Washington," *Colored American*, October 1901, 441. For a more laudatory sketch of Booker T. Washington published by an ally, see William H. Foote, "Character Sketch of Booker T. Washington," *Colored American*, December 1904, 706–16.

70 Hopkins's series "Famous Negro Men" in the *Colored American* included "Toussaint L'Ouverture," November 1900, 9–24; "Hon. Frederick Douglass," December 1900, 122–32; and "William Wells Brown," January 1901, 232–36.

71 Hopkins, "Toussaint L'Ouverture," 10–11, "Hon. Frederick Douglass," 125, and "William Wells Brown," 236.

72 The following Hopkins biographies of "Famous Men of the Negro Race" appeared in *Colored American*: "Lewis Hayden," April 1901, 473–77; "Edwin Garrison Walker," March 1901, 358–66; "Charles Lennox Remond," May 1901, 34–39; and "Robert Browne Elliott," July 1901, 294–312.

73 Hopkins, "Robert Browne Elliott," 301. Also see Pauline Hopkins, "Senator Blanche K. Bruce," *Colored American*, August 1901, 257–61, and "John Mercer Langston," *Colored American*, July 1901, 177–84.

74 Pauline Hopkins, "Sergeant William H. Carney," *Colored American*, June 1901, 84–89; Wilson, *Black Phalanx*; George Washington Williams, *History of the Negro Troops*. Also see Arnold, "Colored Soldiers in the Union Army," 257–66.

75 Hopkins's "Famous Women of the Negro Race" series in the *Colored American* included "Sojourner Truth," December 1901, 45–53; "Harriet Tubman," January/February 1902, 206–13; "Literary Workers," April 1902, 366–402; "Educators," May 1902, 41–46; "Educators (Continued)," June 1902, 125–30; and "Educators (Concluded)," July 1902, 206–13.

76 Biographical information on Lelia Amos Pendleton is found in Mather, *Who's Who of the Colored Race*, 214. She also published *An Alphabet for Negro Children* in 1915.

77 William Alexander opined, "Women are formed to become instructors, for while they immediately hold in their hands the mortality of children, those future sovereigns of the earth, the example they may give and the charm they may diffuse over other periods of life, furnish to them means for the amelioration of every evil." W. Alexander, *History of the Colored Race*, 462.

78 Pendleton, *Narrative of the Negro*, 90–100, 133–45.

79 Biographical information and treatments of the life of Anna Julia Cooper are contained in the following sources: Mather, *Who's Who of the Colored Race*, 76; Hine, Brown, and Terborg-Penn, *Black Women in America*; Hutchinson, *Anna Julia Cooper*; Gabel, *From Slavery to the Sorbonne*; Chateauvert, "Third Step"; Fletcher-Baker, *Singing Something*; Lemert and Bhan, *Voice of Anna Julia Cooper*.

80 Cooper, *Voice from the South*, 9–11. See Bederman, *Manliness and Civilization*, 11–12.

81 The best treatment of Cooper's incorporation of the female voice into her writing is E. Alexander, "'We Must Be About.'"

82 Cooper, *Voice from the South*, 25.

83 Ibid., 26.

84 Ibid., 33–48.

85 Crummell, "The Black Woman of the South: Her Neglects and Her Needs," in Moses, *Destiny and Race*, 211–23. Cooper, *Voice from the South*, 42–43. Cooper offered a similar assessment of Africans Americans.

86 See F. B. Williams, "The Intellectual Progress of the Colored Women of the United States since the Emancipation Proclamation" (1894), and A. J. Cooper, "Discussion of the Same Subject by Mrs. A. J. Cooper of Washington, D.C.," in Sewall, *World's Congress of Representative Women*, 696–711, 711–15. Also see Washington, Wood, and Williams, *New Negro for a New Century*, 384, 392–94, 406–28; and Fannie Barrier Williams, "The Negro and Public Opinion," 31–32, and "An Extension of the Conference Spirit," 300–303.

87 Cooper, "The Ethics of the Negro Question," in Lemert and Bhan, *Voice of Anna Julia Cooper*, 206–15.

88 Ibid., 212.

89 For an assessment of Cooper's positions on labor, Gaines, *Uplifting the Race*, 128–51.

90 Cooper, "Ethics of the Negro Question," 212–13.

91 For an assessment of Cooper's positions on labor, see Gaines, *Uplifting the Race*, 128–51; and Cooper, "Ethics of the Negro Question," 212–13, 215.

Chapter Six

1 Information on the qualities of early historians can be found in Higham, *History*, 6–11.

2 Ibid., 15. For additional information on the work of Henry Baxter Adams, see H. Adams, *Education of Henry Adams*; and W. Stull Holt, *Historical Scholarship*.

3 Higham, *History*, 16. Information on the founding of the American Historical Association can be found in Van Tassel, "From Learned Society to Professional Organization." Information on J. Franklin Jameson's career and publications is found in Rothenberg and Goggin, *John Franklin Jameson*.

4 For discussion of the uses and meanings of science in the American historical profession, see W. Stull Holt, *Historical Scholarship*, 18; Novick, *That Noble Dream*, 1–110; Noble, "Perhaps the Rise and Fall"; and Kloppenberg, "Objectivity and Historicism."

5 Higham, *History*, 28–31, 33–34.

6 Studies of professionalization in the black academy include Hesseltine and Kaplan, "Negro Doctors of Philosophy"; Boardman, "Rise of the Negro Historian," and "Negro Historians of Our Times"; Greene, *Holders of Doctorates*, 26; Robert Harris, "Coming of Age"; "J. Franklin Jameson, Carter G. Woodson, and the Foundations of Black Historiography," in Meier and Rudwick, *Black History*, 1005–15; Goggin, "Carter G. Woodson," and *Carter G. Woodson*.

7 For a characterization of the early black historical academy, see Meier and Rudwick, *Black History*, 1–8; and J. Goggin, "Carter G. Woodson." Also see C. Wesley, "Racial Historical Societies." For an assessment of the treatment of black scholars in the nascent historical profession, see E. Lewis, "To Turn as on a Pivot." While Lewis explores the relationship between black historians and the American historical profession through an examination of the number of articles published by the *American Historical Review*, book reviews and commentaries suggest a larger amount of interest in the nascent field of African American history. Most volumes included reviews of works by black historians or about black history. See the following reviews and documents, which appeared in the *American Historical Review* between 1895 and 1915: "Colonel William Byrd on Slavery and Indentured Servants, 1736, 1739," 1 (October 1895): 88–90; Henry Pratt Ingram, "Review of *A History of Slavery and Serfdom* by John Kells Ingram," 1 (October 1895): 153–56; Wilbur Siebert, "Light on the Underground Railroad," 3 (April 1896): 455–63; "Review of *Underground Railroad: From Slavery to Freedom*, by Wilbur H. Siebert," 3 (April 1899): 557–60; "Review of *Contemporaries*, by Thomas Wentworth Higginson," 3 (April 1900): 591–92; "Minutes of Abolition Conventions, 1794–1829," 4 (July 1900): 804–6; James A. Woodburn, "Review of *A Political History of Slavery*, by William Henry Smith," 9 (January 1904): 385–89; Ulrich Bonnell Phillips, "The Origin and Growth of the Southern Black Belts," 11 (July 1906): 798–816; W. E. B. Du Bois, "Reconstruction and Its Benefits," 15 (October 1909): 781–99; E. J. Corwin, "The Dred Scott Decision in the Light of Contemporary Legal Doctrines," 17 (October 1911): 52–69; Ulrich Bonnell Phillips, "A Jamaica Slave Plantation," 19 (April 1914): 543–58; "Estimates of the Value of Slaves, 1815," 19 (July 1914): 808–13; Ulrich Bonnell Phillips, "Slave Crimes in Virginia," 20 (January 1915): 336–40; A. H. Stone, "The Cotton Factorage System of the Southern States," 20 (April 1915): 557–65; Marcus Jernigan, "Slavery and Conversion in the American Colonies," 21 (April 1916): 504–27.

8 Anderson, introduction, *Education of Blacks*.

9 *Annual Catalogue of Virginia Union University Combining Wayland Seminary and Richmond Theological Seminary* (Richmond: Virginia Union University, 1905), 21–31; "History Teachers, Virginia Union University, 1906–1915," and "History Courses, Virginia Union University, 1906–1915," compiled by Dr. Vonita Foster, library director, Virginia Union University, August 29, 1996, in the author's possession. Biographical information on Charles H. A. Bulkey is included in Winston, *Howard University Department of History*, 8–11. Biographical information on William Tunnell can be found in William V. Tunnell Biographical File, Moorland-Springarn Research Center, Howard University; Dyson, *Howard University*, 176; Logan, *Howard University*, 128; and Winston, *Howard University Department of History*, 9–11.

10 Information on the transition of colleges from a morally based construction to institutions based on knowledge and facts is chronicled in Reuben, *Making of the Modern University*.

11 For biographical information on Charles Chaveau Cook, see "Death of Prof. Charles Cook," *Howard University Journal*, September 30, 1910, 1. Also see Winston, *Howard University Department of History*, 5–7. A listing of courses offered under Cook is included in the *Howard University Catalogue, 1907–1908*, 36, 43–44.

12 An overview of Tunnell's tenure at Howard is provided in the Tunnell Biographical File, Howard University; and Winston, *Howard University Department of History*, 11. For a listing and description of courses offered by Tunnell, see *Howard University Catalogues: 1909–1910*, 42–43, 81–82; *1912–1913*, 52–53; and *1913–1914*, 38.

13 Histories of Howard University include Dyson, *Howard University*; and Logan, *Howard University*.

14 Biographical information on Walter Dyson is found in Mather, *Who's Who of the Colored Race*, 97–98; and Dyson, *Howard University*, 173. Also see Winston, *Howard University Department of History*, 25–27. Biographical information on Charles Wesley is found in Charles Wesley Biographical File, Moorland-Springarn Research Center. Doctoral dissertations on Charles Wesley's life include Harris, "Charles H. Wesley"; and L. Goggin, "Evolution of Central State College." An assessment of Wesley's work is in Conyers, *Charles H. Wesley*.

15 For information on Jesse Moorland's contribution of African and African American historical materials to Howard University, see Jesse E. Moorland to Carter G. Woodson, September 2, 1915, in folder 614, Jesse Moorland Papers, Moorland-Springarn Research Center; and "Negro Americana at Howard University," *Washington*, January 2, 1915.

16 On the administrations of Edmund Asa Ware, Horace Bumstead, and Edmund Trichell Ware see M. Adams, *History of Atlanta University*, 14–40. Bumstead's administration is discussed at length in Bacote, *Story of Atlanta University*, 103–48. For information on Bumstead's role in recruiting Du Bois, see ibid., 130–33. Du Bois's early studies included "The Enforcement of the Slave Trade Laws," *Annual Report of the American Historical Association for the Year 1891* (1892), 161–74; and *Suppression of the African Slave Trade*. Shortly before his arrival and during his tenure at Atlanta University, Du Bois published several essays that would serve as the foundation of his 1903 study, *The Souls of Black Folk*. See "Strivings of the Negro People"; "Storm and Stress in the Black World"; "Evolution of Negro Leadership"; and "Freedmen's Bureau." For an assessment of Du Bois's work at Atlanta University, see D. L. Lewis, *W. E. B. Du Bois*, 218–25.

17 Information on the Hampton and Tuskegee Conferences is included in D. L. Lewis, *W. E. B. Du Bois*, 218. See "Form of Certificate Admitting to Atlanta University: Entrance Requirements, 1910–1915," in box 33, Atlanta University Archives, Robert Woodruff Library, Clark Atlanta University.

18 Vernon Williams discusses the impact of Boas's work on race in *From a Caste to a Minority* and *Rethinking Race*. A description of the department's mission is included in *Catalogue of the Officers and Students of Atlanta University, 1898–1899*, 13. Shifting ideas on race are discussed in Baker, *From Savage to Negro*; Gossett, *Race*, 409–59; and Smedley, *Race in North America*, 250–91.

19 Changes instituted in the Sociology and History Department are described in the annual *Catalogue of the Officers and Students of Atlanta University: 1898–1899*, 13; *1899–1900*, 14; *1902–1903*, 14–15.

20 Ibid., *1903–1904*, 12–13; *1904–1905*, 15; *1905–1906*, 14; *1909–1910*, 13.

21 Description of the Atlanta University Library and the Marblehead Library operation can be found in "Library of Atlanta University," in Edward Ware Papers, Atlanta

University Archives. Endorsements of the Marblehead Library and descriptions of its operation can be found in Miss Frances B. Clemmer, Local Secretary of Atlanta University, to Friends of the University, February 1906, in box 33, Ware Papers; "Appeal for Marblehead Libraries," Edmund Ware to Trustees of the Anna T. Jeanes Foundation for the Negro Rural Schools, 1910, in box 34, Ware Papers; G. S. Dickerman to Edmund Ware, March 25, and December 21, 1909, in ibid. Also see G. S. Dickerman, "Education in the Love of Reading," reprinted from *Southern Workman*, August and September 1910, in ibid.

22 The books included in the series are drawn from the shipping invoices; see J. J. Gregory to Edward Ware, February 2, 1910; Shipping Invoice, Library #12, July 7, 1910; and Shipping Invoice, Library #10, Risley Public School, Brunswick, Ga., May 20, 1910, all in box 34, Ware Papers. For an endorsement and assessment of the program, see D. D. Little to Edmund Ware, January 10, 1909, in box 33, Ware Papers. While Little was grateful for the collection, he was also critical of the fact that it contained so few books by or about African Americans: "I must confess to a little disappointment, however, in that there were so few books in the collection that were written especially for Negroes. We find that our students devour eagerly everything that they can find that was written by a Negro or about Negro achievement." D. D. Little to Edmund T. Ware, April 23, 1910, in ibid.

23 The purpose of the Marblehead collections was to provide libraries to schools and colleges that lacked adequate facilities. Each collection of books included a copy of the pamphlet "From Servitude to Service," describing the work of black schools throughout the South. The collection also contained public documents from various federal agencies, which addressed the practical issues of "agriculture, cooking, hygiene and sanitation." Also see "Appeal for Marblehead Libraries," in Ware Papers.

24 Biographical information on Benjamin Brawley can be found in Mather, *Who's Who of the Colored Race*, 36; and Winston and Logan, *Dictionary of American Negro Biography*, 60–61.

25 The early history of Gammon Theological Seminary is explored in a number of works; see McPheeters, "Origin and Development"; Taylor, "History of Gammon"; and Bronson, "Origin and Significance." A contemporary sketch of Elijah Gammon is in Wilbur P. Thirkield, "Reverend Elijah H. Gammon: A Memorial Address Delivered on Founder's Day, Twenty-third of October, 1891," *Quarterly Bulletin: Gammon Theological Seminary*, 1891.

26 Taylor, "History of Gammon," 49–50; Bronson, "Origin and Significance," 16–19.

27 Taylor, "History of Gammon," 59–61.

28 One of the earliest descriptions of the historical society is found in *Catalogue of the Gammon Theological Seminary, 1894*, 22–24.

29 For information on the Stewart Missionary Society, see *Catalogue of the Gammon Theological Seminary, 1895*, 25–28. A complete biographical assessment of Reverend Stewart can be found in Edward L. Parks, "Reverend William Fletcher Stewart, A.M.: A Memorial Address Delivered May 5th, 1901," *Quarterly Bulletin: Gammon Theological Seminary*, May 1901. Stewart died in 1900; see ibid., 27. For a detailed description of Stewart's plan, see *Quarterly Bulletin: Gammon Theological Seminary*, Stewart Foundation Edition, November 1895, 10–18. A description of the program

of the Stewart Missionary Foundation in 1895 can be found in ibid., 10–16; and *Catalogue of the Gammon Theological Seminary, 1895*, 25–28.

30 Announcements for the Congress on Africa appeared in *Quarterly Bulletin: Gammon Theological Seminary*, Stewart Foundation Edition, November 1895, 30–31. T. Thomas Fortune, editor of the *New York Age* and an invited speaker at the congress, also agreed to place a full-page editorial notice of the conference in his paper; see T. Thomas Fortune to Wilbur Thirkield, November 9, 1895, in reel 1, Papers of President Thirkield, Gammon Theological Seminary Records, Atlanta University Archives. For information on the solicitation of papers and other preparations for the conference, see Orishatukeh Faduma to Thirkield, October 31, 1895; T. Thomas Fortune to Thirkield, October 26, November 7 and 15, 1895; Alexander Crummell to Thirkield, September 30, October 10 and 26, 1895; E. M. Cravath, President of Fisk University, to Thirkield, October 30 and December 9, 1895; W. H. Council to Thirkield, November 11, 1895; and L. L. Denton, President of Claflin College, to Thirkield, December 2, 1895, all in ibid. The role of African American missionaries in Africa is discussed in a number of studies; see Jacobs, *Black Americans and the Missionary Movement*; W. Williams, *Black Americans and the Evangelization*; Willis and Newman, *Black Apostles at Home*; and Chirenje, *Ethiopianism and Afro-Americans*. See Wilbur B. Thirkield, "Opening Remarks," in Bowen, *Africa and the American Negro*, 13.

31 All of the following speeches are located in Bowen, *Africa and the American Negro*: Blyden, "Letter of Greeting and Commendation," 16–17; Noble, "Outlook for African Missions in the Twentieth Century," 61–69; John Smyth, "The African in Africa and the American in Africa," 69–84; Chatelain, "African Slavery: Its Status; The Antislavery Movement in Europe," 103–12; French-Sheldon, "Practical Issues of an African Experience," 95–102; Holderness, "My Life in Africa," 113–16; and Crummell, "Civilization: A Collateral Agency in Planting the Church in Africa," 119–24, and "The Absolute Need of an Indigenous Missionary Agency in Africa," 137–42.

32 All of the following articles can be found in Bowen, *Africa and the American Negro*: Bowen, "Comparative Status of the Negro at the Close of the War and To-day," 163–74; Turner, "The American Negro and His Fatherland," 195–98; and Fortune, "The Nationalization of Africa," 199–204. The congress was received favorably by Cyrus Adams, editor of the *New York Sun*. "I haven't seen one volume which includes at once more accurate and useful information about Africa and her peoples, and also so many practical suggestions as to methods of missionary work, health conditions, and other facts that are most important to bear in mind in working for Africa." See Adams's comments quoted in "The Assembly, the Alumni, the History," *Quarterly Bulletin: Gammon Theological Seminary*, June 1898, 28. Another reviewer characterized the conference in the following way: "The Stewart Missionary Foundation has done a good thing in planning and carrying out a Congress on Africa, as a means of keeping alive the interest that all American Negroes should have in the home of their ancestors and of their kindred. No one who attended the sessions of the Congress at Atlanta will soon forget the enthusiasm excited by the proceedings of those three days, or will doubt for one moment in regard to the value of just such a symposium on the relation of Africa to the American Negro and of the American Negro to Africa." "Review of J. W. E. Bowen, ed., *Africa and the American Negro: Addresses and*

Proceedings of the Congress on Africa, December 13–15, 1895," *Southern Workman,* August 1896, 154. Good secondary assessments of the meeting's import are found in Skinner, *African Americans and U.S. Policy,* 160–64; and W. Williams, *Black Americans and the Evangelization,* 8–9.

33 Information on the involvement of the members of the Stewart Missionary Fund in missionary work is included in the *Quarterly Bulletin: Gammon Theological Seminary, Catalogue Edition, 1904–1905,* 16. Information on the inauguration of courses on African history and geography is discussed in the *Quarterly Bulletin: Gammon Theological Seminary,* July 1909, 18–19. The changes in 1910 can be found in the *Quarterly Bulletin: Gammon Theological Seminary,* 1909–10, 7–8. Information on the formal offering of courses is in *Quarterly Bulletin: Gammon Theological Institute, Catalogue Edition, 1910–1911,* 17–18, 21.

34 *Quarterly Bulletin: Gammon Theological Seminary, Catalogue Edition, 1904–1905,* 14–16. For the initial description of the courses on Africa, see *Quarterly Bulletin: Gammon Theological Institute,* July 1909, 18–19. The shift in the foundation's policies on the mission class is contained in *Quarterly Bulletin: Gammon Theological Seminary,* November 1910, 7. See also *Quarterly Bulletin: Gammon Theological Seminary,* February 1911, 7–8. For an assessment of the early planning for the mission course, see Dr. Atkinson, President and Treasurer of the Stewart Foundation, to Earl Taylor, November 25, 1908, in Stewart Missionary Association, Gammon Theological Seminary Records, reel 13, Atlanta University Archives. In addition to Gammon Theological Seminary, Morris Brown College, established by the African Methodist Episcopal Church in 1881, also pursued a quasi-historical program in its course offerings and lecture components. From the scant records that exist, Morris Brown did not begin to offer a well defined set of history courses until the beginning of the twentieth century. These courses consisted of the standard offerings in ancient, medieval, and modern history. Courses were offered in English history and government as well as American history and government. The primary focus of these courses included the "social, religious, commercial and political lives of the races of mankind, together with the causes leading to the rise and fall of different nations and the general progress of civilization." *Catalogue: Morris Brown College, 1904–1905,* 54–55, and *Catalogue: Morris Brown College, 1907–1908,* 54–55. Information on the historical development of Morris Brown College can be found in Thomas, *Morris Brown College;* and Sewell and Troup, *Morris Brown College.*

35 For an outline of the historical program, see *Catalogue of the Hampton Normal and Agricultural Institute for the Academical Year 1871–1872* (Hampton, Va.: Normal School Press, 1872), 14. Information on the academic and work regimen at Hampton University is outlined in *Catalogue of the Hampton Institute for the Academical Year 1882–1883* (Hampton, Va.: Hampton Institute Steam Press, 1883), 29–31.

36 Discussions of Washington's program of industrial civilizationism include Harlan, *Booker T. Washington: Wizard,* 143–201; Morton, *Afro-American Women of the South,* 122–38; and Anderson, *Education of Blacks,* 79–109.

37 *The Forty-seventh Annual Catalogue: Hampton Normal and Agricultural Institute* (Hampton, Va.: Hampton Institute Press, 1915), 50.

38 *Catalogue of the Tuskegee State Normal School, . . . 1881–1882* (Hampton, Va.: Normal

School Steam Press, 1882), 7–9. An outline of the historical program is contained in *Catalogue of the Hampton Normal and Agricultural Institute for the Academical Year 1871–1872* (Hampton, Va.: Normal School Press, 1872), 14. Information on the academic and work regimen at Hampton University is outlined in *Catalogue of the Hampton Institute for the Academical Year 1882–1883* (Hampton, Va.: Hampton Institute Steam Press, 1883), 29–31. The proceedings of several meetings of the Hampton Negro Conference published by the Hampton Institute Press include *Hampton Negro Conference, Number I, 1897*; *Number II, July 1898*, 8–9; *Number III, July 1899*, 11–15; *Proceedings of the Hampton Negro Conference, Number VI, July 1902*, 65–73; and *Proceedings . . . Number VIII, July 1904*, 79–83.

39 Information on the faculty of Hampton is found in Anderson, *Education of Blacks*, 31–78.

40 Biographical information on Mary Dibble is located in Mary Dibble Biographical File, Hampton University Archives, Hampton, Virginia. Dibble's assessment of the history program can be found in *Report of the Hampton Normal and Agricultural Institute for the Year Ending June 30, 1883* (Richmond, Va.: R. F. Walker, 1883), 14–15. Dibble's comments on the program can be found in *Hampton Normal and Agricultural Institute: Annual Reports for the Academical and Fiscal Year Ending June 30, 1883* (Hampton, Va.: Normal School Steam Press, 1883), 23–25.

41 Biographical information on Anne Scoville can be found in Anne Scoville Biographical File, Hampton University Archives). Examples of Scoville's scholarship on Native Americans includes "Revolutionary Hampton," *Southern Workman*, November 1896, 214–15; "The Moral Status of the Primitive Indian," *Southern Workman*, January 1897, 11–13; and "An Old Church," *Southern Workman*, January 1895, 7. For Scoville's assessment of African Americans and the Bible, see Anne Scoville, "The Negro and the Bible," *Southern Workman*, September 1895, 145–47.

42 Scoville, "Negro and the Bible," 146, 147.

43 Ibid., 147.

44 Even as most colleges turned toward a more scientific curriculum, Hampton continued to emphasize the importance of Bible Study. In fact, the institute maintained a department devoted to this purpose. Despite the school's nondenominational status (as Scoville pointed out in her article), "Hampton claims that it is the duty of the school to lay the broadest foundation for church and state, and within the covers of the Bible may be found not only the words of eternal life, but the widest training for the American citizen." Examples of the institute's program in Bible study can be found in *Catalogue of the Hampton Normal and Agricultural Institute for the Academic Year 1895–1896* (Hampton, Va.: Hampton Institute Press, 1896), 20–21; and Scoville, "Negro and the Bible," 147.

45 Information on Helen Wilhelmina Ludlow can be found in the Helen Ludlow biographical file at Hampton Institute Archives, Hampton University. Some of Ludlow's representative publications include a coauthored book, *Hampton and Its Students*; an edited book, *Twenty-two Years*; an article, "Some Interesting Things at Hampton Institute," and a biographical note in Samuel Chapman Armstrong's *Education for Life*. Ludlow produced over one hundred editorials and short opinion pieces for the *Southern Workman*. She died of cancer in 1924.

46 The best assessment of the Hampton-Tuskegee model is in Anderson, *Education of Blacks*, 33–78. Other works that provide a more celebratory history of Hampton include Samuel Chapman Armstrong, *Education for Life*; Hollis Burke Frissell, "Aims and Methods of Hampton"; Peabody, *Education for Life*.

47 Hampton continued to emphasize biblical study as it instituted a more scientific curriculum. Information can be found in *Hampton Normal and Agricultural Institute: Annual Reports for the Year Ending June 30, 1890* (Hampton, Va.: Normal School Steam Press, 1890), 40–41. The changes in the history curriculum began in 1891. The faculty thought this change might be beneficial to all parties involved. *Hampton . . . Annual Reports for the Year Ending June 30, 1891* (Hampton, Va.: Normal School Steam Press, 1891), 41; and *Hampton . . . Annual Reports for the Year Ending June 30th, 1892* (Hampton, Va.: Normal School Steam Press, 1892), 36–37. The shift in the history curriculum, which included the incorporation of history and geography, was also discussed in the university's organ, see M. R. Hamlin, "Geography Teaching," *Southern Workman*, March 1896: 62–63. The economic aspects of the program are discussed in Bryce, *Economic Crumbs*. From the mid-1890s through the turn of the century, Hampton catalogues provided a complete overview of historical courses; see *Catalogue of the Hampton Normal and Agricultural Institute for the Academic Year 1895–1896* (Hampton, Va.: Hampton Institute Press, 1896), 21–23; *Catalogue . . . for the Academic Year 1896–1897* (Hampton, Va.: Hampton Institute Press, 1897), 25–26; and *Catalogue . . . for the Academic Year 1899–1900* (Hampton, Va.: Hampton Institute Press, 1900), 33–34. Descriptions of the history courses after 1895 are especially complete, including the listing of texts.

48 *Catalogue of the Hampton Normal and Agricultural Institute, 1904–1905* (Hampton, Va.: Hampton Institute Press, 1904), 43; *Fortieth Annual Catalogue: Hampton Normal and Agricultural Institute, 1908* (Hampton, Va.: Hampton Institute Press, 1908), 39–41; *Forty-first Annual Catalogue . . . 1909* (Hampton, Va.: Hampton Institute Press, 1909), 34–35; *Forty-fourth Annual Catalogue . . . 1912* (Hampton, Va.: Hampton Institute Press, 1912), 42–44; and *Forty-seventh Annual Catalogue . . . 1915* (Hampton, Va.: Hampton Institute Press, 1915), 50. For a definitive statement on the civilizationist and religious goals of the race, see Hugh Browne, "Race Loyalty," *Southern Workman*, March 1898, 44–47. Also see Thomas Jesse Jones, "Social Studies in the Hampton Curriculum," and R. R. Moton, "Some Elements Necessary to Race Development," *Southern Workman*, July 1912, 399–408. Anne Goodrich, an instructor at Hampton Institute, also prepared an extensive outline for courses in biblical history; see *Outlines of Bible History*, and *Outlines of History*.

49 Washington's building program at Tuskegee is discussed in Booker T. Washington, *Up from Slavery*, 67–97. Washington's consolidation of power after the Atlanta Compromise speech can be found in D. L. Lewis, *W. E. B. Du Bois*, 211–37; and Harlan, *Booker T. Washington: The Making of a Black Leader*, 204–8.

50 *Catalogue of the Tuskegee State Normal School at Tuskegee, 1881–1882*, 5–7; The 1884–85 catalogue mentioned the library contained 800 volumes. See *Catalogue . . . 1884–1885*; *Catalogue . . . 1886–1887*, 394. During the 1891–92 academic year, the university announced there were 10,000 volumes in the library. *Catalogue of the Tuskegee Normal and Industrial Institute, 1891–1892*, 23.

51   The collection of materials on African Americans is discussed in *Catalogue of Tuskegee Normal and Industrial Institute, 1899–1900*, 13.

52   For hiring information on Edna Hawley, John Mercer Langston Jr., and Ethel Chesnutt, see Booker T. Washington to T. Thomas Fortune, April 15, 1888, Roscoe C. Bruce to Booker T. Washington, and Ethel Perry Chesnutt to Booker T. Washington, March 27, 1901, in *Booker T. Washington Papers*, 6:435–36, 409, 66–67.

53   The 1901–2 catalog indicated the Carnegie Library was built on campus at a cost of $20,000 and featured a colonial style of architecture; see *Catalogue of the Tuskegee Normal and Industrial Institute, 1901–1902*, 14–15; and *Catalogue . . . 1902–1903*, 14–15.

54   *Twenty-third Annual Catalogue of the Tuskegee Normal and Industrial Institute, 1903–1904*, 30; *Twenty-fifth Annual Catalogue . . . 1905–1906*, 41; *Twenty-sixth Annual Catalogue . . . 1906–1907*, 43; *Twenty-eighth Annual Catalogue . . . 1908–1909*, 33–34.

55   *Thirty-first Annual Catalogue of the Tuskegee Normal and Industrial Institute, 1911–1912*, 32; *Thirty-third Annual Catalogue . . . 1913–1914*, 33.

56   *Twenty-eighth Annual Catalogue of the Tuskegee Normal and Industrial Institute, 1909–1910*, 31, 33. Other catalog descriptions of the course on Africa include *Thirtieth Annual Catalogue . . . 1910–1911*, 33; *Thirty-first Annual Catalogue . . . 1911–1912*, 33; and *Thirty-third Annual Catalogue . . . 1913–1914*, 33.

57   Washington's international affiliations are discussed in Harlan, *Booker T. Washington: Wizard*, 262–94. Also see Zimmerman, "German Alabama in Africa," 1362–98.

58   On the speeches at the International Conference of the Negro, see "The First International Conference of the Negro, April 8, 1912"; Emmett Scott to Robert Park, May 13, 1912; "Program: The International Conference of the Negro to Be Held at Tuskegee Institute, Alabama, April 17, 18, 19"; and "Summary of the First International Conference of the Negro," all in box 96, Booker T. Washington Papers, Tuskegee University Archives, Tuskegee, Alabama.

59   Information on the relationship between Washington and other black intellectuals is explored in Harlan, *Booker T. Washington: Wizard*, 3–62. Washington's influence and ability to promote historical works was no secret to anyone after the turn of the century. And people regularly solicited his help. Edward Augustus Johnson, a personal friend of Washington and later a member of the National Negro Business League (which Washington founded), mailed a copy of his book *School History of the Negro Race in America* (1891), urging him to adopt it as part of the historical curriculum at Tuskegee and boasting that it was already being used at Shaw University. Johnson promoted the book to Washington as containing "information that every colored child should know." Whether or not Washington incorporated Johnson's book into Tuskegee's curriculum, he did send the book to Edward Atkinson, a Boston industrialist, suggesting the work "contained some facts on the Negro's progress." Washington's formal or implicit endorsement of a book suggested to the public that it was a reliable source. One apparent endorsement of a work created some difficulties for Washington. In 1900, J. E. MacBrady, president of the American Publishing Company, solicited Washington's assistance in the production of a volume titled *A New Negro for a New Century*. Washington also wrote the introduction for H. F. Kletzing and William Crogman's *Progress of a Race* (discussed at length in the previous chapter) and assisted in the production of another quasi-historical work, *New Negro for a New*

Century. Washington also influenced the direction of the Negro history movement in very subtle ways. Thomas Junius Calloway, Tuskegee's northern agent, secured Washington an invitation to speak before the Bethel Literary and Historical Association in Washington, D.C., in 1891. In 1897, when Alexander Crummell organized the American Negro Academy, John Cromwell, the organization's secretary and author of *The Negro in American History*, informed Washington of the group's initial meeting. In 1900, Du Bois, Calloway, and Murray contributed materials on African American culture and life, including copies of Washington's books and pamphlets, to the Paris Exposition. Washington also corresponded with Daniel Murray, the first African American reference librarian at the Library of Congress. Murray sought Washington's assistance in securing information on various notables of African descent for his proposed "Murray's Historical and Biographical Encyclopedia of the Colored Race Throughout the World" in 1908. After describing the book's plan to Washington, Murray asked for any support that Tuskegee could offer. For information on Washington's relationship with Edward Johnson, see Edward Augustus Johnson to Booker T. Washington, January 12, 1891, in *Booker T. Washington Papers*, 3:121; and Booker T. Washington to Edward Atkinson, November 7, 1897, in ibid., 4:318–19. Washington's engagement with the American Negro Academy is discussed in correspondence with Junius Calloway, Tuskegee's Northern agent. See Thomas Junius Calloway to Booker T. Washington, October 31, 1891, in ibid., 3:176–77; John Cromwell to Booker T. Washington, January 19, 1896, in ibid., 4:255. Also see Daniel Murray to Booker T. Washington, February 2, 1900, in reel 62, frames 67–68, Booker T. Washington Papers, Library of Congress.

60 Harlan, *Booker T. Washington: Wizard*, 77–83; D. L. Lewis, *W. E. B. Du Bois*, 305–11; Booker T. Washington to E. H. Morris, November 19, 1903, in box 8, folder 78, Washington Papers, Library of Congress.

61 The group's membership consisted of Dr. I. B. Scott, editor of the *Southwestern Christian Advocate*, a black Methodist journal, and later a bishop in the Methodist Episcopal Church; H. T. Kealing, editor of the *A.M.E. Church Review*; George Clinton, author and bishop in the African Methodist Episcopal Zion Church; T. Thomas Fortune, editor of the *New York Age*; Dr. C. E. Bentley, a member of the anti-Washington faction from Chicago; Charles W. Anderson, Washington's operative who served as an internal revenue collector under several Republican presidents; E. H. Morris, a Chicago lawyer; Kelly Miller, dean of the Arts and Sciences at Howard University; Archibald Grimké, a Harvard-educated lawyer; and Hugh Browne, secretary of the organization. Hugh Browne to Booker T. Washington, July 18, 1904, in *Booker T. Washington Papers*, 8:22.

62 Browne to Washington, July 18, 1904.

63 "Self-Help in Negro Education: A Social Study; Questionnaire Compiled by R. R. Wright Jr.," and D. W. Woodward, "A Study of the Conditions of Negroes in Jackson, Mississippi," in box 7, folder 77, Washington Papers, Library of Congress; Washington to Browne, July 29, 1906, and June 5, 1908, in box 7, folder 71, ibid.

64 Washington to Alphonsus Orenzo Stafford, November 1, 1907, in *Booker T. Washington Papers*, 8:462. For information on the role of Park, see Robert E. Park to Washing-

ton, October 18, 1909, in box 2, Monroe Nathan Work Papers, Tuskegee University Archives. Also see Booker T. Washington, *Story of the Negro*.

65 Biographical information on Monroe Nathan Work can be found in Linda O. Mc-Murry, *Recorder of the Black Experience*; "Biographical statement," in box 2, Work Papers.

66 The relationship between Du Bois and Work is discussed in McMurry, *Recorder of the Black Experience*, 31–47; W. E. B. Du Bois to the Members of the Negro Movement, the Niagara Movement—Office of the General Secretary, September 13, 1905; W. E. B. Du Bois to Monroe N. Work, June 15, 1905, and July 17, 1908, in box 2, Work Papers. Also see Monroe Work, "Self-Help among Negroes," *Survey*, August 9, 1909, 616–17.

67 See McMurry, *Recorder of the Black Experience*, 48–49; "Mr. Work's Conference with Mr. Washington concerning the Establishment of the Department of Records and Research," and "Plans for Making Tuskegee a Greater Center for Information Relating to the Negro," December 21, 1908, in box 2, Work Papers.

68 "Plans for Making Tuskegee," in box 2, Work Papers.

69 McMurry, *Recorder of the Black Experience*, 75–77.

70 "Fact Gathering and the Negro: Address Delivered at the Alabama State Teacher's College," February 19, 1933, in box 4, Work Papers; "Negro Yearbook Historical Statement," in box 2, Work Papers. The *Negro Yearbook* continued publication until 1938, appearing in more than nine editions. Work also published numerous articles on African folklore and customs between 1906 and 1919. See McMurry, *Recorder of the Black Experience*, 90–96; and Work, *Bibliography of the Negro*.

71 An assessment of Woodson's doctoral training is contained in Charles Wesley, "Carter G. Woodson," *Journal of Negro History* 38 (January 1951): 17. Also see Romero, "Carter G. Woodson"; and J. Goggin, "Carter G. Woodson," and *Carter G. Woodson*.

72 Biographical information on George Cleveland Hall is contained in Mather, *Who's Who of the Colored Race*, 128. The best treatments of the founding of the ASNLH are Meier and Rudwick, *Black History*, 14–16; Scally, "Woodson and the Genesis of ASNLH"; R. Logan, "Carter G. Woodson"; Charles Wesley, "Our Fiftieth Year: The Golden Anniversary, 1965," 172, 195, and "Creating and Maintaining an Historical Tradition"; W. Sherman Savage, "Twenty Years of the Association"; "History of the Association for the Study of Negro Life and History"; and Woodson, "Ten Years of Collecting."

73 Du Bois, "A Portrait of Carter G. Woodson," 25. An in-depth analysis of the journal's seminal role in promoting black history is contained in J. Goggin, "Countering White Racist Scholarship." For a historical assessment of Woodson and the journal, see Winston, "Through the Backdoor."

74 Articles in the *JNH* include "Letters Showing the Rise and Progress of the Early Negro Churches of Georgia and the West Indies," 1 (January 1916): 69–92; "Letters of Richard Allen and Absalom Jones," 1 (October 1916): 436–43; "Letters, Narratives, Laws, and Comments Bearing on the Danish West Indies," 2 (April 1917): 289–324; "Petition for Compensation for the Loss of Slaves by Emancipation in the Danish West Indies," 2 (October 1917): 423–28; "California Freedom Papers," 3 (January

1918): 45–54; "Letters of Governor Edward Coles Bearing on the Struggle of Freedom and Slavery," 2 (April 1917): 158–95; "Letters of Negro Migrants of 1916–1918, Collected under the Direction of Emmett J. Scott," 4 (July 1918): 290–340; "More Letters of Negro Migrants of 1916–1918, Collected under the Direction of Emmett Scott," 4 (October 1918): 412–65.

75   An announcement of Arthur Schomburg's book is contained in *Journal of Negro History* 2 (January 1917): 103; announcements of Benjamin Brawley's book are in ibid.; and in *Journal of Negro History* 3 (April 1918): 210. A discussion of ASNLH's work is found in *Journal of Negro History* 4 (January 1919): 108.

76   John Lynch, "Some Historical Errors of James Ford Rhodes," *Journal of Negro History* 2 (October 1917): 345–68, and "More about the Historical Errors of James F. Rhodes," *Journal of Negro History* 3 (April 1918): 139–57.

77   Edward Channing to Carter G. Woodson, January 31, 1916, in reel 3, Carter G. Woodson Papers, Library of Congress. All materials cited from the Woodson Papers are on reel 3. George W. Cable to Woodson, November 7, 1916; Casely Hayford to Woodson, June 15, 1916; and Dada Adeshigbin to Woodson, January 10, 1917, all in Woodson Papers. In the first volume, as a fund-raising tactic, Woodson included a section entitled "How the Public Received the *Journal of Negro History*," *Journal of Negro History* 1 (April 1916): 225–31.

78   *Journal of Negro History* 1 (October 1916): advertisement section. Also see Woodson, "Ten Years of Collecting," 600–601, and "An Accounting for Twenty-Five Years," *Journal of Negro History* (October 1940): 423. For biographical information on Wilkinson, see Mather, *Who's Who of the Colored Race*, 198.

79   *Journal of Negro History* 1 (October 1916): advertisement section.

80   J. A. Bigham, W. B. Hartgrove, and J. E. Stampps each donated $5. See "Help Us Raise a Research Fund," *Journal of Negro History* 1 (October 1916): advertisement section. An account of Rosenwald's initial interest in the *Journal* is found in "The First Third of a Century of the Association for the Study of Negro Life and History," 47, 48. For a discussion of Moorland's influence on Rosenwald, see Meier and Rudwick, *Black History*, 15; and Woodson, "Ten Years of Collecting," 601.

81   Du Bois, "Portrait of Carter G. Woodson," 22, and Meier and Rudwick, *Black History*, 20–21.

82   See Charles W. Chesnutt to Woodson, January 3, 1917; Walter Brooks to Woodson, June 22, 1917; and Mary W. Talbert to Woodson, July 9, 1917, all in Woodson Papers.

83   A report on the first meeting of the association is found in "The First Biennial Meeting of the Association for the Study of Negro Life and History at Washington," *Journal of Negro History* 2 (October 1917): 442–48. Both Work and Haynes had been avid supporters of the association from its inception. In the first volume of the *Journal*, both men were listed as contributors. See *Journal of Negro History* 1 (October 1916): advertisement section. Biographical information on Monroe N. Work can be found in McMurry's *Recorder of the Black Experience*. For biographical information on George E. Haynes, see Perlman, "Stirring the White Conscience."

84   "First Biennial Meeting," 442–44.

85   Many of the new members of the executive council represented major philanthropic

interests and accommodationist elements within the black community. For information on the new black members of the council, see entries for John R. Hawkins and Robert E. Jones in Mather, *Who's Who of the Colored Race*, 132, 162. Robert Russa Moton to Woodson, September 12, 1917, Woodson Papers. For information on Rosenwald's agreement to serve on the executive council, see Julius Rosenwald to Woodson, August 27 and September 8, 1917, Woodson Papers.

86   Woodson, *A Century of Negro Migration*, 3–17, 159–65. Also see *Journal of Negro History* 3 (January 1918): 98.

87   Henry B. F. MacFarland to Woodson, March 12, 1918; Robert R. Moton to Woodson, June 1, 1918; and Moton to George Foster Peabody, May 28, 1918, all in Woodson Papers.

88   Carter G. Woodson to W. E. B. Du Bois, October 27, 1918; Du Bois to Woodson, October 30 and November 12, 1918; Woodson to Du Bois, November 9, 1918; Woodson to Colonel Charles Young, November 14, 1918; and Young to Woodson, November 30, 1918, all in W. E. B. Du Bois Papers, University of Massachusetts at Amherst. On the Wilcox appointment, see William G. Wilcox to Woodson, December 26, 1918, and Wilcox to Woodson, May 16, 1919, in Woodson Papers. Information on Moorfield Storey's and Cleveland Dodge's contributions to the association is found in *Journal of Negro History* 4 (January 1919): 110. Information on J. E. Ormes and the black history clubs is found in *Journal of Negro History* 4 (April 1919): 237. For information on plans to publish *The Negro in Our History*, see *Journal of Negro History* 4 (October 1919): 474.

89   For the initial announcement of the meeting, see the *Journal of Negro History* 4 (July 1919): 347–48. For a complete summary of the meeting, see "Proceedings of the Second Biennial Meeting of the Association for the Study of Negro Life and History," *Journal of Negro History* 4 (October 1919): 475–82. See "Proceedings of the Second Biennial Meeting," 479–480.

90   See Arnett G. Lindsay, "Dr. Woodson as a Teacher," *Negro History Bulletin* 13 (May 1950): 183. A portion of Lindsay's thesis, "Diplomatic Relations between the United States and Great Britain bearing on the Return of Negro Slaves, 1788–1828," was published in the *Journal of Negro History* 5 (October 1920): 391–419.

91   Reddick, "As I Remember Woodson." Woodson's letter is quoted and information on Woodson's tenure at Howard are in Winston, *Howard University Department of History*, 37–39; Logan, *Howard University Department of History*, 35–39; Logan, *Howard University: The First Hundred Years*, 171, 208. A general overview of black historical studies is found in Van De Burg, "Development of Black Historical Studies"; and Brundage, *Southern Past*.

92   A complete account of the relationship between Jameson and Woodson is found in "J. Franklin Jameson, Carter G. Woodson, and the Foundations of Black Historiography," in Meier and Rudwick, *Black History*, 1005–15.

93   Woodson, *Negro in Our History*, 93, 135.

94   Ibid., 142–43. See Novick, *That Noble Dream*.

95   Du Bois, *Black Reconstruction*.

96   Du Bois critiques the Tragic Era in *Black Reconstruction*, 711–29. See Lynch, *Facts of Reconstruction* and Sinclair, *Aftermath of Slavery*.

97 An examination of Alrutheus Ambush Taylor's life appears in Hall, "Research as Opportunity." On *the Dunning and Burgess school of Reconstruction historiography see E. Foner, Reconstruction: America's Unfinished Revolution.*

Conclusion

1 Two recent studies that present a 1960s narrative for the emergence of black studies are Rojas, *Black Power to Black Studies*; and Rooks, *White Money/Black Power*. For studies that locate professionalism in the late nineteenth or early twentieth centuries, see Franklin, "On the Evolution of Scholarship"; and Meier and Rudwick, *Black History*.

2 Scott, *Domination and the Arts of Resistance.*

3 See Gates, *Signifying Monkey*; Baym, *American Women Writers*; Zafar, *We Wear the Mask*; Carretta, *Unchained Voices*; McHenry, *Forgotten Readers*; and Ernest, *Liberation Historiography.*

4 Winch, *Gentleman of Color*; Saillant, *Black Puritan, Black Republican*; Rael, *Black Identity and Black Protest*; Dain, *Hideous Monster*; Newman, *Freedom's Prophet*; Hinks, *To Awaken My Afflicted Brethren*; Bethel, *Roots of African America Identity*; Kachun, *Festivals of Freedom*; Stauffer, *Black Hearts of Men*. For a good study of the connections between the African past and the American present, see Stuckey, *Going through the Storm*, 103–40.

5 Dagbovie, *Early Black History Movement*. See Meier and Rudwick, *Black History*. For an insightful discussion of black women in the twentieth century as librarians and historians, see Des Jardins, *Women and the Historical Enterprise*, 145–76.

6 Lowenthal, *The Past Is a Foreign Country.*

Bibliography

Manuscript Collections

Amherst, Massachusetts
   University of Massachusetts–Amherst
   W. E. B. Du Bois Papers
Atlanta, Georgia
   Clark Atlanta University, Robert Woodruff Library
   Atlanta University Archives
   Horace Bumstead Papers
   Henry P. Slaughter Collection
   Edward Trichell Papers
   Edmund Asa Ware Papers
   Gammon Theological Seminary Records
   J. W. E. Bowen Papers
   Wilbur P. Thirkield Papers
Detroit, Michigan
   University of Detroit
   Black Abolitionist Papers, 1830–1865 (Microfilm)
Hampton, Virginia
   Hampton University Archives
   William T. Aery Papers
   General Samuel Chapman Armstrong Papers
   Hollis Burke Frissell Papers
Madison, Wisconsin
   State Historical Society of Wisconsin
   Daniel Alexander Murray Papers
New Brunswick, New Jersey
   Rutgers University, Archibald Stevens Alexander Library, Special Collections
      and University Archives
   Peter Still Papers
New Orleans, Louisiana
   Tulane University, Amistad Research Center
   American Missionary Association Archives
   James W. C. Pennington Letters, 1840–1870
Philadelphia, Pennsylvania
   Historical Society of Pennsylvania
   American Negro Historical Society Collection, 1790–1905 (Microfilm)

Leon Gardiner Collection
William Still Letterbook, 1873–1874
Tuskegee, Alabama
Tuskegee University Archives
Booker T. Washington Papers
Monroe Nathan Work Papers
Washington, D.C.
Howard University
Moorland-Springarn Research Center
Bethel Literary and Historical Association Papers
Bethel Metropolitan A.M.E. Church Papers
Kelly Miller Papers
Jesse Moorland Papers
Library of Congress
Frederick Douglass Papers
Daniel Murray Pamphlet Collection
Joseph Meredith Toner Collection
Booker T. Washington Papers
Carter G. Woodson Papers

Newspapers and Periodicals

African Times and Orient Review
Alexander's Magazine
Aliened American
A.M.E. Church Review
Anglo-African Magazine
Anti-Slavery Bugle
Baltimore and Washington Afro-American
Chicago Defender
Christian Recorder
Colored American
Crisis
Douglass Monthly
Frederick Douglass' Paper
Freedom's Journal
Impartial Citizen
Liberator

Mirror of the Times
National Antislavery Standard
North American Review
Negro World
New National Era
New York Age
North Star
People's Advocate
Pine and Palm
Provincial Freeman
Rights of All
Southern Workman
Voice of the Fugitive
Voice of the Negro
Washington Bee
Weekly Anglo-African

University Catalogs

Atlanta University, Atlanta, Georgia, 1898–1915.
Hampton University, Hampton, Virginia, 1872–1915.
Howard University, Washington, D.C., 1913–1915.
Tuskegee University, Tuskegee, Alabama, 1883–1915.

Primary Sources

Adams, Henry. *The Education of Henry Adams*. 1916. Reprint, New York: Vintage Books, 1993.

Alexander, William. *History of the Colored Race in America: Containing also Their Ancient and Modern Life in Africa, Modes of Living, Employment, Customs, Habits, Social life, etc.; the Origin and Development of Slavery . . . The Civil War, Emancipation, Education and Advancement of the Colored Race; Their Civil and Political Rights*. New Orleans: Palmetto Publishing, 1887.

Anthon, Charles. *A Classical Dictionary: Containing an Account of the Principal Names Mentioned in Ancient Authors and Intended to Elucidate All the Important Points Connected with the Geography, History, Biography, Mythology and Fine Arts of the Greeks and Romans. Together with an Account of Coins, Weights, Measures, with Tabular Values of the Same*. New York: Harper & Brothers, 1841.

Armstrong, M. F., Helen Wilhelmina Ludlow, and Thomas P. Fenner. *Hampton and Its Students*. New York: G. P. Putnam's Sons, 1874.

Armstrong, Samuel Chapman. *Education for Life*. Hampton, Va.: Hampton Normal and Agricultural Institute, 1913.

Ball, Terence, ed. *Hamilton, Madison, and Jay: The Federalist Writings with the Letters of Brutus*. New York: Cambridge University Press, 2003.

Bancroft, George. *History of the United States from the Discovery of the American Continent*. Vols. 2 and 3. Boston: Charles C. Little and James Brown, 1844.

Barth, Heinrich. *Travels and Discoveries in North and Central Africa: Being a Journal of an Expedition Undertaken under the Auspices of HBM's Government in the Years 1849–1855*. 3 vols. New York: Harper and Brothers, 1857.

Beard, John Reilly. *The Life of Toussaint L'Ouverture: The Negro Patriot of Hayti; Comprising an Account of the Struggle for Liberty in the Island, and a Sketch of Its History to the Present Period*. London: Ingram, Cooke and Co., 1853.

Beattie, James. *An Essay on the Nature and Immutability of Truth in Opposition to Sophistry and Skepticism*. 1770.

Bell, Howard Holman, James Theodore Holly, and J. Dennis Harris. *Black Separatism and the Caribbean*. 1860. Reprint, Ann Arbor: University of Michigan Press, 1970.

Bentley, Mrs. Fannie C. "The Women of Our Race Worthy of Imitation." *A.M.E. Church Review* 6 (April 1890): 473–77.

Botta, Carlo. *History of the War of Independence of the United States of America*. 3 vols. Philadelphia: J. Maxwell, 1821.

Bowen, J. W. E., ed. *Africa and the American Negro: Addresses and Proceedings of the Congress on Africa Held under the Auspices of the Stewart Missionary Foundation of Gammon Theological Seminary in connection with the Cotton States and International Exposition, December 13–15, 1895*. Atlanta: Gammon Theological Seminary, 1896.

Bragg, George F. *History of the Afro-American Group of the Episcopal Church*. Baltimore: Church Advocate Press, 1922.

Brawley, Benjamin. *Negro Builders and Heroes*. Chapel Hill: University of North Carolina Press, 1937.

Brown, William Wells. *The Black Man, His Antecedents, His Genius, and His Achievements.* New York: T. Hamilton, 1863.

———. *The Negro in the American Rebellion: His Heroism and His Fidelity.* Boston: Lee and Shephard, 1867.

———. *The Rising Son: The Antecedents and Achievements of the Colored Race.* Boston: A. G. Brown, 1874.

———. *St. Domingo: Its Revolutions and Its Patriots.* A lecture delivered before the Metropolitan Athenaeum, London, May 16, and at St. Thomas's Church, Philadelphia, December 20, 1854. Boston: Bela Marsh, 1855.

Bryce, T. T. *Economic Crumbs; or, Plain Talks for the People about Labor, Capital, Money, Tariff, etc.* Hampton, Va.: Hampton Institute Press, 1879.

Buffon, Georges Louis Leclerc. *Natural History, General and Particular.* London: T. Cadell and W. Davies, 1812.

Butler, Frederick. *Sketches of Universal History Sacred and Profane, from the Creation of the World to the Year 1818.* Hartford, Conn.: Cooke and Hale, 1818.

Carretta, Vincent, ed. *Unchained Voices: An Anthology of British Authors in the English-Speaking World of the Eighteenth Century.* Lexington: University Press of Kentucky, 1996.

Child, Lydia Maria Francis. *An Appeal in Favor of That Class of Americans Called Africans.* Boston: Allen and Ticknor, 1833.

Clark, Peter. *The Black Brigade of Cincinnati: Being a Muster-Roll of Its Members; Together with Various Orders, Speeches, etc. Relating to It.* Cincinnati: Joseph Boyd, 1864.

"Class Distinctions among American Negroes." *Southern Workman*, October 1899.

Coffin, Levi. *Reminiscences of Levi Coffin.* Self-published, 1876.

Coker, Daniel. *A Dialogue between a Virginian and an African Minister.* Baltimore: Benjamin Edes, 1810.

Cooper, Anna J. *A Voice from the South.* The Schomburg Library of Nineteenth-Century Black Women Writers. New York: Oxford University Press, 1988.

Coppin, Fanny J. *Reminiscences of School Life and Hints on Teaching.* Philadelphia: A.M.E. Book Concern, 1913.

Council, William Hooper. *Lamp of Wisdom; or, Race History Illuminated: A Compendium of Race History Comprising Facts Gleaned from Every Field for Millions of Readers.* Nashville: J. T. Haley and Co., 1898.

Crogman, William H. *Talks for the Times.* 1896. Reprint, Freeport, N.Y.: Books for Libraries, 1971.

Cromwell, John W. "History of the Bethel Literary and Historical Association." Paper Read before the Association on Founder's Day, February 24, 1896.

———. *The Negro in American History.* Washington, D.C.: Negro Academy, 1914.

———. "Our Colored Churches." *A.M.E. Church Review* 1 (October 1884): 89–100.

Crummell, Alexander. *The Greatness of Christ and Other Sermons.* New York: Thomas Whittaker, 1882.

———. "The Need of New Ideas and New Aims for Afro-Americans for a New Era." *A.M.E. Church Review* 2 (October 1885).

Cuffee, Paul. *A Brief Account of the Settlement and Present Situation of the Colony of Sierra Leone.* 1812.

Culp, Daniel Wallace. *Twentieth Century Negro Literature; or, A Cyclopedia of Thought on the Vital Topics relating to the American Negro*. Naperville, Ill.: J. L. Nichols and Co., 1902.

Day, William Howard. *The Loyalty and Devotion of Colored Americans in the Revolution and War of 1812*. Boston: R. F. Walcutt, 1861.

Delany, Martin. *Blake; or, The Huts of America*. Boston: Beacon, 1970. Originally serialized in the *Weekly Anglo-African*, 1861–62.

———. *The Condition, Elevation, Emigration and Destiny of the Colored People of the United States*. 1852. Reprint, New York: Arno, 1968.

———. *Official Report of the Niger Valley Exploring Party*. New York: Thomas Hamilton, 1861.

———. *The Origins and Objects of Ancient Freemasonry; Its Introduction and Legitimacy among Colored Men: A Treatise Delivered before St. Cyrian Lodge No. 13.*, June 24, 1853. Pittsburgh: W. S. Haven, 1853.

Diaz, Bernal. *The Conquest of New Spain*. Baltimore: Penguin, 1963.

Douglass, Frederick. "Future of the Race: As Carefully Reviewed by Mr. Douglass." *A.M.E. Church Review* 2 (October 1885).

Du Bois, W. E. B. *Black Reconstruction: A History of the Part Which Black Folk Played in the Attempt to Reconstruct Democracy in America, 1860–1880*. New York: Russell and Russell, 1935.

———. "The Evolution of Negro Leadership." *Dial*, July 16, 1901, 53–55.

———. "The Freedmen's Bureau." *Atlantic Monthly*, March 1901, 354–65.

———. "A Portrait of Carter G. Woodson." *Masses and Mainstream*, June 1950, 19–25.

———. "The Storm and Stress in the Black World." *Dial*, April 16, 1901, 262–64.

———. "Strivings of the Negro People." *Atlantic Monthly*, August 1897, 194–98.

———. *The Suppression of the African Slave Trade to the United States, 1638–1870*. New York: Longmans, Green, 1896.

Easton, Hosea. *Appeal to the Christian Public on Behalf of the Methodist Episcopal Church West-Center Boston, Organized under the Rules and Regulations, Recently Adopted by the People of Color at New York Entitled the Asbury Connexion*. Boston: David Hooton/Matthew Teprell, 1828.

———. *A Treatise on the Intellectual Character, and the Civil and Political Condition, of the Colored People of the United States; and the Prejudice Exercised toward Them; with a Sermon on the Duty of the Church to Them*. Boston: Issac Knapp, 1837.

Equiano, Olaudah. *Interesting Narrative of the Life of Olaudah Equiano or Gustavus Vassa, the African* (London, 1996).

Foner, Philip, and Robert James Branham, eds. *Lift Every Voice: African American Oratory, 1787–1900*. Tuscaloosa: University of Alabama Press, 1998.

Forten, James. *Letters by a Man of Colour on a Late Bill before the Senate of Pennsylvania*. Philadelphia, 1813.

Forten, James, and Russell Parrot. *To the Humane and Benevolent Inhabitants of the City and County of Philadelphia*. 1817.

Frazier, S. Elizabeth. "Some Afro-American Women of Mark; Read before the Brooklyn Literary Union, February 18, 1892." *A.M.E. Church Review* 8 (April 1892): 373–86.

Frissell, Hollis Burke. *The Aims and Methods of Hampton: An Address Delivered before a Meeting in New York City, February 12, 1904.* New York: Armstrong Association, 1902.

Fuller, Thomas Oscar. *Pictorial History of the Negro.* Memphis, Tenn.: Pictorial History, 1933.

Garnet, Henry Highland. *The Past and the Present Condition, and the Destiny, of the Colored Race: A Discourse Delivered at the Fifteenth Anniversary of the Female Benevolent Society of Troy, N.Y., February 14, 1848.* Troy, N.Y.: Kneeland and Co., 1848.

———. *Walker's Appeal, with a Brief Sketch of the Life; and also Garnet's Address to the Slaves of the United States of America.* New York: J. H. Tobitt, 1848.

Gibbon, Edward. *Decline and Fall of the Roman Empire.* Vols. 1–3 (1776, 1781, and 1788). Edited by David Womersley. Reprint, New York: Penguin Books, 1994.

Gibson, John, and William Crogman. *The Colored American from Slavery to Honorable Citizenship.* Naperville, Ill.: J. L. Nichols, 1902.

Gloucester, S. H. *A Discourse Delivered on the Occasion of Mr. James Forten Jr. in the Second Presbyterian Church of Color of the City of Philadelphia, April 17, 1842, before the Young Men of the Bible Association of Said Church.* Philadelphia: I. Ashmead and Co., 1843.

Goodrich, Anne. *Outlines of Bible History.* Hampton, Va.: Institute Press, 1906.

———. *Outlines of Bible History,* part 2. Hampton, Va.: Institute Press, 1908.

Green, Alfred M. *Letters and Discussions on the Formation of Colored Regiments, and the Duty of the Colored People in regard to the Great Slave Holders Rebellion in the United States of America.* Philadelphia: Ringwalt and Brown, 1862.

Grégoire, Henri. *An Enquiry concerning the Intellectual and Moral Faculties and Literature of Negroes; Followed with an Account of the Life and Works of Fifteen Mulattoes Distinguished in Science, Literature and the Arts.* New York: Thomas Kirk, 1810.

Griffiths, Julia. *Autographs for Freedom,* 2 vols. Rochester, N.Y.: Wander, Beardsley and Co., 1854.

Grimshaw, William. *Official History of Freemasonry among the Colored People of North America.* New York: Broadway, 1903.

Hall, Prince, and Arthur Alfonso Schomburg. *A Charge Delivered to the African Lodge, June 24, 1797, at Menotomy, Mass.* 1920.

Halley, James T. *Afro-American Encyclopedia of Thoughts, Doings and Sayings of the Race: Embracing Addresses, Lectures, Biographical Sketches, Sermons, Poems, Names of Universities, Colleges Seminaries, Newspapers, Books, and a History of the Denominations, Giving the Numerical Strength of Each: In Fact, It Teaches Every Subject of Interest to the Colored People, as Discussed by More than One Hundred of Their Wisest and Best Men and Women: Illustrated with Beautiful Half-Tone Engravings.* Nashville: Haley and Florida, 1895.

Hamilton, William. *O' Africa.* 1815. Reprinted in *Lift Every Voice: African American Oratory, 1787–1900,* edited by Philip Foner and Robert James Branham, 91–97. Tuscaloosa: University of Alabama Press, 1998.

Harper, Frances Ellen. "The Democratic Return to Power—Its Effects." *A.M.E. Church Review* 1 (January 1885).

Hegel, Georg Wilhelm Friedrich. *The Philosophy of History.* New York: Dover, 1956.

Herder, Johann Gottfried. *Reflections on the Philosophy of the History of Mankind.* Edited by Frank Edward Manuel. Classic European Historians. Chicago: University of Chicago Press, 1968.

Herodotus. *The Histories*. Translated by Robin Waterfield, with an introduction and notes by Carolyn Dewald. New York: Oxford University Press, 1998.

"History of the Association for the Study of Negro Life and History." *Negro History Bulletin*, February 1938.

Hoffman, Frederick. "Race Traits and Tendencies of the Negro." *American Economic Association Publications* 1, no. 11 (August 1896): 33–148, 250–309.

————. "Vital Statistics of the Negro." *Arena* 15 (April 1892): 529–42

Holly, James Theodore. *A Vindication of the Capacity of the Negro Race for Self-Government and Civilized Progress as Demonstrated by Historical Events of the Haytian Revolution and Subsequent Acts of that People since Their National Independence*. New Haven: Afric-American Printing, 1857. Reprinted in Bell, Holly, and Harris, *Black Separatism*, 19–66.

Hope, Ascott. *Heroes in Homespun: Scenes and Stories from the American Emancipation Movement*. London: Wilsons and Milne, 1894.

Hume, David. "Of Natural Characters." 1748. In *The Cambridge Companion to Hume*, ed. David Fate Norton. Cambridge: Cambridge University Press, 1993.

Jefferson, Thomas. *Notes on the State of Virginia*. New York: W. W. Norton, 1954.

Johnson, Edward. "The Importance of Instructing the Youth of the Race in Negro History." Address before the Association of Educators of Colored Youth, Baltimore, Maryland, July 24–27, 1894.

————. *A School History of the Negro Race in America from 1619 to 1890, Combined with the History of the Negro Soldiers in the Spanish-American War*. 1911. Reprint, New York: AMS, 1969.

Jones, Absalom, and Richard Allen. *A Narrative of the Proceedings of the Black People during the Awful Calamity in Philadelphia in the Year 1793; and a Refutation of Some Censures Thrown upon Them in Some Late Publications*. 1794. Reprint, New York: Arno Press and the New York Times, 1969.

Jones, Thomas Jesse. *Social Studies in the Hampton Curriculum*. Hampton, Va.: Hampton Institute Press, 1908.

Josephus, Flavius. *The Antiquities of the Jews*. Translated by William Whiston. New York: Echo Library, 2006.

————. *The Works of Josephus: Complete and Unabridged*. Translated by William Whiston. Peabody, Mass.: Hendrickson, 2003.

Kant, Immanuel. *Immanuel Kant's Physical Geography*. Translated and annotated by Ronald L. Bolin. Thesis, Indiana University, 1968.

Kletzing, Henry F., and William H. Crogman. *Progress of a Race; or, The Remarkable Advancement of the Afro-American Negro*. Atlanta: J. L. Nichols and Co., 1897.

Lander, Richard, and John Lander. *Journal of an Expedition to Explore the Course and Termination of the Niger; With a Voyage Down That River to Its Termination*. 3 vols. London: John Murray, 1828.

Las Casas, Bartolomé de. *The Devastation of the Indies: A Brief Account*. 1152. Reprint, Baltimore: Johns Hopkins University Press, 1994.

Lee, B. F. "Negro Organizations." *Annals of the American Academy of Political and Social Science* 49 (1913): 139–43.

Lewis, Robert Benjamin. *Letter to Louis Kossuth concerning Freedom and Slavery in the United States on Behalf of the American Antislavery Society*. Boston: R. F. Walcutt, 1852.

————.*Light and Truth: Collected from the Bible and Ancient and Modern History, Containing the Universal History of the Colored and Indian Race, from the Creation of the World to the Present Time.* Boston: Benjamin J. Roberts, 1844.

————. *Light and Truth: From Sacred and Ancient History.* Portland: Colesworthy, 1836.

Livermore, George. *An Historical Research respecting the Opinions of the Founders of the Republic on Negroes as Slaves, as Citizens and as Soldiers.* Boston: A. Williams, 1863.

Lossing, Benson. *Pictorial History of the Civil War in the United States of America.* 3 vols. Philadelphia: David McKay, 1866.

Ludlow, Helen Wilhelmina. "Some Interesting Things at Hampton Institute." *Evangelist* 1 (1900).

————. *Twenty-two Years: Works, Records of Negro and Indian Graduates.* Hampton, Va.: Normal School Press, 1893.

MacFarlane, Charles. *Seven Apocalyptic Churches.* London, 1832.

Majors, Monroe. *Noted Negro Women: Their Triumphs and Activities.* Jackson, Tenn.: M. V. Lynk, 1893.

Marrant, John. *You Stand on the Level with the Greatest of Kings.* 1789. Reprinted in Foner and Branham, *Lift Every Voice*, 27–38.

Martineau, Harriet. *The Hour and the Man: An Historical Romance.* New York: Harper and Brothers, 1841.

Mather, Frank Lincoln. *Who's Who of the Colored Race: A General Biographical Dictionary of Men and Women of African Descent.* Chicago, 1915.

A Memorial of Crispus Attucks, Samuel Maverick, James Caldwell, Samuel Gray, and Patrick Carr from the City of Boston. 1889. Reprint, Miami: Mnemosyne, 1969.

Memorial of Thirty Thousand Disenfranchised Citizens of Philadelphia to the Honorable Senate and House of Representatives. Philadelphia, 1855.

Mitchell, Rev. W. M. *The Underground Railroad.* 1860.

Mossell, N. F. *The Work of the Afro-American Woman.* Philadelphia: George S. Ferguson and Co., 1894, 1908.

Mossell-Griffin, Mary C. *Afro-American Men and Women Who Count.* Philadelphia[?], 1900.

Nell, William C. *Colored Patriots of the American Revolution, with Sketches of Several Colored Persons; to Which Is Added a Brief Survey of the Condition and Prospects of Colored Americans.* Boston: Robert Walcutt, 1855.

————. *Services of the Colored Americans in the Wars of 1776 and 1812.* Boston: Primus and Sawyer, 1852.

Newman, Richard, Patrick Rael, and Philip Lapansky, eds. *Pamphlets of Protest: An Anthology of Early African Protest Literature, 1790–1860.* New York: Routledge, 2001.

Oson, Jacob. *A Search for Truth; or, An Inquiry for the Origin of the African Nation: An Address Delivered in New Haven in March and in New York in April, 1817.* New York and New Haven: Christopher Rush, 1817.

Parker, Theodore. *The Boston Kidnapping: A Discourse to Commemorate the Rendition of Thomas Simms, Delivered on the First Anniversary Thereof, April 12, 1852, before the Committee of Vigilance at the Melodeon in Boston.* Boston: Crosby, Nichols and Co., 1852.

Parrott, Russell. *An Oration on the Abolition of the Slave Trade; Delivered on the First of January 1814 at the African Church of St Thomas.* Philadelphia, 1814.

Peabody, Francis Greenwood. *Education for Life: The Story of Hampton Institute.* New York: Doubleday, Page and Co., 1918.

Pendleton, Lelia Amos. *An Alphabet for Negro Children.* 1915.

———. *Narrative of the Negro.* 1912. Reprint, Freeport, N.Y.: Books for Libraries, 1971.

Pennington, James W. C. *The Fugitive Blacksmith; or, The Events in the History of James W. C. Pennington, Formerly a Slave in Maryland.* London: Gilpin, 1849.

———. *A Textbook of the Origin and History of the Colored People.* Hartford, Conn.: L. Skinner, 1841.

Perdue, Theda, ed. *Cherokee Editor: The Writings of Elias Boudinot.* Knoxville: University of Tennessee Press, 1983.

Pettit, Eber. *Sketches in the History of the Underground Railroad, Comprising Many Thrilling Incidents of the Escape of Fugitives from Slavery, and the Perils of Those Who Aided Them.* Fredonia, N.Y.: W. McKinstry & Son, 1879.

Pickard, Kate E. R. *The Kidnapped and the Ransomed: Being the Personal Recollections of Peter Still and His Wife "Vina" after Forty Years of Slavery.* Syracuse, N.Y.: William T. Hamilton, 1856.

Pickens, William. *Bursting Bonds: Enlarged Edition [of] The Heir of Slaves: The Autobiography of a "New Negro."* Edited by William L. Andrews. Bloomington: Indiana University Press, 1991.

———. *The Heir of Slaves: An Autobiography.* Boston: Pilgrim, 1911.

Plato, Ann. *Essays, Including Biographies and Miscellaneous Pieces in Prose and Poetry.* Hartford: Self-published, 1841.

Porter, Dorothy. *Early Negro Writing, 1760–1837.* 1971. Reprint, Baltimore: Black Classic, 1995.

Price, George R., and James Brewer Stewart, eds. *To Heal the Scourge of Prejudice: The Life and Writings of Hosea Easton.* Amherst: University of Massachusetts Press, 2000.

Price, Richard, and Sally Price, eds. *Narrative of the Five Years' Expedition against the Revolted Negroes of Surinam.* Baltimore: Johns Hopkins University Press, 1988.

"Professor Edward A. Johnson and His Books." *Alexander's Magazine,* August 15, 1905, 41–42.

Putnam, Lewis H. *The Review of the Revolutionary Elements of the Rebellion, and of the Aspect of Reconstruction; with a Plan to Restore Harmony between the Two Races in the Southern States.* Brooklyn: Lewis Putnam, 1868.

Ramsay, David. *A History of the American Revolution.* 1793. 2 vols. Reprint, New York: Russell and Russell, 1968.

Reason, Charles. "Introduction: The Colored People's Industrial College." In *Autographs for Freedom,* edited by Julia Griffiths, 11–14. Rochester, N.Y.: Wanzer, Beardsley and Co., 1854. Reprint, Miami: Mnemosyne Publishing, 1969.

Redpath, James, ed. *A Guide to Haiti.* New York: Woolworth Colton, 1861.

———, ed. *Toussaint L'Ouverture: A Biography and Autobiography.* 1863. Reprint, Freeport, N.Y.: Books for Libraries, 1971.

Reinhold, Meyer. *The Classick Pages: Classical Reading of Eighteenth-Century Americans.* University Park: American Philological Association, 1975.

Review of the *Biography of the Indians of North America: From the First Discovery to the Present Time, with an Account of the Antiquities, Manners, Customs and Laws,* by Samuel Drake. *North American Review* 26 (April 1837): 301–31.

Review of the *Complete History of the United States of America: Embracing the Whole Period from the Discovery of North America down to the year 1820,* by Frederick Butler. *North American Review* 16 (January 1823): 156–63.

Review of the *Latin Reader,* by Frederick Jacobs. *North American Review* 21 (July 1825): 246–48.

Richardson, Marilyn, ed. *Maria W. Stewart, America's First Black Woman Political Writer: Essays and Speeches.* Bloomington: Indiana University Press, 1987.

Robinson, Edward. *A Dictionary of the Holy Bible, for the Use of Schools and Young Persons.* Boston: Crocker and Brewster, 1835.

Rollin, Charles. *The Ancient History of the Egyptians, Carthaginians, Assyrians, Babylonians, Medes and Persians, Grecians and Macedonians: Including a History of the Arts and Sciences of the Ancients.* Philadelphia: Brown and Peters, 1829.

———. *The Ancient History of the Egyptians, Carthaginians, Babylonians, Medes, Persians, Macedonians and Grecians.* London, 1808.

Rothenberg, Morey, and Jacqueline Goggin, eds. *John Franklin Jameson and the Development of Humanistic Scholarship in America.* Vol. 1: *Selected Essays.* Athens: University of Georgia Press, 1993.

Russwurm, John. "The Conditions and Prospects of Haiti." Bowdoin College, Commencement Address, 1826.

Saunders, Prince. *An Address Delivered at Bethel Church, Philadelphia, on the 30th of September, 1818, before the Pennsylvania Augustine Society for the Education of People of Colour.* Philadelphia: Joseph Rakestraw, 1818.

Schomburg, Arthur Alonso. "The Negro Digs Up His Past." In *The New Negro,* edited by Alain Locke, 231–37. New York: Albert and Charles Bomi, 1925.

Scruggs, Lawson. *Women of Distinction: Remarkable in Works and Invincible in Character.* Raleigh, N.C., 1893.

Sears, Robert. *A New and Complete History of the Holy Bible as Contained in the Old and New Testaments from the Creation of the World to the Full Establishment of Christianity; . . . with Copious Notes, Critical and Explanatory, Forming an Illustrated Commentary of the Sacred Text with Numerous Engravings.* 2 vols. in 1. New York: Robert Sears, 1842.

Sewall, May Wright. *The World's Congress of Representative Women: A Historical Resume for Popular Circulation of the World's Congress of Representative Women, Convened in Chicago on May 15 and Adjourned on May 22, 1893, under the Auspices of the Women's Branch of the World's Congress Auxiliary.* Chicago and New York: Rand, McNally and Co., 1894.

Shepard, James. *History of St Mark's Church, New Britain, Connecticut, and of Its Predecessor, Christ Church, the Wethersfield and Berlin, from the First Church of England Service in America to Nineteen Hundred and Seven.* New Britain, Conn.: Tuttle, Morehouse and Taylor, 1907.

Sherman, Joan, ed. *African American Poetry of the Nineteenth Century: An Anthology.* Urbana: University of Illinois Press, 1992.

Shorter, Susie. *The Heroines of African Methodism.* Jacksonville, Fla., 1891.

Sidney, Joseph. *An Oration Commemorative of the Abolition of the Slave Trade in the United States Delivered before the Wilberforce Philanthropic Association, in the City of New-York, on the Second of January, 1809.* New York, 1809.

Siebert, Wilbur Henry. *The Underground Railroad from Slavery to Freedom: The American Negro, His History and Literature*. 1898. Reprint, New York: Arno, 1968.

Simmons, William. *Men of Mark: Eminent, Progressive and Rising*. Cleveland: G. Rewell and Co., 1887. Reprint, New York: Arno Press and New York Times, 1968.

Sipkins, Henry. *An Oration on the Abolition of the Slave Trade; Delivered in the African Church in the City of New York, January 2, 1809*. New York: J. C. Totten, 1809.

Smedley, R. C. *The Underground Railroad in Chester and Neighboring Counties of Pennsylvania*. 1883. Reprint, New York: Negro Universities Press, 1968.

Smith, Amanda. *An Autobiography: The Story of the Lord's Dealings with Mrs. Amanda Smith, the Colored Evangelist*. 1836. Reprint, New York: Oxford University Press, 1988.

Smith, Anna Amelia. *Reminiscences of Colored People of Princeton, N.J.* Philadelphia: P. V. Baugh, 1913.

Smith, Ethan. *A View of the Hebrews; or, The Tribes of Israel in America*. Poultney, Vt.: Simon and Shute, 1825.

Smith, James McCune. *The Destiny of the People of Color*. A Lecture Delivered before the Philomethan Society and Hamilton Lyceum in January 1841. New York: Self-published, 1841.

————. *A Lecture on the Haytien Revolution: With a Sketch of the Character of Toussaint L'Ouverture*. Speech delivered at the Stuyvesant Institute, February 26, 1841. New York: Daniel Farnshaw, 1841.

Sparks, Jared. *The Diplomatic Correspondence of the American Revolution*. Boston: Nathan Hale and Gray & Bowen, 1830.

Stevens, Charles Emery. *Anthony Burns: A History*. Boston: John P. Jewett, 1856.

Still, William. *Still's Underground Rail Road Records, with a Life of the Author: The Only Book that Fully Explains the Secret Work of the U.G.R.R.* William Still, 1883.

————. *The Underground Railroad: A Record of Facts, Authentic Narratives, Letters, etc., Narrating the Hardships, Hair-breadth Escapes and Death Struggles of the Slaves in Their Efforts for Freedom, as Related by Themselves, and Others, or Witnessed by the Author*. Philadelphia: Porter and Coates, 1872.

Tacitus, Cornelius. *Agricola and Germania*. New York: Penguin Books, 1970.

Toner, Joseph Meredith. *Boston Slave Riot, and Trial of Anthony Burns: Containing the Report of the Faneuil Hall Meeting, the Murder of Batchelder, Theodore Parker's Lesson for the Day, Speeches of Counsel on Both Sides, Corrected by Themselves, Verbatim Report of Judge Loring's Decision, and a Detailed Account of the Embarkation*. Boston: Fetridge and Co., 1854.

Tytler, Alexander Fraser. *Elements of General History, Ancient and Modern: From the British 7th ed., the Whole Work Revised and Continued to the General Peace in Europe in 1815, and the Chronological Table Improved by Thomas Ruffin; . . . with Questions Adapted to the Use of Schools and Academics*. Hartford, Conn.: Huntington, 1823.

————. *Elements of General History, Ancient and Modern: With a Continuation, Terminating at the Demise of King George III, 1820, by Rev. Edward Nares, DD, to Which Are Added a Succinct History of the United States . . . with an Improved Table of Chronology, a Comparative View of Ancient and Modern Geography, and Questions on Each Section; Adapted for the Use of Schools and Academies by an Experienced Teacher*. Concord, N.H.: Isaac Hill, 1825.

Tytler, Alexander Fraser, and Reverend Edward Nares, D.D. *Universal History from the*

Creation of the World to the Decease of George III. Vol 1. New York: Harper & Brothers, 1854.

Uriah, Homer. *From Dixie to Canada: Romance and Realities of the Underground Railroad.* Orwell, Ohio: H. U. Johnston, 1894.

Ussher, James. *The Annals of the World Deduced from the Origin of Time, and Continued to the Beginning of the Emperor Vespasian's Reign . . . Collected from All History, as well Sacred as Prophane, and Methodically Digested.* London: Printed by E. Tyler, for J. Crook and for G. Bedell, 1658.

Vashon, George Boyer. "Vincent Oge." In *Autographs for Freedom*, ed. Julia Griffiths, 44–60. Auburn, N.Y.: Alden Beardsley and Co., 1854.

Walker, David. *Appeal to the Coloured Citizens of the World.* 1829. Reprint, State College: Pennsylvania State University Press, 2000.

Ward, Samuel Ringold. "Origin, History and Hopes of the Negro Race." *Pennsylvania Freeman*, December 29, 1853.

Washington, Booker T. *Booker T. Washington Papers.* Edited by Louis Harlan, 14 vols. Urbana: University of Illinois Press, 1972.

———. *The Story of the Negro: The Rise of the Race from Slavery.* 2 vols. London: T. Fisher Urwin, 1909.

———. *Up from Slavery.* Edited and with an introduction by William L. Andrews. Oxford World Classics. New York: Oxford University Press, 2008.

Washington, Booker T., N. B. Wood, and Fannie Barrier Williams. *A New Negro for a New Century: An Accurate and Up-to-Date Record of the Negro Race.* Chicago: American Publishing House, 1900.

Washington, Margaret Murray. "The Advancement of Colored Women." *Colored American Magazine*, February 1905, 183–89.

Watkins, William. *Our Rights as Men: An Address Delivered in Boston before the Legislative Committee on the Militia, February 24, 1853.* Boston: Benjamin F. Roberts, 1853.

Watson, Richard. *A Biblical Dictionary: Explanatory of the History, Manners and Customs of the Jews and Neighboring Nations, with an Account of the Most Remarkable Places and Persons Mentioned in Sacred Scripture.* New York: B. Waugh and T. Mason, 1832.

Webster, Noah. *Elements of Useful Knowledge, Containing a Historical and Geographical Account of the United States, for the Use of Schools.* Hartford, Conn.: Hudson and Goodwin, 1815.

———. *Elements of Useful Knowledge*, Vol. 3: *Containing a Historical and Geographical Account of the Empires and States in Europe, Asia and Africa, with Their Colonies. To Which Is Added a Brief Description of New Holland and the Pacific and Indian Oceans.* New Haven, Conn.: Bronson and Walter, 1806.

Weems, Parson. *The Life and Memorable Actions of George Washington, General and Commander of the Country.* Philadelphia: George Keating, 1800.

Wells, Ida B. *On Lynchings: Southern Horrors, a Red Record, and Mob Rule in New Orleans.* 1892. Reprint, Salem, N.H.: Ayer, 1993.

Wesley, Charles. "Our Fiftieth Year: The Golden Anniversary, 1965." Special Summer Issue, *Negro History Bulletin* 28 (1965): 172, 195.

Wesley, Dorothy Porter, and Constance Uzelac, eds. *William Cooper Nell: Selected Writings, 1832–1874*. Baltimore: Black Classic, 2002.

Willetts, Gilson. "After Forty Years of Freedom." *Alexander's Magazine*, November 15, 1905, 11–18.

Williams, Daniel Barclay. *Freedom and Progress and Other Choice Addresses on Practical, Scientific, Educational and Philosophic, Historical and Religious Subjects*. Petersburg, Va.: Self-published, 1890.

————. *Science, Art and Methods of Teaching: Containing Lectures on the Science, Art and Methods of Education*. Petersburg, Va.: Self-published, 1887.

Williams, Fannie Barrier. "An Extension of the Conference Spirit." *Voice of the Negro*, July 1904, 300–303.

————. "The Negro and Public Opinion." *Voice of the Negro*, January 1904, 31–32.

Williams, George Washington. *History of the Negro Race in America from 1619 to 1800*. New York: G. P. Putnam and Sons, 1883.

————. *History of the Negro Race in America from 1800 to 1880*. New York: G. P. Putnam and Sons, 1883.

————. *The History of Negro Troops in the War of Rebellion, 1861–1865*. New York, 1888.

Williams, Peter. *Abolition of the Slave Trade*. 1808. Reprinted in *Lift Every Voice: African American Oratory, 1787–1900*, edited by Philip Foner and Robert James Branham, 66–73. Tuscaloosa: University of Alabama Press, 1998.

Wilson, Joseph T. *Black Phalanx: A History of the Negro Soldiers in the Wars of 1775–1812, 1861–1865*. Hartford, Conn.: American Publishing, 1882.

————. *Emancipation: Its Course and Progress from 1481 B.C. to A.D. 1875; With a Review of President Lincoln's Proclamations, the XIII Amendment, and the Progress of Freed People since Emancipation, with a History of the Emancipation Monument*. Hampton, Va.: Normal School Press, 1882. Reprint, New York: Negro Universities Press, 1969.

————. "Some Negro Poets." *A.M.E. Church Review* 4 (January 1888): 236–45.

Woodson, Carter G. *A Century of Negro Migration*. Washington, D.C.: Association for the Study of Negro Life and History, 1918. Reprint, New York: AMS, 1970.

————. *The Education of the Negro prior to 1861*. Washington, D.C.: Associated Publishers, 1919.

————. *The Negro in Our History*. Washington, D.C.: Associated Publishers, 1922.

————. *The Negro Professional Man and the Community, with Special Emphasis on the Physician and the Lawyer*. Washington, D.C.: Associated Publishers, 1934.

————. "Ten Years of Collecting and Publishing the Records of the Negro." *Journal of Negro History* 10 (1925): 598–606.

Work, Monroe. *A Bibliography of the Negro in Africa and America*. 1928. Reprint, Mansfield Center, Conn.: Martino, 2004.

Yates, William B. *Rights of the Colored Men to Suffrage, Citizenship and Trial by Jury: Being of Book of Facts, Arguments and Authorities, Historical Notices and Sketches of Debates—With Notes*. 1838.

Young, Robert Alexander. *The Ethiopian Manifesto; Issued in Defence of the Black Man's Rights in the Scale of Universal Freedom*. New York, 1829.

Secondary Sources

Adamo, David T. *Africa and the Africans in the New Testament*. Lantham, Md.: University Press Of America, 2001.

———. *Africa and the Africans in the Old Testament*. San Francisco: International Scholars, 1998.

———. "The Image of Cush in the Old Testament." In *Interpreting the Old Testament in Africa: Papers from the International Symposium on Africa and the Old Testament in Nairobi, October 1999*, edited by Mary Getui, Knut Holter, and Victor Zinkuartie. New York: Peter Lang, 2001.

Adams, Myron. *A History of Atlanta University, 1865–1929*. Atlanta: Atlanta University Press, 1930.

Adeleke, Tunde. *Without Regard to Race: The Other Martin Robison Delany*. Jackson: University of Mississippi Press, 2003.

Alexander, Elizabeth. "'We Must Be About Our Father's Business': Anna Julia Cooper and the Incorporation of the Nineteenth-Century African American Woman Intellectual." *Signs* 20 (1995): 337–56.

Allen, Carol. *Black Women Intellectuals: Strategies of Nation, Family, and Neighborhood in the Works of Pauline Hopkins, Jessie Fauset, and Maria Bonner*. New York: Garland, 1998.

Allen, Theodore W. *The Invention of the White Race: Racial Oppression and Social Control*. London: Verso, 1994.

Almond, Philip C. *Heretic and Hero: Muhammad and the Victorians*. Wiesbaden, Ger.: Otto Harrassowitz, 1989.

Anbinder, Tyler. *Nativism and Slavery: The Northern Know-Nothings and the Politics of the 1850s*. New York: Oxford University Press, 1992.

Anderson, James. *The Education of Blacks in the South, 1860–1935*. Urbana: University of Illinois Press, 1988.

Andrews, William. "The Representation of Slavery and the Rise of Afro-American Literary Realism, 1865–1920." In *Up from Slavery: Authoritative Texts, Contexts and Composition History*, edited by William Andrews, 249–58. New York: W. W. Norton, 1996.

———. *To Tell a Free Story: The First Century of Afro-American Autobiography, 1760–1865*. Urbana: University of Illinois Press, 1986.

Angell, Stephen Ward. *Bishop Henry McNeil Turner and African American Religion in the South*. Knoxville: University of Tennessee Press, 1992.

Appleby, Joyce, et al. *Telling the Truth about History*. New York: W. W. Norton, 1994.

Arbour, Keith. *Canvassing Books, Sample Books and Subscription Publishers' Ephemera, 1833–1851, in the Collection of Michael Zinman*. Ardsley, N.Y.: The Haydn Foundation for the Cultural Arts, 1996

Arthur, John, and Amy Shapiro, eds. *Campus Wars: Multiculturalism and the Politics of Difference*. Boulder, Colo.: Westview, 1995.

Asante, Molefi Kete. *Afrocentricity*. Trenton, N.J.: Africa World, 1988.

———. *Kemet, Afrocentricity, and Knowledge*. Trenton, N.J.: Africa World, 1988.

Ayers, Edward. *The Promise of the New South: Life after Reconstruction*. New York: Oxford University Press, 1992.

Bacon, Jacqueline. *Freedom's Journal: The First African American Newspaper*. Lanham, Md.: Lexington Books, 2007.

———. *The Humblest May Stand Forth: Rhetoric, Empowerment and Abolition*. Columbia: University of South Carolina Press, 2002.

Bacote, Clarence. *The Story of Atlanta University: A Century of Service, 1865–1965*. Atlanta: Atlanta University Press, 1969.

Bailey, Randall, ed. *Yet with a Steady Beat: Contemporary U.S. Afrocentric Biblical Interpretation*. Atlanta: Society of Biblical Literature, 2003.

Bailyn, Bernard. *To Begin the World Anew: The Genius and Ambiguities of the American Founders*. New York: Knopf, 2003.

Baker, Lee. *From Savage to Negro: Anthropology and the Construction of Race, 1896–1954*. Berkeley: University of California Press, 1998.

Banks, William. *Black Intellectuals: Race and Responsibility in American Life*. New York: W. W. Norton, 1996.

Banton, Michael. *Racial Theories*. New York: Cambridge University Press, 1998.

Barr, James. "the Pre-Scientific Chronology: The Bible and the Origin of the World." *Proceedings of the American Philosophical Society* 143 (September 1993): 379–89.

Basard, Katherine Clay. *Spiritual Interrogations: Culture, Gender, and Community in Early African American Women's Writing*. Princeton, N.J.: Princeton University Press, 1999.

Bay, Mia. *The White Image in the Black Mind: African American Ideas about White People, 1830–1925*. New York: Oxford University Press, 2000.

Baym, Nina. *American Women Writers and the Work of History, 1790–1860*. New Brunswick, N.J.: Rutgers University Press, 1995.

Bederman, Gail. *Manliness and Civilization: A Cultural History of Gender and Race in the United States, 1880–1917*. Chicago: University of Chicago Press, 1995.

Bender, Thomas. *Intellect and Public Life: Essays on the Social History of Academic Intellectuals in the United States*. Baltimore: Johns Hopkins University Press, 1993.

Benedict, Michael Les. *A Compromise of Principle: Congressional Republicans and Reconstruction, 1863–1869*. New York: W. W. Norton, 1974.

———. *The Impeachment and Trial of Andrew Jackson*. New York: W. W. Norton, 1973.

Ben-Jochannan, Yosef. *African Origins of the Major "Western Religions."* New York: Alkebu-lan Books, 1970.

———. *Africa: The Mother of Western Civilization*. New York: Alkebu-lan Books, n.d.

———. *Black Man of the Nile and His Family*. 2nd ed. Baltimore: Black Classic Press, 1989.

Bercovitch, Sacvan. *The American Jeremiad*. Madison: University of Wisconsin Press, 1978.

Berkhofer, Robert F. *Beyond the Great Story: History as Text and Discourse*. Cambridge: Harvard University Press, 1995.

Berlinerblau, Jacques. *Heresy in the University: The Black Athena Controversy and the Responsibility of American Intellectuals*. New Brunswick, N.J.: Rutgers University Press, 1999.

Bernal, Martin. *Black Athena: The Afroasiatic Roots of Classical Civilization*. Vol. 1: *The Fabrication of Ancient Greece, 1785–1985*. New Brunswick, N.J.: Rutgers University Press, 1987.

———. *Black Athena Writes Back: Martin Bernal Responds to His Critics.* Durham, N.C.: Duke University Press, 2001.

Bethel, Elizabeth R. *The Roots of African American Identity: Memory and History in Antebellum Black Communities.* New York: St. Martin's, 1997.

Black, J. B. *The Art of History: A Study of Four Great Historians of the Eighteenth Century.* New York: Russell and Long, 1965.

Blackburn, Robin. "The Old World Background to European Colonial Slavery." *William and Mary Quarterly* 54 (January 1997): 65–102.

Blackett, Richard. *Beating against the Barriers: Biographical Essays in Nineteenth-Century Afro-American History.* Baton Rouge: Louisiana State University Press, 1986.

———. *Building an Antislavery Wall: Black Americans in the Abolitionist Movement, 1830–1860.* Ithaca, N.Y.: Cornell University Press, 1983.

Black Public Sphere Collective, ed. *Black Public Sphere.* Chicago: University of Chicago Press, 1995.

Blight, David. *Frederick Douglass' Civil War: Keeping Faith in Jubilee.* Baton Rouge: Louisiana State University Press, 1989.

——— "In Search of Learning, Liberty and Self-Definition: James McCune Smith and the Ordeal of the Antebellum Black Intellectual." *African Americans in New York Life and History* 9 (July 1985): 7–25.

———. *Passages to Freedom: The Underground Railroad in History and Memory.* Washington, D.C.: Smithsonian Books, 2004.

———. *Race and Reunion: The Civil War in American Memory.* Cambridge: Harvard University Press, 2001.

Blockson, Charles. *The Underground Railroad.* New York: Prentice-Hall, 1987.

Bloom, Alan. *The Closing of the American Mind.* New York: Simon and Schuster, 1987.

Boardman, Helen. "Negro Historians of Our Times." *Negro History Bulletin* 8 (April 1945): 155–59, 166.

———. "The Rise of the Negro Historian." *Negro History Bulletin* 8 (April 1945): 148–54, 166.

Bordewich, Fergus. *Bound for Canaan: The Underground Railroad and the War for the Soul of America.* New York: Amistad, 2005.

Boulton, Alexander O. "The American Paradox: Jeffersonian Equality and Racial Science." *American Quarterly* 47 (September 1995): 467–93.

Brading, D. A. *The First America: The Spanish Monarchy, Creole Patriots, and the Liberal State, 1492–1867.* New York: Oxford University Press, 1991.

Braude, Benjamin. "The Sons of Noah and the Construction of Ethnic and Geographical Identities in the Medieval and Early Modern Periods." *William and Mary Quarterly* 54 (January 1997): 107–42.

Breisach, Ernest. *Historiography: Ancient, Medieval, Modern.* Chicago: University of Chicago Press, 1988.

———. *On the Future of History: The Postmodernist Challenge and Its Aftermath.* Chicago: University of Chicago Press, 2003.

Bronson, Oswald Perry. "The Origin and Significance of the Interdenominational Theological Center." Ph.D. diss., Northwestern University, 1965.

Brooke, John. *The Refiner's Fire: The Making of Mormon Cosmology, 1644–1844.* New York: Cambridge University Press, 1994.

Brooks, Joanna. *American Lazarus: Religion and the Rise of African American and Native American Literatures*. New York: Oxford University Press, 2003.

―――. "The Early American Public Sphere and the Emergence of a Black Print Counterpublic." *William and Mary Quarterly* 62 (2005): 67–93.

―――. "Prince Hall: Freemasonry and Genealogy." *African American Review* 34 (Summer 2000): 197–216.

Brooks, Joanna, and John Saillant, eds. *"Face Zion Forward": First Writers of the Black Atlantic, 1785–1798*. Boston: Northeastern University Press, 2002.

Brooks, Kristina Margaret. "Transgressing the Boundaries of Identity: Racial Pornography, Fallen Women and Ethnic Others in the Works of Pauline Hopkins, Alice Dunbar-Nelson and Edith Wharton." Ph.D. diss., University of California at Berkeley, 1995.

Brown, Lois. *Pauline Elizabeth Hopkins: Black Daughter of the Revolution*. Chapel Hill: University of North Carolina Press, 2008.

Brown, Richard. *Knowledge Is Power: The Diffusion of Information in Early America, 1700–1865*. New York: Oxford University Press, 1989.

Brown, Stewart, ed. *William Robertson and the Expansion of Empire*. New York: Cambridge University Press, 1997.

Bruce, Dickson. *The Origins of African American Literature, 1680–1865*. Charlottesville: University Press of Virginia, 2001.

Brundage, W. Fitzhugh. *Lynching in the New South: Georgia and Virginia, 1880–1930*. Urbana: University of Illinois Press, 1993.

―――. *The Southern Past: A Clash of Race and Memory*. Cambridge: Harvard University Press, 2005.

―――, ed. *Under Sentence of Death: Lynching in the South*. Chapel Hill: University of North Carolina Press, 1997.

Bulmer, Martin, and John Solomos, eds. *Racism*. New York: Oxford University Press, 1999.

Burkett, Randall. "The Reverend Henry Croswell and Black Episcopalians in New Haven, 1820–1860." *The North Star: A Journal of African American Religious History* 7 (Fall 2003): 3–13.

Burns, Thomas S. *Rome and the Barbarians, 100 B.C.–A.D. 400*. Baltimore: Johns Hopkins University Press, 2003.

Calcott, George. *History in the United States, 1800–1860: Its Practice and Purpose*. Baltimore: Johns Hopkins University Press, 1960.

Campbell, James. *Middle Passages: African American Journeys to Africa, 1787–2005*. New York: Penguin, 2006.

―――. *Songs of Zion: The African Methodist Episcopal Church in the United States and South Africa*. Chapel Hill: University of North Carolina Press, 1998.

Canizares-Esguerra, Jorge. "Entangled Histories: Borderland Historiographies in New Clothes?" *American Historical Review* 112 (2007): 787–99.

―――. *How to Write the History of the New World: Histories, Epistemologies and Identities in the Eighteenth-Century Atlantic World*. Palo Alto: Stanford University Press, 2001.

Carby, Hazel. "On the Threshold of the Women's Era: Lynching, Empire and Sexuality in the Black Feminist Theory." In *Race, Writing, and Difference*, edited by Henry Louis Gates, 301–16. Chicago: University of Chicago Press, 1985.

———. *Reconstructing Womanhood: The Emergence of the Afro-American Woman Novelist.* New York: Oxford University Press, 1987.

Casement, William. *The Great Canon Controversy: The Battle of the Books in Higher Education.* New Brunswick, N.J.: Transaction, 1996.

Casper, Scott. *Constructing American Lives: Biography and Culture in Nineteenth-Century America.* Chapel Hill: University of North Carolina Press, 1999.

Chateauvert, Melinda. "The Third Step: Anna Julia Cooper and Black Education in the District of Columbia, 1910–1960." *Sage* (Supplement, 1988): 7–13.

Chirenje, J. Mutero. *Ethiopianism and Afro-Americans in Southern Africa, 1883–1916.* Baton Rouge: Louisiana State University, 1987.

Clegg, Claude. *The Price of Liberty: African Americans and the Making of Liberia.* Chapel Hill: University of North Carolina Press, 2004.

Clinton, Catherine. *Harriet Tubman: The Road to Freedom.* New York: Little, Brown, 2004.

Collins, Bruce. "The Ideologies of Antebellum Northern Democrats." *Journal of American Studies* 11 (1977): 103–20.

Collison, Gary Lee. *Shadrach Minkins: From Fugitive Slave to Citizen.* Cambridge: Harvard University Press, 1997.

Conn, Steven. *History's Shadow: Native Americans and Historical Consciousness in the Nineteenth Century.* Chicago: University of Chicago Press, 2004.

Conrad, Susan. *Perish the Thought: Intellectual Women in Romantic America, 1830–1860.* Secaucus, N.J.: Citadel, 1976.

Conyers, James L., ed. *Charles H. Wesley: The Intellectual Tradition of a Black Historian.* New York: Garland, 1997.

Copher, Charles. "The Black Presence in the Old Testament." In *Stony the Road We Trod: African American Biblical Interpretations,* edited by Cain Hope Felder, 146–64. Minneapolis: Fortress, 1991.

Cornelius, Janet Duitsman. *"When I Can Read My Title Clear": Literacy, Slavery, and Religion in the Antebellum South.* Columbia: University of South Carolina Press, 1991.

Cornell, Saul. *The Other Founders: Anti-Federalism and the Dissenting Tradition in America, 1788–1828.* Chapel Hill: University of North Carolina Press, 1999.

Cornish, Dudley. *The Sable Arm: Black Troops in the Union Army, 1861–1865.* Lawrence: University of Kansas Press, 1987.

Cotkin, George. *Reluctant Modernism, American Thought and Culture, 1880–1900.* New York: Twayne, 1992.

Courtes, Jean Marie. "The Theme of Ethiopia and Ethiopians in Patristic Literature." In *The Image of the Black in Western Art: From the Christian Era to the Age of Discovery,* edited by Jean Devisse, 2:9–34. New York: William Morrow, 1979.

Crawford, George W. *Prince Hall and His Followers: Being a Monograph on the Legitimacy of Negro Masonry.* 1914. Reprint, New York: AMS Press, 1971.

Cromwell, *Adelaide.* "The Black Presence in the West End of Boston, 1800–1864." In *Courage and Conscience: Black and White Abolitionists in Boston ,* edited by Donald Jacobs. Bloomington: Indiana University Press, 1993.

———. *The Other Brahmins: Black Upper Class, 1750–1950.* Little Rock: University of Arkansas Press, 1994.

Crowder, Ralph. "John Edward Bruce and the Value of Knowing the Past: Politician,

Journalist, and Self-Trained Historian of the African Diaspora, 1856–1924." Ph.D. diss., University of Kansas, 1994.

———. *John Edward Bruce: Politician, Journalist and Self-Trained Historian of the African Diaspora*. New York: New York University Press, 2004.

Curry, Leonard. *The Free Black in Urban America, 1800–1859: The Shadow of the Dream*. Chicago: University of Chicago Press, 1981.

Curtin, Philip. *The Image of Africa: British Ideas and Action, 1780–1850*. Madison: University of Wisconsin Press, 1964.

———, ed. *Africa Remembered: Narratives by West Africans from the Era of the Slave Trade*. Madison: University of Wisconsin Press, 1967.

Dagbovie, Pero. *The Early Black History Movement: Carter G. Woodson and Lorenzo Johnston Greene*. Urbana: University of Illinois Press, 1987.

Dain, Bruce. "Haiti and Egypt in the Early Black Radical Discourse in the United States." *Slavery and Abolition* 14 (December 1993): 140–61.

———. *A Hideous Monster of the Mind: American Race Theory in the Early Republic*. Cambridge: Harvard University Press, 2002.

Dalton, Karen Chambers. "'The Alphabet Is an Abolitionist': Literacy and African Americans in the Emancipation Era." *Massachusetts Review* (Winter 1991): 545–55.

Dann, Martin. *The Black Press, 1827–1890: The Quest for National Identity*. New York: Putnam and Sons, 1971.

Davidson, Cathy N. *Revolution and the Word: The Rise of the Novel in America*. New York: Oxford University Press, 1986.

Davis, David Brion. *The Problem of Slavery in the Age of Revolution, 1780–1823*. Ithaca, N.Y.: Cornell University Press, 1975.

Davis, John. *The Landscape of Belief: Encountering the Holy Land in Nineteenth-Century American Art and Culture*. Princeton, N.J.: Princeton University Press, 1996.

Dean, David. *Defender of the Race: James Theodore Holly, Nationalist Black Bishop*. Boston: Lambeth, 1979.

Delia, Dianna. "The Alexandrian Library in Classical and Islamic Traditions." *American Historical Review* 97 (December 1992): 1449–67.

Denby, David. *Great Books: My Adventures with Homer, Rousseau, Woolf, and Other Indestructible Writers of the Western World*. New York: Simon and Schuster, 1996.

Des Jardins, Julie. *Women and the Historical Enterprise in America: Gender, Race, and the Politics of Memory, 1880–1945*. Chapel Hill: University of North Carolina Press, 2003.

Devisse, Jean, ed. *The Image of the Black in Western Art: From the Christian Era to the "Age of Discovery."* Vol. 2. New York: William Morrow, 1979.

Dorieski, C. K. "Inherited Rhetoric and Authentic History: Pauline Hopkins at the *Colored American Magazine*." In *The Unruly Voice: Rediscovering Pauline Hopkins*, edited by John Grusser, 71–96. Urbana: University of Illinois Press, 1996.

Doyle, Don. *New Men, New Cities, New South: Atlanta, Nashville, Charleston, and Mobile, 1860–1910*. Chapel Hill: University of North Carolina Press, 1990.

Drake, St. Clair. *Black Folk Here and There*. Vol. 2. Los Angeles: UCLA Center for African American Studies, 1987.

Dubois, Laurent. *Avengers of the New World: The Story of the Haitian Revolution*. Cambridge, Mass: Belknap Press of Harvard University Press, 2004.

————. *A Colony of Citizens: Revolution and Slave Emancipation in the French Caribbean, 1787–1804*. Published for the Omohundro Institute of Early American History and Culture, Williamsburg, Va. Chapel Hill: University of North Carolina Press, 2004.

Dyson, Walter. *Howard University: The Capstone of Negro Education; A History, 1867–1940*. Washington, D.C.: Graduate School of Howard University, 1941.

Ernest, John. *Liberation Historiography: African American Writers and the Challenge of History, 1794–1861*. Chapel Hill: University of North Carolina Press, 2004.

————, ed. *The Narrative of the Life of Henry Box Brown, Written by Himself*. Chapel Hill: University of North Carolina Press, 2008.

Eze, Emmanuel Chukwudi. *Race and the Enlightenment*. Oxford: Blackwell, 1997.

Fabre, Geneviève, and Robert O'Meally, eds. *History and Memory in African American Culture*. New York: Oxford University Press, 1994.

Farrison, William Edward. *Williams Wells Brown, American Reformer*. Chicago: University of Chicago Press, 1969.

Faust, Drew Gilpin, ed. *The Ideology of Slavery: Proslavery Thought in the Antebellum South, 1830–1860*. Baton Rouge: Louisiana State University Press, 1981.

Felder, Cain Hope, ed. *Stony the Road We Trod: African American Biblical Interpretation*. Minneapolis: Fortress, 1991.

Feldman, Louis. *Josephus and Modern Scholarship, 1937–1980*. New York: W. de Gruyter, 1984.

Feldman, Louis, and Cohei Huta. *Josephus, the Bible and History*. Detroit: Wayne State University Press, 1988.

Ferguson, Robert A. *American Enlightenment, 1750–1820*. Cambridge, Mass.: Harvard University Press, 1997.

Fikes, Robert. "African American Scholars of Greco-Roman Heritage." *Journal of Blacks in Higher Education* 35 (2002): 120–24.

————. "It Was Never Greek to Them: Black Affinity for Ancient Greek and Roman Culture." *Negro Educational Review* 53 (2002): 3–12.

Fletcher-Baker, Karen. *A Singing Something: Womanist Reflections on Anna Julia Cooper*. New York: Crossroads, 1994.

Foner, Eric. *Free Labor, Free Men: The Ideology of the Republican Party before the Civil War*. New York: Oxford University Press, 1970.

————. *Reconstruction: America's Unfinished Revolution, 1863–1877*. New York: Oxford University Press, 1996.

Foner, Philip. "The Battle to End Discrimination on the Philadelphia Streetcars." Part 1: "Background and the Beginning of the Battle." *Pennsylvania History* 40 (July 1973): 275–80.

Fortune, T. Thomas. *Black and White: Land, Labor and Politics in the South*. New York: Fords, Howard and Hubert, 1884.

Foster, Frances Smith. *Written by Herself: Literary Production by African American Women, 1746–1892*. Bloomington: Indiana University Press, 1993.

Francesconi, Daniele. "William Robertson on Historical Causation and Unintended Consequences." *Cromohs* 4 (1999): 1–18.

Franklin, John Hope. "Dilemma of the Negro Scholar." In *Race and History: Selected Essays, 1938–1988*, edited by John Hope Franklin, 293–308. Baton Rouge: Louisiana State University Press, 1988.

———. *The Free Negro in North Carolina, 1790–1860*. Chapel Hill: University of North Carolina Press, 1945.

———. *George Washington Williams: A Biography*. Chicago: University of Chicago Press, 1985.

———. "On the Evolution of Scholarship in Afro-American History." In *The State of Afro-American History: Past, Present and Future*, edited by Darlene Clark Hine, 1–22. Baton Rouge: Louisiana State University Press, 1986.

———, ed. *Race and History: Selected Essays, 1938–1988*. Baton Rouge: Louisiana State University Press, 1988.

Frazier, E. Franklin. *Black Bourgeoisie: The Rise of a New Black Middle Class in the United States*. New York: Collier Books, 1957.

Frederickson, George. *The Black Image in the White Mind: The Debate on Afro-American Culture, 1817–1914*. Middletown, Conn.: Wesleyan University Press, 1987.

———. *The Inner Civil War: Northern Intellectuals and the Crisis of the War*. Urbana: University of Illinois Press, 1993.

Freehling, William. *The Road to Disunion: Secessionists at Bay, 1776–1854*. New York: Oxford University Press, 1990.

Freimarck, Vincent, and Bernard Rosenthal, eds. *Race and the American Romantics*. New York: Schocken Books, 1971.

Freund, Bill. *The Making of Contemporary Africa: The Development of Society since 1800*. Bloomington: Indiana University Press, 1984.

Frick, Carolyn E. *The Making of Haiti: The Saint Dominique Revolution from Below*. Knoxville: University of Tennessee Press, 1980.

Fulop, Timothy. "The Future Golden Day of the Race: Millenarianism and Black Americans in the Nadir, 1877–1901." In *African American Religion: Interpretative Essays on History and Culture*, edited by Timothy Fulop and Albert Raboteau, 227–56. New York: Routledge, 1997.

Gabel, Leona C. *From Slavery to the Sorbonne and Beyond: The Life and Writings of Anna Julia Cooper*. Northampton, Mass.: Smith College Department of History, 1982.

Gaines, Kevin K. *Uplifting the Race: Black Leadership, Politics, and Culture in the Twentieth Century*. Chapel Hill: University of North Carolina Press, 1997.

Gara, Larry. "William Still and the Underground Railroad." *Pennsylvania Magazine of History*, January 1961, 33–44.

Gates, Henry Louis. "The Master's Pieces: On Canon Formation and the African American Tradition." *South Atlantic Quarterly* 89 (Winter 1996): 89–111.

———. *The Signifying Monkey: A Theory of Afro-American Literary Criticism*. New York: Oxford University Press, 1988.

———. "The Trope of the New Negro and the Reconstruction of the Image of the Black." *Representations* 24 (Fall 1984): 129–55.

Gatewood, Willard. "Aristocrats of Color, North and South: The Black Elite, 1880–1920." *Journal of Southern History* 54 (February 1988): 3–20.

———. *Aristocrats of Color: The Black Elite, 1880–1920*. Bloomington: Indiana University Press, 1990.

Gay, Peter. *The Enlightenment: The Rise of Modern Paganism*. New York: W. W. Norton, 1996.

————. *A Loss of Mastery: Puritan Historians in Colonial America.* Berkeley: University of California Press, 1960.

Genovese, Eugene. *From Rebellion to Revolution: Afro-American Slave Revolts in the Making of the Modern World.* Baton Rouge: Louisiana State University Press, 1971.

Gerteis, Louis. "The Slave Power and Its Enemies." *Reviews in American History* 16 (September 1988): 390–95.

Gibson, Charles, ed. *The Black Legend: Anti-Spanish Attitudes in the Old World and the New.* New York: Knopf, 1971.

Giddings, Paula. *When and Where I Enter: The Impact of Black Women on Race and Sex in America.* Toronto: Bantam Books, 1984.

Gilman, Susan. "Pauline Hopkins and the Occult: African American Revisions of Nineteenth-Century Sciences." *American Literary History* 8 (1996): 57–82.

Gilroy, Paul. *The Black Atlantic: Modernity and Double Consciousness.* Cambridge, Mass: Harvard University Press, 1993.

Gladstone, William. *United States Colored Troops, 1863–1867.* Gettysburg, Pa.: Thomas, 1990.

Glatthaar, Joseph T. *Forged in Battle: The Civil War Alliance of Black Soldiers and White Officers.* New York: Macmillan, 1990.

Glaude, Eddie. *Exodus! Religion, Race, and Nation in Nineteenth-Century Black America.* Chicago: University of Chicago Press, 2000.

Goggin, Jacqueline. "Carter G. Woodson and the Movement to Promote Black History." Ph.D. diss., University of Rochester, 1984.

————. *Carter G. Woodson: Life in Black History.* Baton Rouge: Louisiana State University Press, 1993.

————. "Countering White Racist Scholarship: Carter G. Woodson and the *Journal of Negro History*." *Journal of Negro History* 68 (Fall 1983): 355–75.

Goggin, Lathardus. "The Evolution of Central State College under Charles H. Wesley from 1942–1965: An Historical Analysis." Ed.D. diss., University of Akron, 1983.

Goldberg, David Theo. *Racist Culture: Philosophy and the Politics of Meaning.* Cambridge: Blackwell, 1993.

Goldenberg, David M. *The Curse of Ham: Race and Slavery in Early Judaism, Christianity, and Islam.* Princeton, N.J.: Princeton University Press, 2003.

Gossett, Thomas. *Race: The History of an Idea in America.* New York: Schocken Books, 1963.

Gould, Stephen G. *Eight Little Piggies: Reflections in Natural History.* New York: W. W. Norton, 1993.

Grafton, Anthony. *New Worlds, Ancient Texts: The Power of Tradition and the Shock of Discovery.* Cambridge: Harvard University Press, 1992.

Grantham, Dewey. *Southern Progressivism: The Reconciliation of Progress and Tradition.* Knoxville: University of Tennessee Press, 1983.

Green, Constance McLaughlin. *The Secret City: A History of Race Relations in the Nation's Capital.* Princeton, N.J.: Princeton University Press, 1967.

Greene, Harry Washington. *Holders of Doctorates among American Negroes: An Educational and Social Study of Negroes Who Earned Doctoral Degrees.* Boston: Meador, 1946.

Greene, Lorenzo, and Carter G. Woodson. *The Negro Wage Earner.* New York: Associated Publishers, 1930.

Griffler, Keith. *Frontline of Freedom: African Americans and the Forging of the Underground Railroad in the Ohio Valley*. Lexington: University Press of Kentucky, 2004.

Gruesser, John. *The Unruly Voice: Rediscovering Pauline Hopkins*. Urbana: University of Illinois Press, 1996.

Gubert, Betty Kaplan. *Early Black Bibliophiles, 1863–1918*. New York: Garland, 1982.

Gunning, Sandra. *Race, Rape, and Lynching: The Red Record of American Literature, 1890–1912*. New York: Oxford University Press, 1996.

Gustafson, Sandra. *Eloquence Is Power: Oratory and Performance in Early America*. Chapel Hill: University of North Carolina Press, 2000.

Habermas, Jürgen. *The Structural Transformation of the Public Sphere: An Inquiry into a Category of Bourgeois Society*. Cambridge, Mass.: MIT Press, 1989.

Habtu, Tewoldemedhim. "The Images of Egypt in the Old Testament: Reflections of African Hermeneutics." In *Interpreting the Old Testament*, edited by Mary Getui, Knut Holter, and Victor Zinkuartie, 55–64. New York: Peter Lang, 2001.

Hall, Stephen G. "To Render the Private Public: William Still and the Selling of the Underground Railroad." *Pennsylvania Magazine of History and Biography* 127 (January 2003): 35–55.

Handlin, Lillian. *George Bancroft: The Intellectual as Democrat*. New York: Harper and Row, 1984.

———. "Research as Opportunity: Alrutheus Ambush Taylor, Black Intellectualism and the Remaking of Reconstruction Historiography, 1893–1954." *UCLA Historical Journal* 16 (1996): 39–60.

———. "'A Search for Truth': Jacob Oson and the Beginnings of Textual Historical Discourse among African Americans in the Early Republic." *William and Mary Quarterly* 64, no. 1 (January 2007): 139–48.

Harlan, Louis. *Booker T. Washington: The Making of a Leader, 1856–1901*. London: Oxford University Press, 1972.

———. *Booker T. Washington: Wizard of Tuskegee, 1901–1915*. New York: Oxford University Press, 1983.

Harris, Abram. *The Negro as Capitalist: A Study of Banking and Business among American Negroes*. 1935. Reprint, New York: Negro Universities Press, 1969.

Harris, Janette Hotson. "Charles H. Wesley: Educator and Historian." Ph.D. diss., Howard University, 1975.

Harris, Joseph, ed. *Africa and Africans as Seen by Classical Writers: The William Leo Hansberry African History Notebook*. Vol. 2. Washington, D.C.: Howard University Press, 1981.

———. *Pillars in Ethiopian History: The William Leo Hansberry African History Notebook*. Vol. 1. Washington, D.C.: Howard University Press, 1974.

Harris, Robert. "Coming of Age: The Transformation of Afro-American Historiography." *Journal of Negro History* 67 (Summer 1982): 107–21.

Hartman, Saidiya. *Scenes of Subjection: Terror, Slavery, and Self-making in Nineteenth-Century America*. New York: Oxford University Press, 1997.

Harvey, Bruce. *American Geographics: U.S. National Narratives and Representation of the Non-European World, 1830–1865*. Stanford, Calif.: Stanford University Press, 2001.

Hatch, Nathan, and Mark Noll, eds. *The Bible in America: Essays in Cultural History*. New York: Oxford University Press, 1982.

Hatchett, Catherine. "George Boyer Vashon, 1824–1878: Black Educator, Poet and Fighter for Equal Justice, Part 1." *Western Pennsylvania Historical Magazine* 68 (July 1985): 205–19.

Haywood, Chanita. "Prophesying Daughters: Nineteenth-Century Black Religious Women, the Bible and Literary History." In *African Americans and the Bible: Sacred Texts and Social Textures,* edited by Vincent Winbush, 355–66. New York: Continuum, 2001.

Hertzberg, Arthur. *The Jews in America: Four Centuries of Uneasy Encounter; A History.* New York: Simon and Schuster, 1989.

Hesseltine, William B., and Louis Kaplan. "Negro Doctors of Philosophy in History." *Negro History Bulletin* 4 (December 1942): 59 and 67.

Higginbotham, Elizabeth. *Righteous Discontent: The Women's Movement in the Black Baptist Church, 1880–1920.* Cambridge: Harvard University Press, 1993.

Higham, John. *History: Professional Scholarship in America.* Baltimore: Johns Hopkins University Press, 1965.

Hine, Darlene Clark. *Black Women in White: Racial Conflict and Cooperation in the Nursing Profession, 1890–1950.* Bloomington: Indiana University Press, 1989.

———, ed. *The State of Afro-American History.* Baton Rouge: Louisiana State University Press, 1986.

Hine, Darlene Clark, Elsa Barkley Brown, and Rosalyn Terborg-Penn, eds. *Black Women in America: An Historical Encyclopedia.* 2 vols. Bloomington: Indiana University Press, 1993.

Hinks, Peter. *To Awaken My Afflicted Brethren: David Walker and the Problem of Antebellum Slave Resistance.* State College: Pennsylvania State University Press, 1997.

Holt, Thomas. *Black over White: Negro Political Leadership in South Carolina during Reconstruction.* Urbana: University of Illinois Press, 1979.

———. *The Problem of Freedom: Race, Labor, and Politics in Jamaica and Britain, 1832–1938.* Baltimore: Johns Hopkins University Press, 1992.

Holt, W. Stull. *Historical Scholarship in the United States, and Other Essays.* Seattle: University of Washington Press, 1967.

Holter, Knut, ed. *Old Testament Research for Africa: A Critical Analysis and Bibliography of African Old Testament Dissertations, 1967–2000.* New York: Peter Lang, 2002.

Hornblower, Simon, and Anthony Spatworth, eds. *The Oxford Classical Dictionary.* Oxford: Oxford University Press, 1996.

Horner, Charles. *The Life of James Redpath.* New York: Barse and Hopkins, 1926.

Horsman, Reginald. *Race and Manifest Destiny: The Origins of American Racial Anglo-Saxonism.* Cambridge: Harvard University Press, 1981.

Horton, James O., and Lois Horton. *Black Bostonians: Family Life and Community Struggle in the Antebellum North.* New York: Holmes and Meier, 1979.

———. *In Hope of Liberty: Culture, Community, and Protest among Northern Free Blacks, 1700–1860.* New York: Oxford University Press, 1997.

Hountondji, Paulin J. *African Philosophy: Myth and Reality.* Bloomington: Indiana University Press, 1983.

Howard-Pitney, David. *The Afro-American Jeremiad: Appeals for Justice in America.* Philadelphia: Temple University Press, 1990.

Howe, Stephen. *Afrocentricism: Mythical Pasts and Imagined Homes.* London: Verso, 1998.

Hrbek, Ivan, ed. *General History of Africa.* Vol. 3: *Africa from the Seventh to the Eleventh Century.* Berkeley: University of California Press, 1992.

Hunt, Alfred. *Haiti's Influence on Antebellum America: Slumbering Volcano in the Caribbean.* Baton Rouge: Louisiana State University Press, 1988.

Hutchinson, Louisa Daniel. *Anna Julia Cooper: A Voice from the South.* Washington, D.C.: Smithsonian Institution Press, 1981.

Hutton, Frankie. *The Early Black Press in America, 1827 to 1860.* Westport, Conn.: Greenwood, 1993.

Iggers, George G., and James M. Powell, eds. *Leopold von Ranke and the Shaping of the Historical Discipline.* New York: Syracuse University Press, 1990.

Irwin, John. *American Hieroglyphics: The Symbol of the Egyptian Hieroglyphics in the American Renaissance.* New Haven: Yale University Press, 1980.

Isichei, Elizabeth. *A History of Christianity in Africa.* Grand Rapids, Mich.: William B. Eerdmans, 1995.

Issac, Benjamin. *The Invention of Racism in Classical Antiquity.* Princeton, N.J.: Princeton University Press, 2004.

Jackson, Blyden. *A History of Afro-American Literature.* Baton Rouge: Louisiana State University Press, 1989.

Jackson, John G. *Introduction to African Civilizations.* New York: Citadel, 1970.

———. *Man, God, and Civilization.* New York: Citadel, 1972.

Jacobs, Sylvia, ed. *Black Americans and the Missionary Movement in Africa.* Westport, Conn.: Greenwood, 1982.

James, Cyril Lionel Robert. *The Black Jacobins: Toussaint L'Ouverture and the San Domingo Revolution.* London: Allison and Busby, 1980.

James, George G. M. *Stolen Legacy.* New York: Philosophical Library, 1954.

Jaynes, Gerald. *Branches without Roots: Genesis of the Black Working Class in the American South, 1862–1882.* New York: Oxford University Press, 1986.

Jeffrey, Julie Roy. *Abolitionists Remember: Antislavery Autobiographies and the Unfinished Work of Emancipation.* Chapel Hill: University of North Carolina Press, 2008.

Jenkins, Keith. *Re-Thinking History.* New York: Routledge, 1991.

Johannsen, Robert. *To the Halls of the Montezumas: The Mexican American War in the America Imagination.* New York: Oxford University Press, 1985.

Jones, Martha. *All Bound Up Together: The Woman Question in African American Public Culture, 1830–1900.* Chapel Hill: University of North Carolina Press, 2007.

Jordan, Erwin L. *Black Confederates and Afro-Yankees in the Civil War.* Charlottesville: University of Virginia Press, 1995.

Joyce, Donald Franklin. *Gatekeepers of Black Culture: Black-Owned Publishing in the United States, 1817–1981.* New York: Greenwood, 1983.

July, Robert. *A History of the African People.* New York: Charles Scribner and Sons, 1980.

Kachun, Mitch. "African Americans, Public Commemorations and the Haitian Revolution: A Problem of Historical Mythmaking." *Journal of the Early Republic,* Summer 2006, 249–74.

———. *Festivals of Freedom, Memory, and Meaning in African American Emancipation Celebrations, 1808–1915.* Amherst: University of Massachusetts Press, 2003.

Kaplan, Sidney. *The Black Presence in the Era of the American Revolution*. Washington, D.C.: Smithsonian Institution, 1973.

Keita, Maghan. "Deconstructing the Classical Age: Africa and the Unity of the Mediterranean World." *Journal of Negro History* 79 (Spring 1994): 147–66.

———. *Race and the Writing of History: Riddling the Sphinx*. New York: Oxford University Press, 2000.

Kendrick, Ruby M. "They Also Serve: The National Association of Colored Women, Inc." *Negro History Bulletin* 17 (March 1954): 171–75.

Kidd, Colin. *The Forging of Races: Race and Scripture in the Protestant Atlantic World, 1600–2000*. Cambridge: Cambridge University Press, 2006.

Kloppenberg, James. "Objectivity and Historicism: A Century of American Historical Writing." *American Historical Review* 96 (June 1991): 1011–30.

Konkle, Maureen. *Writing Indian Nations: Native Intellectuals and the Politics of Historiography, 1827–1863*. Chapel Hill: University of North Carolina Press, 2004.

Kraus, Michael, and David Joyce. *The Writing of American History*. Norman: University of Oklahoma Press, 1987.

Kuklick, Bruce. *Puritans in Babylon: The Ancient Near East and American Intellectual Life, 1880–1930*. Princeton, N.J.: Princeton University Press, 1996.

Kupperman, Karen Ordahl, ed. *America in European Consciousness, 1493–1750*. Chapel Hill: University of North Carolina Press, 1995.

Landry, Bart. *The New Black Middle Class*. Berkeley: University of California Press, 1987.

Landsman, Ned. *From Colonials to Provincials: American Thought and Culture, 1680–1760*. New York: Twayne, 1997.

Lane, Roger. *William Dorsey's Philadelphia and Ours: On the Past, Present and Future of the Black City in America*. New York: Oxford University Press, 1991.

Lapansky, Phil. "Aboard William Still's Underground Railroad Celebrating an African American Classic." Paper delivered to the Philobibion Club of Philadelphia, February 9, 1993.

Larsen, Mogens Trolle. *The Conquest of Assyria: Excavations in an Antique Land, 1840–1860*. New York: Routledge, 1994.

Lavik, Marta Høyland. "The 'African' Texts of the Old Testament and Their African Interpretation." In *Interpreting the Old Testament in Africa*, edited by Mary Getui, Knut Holter, and Victor Zinkuratire, 43–54. New York: Peter Lang, 1999.

Lears, T. Jackson. *No Place of Grace: Antimodernism and the Transformation of American Culture*. Chicago: University of Chicago Press, 1981.

Lefkowitz, Mary. *Not Out of Africa: How Afrocentrism Became an Excuse to Teach Myth as History*. New York: Basic Books, 1996.

Lemert, Charles, and Esme Bhan, eds. *The Voice of Anna Julia Cooper*. Lanham, Md.: Rowan and Littlefield, 1997.

Lerner, Gerda, ed. *Black Women in White America: A Documentary History*. New York: Vintage Books, 1972.

Levin, David. *History as Romantic Art: Bancroft, Prescott, Motley, and Parkman*. Stanford, Calif.: Stanford University Press, 1959.

Levine, Bruce. *Half Slave, Half Free: The Roots of the Civil War*. New York: Hill and Wang, 1972.

Levine, Robert. "Circulating the Nation: David Walker, the Missouri Compromise, and the Rise of the Black Press." In *The Black Press: New Literary and Historical Essays*, edited by Todd Vogel, 17–36. New Brunswick, N.J.: Rutgers University Press, 2001.

———. *Martin Delany, Frederick Douglass, and the Politics of Representative Identity*. Chapel Hill: University of North Carolina Press, 1997.

———, ed. *Martin R. Delany: A Documentary Reader*. Chapel Hill: University of North Carolina Press, 2003.

Lewis, David Levering. *The Race to Fashoda: Colonialism and Resistance*. New York: Henry Holt, 1987.

———. *W. E. B Du Bois: Biography of a Race, 1868–1919*. New York: Henry Holt, 1997.

Lewis, Earl. "To Turn as on a Pivot: Writing African Americans into a History of Overlapping Diasporas." *American Historical Review* 100 (June 1995): 765–87.

Little, Lawrence S. *Disciples of Liberty: The African Methodist Episcopal Church in the Age of Imperialism, 1884–1916*. Knoxville: University of Tennessee Press, 2000.

Logan, Rayford. "The Attitude of the Church toward Slavery prior to 1500." *Journal of Negro History* 17 (October 1932): 466–80.

———. *The Betrayal of the Negro: From Rutherford B. Hayes to Woodrow Wilson*. New York: Macmillan, 1954.

———. "Carter G. Woodson: Mirror and Molder of His Time." *Journal of Negro History* 58 (July 1973): 1–17.

———. *Howard University: The First Hundred Years, 1867–1967*. New York: New York University Press, 1969.

Logan, Shirley. *"We Are Coming": The Persuasive Discourse of Nineteenth-Century Black Women*. Carbondale: Southern Illinois University Press, 1999.

Loggins, Vernon. *The Negro Author: His Development to 1900*. Port Washington, N.Y.: Kennikat, 1939.

Lowenberg, Bert James. *American History in American Thought: Christopher Columbus to Henry Adams*. New York: Simon and Schuster, 1972.

Lowenthal, David. *The Past Is a Foreign Country*. New York: Cambridge University Press, 1999.

Lynch, John. *The Facts of Reconstruction*. New York: Neale, 1914.

Mabee, Carlton. "A Negro Boycott to Integrate Boston Schools." *New England Quarterly* 41 (September 1968): 341–61.

MacCormack, Sabine. "Limits of Understanding: Perceptions of Greco-Roman and Amerindian Paganism in Early Modern Europe." In *America in European Consciousness, 1493–1750*, edited by Karen Kupperman, 79–130. Chapel Hill: University of North Carolina Press, 1995.

Maffly-Kipp, Laurie. "Mapping the World, Mapping the Race: The Negro Race History, 1874–1915." *Church History* 64 (December 1995): 610–26.

Mahan, Harold. *Benson Lossing and Historical Writing in the United States, 1830–1890*. Westport, Conn.: Greenwood, 1997.

Maltby, William S. *The Black Legend in England: The Development of Anti-Spanish Sentiment, 1558–1600*. Durham, N.C.: Duke University Press, 1971.

Mandelbaum, Maurice. *History, Man, and Reason: A Study in Nineteenth-Century Thought*. Baltimore: Johns Hopkins University Press, 1971.

Martin, Waldo. *The Mind of Frederick Douglass*. Chapel Hill: University of North Carolina Press, 1984.

Matthews, Jean. *Toward a New Society: American Thought and Culture, 1800–1830*. Boston: Twayne, 1991.

May, Henry. *The Enlightenment in America*. New York: Harper Brothers, 1960.

May, Robert. "The Slave Conspiracy Revisited: United States Presidents and Filibustering, 1848–1861." In *Union and Emancipation: Essays on Politics and Race in the Civil War*, edited by David W. Blight and Brooks D. Simpson, 7–28. Kent, Ohio: Kent State University Press, 1997.

McGlynn, Frank, and Seymour Drescher, eds. *The Meaning of Freedom: Economics, Politics and Culture after Slavery*. Pittsburgh: University of Pittsburgh Press, 1992.

McHenry, Elizabeth. "'Dreaded Eloquence': The Origins and Rise of African American Literary Societies and Libraries." *Harvard Library Bulletin* 6 (Spring 1995): 32–56.

———. *Forgotten Readers: Recovering the Lost History of African American Literary Societies*. Durham, N.C.: Duke University Press, 2002.

McKittrick, Eric L. *Andrew Johnson and Reconstruction*. New York: Oxford University Press, 1960.

McMurry, Linda O. *Recorder of the Black Experience: A Biography of Monroe Nathan Work*. Baton Rouge: Louisiana State University Press, 1985.

McPheeters, Alphonso. "The Origin and Development of Clark University and Gammon Theological Seminary." Ph.D. diss., University of Cincinnati, 1944.

McPherson, James. *The Negro's Civil War: How American Negroes Felt and Acted during the War for the Union*. New York: Pantheon Books, 1985.

Meier, August. "Negro Class Structure and Ideology in the Age of Booker T. Washington." *Phylon* 23 (Fall 1962): 258–66.

———. *Negro Thought in America, 1880–1915: Racial Ideologies in the Age of Booker T. Washington*. Ann Arbor: University of Michigan Press, 1966.

Meier, August, and Elliott Rudwick. *Black History and the Historical Profession, 1915–1980*. Urbana: University of Illinois Press, 1986.

Miller, Perry. *The New England Mind: The Seventeenth Century*. Cambridge: Harvard University Press, 1953.

Miller, William Lee. *Arguing about Slavery: The Great Battle in the United States Congress*. New York: Alfred Knopf, 1996.

Mitchell, Michele. *Righteous Propagation: African Americans and the Politics of Racial Destiny after Reconstruction*. Chapel Hill: University of North Carolina Press, 2004.

Moody, Joycelyn Cathleen. *Sentimental Confessions: Spiritual Narratives of Nineteenth-Century African American Women*. Athens: University of Georgia Press, 2001.

Morgan, Edmund S. *American Slavery, American Freedom: The Ordeal of Colonial Virginia*. New York: W. W. Norton, 1975.

Morrison, Michael, and James Brewer Stewart, eds. *Race and the Early Republic: Racial Consciousness and Nation-Building in the Early Republic*. New York: Rowan and Littlefield, 2002.

Morton, Patricia. *Disfigured Images: The Historical Assault on Afro-American Women*. New York: W. W. Norton, 1985.

Moses, Wilson Jeremiah. *Afrotopia: The Roots of African American Popular History*. Cambridge: Oxford University Press, 1998.

———. Alexander Crummell: *A Study of Civilization and Discontent*. New York: Oxford University Press, 1989.

———. *Black Messiahs and Uncle Toms: Social and Literary Manipulations of a Religious Myth*. University Park: Pennsylvania State University Press, 1982.

———. *Destiny and Race: Selected Writings, 1840–1898*. Amherst: University of Massachusetts Press, 1992.

———. *The Golden Age of Black Nationalism, 1850–1925*. New York: Oxford University Press, 1978.

———. *The Wings of Ethiopia: Studies in African American Life and Letters*. Ames: University of Iowa Press, 1990.

Moss, Alfred. *The American Negro Academy: Voice of the Talented Tenth*. Baton Rouge: Louisiana State University Press, 1981.

Mosse, George. "Eighteenth-Century Foundations." In *Racism*, edited by Martin Bulmer and John Solomos, 40–45. New York: Oxford University Press, 1999.

Mudimbe, V. Y. *The Idea of Africa*. Bloomington: Indiana University Press, 1994.

Mulvey, Christopher. "The Fugitive Self and the New World of the North: William Wells Brown's Discovery of America." In *The Black Columbiad: Defining Moments in African American Literature*, edited by Werner Sollors and Maria Diedrich, 99–111. Cambridge: Harvard University Press, 1994.

Muraskin, William A. *Middle-Class Blacks in a White Society: Prince Hall and Freemasonry in America*. Columbia: University of Missouri Press, 1980.

Nederveen Pieterse, Jan. *White on Black: Images of Africa and Blacks in Western Popular Culture*. New Haven: Yale University Press, 1995.

Neverdon-Morton, Cynthia. *Afro-American Women of the South and the Advancement of the Race*. Knoxville: University of Tennessee Press, 1989.

Newman, Richard S. *Freedom's Prophet: Bishop Richard Allen, the AME Church, and the Black Founding Fathers*. New York: New York University Press, 2008.

Nicholls, David. *From Dessalines to Duvalier: Race, Colour and National Independence in Haiti*. New Brunswick, N.J.: Rutgers University Press, 1996.

Noble, David W. "Perhaps the Rise and Fall of Scientific History in the American Historical Profession." *Reviews in American History* 17 (December 1989): 519–22.

Noll, Mark. "The Image of the United States as a Biblical Nation, 1776–1865." In *The Bible in America: Essays in Cultural History*, edited by Nathan Hatch and Mark Noll, 39–57. New York: Oxford University Press, 1994.

Norton, Mary Beth. *Founding Mothers and Fathers: Gendered Power and the Forming of American Society*. New York: A. A. Knopf, 1996.

Novick, Peter. *That Noble Dream: The Objectivity Question and the American Historical Profession*. New York: Cambridge University Press, 1988.

Numbers, Ronald L. "'The Most Important Biblical Discovery of Our Time': William Henry Green and the Decline of Ussher's Chronology." *Church History* 69 (2000): 257–76.

Obenzinger, Hilton. *American Palestine: Melville, Twain, and the Holy Land Mania*. Princeton, N.J.: Princeton University Press, 1996.

O'Leary, Cecilia Elizabeth. *To Die for: The Paradox of American Patriotism*. Princeton, N.J.: Princeton University Press, 1999.

Oshinsky, David M. *"Worse than Slavery": Parchman Farm and the Ordeal of Jim Crow Justice*. New York: Free Press, 1996.

Ott, Thomas, *The Haitian Revolution, 1789–1894*. Knoxville: University of Tennessee Press, 1971.

Otten, Thomas. "Pauline Hopkins and the Hidden Self of Race." *English Literary History* 59 (1992): 227–56.

Painter, Nell Irvin. *Black Exodusters: Black Migration to Kansas after Reconstruction*. New York: Knopf, 1976.

———. *Sojourner Truth: A Life, a Symbol*. New York: W. W. Norton, 1996.

Patterson, Martha Helen. "'Survival of the Best Fitted': The Trope of the New Women in Margaret Murray Washington, Pauline Hopkins, Sui Sin Far, Edith Wharton and Mary Johnston, 1895–1913." Ph.D. diss., University of Iowa, 1996.

Patterson, Orlando. *Freedom in the Making of the Western Culture*. New York: Basic Books, 1991.

Peckham, Morse. *Romanticism: The Culture of the Nineteenth Century*. New York: Braziller, 1965.

Penn, I. Garland. *The Afro-American Press and Its Editors*. Springfield, Mass: Wiley & Co., 1891.

Perkins, Linda. *Fanny J. Coppin and the Institute for Colored Youth, 1865–1902*. New York: Garland, 1987.

Perlman, Daniel. "Stirring the White Conscience: The Life of George Edmund Haynes." Ph.D. diss., New York University, 1972.

Perry, Lewis. *Intellectual Life in America: A History*. Chicago: University of Chicago Press, 1989.

Person-Lynn, Kwaku, ed. *First Word: Black Scholars, Thinkers, Warriors; Knowledge, Wisdom, Mental Liberation*. New York: Harlem River, 1996.

Persuitte, Joseph. *Joseph Smith and the Origins of the Book of Mormon*. Jefferson, N.C.: McFarland, 1985.

Peterson, Carla. *Doers of the Word: African-American Women Speakers and Writers in the North (1830–1880)*. New York: Oxford University Press, 1995.

Phillipson, Nicholas. "Providence and Progress: An Introduction to the Historical Thought of William Robertson." In *William Robertson and the Expansion of Empire*, edited by Stewart Brown, 55–73. New York: Cambridge University Press, 1997.

Piersen, William. *Black Yankees: The Development of an Afro-American Subculture in Eighteenth-Century New England*. Amherst: University of Massachusetts Press, 1988.

Plummer, Brenda Gayle. *Haiti and the Great Powers*. Baton Rouge: Louisiana State University Press, 1988.

———. *Haiti and the United States: The Psychological Moment*. Athens: University of Georgia Press, 1992

Potkay, Adam, and Sandra Burr, eds. *Black Atlantic Writers of the Eighteenth Century: Living the New Exodus in England and the Americas*. New York: St Martin's, 1995.

Potter, David. *The Impending Crisis, 1848–1861*. New York: Oxford University Press, 1976.

Prah, Kwesi Kwaa. *Jacobus Eliza Johannes Capitein, 1717–1747: A Critical Study of an Eighteenth Century African*. Trenton, N.J: Africa World Press, 1992.

Pratt, Mary Louise. *Imperial Eyes: Travel Writing and Transculturation*. New York: Routledge, 1992.

Price, George R., and James Brewer Stewart, eds. *To Heal the Scourge of Prejudice: The Life and Writings of Hosea Easton*. Amherst: University of Massachusetts Press, 2000.

Quarles, Benjamin. "Black History's Antebellum Origins." In *Black Mosaic: Essays in Afro-American History and Historiography*, edited by Benjamin Quarles, 109–34. Amherst: University of Massachusetts Press, 1988.

———. *The Negro in the American Revolution*. Chapel Hill: University of North Carolina Press, 1961.

———. *The Negro in the Civil War*. Boston: Little, Brown, 1953.

———. "The Revolutionary War as a Declaration on Independence." In *Slavery and Freedom in the Age of the American Revolution*, edited by Ira Berlin and Ronald Hoffman, 283–301. Urbana: University of Illinois Press, 1986.

Rael, Patrick. *Black Identity and Black Protest in the Antebellum North*. Chapel Hill: University of North Carolina Press, 2002.

Reddick, L. D. "A New Interpretation of Negro History." *Journal of Negro History* 23 (January 1937): 17–28.

———. "As I Remember Woodson." *Negro History Bulletin* 17 (November 1953): 37.

Redford, Donald D. *From Slave to Pharaoh: The Black Experience in Ancient Egypt*. Baltimore: Johns Hopkins University Press, 2004.

Redkey, Edwin. *Black Exodus: Black Nationalist and Back-to-Africa Movements, 1890–1910*. New Haven: Yale University Press, 1969.

Reed, Adolph. *W. E. B Du Bois and Political Thought: Fabianism and the Color Line*. New York: Oxford University Press, 1997.

Reed, Harry. *Platform for Change: The Foundations of the Northern Free Black Community, 1827–1860*. Westport, Conn.: Greenwood, 1993.

Reed, Traci Carroll. "Subjects of Consumption: Nineteenth-Century African American Writers." Ph.D. diss., Northwestern University, 1992.

Reinhold, Meyer. *Classica Americana: The Greek and Roman Heritage in the United States*. Detroit: Wayne State University Press, 1984.

Remini, Robert. *Andrew Jackson and His Indian Wars*. New York: Viking, 2001.

Reuben, Julie. *The Making of the Modern University: Intellectual Transformation and the Marginalization of Morality*. Chicago: University of Chicago Press, 1996.

Reynolds, David. *Walt Whitman's America: A Cultural Biography*. New York: Alfred A. Knopf, 1995.

Rogers, J. A. *The World's Greatest Men of Color*. 1945. Vols. 1 and 2. Reprint, New York: Macmillan, 1972.

Rojas, Fabio. *From Black Power to Black Studies: How a Radical Social Movement Became an Academic Discipline*. Baltimore: Johns Hopkins University Press, 2007.

Romero, Patricia. "Carter G. Woodson: A Biography." Ph.D. diss., Ohio State University, 1972.

Ronnick, Michele. *The First Three African American Members of the American Philological Society*. Philadelphia: American Philological Society, 2001.

———. "The Latin Quotations in the Correspondence of Edward Wilmot Blyden." *Negro Educational Review* 46 (1994): 101–6.

———. "A Pick instead of Greek and Latin: The Afro-American Quest for Useful Knowledge, 1880–1920." *Negro Educational Review* (1996): 60–66.

———. "Racial Ideology and the Classics in the African American University Experience." *Classical Bulletin* 76 (2001): 169–80.

———. "Twelve Black Classicists." *Arion* 11 (2004): 85–102.

———, ed. *The Autobiography of William Sanders Scarborough: An American Journey from Slavery to Scholarship.* Detroit: Wayne State University Press, 2005.

Rooks, Noliwe. *White Money/Black Power: The Surprising History of African American Studies and the Crisis of Race in Higher Education.* Boston: Beacon, 2006.

Ross, Dorothy. "Historical Consciousness in Nineteenth-Century America." *American Historical Review* 89 (October 1984): 909–28.

———. *The Origins of the Social Sciences.* New York: Cambridge University Press, 1991.

Ruggles, Jeffrey. *The Unboxing of Henry Brown.* Richmond: Library of Virginia, 2003.

Saillant, John. *Black Puritan, Black Republican: The Life and Thought of Lemuel Haynes, 1753–1833.* New York: Oxford University Press, 2003.

———. "'Wipe Away All Tears from Their Eyes': John Marrant's Theology in the Black Atlantic, 1785–1808." *Journal of Millennial Studies* 1, no. 1 (Winter 1999), http://www.mille.org/publications/winter98/journvol1issue1.html.

Sanneh, Lamin. *Abolitionists Abroad: American Blacks and the Making of Modern West Africa.* Cambridge: Harvard University Press, 1999.

Savage, Kirk. *Standing Soldiers, Kneeling Slaves: Race, War, and Monument in Nineteenth-Century America.* Princeton, N.J.: Princeton University Press, 1997.

Savage, W. Sherman. "Twenty Years of the Association for the Study of Negro Life and History." *Journal of Negro History* 20 (January 1935): 379–80.

Scally, Sister Anthony. "Woodson and the Genesis of ASNLH." *Negro History Bulletin* 40 (January–February 1977): 633–55.

Schaffer, Arthur. *To Be an American: David Ramsay and the Making of American Consciousness.* Columbia: University of South Carolina Press, 1991.

Schlesinger, Arthur. *The Disuniting of America: Reflections on a Multicultural Society.* New York: W. W. Norton, 1998.

Schorr, Joel. *Henry Highland Garnet: A Voice of Black Radicalism in the Nineteenth Century.* New York: Garland, 1995.

Scott, James C. *Domination and the Arts of Resistance.* New Haven: Yale University Press, 1990.

Sernett, Milton. *Abolition's Axe: Beriah Green, Oneida Institute, and the Black Struggle for Freedom.* Syracuse, N.Y.: Syracuse University Press, 1986.

Sewell, George A., and Cornelius Troup. *Morris Brown College, the First Hundred Years, 1881–1981: A Saga of a Century of Educational Achievement That Began through Self-Help.* Atlanta, Ga.: Morris Brown College, 1981.

Sewell, Richard. *Ballots for Freedom: Antislavery Politics in the United States, 1837–1860.* New York: Oxford University Press, 1978.

Sha'ban, Fuad. *Islam and the Arabs in Early American Thought: The Roots of Orientalism in America.* Durham, N.C.: Acorn, 1991.

Shalhope, Robert E. *The Roots of Democracy: American Thought and Culture, 1760–1800*. Boston: Twayne, 1990.

Shamit, Yaacov. *History in Black: African Americans in Search of an Ancient Past*. London: Frank Cass, 2001.

Shaw, Stephanie. *What a Woman Ought to Be and Ought to Do: Black Professional Women Workers during the Jim Crow Era*. Chicago: University of Chicago Press, 1996.

Shockley, Ann Allen. "Pauline Elizabeth Hopkins: A Biographical Excursion into Obscurity." *Phylon* 33 (1972): 22–26.

Sims, William Gilmore. *The Life of Francis Marion*. Cincinnati: H. W. Derby, 1844.

Sinclair, William. *Aftermath of Slavery*. 1905. Reprint, New York: Arno Press and the New York Times, 1969.

Sinnette, Elinor Des Verney, W. Paul Coates, and Thomas C. Battle. *Black Bibliophiles and Collectors, Preservers of Black History*. Washington, D.C.: Howard University Press, 1980.

Skinner, Elliott. *African Americans and U.S. Policy toward Africa, 1850–1924: In Defense of Black Nationality*. Washington, D.C.: Howard University Press, 1992.

Smedley, Audrey. *Race in North America: Origin and Evolution of a Worldview*. 2nd ed. Boulder, Colo.: Westview, 1999.

Smith, Robert P. "William Cooper Nell: Crusading Black Abolitionist." *Journal of Negro History* 55 (July 1970): 182–99.

Smith, Theophus. *Conjuring Culture: Biblical Formations of Black America*. New York: Oxford Press, 1994.

Smitten, Jeffrey. "Impartiality in Robertson's History of America." *Eighteenth Century Studies* 19 (Autumn 1985): 56–77.

Snowden, Frank. *Before Color Prejudice: The Ancient View of Blacks*. Cambridge: Harvard University Press, 1983.

———. *Blacks in Antiquity: Ethiopians in the Greco-Roman Experience*. Cambridge: Harvard University Press, 1970.

Sollors, Werner. *Neither Black nor White yet Both: Thematic Explorations of Interracial Literature*. New York: Oxford University Press, 1997.

Spady, James P. "The Afro-American Historical Society: The Nucleus of Black Bibliophiles (1897–1923)." *Negro History Bulletin* 37 (June/July 1974): 254–55.

Stauffer, John. *The Black Hearts of Men: Radical Abolitionists and the Transformation of Race*. Cambridge: Harvard University Press, 2002.

Staundenraus, P. J. *The American Colonization Movement*. New York: Columbia University Press, 1961.

Stringfellow, Thornton. "A Brief Examination of Scripture Testimony on the Institution of Slavery." In *The Ideology of Slavery: Proslavery Thought in the Antebellum South, 1830–1860*, edited by Drew Gilpin Faust, 136–67. Baton Rouge: Louisiana State University Press, 1981.

Stuckey, Sterling. *Going through the Storm: The Influence of African American Art in History*. New Haven: Yale University Press, 1994.

———. *The Ideological Origins of Black Nationalism*. Boston: Beacon, 1972.

———. "A Last Stern Struggle: Henry Highland Garnet and Liberation Theology." In *Going through the Storm: The Influence of African American Art in History*, edited by Sterling Stuckey, 103–19. New York: Oxford University Press, 1994.

——. *Slave Culture: Nationalist Theory and the Foundations of Black America*. New York: Oxford University Press, 1987.

Sundquist, Eric. *To Wake the Nations: Race in the Making of American Literature*. Boston: Harvard University Press, 1993.

Sweet, John Wood. *Bodies Politic: Negotiating Race in the American North, 1730–1830*. Baltimore: Johns Hopkins University Press, 2003.

Sweet, Leonard. *Black Images in White America, 1784–1870*. New York: W. W. Norton, 1976.

Swift, David. *Black Prophets of Justice: Activist Clergy before the Civil War*. Baton Rouge: Louisiana State University Press, 1989.

Switala, William. *Underground Railroad in Delaware, Maryland and West Virginia*. Mechanicsburg, Pa.: Stackpole Books, 2004.

Takaki, Ronald. *Iron Cages: Race and Culture in Nineteenth-Century America*. New York: Oxford University Press, 1979.

Tate, Claudia. *Domestic Allegories and Political Desires*. New York: Oxford University Press, 1992.

Taylor, Prince A. "A History of Gammon Theological Seminary." Ph.D. diss., New York University, 1948.

Thomas, Annie B. *Morris Brown College: From Its Beginnings in 1885 to Time of Removal*. 1932.

Thomas, Herman. *James W. C. Pennington: African American Church Man and Abolitionist*. New York: Garland, 1995.

Thompson, Lloyd. *Romans and Blacks*. Norman: University of Oklahoma Press, 1989.

Thorpe, Earl. *Black Historians: A Critique*. New York: W. W. Norton, 1961.

——. *Negro Historians in the United States*. Baton Rouge, La.: Fraternal Press, 1958.

——. "Negro Historiography in the United States." Ph.D. diss., Ohio State University, 1953.

——. Review of *Black History and the Historical Profession, 1915–1980*, by August Meier and Elliott Rudwick. *Journal of Negro History* 58 (Spring 1993): 123–27.

Tolnay, Stewart, and E. M. Beck. *A Festival of Violence: An Analysis of Southern Lynching, 1882–1930*. Urbana: University of Illinois Press, 1995.

Trafton, Scott. *Egypt Land: Race and Nineteenth-Century Egyptomania*. Durham, N.C.: Duke University Press, 2004.

Trouillot, Michel-Rolph. *Haiti: State against Nation, Origins and Legacy of Duvalierism*. New York: Monthly Review, 1990.

——. *Silencing the Past: Power and the Production of History*. Boston: Beacon Press, 1995.

Ullman, Victory. *Martin Delany: The Beginnings of Black Nationalism*. Boston: Beacon, 1972.

Van DeBurg, William L. "The Development of Black Historical Studies in American Higher Education." *Canadian Review of American Studies* 11 (Fall 1980): 175–91.

Van Tassel, David D. "From Learned Society to Professional Organization: The American Historical Association, 1884–1900." *American Historical Review* 89 (October 1984): 929–56.

Vogel, Todd, ed. *The Black Press: New Literary and Historical Essays*. New Brunswick, N.J.: Rutgers University Press, 2001.

Walker, Clarence. "The American Negro as Historical Outsider, 1836–1935." In
  Deromanticizing Black History: Critical Essays and Reappraisals. 87–108. Knoxville:
  University of Tennessee Press, 1991.

———. *We Can't Go Home Again: An Argument about Afrocentrism.* New York: Oxford
  University Press, 2003.

Wallace, Maurice. *Constructing the Black Masculine: Identity and Ideality in African American
  Men's Literature and Culture, 1775–1995.* Durham, N.C.: Duke University Press, 2002.

Warner, Robert Austin. *New Haven Negroes: A Social History.* New York: Arno Press and
  the New York Times, 1969.

Wayman, Harris. "The American Negro Historical Society of Philadelphia and Its
  Officers." *Colored American Magazine,* February 1903, 287–94.

Wells, Peter S. *The Barbarians Speak: How the Conquered Peoples Shaped the Roman Empire.*
  Princeton, N.J.: Princeton University Press, 1999.

Wertheimer, Eric. *Imagined Empires: Incas, Aztecs and the New World of American Literature,
  1771–1876.* New York: Cambridge University Press, 1999.

Wesley, Charles. "Creating and Maintaining an Historical Tradition." *Journal of Negro
  History* 37 (1952): 13–33.

———. *Ohio Negroes in the Civil War.* Columbus: Ohio State University Press, 1962.

———. "Racial Historical Societies and the American Heritage." *Journal of Negro History*
  37 (January 1952): 11–35.

Whelchel, L. H. *My Chains Fell Off: William Wells Brown, Fugitive Abolitionist.* Lanham,
  Md.: University Press of America, 1985.

White, Deborah Gray. *Ar'n't I a Woman: Female Slaves in the Plantation South.* New York,
  1985.

White, Hayden. *Content and Form: Narrative Discourse and Historical Representation.*
  Baltimore: Johns Hopkins University Press, 1990.

———. *Metahistory: The Historical Imagination in Nineteenth-Century Europe.* Baltimore:
  Johns Hopkins University Press, 1974.

White, Shane, and Graham White. *Stylin': African American Expressive Culture from Its
  Beginnings to the Zoot Suit.* Ithaca, N.Y.: Cornell University Press, 1998.

Wickett, Murray. *Contested Territory: Whites, Native Americans, and African Americans in
  Oklahoma, 1865–1907.* Baton Rouge: Louisiana State University Press, 2000.

Wiebe, Robert H. *The Search for Order, 1877–1920.* New York: Hill and Wang, 1967.

Williams, Chancellor. *The Destruction of Black Civilization: Great Issues of a Race from 4500
  B.C to 2000 A.D.* Chicago: Third World Press, 1987.

Williams, Gilbert Anthony. *The Christian Recorder, Newspaper of the African Methodist
  Episcopal Church: History of a Forum of Ideas, 1854–1902.* McFarland, 1996.

Williams, Heather Andrea. *Self-Taught: African American Education in Slavery and Freedom.*
  Chapel Hill: University of North Carolina Press, 2005.

Williams, Loretta. *Black Freemasonry and Middle-Class Realities.* Columbia: University of
  Missouri Press, 1980.

Williams, Vernon. *From a Caste to a Minority: Changing Attitudes of American Sociologists
  toward Afro-Americans, 1896–1945.* New York: Greenwood, 1968.

———. *Rethinking Race: Franz Boas and His Contemporaries.* Lexington: University Press
  of Kentucky, 1996.

Williams, Walter. *Black Americans and the Evangelization of Africa, 1877–1900*. Madison: University of Wisconsin Press, 1982.

Willis, David, and Richard Newman, eds. *Black Apostles at Home and Abroad: Afro-Americans and the Christian Mission from Revolution to Reconstruction*. Boston: G. K. Hall, 1982.

Wills, Gary. *Cincinnatus: George Washington and the Enlightenment*. New York: Doubleday, 1984.

———. *Lincoln at Gettysburg: The Words That Remade America*. New York: Simon and Schuster, 1992.

Wilmore, Gayraud. *Black Religion and Black Radicalism*. New York: Doubleday, 1972.

Wimbush, Vincent, ed. *African Americans and the Bible: Sacred Texts and Social Textures*. New York: Continuum, 2001.

Winch, Julie. *A Gentleman of Color: The Life of James Forten*. New York: Oxford University Press, 2002.

Winston, Michael. *The Howard University Department of History, 1913–1973*. Washington, D.C.: Howard University Department of History, 1973.

———. "Through the Backdoor: Academic Racism and the Negro Scholar in Historical Perspective." *Daedalus* 100 (Summer 1971): 678–719.

Winston, Michael, and Rayford Logan, eds. *Dictionary of American Negro Biography*. New York: W. W. Norton, 1972.

Winterer, Caroline. *The Culture of Classicism: Ancient Greece and Rome in American Intellectual Life, 1780–1910*. Baltimore: Johns Hopkins University Press, 2002.

———. *The Mirror of Antiquity: American Women and the Classical Tradition, 1750–1900*. Ithaca, N.Y.: Cornell University Press, 2007.

Wood, Leonard. *A History of South Africa*. New Haven: Yale University Press, 1990.

Yamauchi, Edwin M. *Africa and the Bible*. Grand Rapids, Mich.: Baker Academic, 2004.

Young, Alfred F. *The Shoemaker and the Tea Party: Memory and the American Revolution*. Boston: Beacon, 1999.

Zafar, Rafia. *We Wear the Mask: African American Writers Write American Literature, 1760–1870*. New York: Columbia University Press, 1997.

Zboray, Robert. "Antebellum Reading and the Ironies of Technological Innovation." In *Reading in America: Literature and Social History*, edited by Cathy Davidson, 180–200. Baltimore: Johns Hopkins University Press, 1989.

———. *A Fictive People: Antebellum Economic Development and the American Reading Public*. New York: Oxford University Press, 1993.

Zimmerman, Andrew. "German Alabama in Africa: The Tuskegee Expedition to German Togo and the Transnational Origins of West African Cotton Growers." *American Historical Review* 110 (December 2005): 1362–98.

Index